HOMEY DON'T PLAY THAT!

HOMEY DON'T PLAY THAT!

THE STORY OF *IN LIVING COLOR* AND THE BLACK COMEDY REVOLUTION

DAVID PEISNER

37INK

ATRIA

New York   London   Toronto   Sydney   New Delhi

37INK

ATRIA

An Imprint of Simon & Schuster, Inc.
1230 Avenue of the Americas
New York, NY 10020

First 37INK/Atria Books hardcover edition February 2018

37INK / ATRIA BOOKS and colophon are trademarks of Simon & Schuster, Inc.

For information about special discounts for bulk purchases, please contact Simon & Schuster Special Sales at 1-866-506-1949 or business@simonandschuster.com.

The Simon & Schuster Speakers Bureau can bring authors to your live event. For more information or to book an event, contact the Simon & Schuster Speakers Bureau at 1-866-248-3049 or visit our website at www.simonspeakers.com.

Interior design by Amy Trombat

Manufactured in the United States of America

10 9 8 7 6 5 4 3 2 1

Library of Congress Cataloging-in-Publication Data has been applied for.

ISBN 978-1-5011-4332-8
ISBN 978-1-5011-4336-6 (ebook)

Contents

"When Americans can no longer laugh at each other,
they have to fight one another."

—RALPH ELLISON

"Heroes ain't born, they're cornered."

—REDD FOXX

Preface

Keenen Ivory Wayans stood up, kissed his mom on the cheek, high-fived his younger brother Shawn, and hugged his dad. Smiling broadly, dressed in a sharp, black tuxedo, he paused for a split second, as if to take in the moment, just for himself.

It would've been hard to script a triumph any more complete than the one he was in the middle of. He'd just heard his old friend Jerry Seinfeld say it, "And the winner of this year's Emmy is . . . *In Living Color.*" The show had been on the air barely five months. And it was on Fox, which was barely considered a television network, programming only four nights a week. Fox had hemmed and hawed for the better part of a year deciding whether to air the show. They worried it was too black, that white people wouldn't get it, that black people would be offended, that gay people would protest, that Keenen's siblings weren't as funny as he thought they were, or simply that nobody would watch. Keenen had resisted their attempts to bend the show to their ideas, to water it down. He'd come too far. If he was going down, he was going down swinging on his own terms.

Keenen took one step toward the stage inside the Pasadena Civic Auditorium and wrapped the show's line producer, Michael Petok, in a bear hug. Petok's fiancée wiped lipstick from Keenen's face and then Keenen embraced the show's other producer, Tamara Rawitt, a short, Jewish former marketing exec who'd become his somewhat unlikely lieutenant. As the three of them strode down the aisle toward the dais, they were trailed by Kevin Bright, a supervising producer on the show's pilot. All four walked onstage, Keenen nodded at Seinfeld, whom he'd known since the two were young standups at the Improv in New York, took the gold statue from the other presenter, Patrick Stewart, and looked out across the three thousand or so people staring back at him.

At thirty-two, Keenen was hardly a fresh, young face anymore. He'd spent years slugging it out as a standup. He'd been turned down by *Saturday Night Live*. He'd played forgettable roles on forgotten television shows. For years, he'd watched the friends he'd come up with—Eddie Murphy, Arsenio Hall, Robert Townsend—achieve their dreams. He'd done okay too, but sometimes couldn't escape the feeling he was being left behind. Eddie was the biggest comedy star in the world. Robert and Keenen had worked together on a pretty great movie, *Hollywood Shuffle*, but afterward, Robert got all the shine. Arsenio debuted his hit late-night talk show more than a year before *In Living Color* launched. For a long time, even Keenen's younger brother Damon's star seemed to be eclipsing his. But this was, finally and undeniably, Keenen's moment. *His* show was a hit. *He* just won an Emmy. And to make it a little sweeter, the nominees he beat out included both *Saturday Night Live* and his old friend and rival Arsenio.

"All right," he said, looking down at the floor, clearing his throat and exhaling in a short, shallow breath. "I'd like to thank the people who helped make the vision become a reality." He rolled through the expected list of thank-yous—his producers, his writers, Fox bigwigs like Barry Diller and Peter Chernin, his manager Eric Gold.

"I could tell he was beginning to forget people," says Rawitt, recalling the moment. "You could see my mouth moving behind him, like 'Thank this one,' 'Thank that one.' I remember before the ceremony Eric Gold frantically rushing over to me and going, 'Please make him thank me.'"

Keenen had grown up one of ten kids in the projects in Manhattan, and as he turned his speech toward his family, emotion overwhelmed him. "Above all, I'd like to thank my family. Those are the ones I've been doing this for all my life." He covered his mouth, stepped back a half step from the microphone, and quietly told himself, "Okay, let me chill."

Keenen had never won anything in his life. *In Living Color* had been nominated in two other categories that year, Outstanding Choreography and Outstanding Writing, and lost both. He figured this would be the same but was prepared in case it wasn't. He'd planned a great speech to salute his mom, who'd been there to support him through all the things he'd never won, through his disappointments and failures.

Composing himself, Keenen tried to continue. "My mother and father are here tonight . . ." Again, he began to choke up, and, out in the crowd, his brother Shawn wiped tears from his own eyes. "I'm gonna get through this," Keenen pledged before abandoning his resolve. "This is for you, Ma, forget it," he said, his voice shooting up a few octaves and cracking. With that, he waved the Emmy, and walked offstage, his arm draped around Rawitt's shoulders.

"It was the worst acceptance speech ever," Keenen says, looking back on it twenty-five years later.

Yet the moment was an unqualified, wide-screen triumph for a show that punctuated the beginning of a new era. There had been black sketch shows before *In Living Color*, including the short-lived but influential *Richard Pryor Show* more than a decade earlier. That this was the first one that found an audience said as much about that audience as it did about the show. The culture was changing. For more than fifty years, black life on screens big and small had looked even more demeaning than it did in the real world. Stereotypes were indulged. The Civil Rights Movement came and went without too many substantive changes in front of or behind the camera. There had been important breakthroughs—Bill Cosby, Flip Wilson, Redd Foxx, Richard Pryor—but the march of progress was exceedingly, agonizingly slow.

Until suddenly it wasn't. Not only were there Eddie and Arsenio and Robert and Keenen, but there were Spike Lee and Oprah Winfrey and Reggie and Warrington Hudlin. Soon there would be Chris Rock and John Singleton and Martin Lawrence and the Hughes Brothers and Chris Tucker and Dave Chappelle. The week before that Emmy broadcast, a new show featuring a former rapper named Will Smith had debuted. Many of the era's other rappers would soon become multi-hyphenate stars themselves: Ice Cube, LL Cool J, Ice-T, Queen Latifah, Tupac Shakur. *In Living Color*—a black show created by a black man that seemed to effortlessly cross over to a mainstream audience ready and waiting for it—was in many ways at the center of it all. As Keenen put it, "We became this bridge in America between white suburban kids and urban kids."

Most great success stories are the sum of small failures overcome. When you zoom tightly in on that Emmy coup, cracks appear in the foundation that offer hints as to why *In Living Color* lasted only five seasons and why Keenen didn't even finish out the fourth: One of the original cast members had been fired a few weeks before the Emmys, nearly the entire writing staff had already turned over, and many of the Fox executives Keenen thanked in his acceptance speech had either left the company or were on their way out soon. Even one of the producers on the podium that night accepting the Emmy alongside Keenen hadn't seen him since he was dismissed after the pilot. This was the unforgiving cauldron in which *In Living Color* was forged. But for at least those few moments on the auditorium stage that night, things were about as perfect as they could be.

"There was the feeling of newness and excitement and *Here we are! We've arrived!*" says David Alan Grier, one of four cast members that survived all five seasons on the show. "Two weeks later it was, 'Let's move on.'"

In Living Color was nominated for fifteen more Emmys over its next four seasons. It would never win another one again.

"If You Ain't Helping Your Brother, Then I'm Beating Your Ass"

t was five blocks from PS 11 to the Wayans family's fifth-floor apart-ment in the Robert Fulton Houses in Chelsea, on the West Side of Manhattan, and Keenen had run the whole way home. He was a skinny, quiet kid, still pretty new to the neighborhood. He wasn't looking for trouble. Nonetheless, trouble found him and had chased him home. A menacing elementary school classmate had insisted that he and Keenen would square off at 3:00 p.m. to settle their grievances—real or imag-ined—so Keenen hightailed it for the safety of home around half past two, his tormentor presumably in pursuit.

Now, safely barricaded in his family's apartment, sweating from his dash home, he took to his afternoon ritual of parking himself in front of the television and watching cartoons. But he'd gotten home so quickly that he arrived before they started. Instead, he turned on the television to find something entirely unexpected: Richard Pryor on a daytime talk show.

This was the midsixties, when Pryor was still "Richie Pryor," a gan-gly kid in a sharp suit, spouting funny, if not exactly weighty, Bill Cosby-isms. He hadn't yet completed the existential transformation into the radical, truth-telling black man who would change comedy forever.

In a sense, that was all the better for Keenen, who looked at the television and saw a vision of himself staring back at him: a skinny black kid unloading tales of childhood poverty, an unusual family, and in fact, his own victimization at the hands of a school bully.

"I was laughing, so amazed that this guy could take this horrible moment and make it funny," Keenen would say years later. "I was like, 'Who is this man? I want to be like this man.'"

As humans, we have a way of imposing a narrative structure on our pasts that rarely exists in real life. *What was the moment when your life changed? What set you down this road? When did you first stumble on this idea?* Clean, easy-to-follow storylines with distinct beginnings, middles, and ends are appealing, but life doesn't usually conform to our storytelling desires. Ideas don't turn on like lightbulbs. Rather, they flare up like a fire on wet wood: lots of sparks, plenty of smoke, much frustration and failure before finally catching and holding—and even then, always in danger of being snuffed out by the whims of fate.

Keenen Ivory Wayans has told this tale about being chased home by a school bully and stumbling on Richard Pryor many times as a way of explaining his path into comedy. There's no reason to doubt that the tale itself is true—though some details have likely been obscured by the intervening fifty years. As a great storyteller, and an unabashed lover of structure, Keenen himself is undoubtedly drawn to this anecdote as a premise, a sensible start to his own tale and to the story of the show he'd create, inspired by that same gangly comedian he saw on television after school that day. But reality, as it turns out, is rarely so sensible.

The Wayans family moved to the Fulton Houses in 1964. The housing project was brand new then. In fact, the 944-unit, 11-building complex that sprawls from 16th Street to 19th Street between Ninth and Tenth Avenues wouldn't be totally complete until the following year. When the Wayanses moved in, monthly rents ranged from $46 for a small three-room apartment in one of the complex's three high-rise towers, to $94 for the largest seven-and-half-room units in one of the six-story low-rises.

Keenen's family had one of the bigger units in a low-rise that opened onto 16th Street. It had four bedrooms, which was already a little tight: His parents shared one room; Keenen, his older brother, Dwayne, and his younger brother Damon split another room; his sisters Kim and Diedra shared another; and the baby at the time, Elvira (named after her mom), had a room to herself, though not for long. Younger sisters Nadia and Devonne entered the picture in 1965 and 1966, and younger brothers Shawn and Marlon further expanded the brood in 1971 and 1972, respectively.

The Chelsea that the Wayanses moved to in 1964 was not the Chelsea of high-end boutiques, world-renowned art galleries, multimillion-dollar apartments, and artisanal food emporiums it is today. It was a loud, busy, rough, working-class neighborhood. Much of the area around the Fulton Houses was still tenements. A freight train ran along Tenth Avenue, on the backside of the projects. Across 16th Street from the Wayans family's dark brick apartment building was the Nabisco factory, where Oreos were made. Facing that, on the opposite side of Ninth Avenue, was a massive Art Deco building that housed the Port Authority headquarters. In 1966, another striking building, with small porthole windows and the general countenance of a large ship, was built across 16th Street as a union hall and dormitory for visiting seamen. Bodegas, pizzerias, record stores, Laundromats, and other small family-owned shops lined Ninth Avenue, including a barbershop owned by a resident of the Fulton Houses and an arcade, both of which were frequent gathering spots. A vaguely gothic-looking building on 20th Street, between Tenth and Eleventh, housed a drug rehab facility and was converted into the Bayview Correctional Facility, a women's prison, in 1974.

The construction of the Fulton Houses and the neighboring Chelsea-Elliott Houses, roughly ten blocks farther north, brought a wave of new families, like the Wayanses, to the area. PS 11, already crowded, braced for a doubling of its enrollment. Many who moved into the Fulton Houses were Irish families, relocating from the collapsing tenements nearby, and Puerto Ricans, who'd begun emigrating to both Chelsea and the Lower East Side in the first part of the century. In addition, there were a smaller number of African-Americans, including a young Gil Scott-Heron, who'd grow up to become a pioneering black poet, spoken-word performer, and one of hip-hop's godfathers. Heron was a teenager in 1964, when he and his mother moved into an apartment on 17th Street, just a block from the Wayans family. Another proto-hip-hop influence, the fiery, militant civil rights activist then known as H. Rap Brown, who had been the chairman of the Student Non-Violent Coordinating Committee and the minister of justice for the Black Panthers—he's currently serving a life sentence for shooting an Atlanta police officer—lived on 18th Street for a stretch in the late sixties. Whoopi Goldberg, who was a few years older than Keenen, lived in the nearby Chelsea-Elliott Houses, as did Antonio Fargas, who'd star in a string of blaxploitation films in the seventies—including *Foxy Brown* and *Across 110th Street*—and as "Huggy Bear" on *Starsky & Hutch*, as well as in Keenen's own 1988 blaxploitation spoof, *I'm Gonna Git You Sucka.*

The racial melting pot of the Fulton Houses was a change for Keenen and his family. The Wayanses had moved from Harlem, which, since the early part of the century, had been the spiritual center for black cultural life in America and home to a population that was, by the midsixties, more than 95 percent black.

Keenen spent the first six years of his life living in a tenement at the corner of 145th Street and Amsterdam Avenue, at the southwest corner of the historic neighborhood of Sugar Hill. From the 1920s through the 1950s, Sugar Hill had been an address of choice for wealthy, prominent African-Americans, including W. E. B. Du Bois, Thurgood Marshall, Cab Calloway, Duke Ellington, Willie Mays, Frankie Lymon, and W. C. Handy.

Keenen's mom, born Elvira Green in 1938, had grown up in Harlem. Though she was born just after the Harlem Renaissance, its ideas—about the arts, literature, music, politics, and black identity—still coursed through the veins of the community. Known then as the "New Negro Movement," Renaissance writers, poets, musicians, and political leaders embraced an assertive, progressive vision for African-American public life. The cultural mix in Harlem included writers such as Du Bois, Langston Hughes, and Zora Neale Hurston, future congressman Adam Clayton Powell Jr., back-to-Africa crusader Marcus Garvey, comedian Jackie "Moms" Mabley, and jazz greats Ellington, Calloway, and Count Basie.

Elvira grew up awash in the Renaissance's legacy. The legendary

Apollo Theater opened on West 125th Street in 1934, joining an already robust theater scene that included the Lafayette—the first integrated theater in the city—and the Lincoln, on West 135th Street, next door to the offices of Garvey's Universal Negro Improvement Association. The neighborhood remained a locus of the jazz world for decades. In fact, two months after Keenen was born, *Esquire* magazine managed to gather together fifty-seven of the world's most prominent jazz musicians, including Basie, Dizzy Gillespie, Charles Mingus, Sonny Rollins, and Thelonious Monk, in front a brownstone on 126th Street for a famous photograph that became known as "A Great Day in Harlem."

Following Garvey's example, Harlem became a magnet for black nationalist and civil rights groups through the middle of the century. In 1954, Malcolm X began preaching out of a storefront mosque on 116th Street known as Temple Number 7. In the fall of 1958, Martin Luther King Jr. was signing books at a department store a little over a mile from the Wayans family's apartment, when he was stabbed with a letter opener by a mentally ill black woman named Izola Curry. King's life was saved by a team of surgeons at the same hospital where Keenen had been born a few months earlier.

Elvira was, in many ways, a product of the crosscurrents sweeping through Harlem. Speaking about her to an interviewer for the Archive of American Television in 2013, Keenen described her as "a radical."

"She was all about civil rights and black power and black is beautiful," he said. Once, when Keenen was in elementary school, he brought home an assignment to make a collage and his mother enthusiastically pitched in. She told him he needed a theme for his collage and she had an idea. In the family's apartment was a framed picture of the children's fable character Little Boy Blue. She took it out of the frame and laid it on the table. Then she and Keenen began cutting out photos from *Ebony* magazine and pasting them on the Little Boy Blue picture.

"We covered everything but his eye," Keenen said. He took his collage into school and presented it to the class. His teacher was pleased. "Miss Jackson goes, 'Oh, that's really nice, Keenen.' I said, 'You know, it got a theme!' And she said, 'Well, what's your theme? Tell the class.'" He held up the collage of black faces surrounding the large eye. "I said, 'Look out, black world, because Whitey got his eye on you!'"

That was Elvira. She taught her children to challenge prevailing wisdom. "My mom would say, 'Of the ghetto doesn't mean you are ghetto.'" As Keenen told Henry Louis Gates Jr. in a 2015 interview, "That kind of stuff stays in your head and teaches you to think a certain way."

As a child, Keenen went to see a performance featuring the famed conductor Leonard Bernstein. "I was a little boy," he said. "My mother got tickets but couldn't go because she couldn't afford a babysitter. She gave me the tickets and said, 'You may not understand this but Mama wants you to go.' So she dressed me as best she could—I had on a plaid shirt and some corduroy pants and everybody else [had] on tuxedos—but she wanted me to have that experience."

Life in Harlem for the young Wayans family was hardly idyllic. Keenen's father, Howell, a diligent Jehovah's Witness born and raised in New York, always had a job, often more than one, but the growing family struggled to make ends meet. Their apartment building was little more than a slum, infested with rats and junkies. A heroin addict that the Wayans kids nicknamed Sleepy used to hang out in front of the building. Keenen and his siblings occasionally enlisted Sleepy to help them cross the street, but Sleepy, true to his moniker, had a habit of nodding off halfway across Amsterdam Avenue. "My mother would look out the window, see us and yell, 'I told you not to go across the street with him!'"

The family's living conditions weren't unique. A series of rent strikes in Harlem, beginning in November of 1963, brought attention to the problems—broken windows, crumbling ceilings, roaches, intermittent heat and water, and in the words of one tenant back then, "rats so big they can open up your refrigerator without you"—but didn't necessarily alleviate them.

Poverty was endemic, unemployment was double that of the rest of the city, and the schools were awful. Around the time that Keenen and his older brother Dwayne were in elementary school, more than three-quarters of Harlem students tested below grade level in reading and math. In 1964, Harlem residents protested by staging two separate school boycotts in which more than 90 percent of students participated.

The racial undertones to Harlem's problems were undeniable, and also a pretty accurate reflection of the state of affairs nationwide. The country often seemed as if it were being ripped apart along color lines. In June of

1963, hours after John F. Kennedy had proposed the Civil Rights Act on national television, NAACP activist Medgar Evers was gunned down in Jackson, Mississippi, by a member of the White Citizens' Council. Three months later—and just a couple of weeks after Martin Luther King Jr. led the March on Washington—a Ku Klux Klan–planted bomb ripped through the 16th Street Baptist Church in Birmingham, Alabama, killing four young black girls. Nine weeks later, John F. Kennedy was assassinated in Dallas.

In Harlem, the gravely substandard living conditions and the rising tide of radical politics created a potent brew. In the summer of 1964—two weeks after new president Lyndon Johnson signed the Civil Rights Act into law—that brew boiled over, when a fifteen-year-old black teenager was shot and killed by a white NYPD officer in front of about a dozen witnesses. Six days of angry rioting consumed Harlem, with protestors looting stores and attacking police officers with bricks, bottles, and Molotov cocktails, and the cops responding first with batons, tear gas, and hoses, and then, later, with live ammunition. The chaos eventually spread to Bedford-Stuyvesant in Brooklyn and kicked off a summer of rage that ignited similar uprisings across the river in Jersey City, Paterson, and Elizabeth, New Jersey, and even farther afield in Philadelphia, Chicago, and Rochester. Race riots became an enduring feature of urban strife in the sixties, as violent demonstrations shook Watts, Cleveland, Omaha, Newark, Detroit, Minneapolis, Chicago, Washington, D.C., and Baltimore before the decade was out. When all was said and done in Harlem that summer of 1964, one protestor was dead, more than five hundred had been injured, nearly another five hundred had been arrested, and there was close to a million dollars in property damage.

Clearly, the Wayanses picked a good time to get the hell out.

The Fulton Houses were a step up for the Wayans family. In contrast to the popular image that the phrase "public housing projects" sometimes conjures, these particular projects were a relatively safe, family-oriented community. Most of the kids attended the same elementary school, PS 11, or junior high, IS 70, and after a few years, many of the families knew each other.

Although the Wayanses were a large family, in a community heavily populated with Irish, Puerto Rican, and African-American families, that didn't necessarily distinguish them. The Fulton Houses were overflowing with children and had been built with them in mind. In the courtyard between the Wayans family's building and the one next door there was a small playground with cement turtles and whales, where younger kids would chase each other, and older ones might play "spin the bottle." In a covered area near the playground and the building's front door was a spot for four square and hopscotch. A block north on 17th was Kelly Park, and a block past that, between 18th and 19th, a basketball court.

The Wayanses' apartment was brand new, and although the four-bedroom unit was cramped for a family that would grow to twelve members by the early seventies, they learned how to use every inch of it. Rooms were crowded with beds—Shawn and Marlon slept head to toe in the same bed for nearly sixteen years—and the two bathrooms were hardly ever empty. Howell seemed to nearly always be occupying one of them; it was his personal refuge from the everyday insanity of the crowded apartment. If any of his children wanted to find a similar serenity, the best option was a closet.

"Each room had a closet," Keenen recalled. "The closet was like our office. We could go there for privacy. At dinner, my mother would count us, and if one was missing she'd go into the closet and see who'd fallen asleep."

Poverty was pretty much the norm throughout the Fulton Houses, but the Wayanses, according to Keenen, were "the poorest of the poor." Breakfast was often puffed rice, bought in bulk. Lunch might be grilled cheese sandwiches with, as Shawn described it, "government cheese where the cheese don't melt." Dinner was, occasionally, nonexistent.

As Damon wrote in his book of comic essays, *Bootleg*, "My mother would look at us and say, 'Look, babies, there ain't no food in the house. We're having sleep for dinner. Now brush your teeth and get ready for bed. Keenen, you make sure everyone gets a little extra toothpaste tonight.'"

There was a phone in the apartment, but it was often disconnected because the family couldn't pay the bill, so anyone who wanted to make or receive a call would have to use the pay phone on the corner across the street. Despite the struggles, the family never went on welfare. Elvira was a proud, resourceful woman and wouldn't think of it.

Their financial problems weren't a result of laziness or apathy, just math. Keenen and his siblings worked from a young age—collecting bottles, shining shoes, delivering groceries—and their father always worked too. There were just too many kids and too little money. For a time, Howell worked as a supermarket manager, as a sales representative for Guinness/Harp, and for Drake's Cakes, but eventually, he quit to go into business for himself.

"My dad wanted to be his own man and have his own business," Keenen said.

What that meant in practice was he would go to the post office and buy whatever surplus items hadn't been picked up—condoms, hair beads, sunglasses, costume jewelry, whatever—and sell them. On occasion, he'd enlist his children to hawk the items door to door. Neighbors referred to the family as the "Haneys," after the junk merchants on the then popular television comedy *Green Acres*. It wasn't exactly a gold mine. As Marlon put it, "My dad had a job at Drake's Cakes and made good money. Then he decided he didn't want to work for the Man. My mother was like, 'You stupid asshole—work for the Man! He gives you benefits!'"

Elvira, who sometimes went by Vi, had been a singer in her youth—she and her sisters sang as "the Green Sisters," and even performed at the Apollo once—and then became a social worker. As the family grew, raising the kids became a full-time job and then some. Many say she was the funniest one in the whole family—but only when she was angry. Nothing could make her angry as reliably as her husband.

Marlon recalled, "My dad would annoy the shit out of my mother and she'd curse him out. When my mom cursed my dad out, she was like Richard Pryor with titties. I thought his name was Motherfucker until I was nineteen." They argued about money, about religion—he was a Jehovah's Witness, she was not—about pretty much anything. She used to mock Howell's inability to grow a mustache by calling him "Horse Lip."

"We got to watch the best buddy comedy ever," Marlon said. "Fuck Tom and Jerry. Fuck Daffy Duck and Bugs Bunny. We got to watch Elvira and Howell."

Shawn and Marlon, in particular, delighted in riling their mother up. Keenen recalled a time when his youngest brothers found a bell that sounded just like their telephone. The two hid under their mother's bed, repeatedly ringing the bell. Their mother came running in from the kitchen to answer the phone, over and over, only to pick it up and hear a dial tone. Eventually, she was convinced it was a woman calling her husband and hanging up, which set off the expletive-laced verbal tirade they were hoping for all along. Getting mad and getting laughs were inextricably linked in the Wayans household.

But it wasn't all fun and games. Howell was a strict, hardworking man. According to Marlon, he started his day at three in the morning. "I used to watch my dad wake up, put his hand on his head, read his Bible for a little while, look up to the sky, take a deep breath, and go, 'How the fuck am I going to feed these ten motherfuckers today?' He'd somehow magically go out and bring dinner home." Besides work, he also went door to door as a Jehovah's Witness. "This is where he gets his work ethic," Marlon said. "He got so many doors slammed in his face."

He tried to impose the same discipline on his children. The kids were supposed to be up at five every morning and back in the apartment before the streetlights came on at night. "We had to be accounted for, and if we weren't, we were going to answer to an ass-whipping," said Marlon.

In fact, ass-whippings became occasions for public amusement in the household.

"If you were getting a whipping from my father, there would be five of us in the room laughing about how you were getting hit," Damon said.

The siblings reacted in different ways to their father's restrictive rules. Kim was a proverbial "good girl" who fell in line, worked hard, got good grades. Keenen didn't rock the boat either.

"I never rebelled, I just developed a plan," he said. "One of my favorite kid stories was 'The Tortoise and the Hare.' I really related to the tortoise. I never looked for immediate results. I always paced things." So Keenen got jobs. Took on more responsibility. Made himself indispensable.

Dwayne and Damon revolted. Damon remembered a night when Dwayne decided that the nighttime curfew was bullshit. He was going out whether his father liked it or not. Howell guarded the door, armed with a belt, and challenged Dwayne, "You want to go outside, you gotta go through me." The other siblings watched the confrontation with nervous, if somewhat gleeful, anticipation.

"My brother took my father, body-slammed him, and went outside," Damon said. "We followed him."

———

Being home by early evening introduced most of the Wayans siblings to their first comedy workshop: the dinner table. It was a raucous, ruthless, and unforgiving venue. "Anything that happened that day, that's what the jokes were about," said Keenen. "We'd start snappin' on each other. Everybody had a twisted sense of humor. We cracked jokes about your most painful experiences."

Damon remembered a game he and his siblings called, "Make Me Laugh or Die." "Everybody would sit down and then one of us would have to get up and make everybody laugh," he said. They'd do impressions, funny dances, sketches. "You couldn't just make one laugh—you had to make everyone laugh at the same time, in unison. If you didn't, we all thought about what your 'die' is. We'd pick something like 'You've got to go drink Daddy's last beer in front of him.' 'Go fart in Mama's face.'"

The idea was to forestall laughing as long as possible, to *not* laugh so as to make your sibling have to endure the "Die" task. (Years later, Keenen's stinginess with laughs became well known among *In Living Color* writers and cast members. Even when he liked something, he was far more apt to offer a straight-faced "That's funny" than to actually break.)

Clowning around aside, the close quarters in the apartment created, at times, an almost uncomfortably intimate relationship between siblings. There were no private conversations. If you took too long in the bathroom, everyone knew about it. If someone had a date, everyone had an opinion. When Keenen lost his virginity, he did so with Shawn and Marlon watching.

"I was babysitting," Keenen said. "I thought, 'This is the perfect time. I'm gonna have my girl come over.'" But every time he'd look over his shoulder, he'd see his two brothers in the doorway of his room, quickly scampering down the hallway.

On the not infrequent occasions when friction between brothers boiled over into an actual fistfight, their mother insisted they make up with a kiss.

"My mother used to make us kiss on the mouth," said Damon. This went on until the boys were well into their teenage years. "We left home because we didn't want to kiss each other on the mouth," he joked.

———

Growing up, Damon and Keenen were very close but very different from each other. Damon was born with a clubfoot—a birth defect where a foot is bent inward at an acute angle—and underwent several surgeries and wore corrective shoes as a child. As a result, his mother showered him with extra attention, which didn't exactly endear him to Keenen and Dwayne.

"Dwayne hated me," Damon said. "He used to beat me up. When my mother made him babysit, he'd hang me on the door hook. If I tried to get down, he'd hit me."

The orthopedic shoes also meant that Damon walked with a severe limp—he later joked that his "crip walk" made people in the neighborhood think he was in a gang—and wasn't allowed to play sports. In gym class, he sat on the side, lest his special shoes scuff up the gym floor. "That's where the comedy started," Damon told the *St. Louis Dispatch* in 1990, "from me heckling the kids that were playing."

He also became a target for abuse. As a defense mechanism, he developed a sharp, unforgiving sense of humor. When kids would play "the dozens" on the playground, snapping each other with "Yo Mama" jokes and the like, nobody wanted to play with Damon, who channeled his insecurities into his verbal jousts. "They knew they couldn't talk about my shoe. If they did, it'd turn ugly and the game was over."

Damon got in lots of fights, even though he didn't like and wasn't particularly good at fighting. It didn't help that he was a small kid well into his teens. While Keenen grew to over six feet tall by sixteen, Damon was under five feet past his fourteenth birthday.

"The doctors thought he was going to be a midget," Keenen said. "He was literally my little brother. I looked after him and he looked up to me."

Damon's height and his physical disabilities seemed to create a certain neediness in him. "All I really wanted was to be accepted and not talked about," he said. As he grew into a teenager, he hung around some rough dudes, smoked a lot of weed, dabbled in petty crime, and eventually dropped out of school during tenth grade. "I never had any goals," he said. "I just wanted to survive."

For the Wayans kids, fistfights were a pretty regular feature of life in Chelsea. As Keenen pointed out, the Fulton Houses were "one of the first integrated projects in Manhattan, and the racial tension was unbelievable." Unbelievable but not unusual. This was the late sixties and early seventies, when the nightly news was cataloguing landmarks and setbacks on the road to racial harmony on a near-daily basis: Congress passes the Voting Rights Act; the Supreme Court strikes down laws against miscegenation and welcomes its first African-American justice, Thurgood Marshall; Martin Luther King is assassinated in Memphis; Black Panther leader Fred Hampton is murdered by law enforcement officers as he sleeps; and two New York City cops are gunned down on an East Village sidewalk by members of the Black Liberation Army. It was like Newton's Third Law, with bullets: For every action, there was an equal and opposite reaction. Progress and regress. A vicious cycle.

The Fulton Houses were certainly subject to these larger forces. In his younger years, Keenen said, the epithet "nigger" was thrown pretty freely at him by white residents. "Every time I'd go outside someone would call me a nigger," he said. On one occasion, after some older kids on the corner had shouted, "Get out of here, li'l nigger!" at him, he came home upset. His mother offered some peculiar advice for her young son.

"You go back out there and if they call you 'nigger' again, you tell them to call you 'Mr. Nigger'!" she told him. Keenen returned to the corner emboldened with a sense of righteous purpose. When the same teenagers spotted him, one called out, "I thought I told you to get out of here, you little nigger!" Keenen puffed his chest out and followed his mom's counsel. His tormentors went silent for a second then burst into laughs. Then came the rejiggered fusillade of racial slurs: "Mr. Nigger," "Dr. Jungle Bunny," "Professor Coon." It was an early lesson in the absurdities of racism. "I'm just like, 'I guess Mom's thing didn't work,'" he said, laughing about it, many years later.

More commonly, problems between Puerto Rican, Irish, and African-American kids in the Fulton Houses were settled with fists.

"You had three of the toughest groups who had never interrelated to each other at all put into this eight-square-block housing development," Keenen said. "Everybody came with their issues and baggage and resentments. It was hell. You walked out the door, you fought."

As Damon recalled, their mother counseled that there was safety in numbers. "There's no reason why we should lose a fight," she told them. "There's ten of you against one, and if you ain't helping your brother, then *I'm* beating your ass."

If one Wayans was in a fight, they were all there, even the girls. Keenen recalled a long-running feud with another family, the Andersons. "Damon got into a fight with the youngest. He went and got his brother. Soon, I was fighting with the middle kid. Then Dwayne was fighting with the older brother. It went on for four years after school."

By the time Shawn and Marlon were growing up, a lot of the racial animosity in the projects had subsided, but Marlon, like Damon before him, had a mouth and an audacity that belied his slight frame.

"I would always find the biggest dude, then 'pop,' one punch and turn around and go 'Shaaaaaawn!'" At which point, Shawn and other family members would join the fray. "My sister would kick him, my nephew would bite him," Marlon recalled. "It was like fighting an octopus. Everybody would jump in."

Which is not to say that they won every fight. In his book, *Bootleg*, Damon recalled watching Keenen getting beat up by a white kid as "the worst day of my life." From a young age, Keenen had studied and practiced karate—or "the arts," as he sometimes called it back then. He took it all very seriously, and for a spell had taken to wearing Chinese slippers. When Damon heard a white kid making fun of said slippers, he dutifully reported the transgression back to Keenen.

"I told Keenen that he had to defend his karate shoes. I figured it was a win-win situation and I'd enjoy seeing Keenen beat on the white boy."

Neighborhood kids gathered around Keenen and his slipper-slandering aggressor for the showdown. Then Keenen started to take off his shirt—standard prefight procedure for black kids in the Fulton Projects at the time, according to Damon—"when this white boy just hauled off and started whuppin' his ass," Damon recalled. "It looked like one of those hockey fights. Keenen couldn't even get one punch off 'cause his arms were stuck in his shirt. I wanted to help out, but I was in such shock because it all happened so fast. Before I knew it, Keenen was lying on the ground in a bloody pulp with his shirt still pulled over his head, crying."

But like soldiers who'd defended each other side by side on a battle-field, all the fighting, and just surviving, day to day, in the face of poverty, racism, kids making fun of your slippers, and a mom who insisted you kiss your brothers on the mouth had an impact. "It bonded us more than any typical family," Keenen said.

"Keenen Was Always the Pioneer"

When Keenen was young, his mother sometimes snuck into his bedroom late at night and woke him up. "That little skinny boy is on TV," she'd whisper. That's what she called Richard Pryor. *That little skinny boy.* She didn't know his name but knew her son loved him. Every time Pryor was on television, clowning with Ed Sullivan or Merv Griffin or Johnny Carson or Dinah Shore, Keenen scrambled to watch. (Unlike his wife, Howell didn't really support his children's burgeoning yen for comedy the same way. He dished out spankings when he found his kids listening to Pryor and Redd Foxx albums. "He'd beat us, but we'd take the beating," Damon said. "That's how funny Pryor was.")

The decade in which Keenen and his siblings were falling for Pryor was an artistically tumultuous one for the pioneering comedian. He had grown up in abject poverty in Peoria, Illinois, living for many years in a brothel where his mother serviced clients and his grandmother was the madam. During his early forays into comedy, Pryor presented himself as "Richie Pryor," a somewhat goofy peddler of largely inoffensive observational humor and physical comedy. His act was solid—he performed on television, he booked lucrative shows in Vegas—it just wasn't *him*. Similarities to Bill Cosby, who, by that time, was already white America's favorite black comedian, were noted by many, including Cosby himself.

As the now infamous legend goes, Pryor had a cathartic onstage breakdown at the Aladdin in Las Vegas in September 1967: He looked out at the almost exclusively white crowd, which included Dean Martin, then muttered to himself, "What the fuck am I doing here?" and walked off to find the real "Richard Pryor"—the one who'd draw from the wellspring of his harrowing childhood and deliver knife-edged jokes that assaulted America's racial fault lines.

The truth is more nuanced. Signs of Pryor's growing disenchantment with his act (and himself) were evident long before his shows at the Aladdin. At a gig opening for singer Trini López, Pryor lay on the floor and delivered his entire set facing the club's ceiling, ignoring the crowd. At the Cafe Wha?, in New York, he attacked a heckler with a plastic fork. As Scott Saul describes in his book *Becoming Richard Pryor*, the incident at the Aladdin hotel was actually two separate incidents that occurred over the course of about ten days. On opening night, seven minutes into his set, Pryor did, in fact, walk offstage, get in his car, and drive to Los Angeles. In his own memoir, Pryor writes, "I didn't know who Richard Pryor was. And in that flash of introspection when I was unable to find an answer, I crashed." But after a brief sojourn in Los Angeles, Pryor returned to the Aladdin to fulfill his contract. He was eventually fired for repeatedly cursing onstage.

While the incidents are now seen as the turning point in Pryor's career, the transformation was far from immediate. He continued appearing on staid television programs and even performing in Vegas before he stepped off the showbiz hamster wheel and moved to a small one-room apartment in Berkeley, California, in 1971. There, he began hanging around black bohemian intellectuals like Claude Brown and Ishmael Reed, and militant Black Panther leaders such as Huey P. Newton and Eldridge Cleaver. Awash in the city's countercultural vibe, the writings of Malcolm X, and the music of Miles Davis and Marvin Gaye, Pryor deconstructed his own act then put it back together anew. When he re-emerged, a comedy revolution was set in motion.

That revolution was foundational for Keenen, as well as for his siblings, but it was only a part of his early comedy education. As a kid, Keenen watched Johnny Carson on *The Tonight Show* nearly every night, sometimes sitting in his grandfather's lap. He was also a big fan of *The*

Carol Burnett Show, *Laugh-In*, *The Jackie Gleason Show*, and *I Love Lucy*, all of which, in their own ways, would exert a substantive influence on *In Living Color*.

During the sixties, when Keenen, Kim, and Damon were first discovering comedy, television was mostly a wasteland for black comics—or African-Americans in general. After the cancellation of *The Amos 'n Andy Show* in 1953, under pressure from the NAACP, who felt—not without cause—that the show reinforced negative stereotypes of black people, African-American comedy pretty much disappeared from television for more than a decade. In 1965, Cosby briefly interrupted that streak, first with a starring role for three years on *I Spy*, then in 1969 with his early sitcom *The Bill Cosby Show*, but it wasn't really until 1970, beginning with the debut of *Flip*, the successful, hour-long comedy-variety show hosted by comedian Flip Wilson, that the prevailing winds shifted.

Wilson, while not the comedy insurrectionist Pryor was, was nonetheless revolutionary in his own way. He spurned a million-dollar check up front from NBC and insisted instead on ownership of his own show. His faith in himself paid off handsomely: The show was a massive hit, and once Wilson walked away from it in 1974, he was able to retire and retreat from public view. Keenen may not have been hip to the financial backstory behind Wilson's deal—after all, he was twelve when *Flip* debuted—but he was an avowed fan.

Flip's success prepped the ground for a slow trickle of black sitcoms. First, in 1972, was *Sanford and Son*, starring Redd Foxx as a junkshop owner; two years later came *Good Times*, featuring a young comic named Jimmie Walker, which focused on an African-American family struggling to make ends meet in the notorious Cabrini-Green housing projects in Chicago; a year after that, *The Jeffersons* spun off from the gleefully controversial sitcom *All in the Family*. Each of these shows, though, was the product of the same white executive producer, Norman Lear.

Opportunities for black actors in mainstream Hollywood movies during this period were scant. But by the early seventies, a parallel film industry sprung up of low-budget so-called blaxploitation films. Coming at the tail end of the civil rights era, films like *Sweet Sweetback's Baadasssss Song*, *Shaft*, *Superfly*, *Cotton Comes to Harlem*, *The Mack*, and *Three the Hard Way* presented the world through a distinctly racial lens:

black heroes unapologetically fighting the white establishment. These films were, for better and worse, a product of their times. The earnest hopes of the sixties had begun to curdle into something harder, angrier. Martin and Malcolm were both dead by assassins' bullets, but in the Panthers, the Black Liberation Army, and other advocates preaching "Black Power," it seemed that Malcolm's vision—as well as that of Huey Newton, H. Rap Brown, and Angela Davis—was the one that was ascendant.

Blaxploitation wasn't bound by any single genre but was nearly always soaked in gratuitous sex and violence. The point wasn't realism, necessarily, but that the extremes portrayed in these films—a hyperviolent, two-tiered world, divided by color, with venal, greedy white men pulling the levers of power—certainly *felt* real for much of black America. The belief that the right black hero, through a combination of strength, smarts, sex appeal, and general badass-ery could, at least momentarily, tilt these otherwise weighted scales in their own direction was understandably appealing. The films spawned a generation of stars including Richard Roundtree, Rudy Ray Moore, Fred Williamson, Bernie Casey, Jim Brown, and Pam Grier, and gave black comics like Pryor, Cosby, Foxx, Wilson, and Godfrey Cambridge some of their first film roles. However, by the late seventies, civil rights groups—the NAACP, the Urban League, the Southern Christian Leadership Conference, among others—were concerned that blaxploitation traded on old, backward stereotypes (which, to be fair, it often did) and helped stop the movement dead.

Keenen saw a lot of these films as a teenager and in his twenties. Years later, he lamented their disappearance. "It caused a lot of really talented people to lose work and slighted a lot of great accomplishments made in that time period. Politics came into play because we were very sensitive to how we wanted to be seen on-screen. We had fought so hard in terms of civil rights—people were sensitive about anything which seemed to undermine that even remotely." He would not only absorb a love and appreciation for these films but also note the lessons behind their downfall.

Keenen was drawn more instinctively to comedy than drama. He has cited his introduction to Pryor as the moment he first wanted to be a comedian, but much like Pryor's own awakening, it was almost certainly a more gradual process. Once, during a family gathering, back when the Wayanses were still living in Harlem, Keenen put on his father's clothes and staggered around with a wine bottle, pretending to be a drunk. As he told an interviewer in 2013, that was the first time he remembered getting an adult laugh. "I was hooked after that." After the family moved to Chelsea, he'd sometimes sit in the relative quiet of his bedroom closet and "dream about being a comedian." But for a long time, he kept his showbiz dreams a closely guarded secret.

When it came time for high school, those performer inclinations began sneaking to the surface. Keenen ventured out of the neighborhood to Seward Park, a high school on Manhattan's Lower East Side. The school was housed in a large, seven-story, block-long monolith built in 1929. In the late sixties, future *Angela's Ashes* author Frank McCourt began working as an English teacher there. In his book *Teacher Man*, McCourt paints a picture of Seward Park as an overcrowded, chaotic melting pot of mostly black, Latino, and Asian kids. Kevin Bright, who later produced the *In Living Color* pilot (and, more famously, *Friends*), graduated from Seward Park three years before Keenen and describes it as "the New York City public high school you got lumped into if you weren't smart enough to get in a specialized high school like Stuyvesant or Bronx High School of Science." Bright recalled a shootout in the cafeteria between Asian gang members during his time there.

A generation earlier, the school had churned out a pretty impressive roster of future actors and actresses, including Tony Curtis, Estelle Getty, Zero Mostel, Walter Matthau, and Jerry Stiller. But Keenen never took a drama class, never auditioned for a school play. "I didn't know anything about performing or show business," Keenen said. "I was just a guy that when my friends would get high, they'd come get me to make them laugh." He crafted jokes and characters for his friends. Around them, Keenen could relax and turn on the charm, but being the center of attention didn't come naturally. "People who knew me would say, 'I never thought this guy would be a comedian.' Most people I went to high school with didn't have any idea. In big groups, I was always very shy and quiet."

Similarly, Damon, who attended a different high school, Murry Bergtraum, showed little interest in drama programs. It was their younger sister Kim, who also went to Seward Park, who was the family's resident performer.

"I came out of the womb, got smacked on the butt, and said, 'I'm going to be an actress,'" Kim said. "As far back as I can remember, I always knew what I was going to do."

Kim was the one putting on shows in the living room, dressed in her mom's hats and wigs. She was a fixture in every school musical, every community play, and every children's dance recital in lower Manhattan. She was constantly hanging around the Hudson Guild, a community center several blocks north of the Fulton Houses that offered art and drama classes, and put on local productions. As Keenen recalled, "Where I had this secret dream to be in show business, Kim had this desperate dream."

Because of the family's financial hardships, Kim often couldn't afford the appropriate accoutrements for all of her extracurricular activities, so she'd improvise. When one production required angel wings and tap shoes, Kim and Vi fashioned a wire hanger and some old curtains into the former, and fastened bottle tops to the bottoms of her shoes to take care of the latter.

"We go to the play," Keenen recalled, laughing, years later, "and she is literally skidding across the floor, banging into everybody because she has no grip on the bottoms of these shoes." Episodes such as these would inspire one of Kim's most memorable characters on *In Living Color*, the ferociously ambitious but equally untalented child actor, Lil' Magic.

"I was Lil' Magic," Kim says. "I was such a little desperado. I was ruining dance recitals across Manhattan because I never could afford the costume, but I'd just show up. Much to the amazement and chagrin of the dance instructor. She couldn't get rid of me."

Keenen and Damon's performances back then were less formal. As early as eleven and thirteen, Damon and Keenen often clowned around for the amusement of family and friends, pretending to be Wiz and Juju, two streetwise kids always trying to pull some sort of scam. Wiz and Juju would one day morph into Wiz and Ice, the two hustlers featured in one of *In Living Color*'s most enduring series of sketches, "The Homeboy Shopping Network."

At the movies, Keenen and Damon often lapsed into Dickie and Donald Davis, two gay brothers, an early template for Antoine Merriweather and Blaine Edwards, the two flamboyant, effeminate film critics played by Damon and David Alan Grier on *In Living Color*'s "Men on Film." On occasion, Keenen and Damon took a version of these characters out into the neighborhood.

"Me and Keenen used to walk around the Village as a gay couple," Damon says. "Sometimes I'd walk up to other guys who were with guys and go, 'You left your robe and toothpaste at my house,' slap him, and just take off running. That just was something we did to humor ourselves."

Although it's perhaps not the most flattering anecdote, it's worth putting it into some context. The Wayanses grew up less than a mile—a fifteen-minute walk—from the Stonewall Inn, the West Village gay bar that became ground zero for the modern gay rights movement in late June of 1969, when patrons rioted to protest repeated police raids. The event cemented Greenwich Village, particularly the West Village, as one of the main hubs of gay life in America. In the seventies, the gay population in the Village began moving north into Chelsea, lured by cheaper housing costs, beginning a massive gentrification of the neighborhood surrounding the Fulton Houses. For teenagers like Keenen and Damon, this manifested itself as the relatively sudden emergence of a previously closeted but now highly visible gay culture. To them, it was all very different, and different was just funny.

"It was a time when it wasn't really acceptable to be gay," says Damon. "But the West Village was super-gay."

———

Keenen's role within the family was often more fatherly than brotherly. Although Dwayne was older, Dwayne had an air of unreliability around him. Some who knew him have surmised he may have suffered from schizophrenia or autism, and he eventually developed a serious drug habit, and died in 2000. Keenen, on the other hand, was solid. He didn't really drink, didn't do drugs, and was a good student at Seward Park—at least until he took a job at McDonald's to help support the family. As he put in more and more hours slinging fast food—he eventually became a manager there—his grades slipped from As to Cs. But, as often as not, it was Keenen who was buying Marlon and Shawn pizza for dinner, or ice cream after school, or a new bike around Christmastime. It was Keenen who took them to get their immunization shots. It was Keenen they turned to with questions about school, about sex, about anything. It was a family dynamic that stuck.

As Keenen got older and took on more responsibility, the rules around the house loosened. He certainly didn't have to be home at six in the evening if he was working a late shift. During summer nights, he'd sometimes venture out to parks and parties beyond the neighborhood, to Harlem or the Bronx. New York City in the seventies is often painted as a dimly romantic tableau of crime, blackouts, and urban decay—and it's worth mentioning that the elevated West Side Highway *did* collapse in 1973, just a few blocks from the Wayanses' apartment—but that's not all Keenen found in the streets beyond Chelsea.

"When I was a teenager, I used to go to parties in parks where people were just out there DJing," Keenen says. Hip-hop was being born in those parks and in basements and in local rec centers, by guys like DJ Kool Herc, Afrika Bambaataa, Busy Bee, Melle Mel, and Lovebug Starski. "I used to go and hear guys like Starski and Busy Bee. That's what we did in the summer."

Despite Kennen's plummeting grades and his general indifference toward the idea of college, an uncle convinced him to apply for a United Negro College Fund scholarship, which he won. After taking time off, in June of 1976 he left for Tuskegee Institute, a historically black school in Alabama, and became the first in his family to go to college. At the time, he'd only been outside the New York area once, to visit his grandmother in South Carolina.

"I can't explain the feelings of pride we had for him," Kim said. "Keenen was always the pioneer. The day he left, we gave him a huge duffel bag full of care packages and letters telling him how proud we were. We thought he was some kind of king." As he rode away from the Fulton Houses in a taxi, his siblings trailed behind him, running after the cab until they could no longer keep up.

3

"This Is the Place"

Tuskegee, Alabama, was a stark change from Manhattan's West Side. A small city of about ten thousand people in the green hills of eastern Alabama, Tuskegee had already played an outsized role in African-American history by the time Keenen arrived in 1976. The college, founded in 1881 by Booker T. Washington, was the site of pioneering agricultural research by George Washington Carver, who taught there for forty-seven years. During World War II, it was home to the training facility for the Tuskegee Airmen, the first squadron of black fighter pilots in the nation's history. *Invisible Man* author Ralph Ellison attended in the thirties, Malcolm X's future wife Betty Shabazz did the same in the early fifties, and civil rights icon Rosa Parks was born in the city.

Tuskegee's recent history was grimmer, though. In 1966, civil rights organizer Sammy Younge Jr., a Tuskegee native and a student at the college, was shot in the back of the head by a white gas station attendant after an argument about using a "whites only" bathroom. Younge, a Student Nonviolent Coordinating Committee member who'd marched from Selma to Montgomery in 1965, and had been beaten and arrested while trying to register voters and integrate businesses, became the first black college student murdered during the Civil Rights Movement. His murderer was acquitted by an all-white jury, sparking angry demonstrations around the city.

In 1972, the Associated Press broke the story of a forty-year-long medical study at Tuskegee conducted by the U.S. Public Health Service, tracking black men with syphilis. The research, intended to follow the natural progression of the disease if untreated, represents perhaps the most egregious ethical transgression in the history of public health in this country: Participants in the study were never told of their diagnosis or offered treatment, despite the fact that by 1947, penicillin had become a common and effective medication for the disease. More than one hundred study participants died, forty of their wives were infected, and nineteen passed the disease on to their children. The study contributed to a high and enduring level of mistrust that African-Americans, particularly in the rural South, had for both the medical community and the federal government.

All that notwithstanding, Keenen described his time in Tuskegee as a "vacation." He was studying to be an engineer, and although he got good grades, that's not necessarily where his focus was. ("God help the person who drove across any bridge I designed," he said.) Most of what he was learning in Tuskegee wasn't coming out of books.

"Being in a city that was predominantly black, I knew for the first time in my life what white people feel every day—that is, what it's like to be in the majority," he said. "You have no blinders on because you look around and the mayor is black, the police chief is black, and the janitor is black. You can take your pick: You can be anyone." Although the city's population had been majority African-American for a long time, it took a 1960 U.S. Supreme Court ruling to wrest power away from the dwindling white population, who had gerrymandered the city's borders to disenfranchise black residents.

There weren't many Tuskegee students from New York City or who'd even been there, so Keenen found himself to be something of an exotic creature on campus. He'd frequently entertain friends with tales of the Big Apple, and slip into impressions of neighborhood characters. One day, one of the few other New Yorkers at the school, an upperclassman, approached Keenen with a little advice.

"Hey, when you go home you should check out the Improv."

"What's that?"

"It's a comedy club. Richard Pryor started there."

On his next trip back home, he looked in the phone book, and found that the club was all of a twenty-minute walk up Ninth Avenue from the Fulton Houses. "The irony was it took me going two thousand miles away to find out about a club that was one mile from my house."

———

Budd Friedman opened the Improvisation in 1963 in a space on the corner of West 44th and Ninth formerly occupied by a Vietnamese restaurant. It was on the rather run-down edge of the theater district, next to Dykes Lumber yard. It's signature redbrick wall behind the stage wasn't an aesthetic choice: When Friedman yanked out the mirrors and wall panels as he readied the club to open, there was the redbrick wall. Hiring someone to put up drywall wasn't in the budget, so the brick stayed.

The place wasn't much to look at, a few rows of tables, wooden chairs, a barely elevated stage, and a small bar. At first, the Improv was mainly a late-night hangout for Broadway performers such as Liza Minnelli and Bette Midler who occasionally got up on the microphone to sing. By the midsixties, comedians had begun to infiltrate. Robert Klein, Lily Tomlin, Dick Cavett, Rodney Dangerfield, George Carlin, and yes, a young Richie Pryor, among others, came there to drink and work out routines between musical acts. Friedman auditioned performers onstage and cobbled together each night's lineup based on who was hanging around. No one got paid. The trade-off was simple: Comics got to try out material in front of an audience that might sometimes include agents, managers, and television bookers; Friedman got free entertainment. Danny Aiello, who'd recently lost his job working for Greyhound, worked as a bouncer at the door for $190 a week.

By the early seventies, the Improv had, somewhat accidentally, become the nation's first comedy club. As the place grew in stature, more and more comedians hung around the bar, waiting for a chance to go on. Comics such as Richard Lewis, Andy Kaufman, Freddie Prinze, Jimmie Walker, Jay Leno, and Elayne Boosler became regulars, and Pryor filmed his first concert film, *Live and Smokin'*, at the club in 1971. The following year, another comedy club, Catch a Rising Star, opened on the Upper East Side, which both ended the Improv's monopoly on the local comedy scene and validated its existence. By 1975, a third club, the Comic Strip, had opened a few blocks from Catch.

By the time Keenen arrived at the Improv in the late seventies, Friedman had opened a second Improv, in California, and had largely left the day-to-day management of the original club to a young former comic named Chris Albrecht and his assistant, Judy Orbach. Years later, Keenen described his first visit to the New York Improv as something like the culmination of a spiritual pilgrimage.

"I walk in the door and there's all these black-and-white photos of all these great comedians up on the wall," he said. "I was just like, 'Wow. This is the place.' I didn't even see the [main] room. It wasn't until you actually get past the door and go in the room that you go, 'This place is a shithole.'"

Regular spots at the club were highly coveted, and the gauntlet a comic had to pass through was intimidating. It typically started on a Sunday: Prospective comics lined up outside the club—sometimes beginning that morning—in hopes of getting a "ticket"—i.e., the right to get onstage that night for five minutes to try to impress the club's management. Orbach normally started handing out tickets from an ice bucket in the early evening.

"We handed out maybe fifty, and everyone who didn't get one would come back the following week," Orbach recalls. Comics who "passed" onstage could start hanging around the club in hopes of getting more stage time; though, particularly for a comic who'd only recently passed, there was no guarantee of that.

"If you were fairly new then you'd come in Tuesday through Thursday and the second show on Friday and Saturday night," says John DeBellis, a regular during the mid-to-late seventies who later went on to write on *Saturday Night Live*. "But I was told by Elayne Boosler to come in every night for every show, just in case a regular act didn't show up. So I'd be there for both shows hoping to get on."

Albrecht was in his midtwenties then, but he carried himself with an authority beyond his years.

"Everybody liked Chris," says DeBellis. "He's really smart and you didn't feel that crazy ambition from him. He just had a way about him that you could tell he was in charge without ever telling you he's in charge. And he was amazing with women."

Keenen was home from Tuskegee on summer break in 1978 the first Sunday he lined up with the other hopefuls. He was there at eight in the morning, and as others began to arrive, he gravitated toward a young black comic who'd moved to New York from Chicago a few years earlier: Robert Townsend. "We were the only two brothers standing in line," Keenen said.

After waiting around all day, Keenen was blessed with a ticket. When he finally got onstage to do his five minutes, the feeling was surreal. It had been more than a decade since he first got chased home from elementary school and chanced upon Richard Pryor on television. He could always crack his friends up, and had learned to make his siblings laugh—or "die" if he didn't. He'd spent countless hours sealed in his bedroom closet daydreaming about his future life as a comedian. But until he stepped on that small stage at the Improv, it had all been his secret, safely tucked away. If no one knew, no one would ever know his failure. Once he stepped out in front of that tiny crowd of drunken New Yorkers, the dream wasn't just his anymore. It was public. It was a declaration of intent. He wasn't just a funny dude on the corner who could always make his stoned friends laugh. He was an aspiring comedian.

It didn't go well.

"I bombed terribly," he said. Yet that didn't fully encapsulate what happened that night for Keenen. "It was an out-of-body experience. I was standing onstage, but at the same time I was able to see myself. [There] was only about five people in the audience and [there] was . . . scattered laughter. Still, I was looking at myself like, *You're doing it*. It was like I'd stepped into my dream—all those years and the feeling was as good as I thought it was going to be. I didn't care about laughter at that moment because I knew I could do this."

Keenen didn't "pass," but he started hanging out at the Improv every night. He took to studying the comics and their routines with an intensity he'd never brought to his college courses.

"I started to understand how you work a stage and tell a joke," he said. "Also, me being a kid from the projects, my audience at the Improv was tourists and people from New Jersey—you know, all white. I had to learn to translate my experiences to a different group of people."

By his third audition, Keenen nailed it. He was officially an Improv regular. Robert Townsend was immediately impressed with his new friend.

"One of his first jokes, he goes, 'I'm from a family of ten kids. My *father* had stretch marks,'" Townsend says. "Even as a young comedian, Keenen was kind of a master craftsman. He knew instinctively how to set up a punch, deliver the joke, rewrite the structure, make it funnier."

At the end of the summer of 1978, Keenen returned to Tuskegee, but flush from his experiences at the Improv, his college days were numbered. Now that he knew what he wanted to do with his life, now that he'd had a taste of it, the idea of studying to be an engineer felt like a waste of time and money. Or worse, a mark of personal cowardice. Albrecht had laid it out for him in stark terms before he left: "If you're serious about this, you need to be here year-round."

He knew this was going to be a difficult conversation with his parents. They'd always emphasized the importance of education and had beamed when he'd become the first person in the family to go to college a few years earlier. But when he returned home to New York later in the school year, he sat on the dryer in the family's apartment one evening and explained to his mother he was dropping out. Marlon, then just in elementary school, watched the conversation unfold.

"My mother cursed Keenen out," he recalled. "My mother said, 'Boy, a standup comedian? I known you your whole life and you ain't never said nothing funny. This shit is the funniest thing you ever said! You're going to be standup comedian? Let me tell you something, boy: You better go out there and get your engineer's degree and a job with some benefits!'"

Howell too tried to reason with Keenen.

"Son, you should finish school. Get the degree so you have something to fall back on."

"I understand that," he told his father. "But if I have a cushion that I know I can fall on, I'll allow myself to fall. If I know there's nothing but hard concrete, I'm going to do my best to stay standing." His parents weren't convinced. "I might as well have said I was going to smoke crack," Keenen said. "But I knew deep in myself what I wanted to be. I knew I was going to do it."

———

Becoming a regular at the Improv was an accomplishment for a kid who was barely twenty. Unfortunately for Keenen, it wasn't the kind of accomplishment that came with a steady paycheck. He moved back into his family's apartment in the Fulton Houses and got a job working the door at the club.

His first actual paying standup gig wasn't a memorable one, or at least not memorable in the way he would've hoped. It had all the hallmarks of a disaster from the outset: He was booked to perform at a racquetball convention.

"It was me, by the juice bar, with a microphone, and racquetball courts all around me," Keenen recalled. "People came to the juice bar [as] I was trying to do my act. Right at the punch line, the blender would go 'Eeeeek-kkk!' or the PA would go 'Court 3 is open.'" But even in this debacle, there was a lesson to be learned. "Distraction is the death of comedy. You can have the audience right there, the setup is going great, and just as you get to the punch line, a waitress puts a glass down—clink!—and it dies."

Eventually more paying gigs materialized, often opening for musicians, at clubs like the Village Gate. The money typically stunk, but Keenen was soaking up the experience like a sponge. The Improv was like a graduate seminar in standup in those days. Larry David, Jerry Seinfeld, Jay Leno, Larry Miller, Robert Wuhl, Joe Piscopo, and Bill Maher were regulars. Guys like Robin Williams and Rodney Dangerfield would stop in to work on material. Sitting in the club, waiting to go on, the conversations were about comedy. *Did you see my set last night? That premise was great, but why didn't the punch line work as well as it should have? Why don't you try doing it this way?* Comics traded standup tips over drinks, recommended movies to each other, analyzed *Tonight Show* sets, tried out material on each other. When the club closed, the comics would continue the conversation at cheap, all-night eateries like the Green

Kitchen or the Market Diner. When they weren't at the club, they'd get together and play poker or touch football.

Keenen hung around the club often and sometimes played on the Improv's softball team. (DeBellis's scouting report: "Really smooth but couldn't hit.") He felt very much part of a community.

"There was a great camaraderie in the clubs back then," Keenen said. "Part of why I think that generation prospered like it did is because we all looked out for each other. If you were a new comic and you did a bit and Jerry Seinfeld had a bit that was similar, he wouldn't have to say anything. I'd come up and go, 'Yo, you can't do that. That's Jerry's bit.' What that did is that forced everyone to be individuals." Those who didn't adhere to this code were ostracized. "It was a brotherhood," he said. "That's what really helped create my voice."

Like in any community—particularly one largely populated with wildly insecure, occasionally drug-addled neurotics who measured their self-worth in a combination of belly laughs and career advancements—there were rivalries, jealousies, and fights. But the stakes, relatively speaking, were still low then. The comedy industry was in its infancy. The goal for most of the comics at the Improv was—best case—a shot on *The Tonight Show*. Other paths forward were just beginning to suggest themselves—Gabe Kaplan, Freddie Prinze, Robin Williams, and Jimmie Walker had all recently graduated from the clubs to network sitcom deals, and *Saturday Night Live* had also started up in 1975, just a few blocks away—but opportunities were few and far enough between that cutthroat, knife-in-the-back competitiveness was relatively rare. Keenen was well liked and even those who weren't blown away by his act felt that he had something intangible.

"His standup was okay, but my ex-wife used to say he was the best-looking guy she's ever seen," says DeBellis. "He had a huge smile and an infectious laugh. It would draw you in."

Keenen's comedy progressed but the cultural gap between him and the mostly white audience sometimes felt unbridgeable. Albrecht, then the club's manager, was a consistent sounding board and mentor for Keenen, often dispensing pearls of advice before or after a set.

"One night, Chris goes, 'When you go on, I want you to say *I* and *me*. Never say *yours* and *ours*,'" Keenen said. "'The more specific you are, the funnier you're going to be.'" Keenen made the adjustment and noticed a difference. "I realized that if I were to come on and say, 'All of our mothers do this,' then people would sit back and go, 'Well, I don't know if my mother does that.' But if I say, 'My mother does this,' then people either go, 'Yeah, my mother does that too!' or, 'Your mom is funny!'" With time, Keenen's comedy became broader, smoother, more inclusive.

The New York comedy scene represented nearly as big a cultural whiplash for Keenen as decamping for Tuskegee had been. There were few black comics, and the ones there tended to congregate around each other. Keenen and Robert Townsend felt an instant kinship. Both had grown up poor—Townsend on Chicago's West Side—but they were decidedly different people. When Keenen first visited Robert at his apartment in Queens, he could see that immediately.

"He invites me over and lays out wine and cheese," Keenen said. "I didn't know if he was classy or gay. And it was different kinds of cheese. I didn't know where to start. The only cheese I knew was the government block."

As a kid, Townsend's mother shielded him from neighborhood gangs in Chicago by keeping him inside, where he spent lots of time in front of the television, honing impressions of James Cagney, Humphrey Bogart, and Bill Cosby. As a young man, he worked as an actor in Chicago, performing with the city's Experimental Black Actors Guild, then enrolled in college, first at Illinois State University and then at Hunter College in New York. Like Keenen, he eventually quit school to follow his dream of being a performer. In New York, Townsend worked and studied with the Negro Ensemble Company, and occasionally scored acting work in commercials. But his frustration with the opportunities available to him as a black actor convinced him to give standup a try.

"I just loved performing," Townsend says. "I had gone to see an all-black and Hispanic version of *Julius Caesar*. Some of the actors had the language down and some sounded like they came off 125th Street. I crafted my first [standup] routine based on that. That started me as a comedian, but I was never a pure standup. I was doing characters."

Unlike Keenen, who "passed" at the Improv quickly, it took Robert longer. Keenen did his best to help.

"He schooled me on how to work the system," Townsend says. "He was like, 'Ask for this spot, not that spot.' 'Show up at this time, not that time.' By the time I worked Keenen's system, I got in."

Robert returned the favor by sharing what he'd learned as a struggling actor.

"It was a good exchange," said Keenen. "He taught me the business of acting and I taught him the business of comedy."

The friendship wasn't simply transactional. These were two guys in their early twenties who'd already made it far enough from their humble beginnings to be imbued with a sense of possibility that outstripped what any clear-eyed, sober assessment might promise. They were funny, handsome, smart, and confident that those qualities would be enough to shrug off all the forces conspiring to crush their ambitions.

"We just clicked," says Townsend. That said, he was occasionally startled at what made Keenen laugh. "I'd visit him in his neighborhood in Chelsea and he'd have his friends try to rob me. He wanted to see what [I] was gonna do. He thought that shit was funny. His sense of humor can be twisted."

———

There were so few black comics in New York in this era that if you ask one of them how many there were, they'll usually start naming them. *Let's see, there was Keenen, Robert Townsend, George Wallace, John Ridley, Barry "Berry" Douglas, that crazy dude Maurice who used to do an impression of Humphrey Bogart on cocaine . . .* Certainly, you could count them on your fingers and still have a few fingers left over to hold your cigarette. So when a new one emerged, the others heard about him.

In 1978, Keenen was working the door at the Improv, when a short, skinny black guy—a kid, really—walked up and stuck out his hand.

"Hey, I'm Eddie Murphy. I thought I was the only funny black man in New York. Now I see there are two."

Keenen had heard about Eddie. He was barely seventeen and cocky as hell. He'd mostly been performing in clubs on Long Island, near where he'd grown up in Roosevelt, but carried himself like a guy poised to take Manhattan. Keenen liked him right away and helped get him an audition at the Improv. Silver Friedman, Budd's ex-wife, had recently won control of the club in their divorce, and was running the Sunday tryouts.

"Silver was different from Budd or Chris Albrecht in that she wanted clean humor," Keenen said. "It wasn't that Eddie was dirty, but he was young." His material at the time, Keenen explained, revolved mostly around "boogers and farts and doo-doo. So he goes on and he does his booger set. Silver is horrified. She's like, 'I don't allow toilet humor in my club.'" Keenen cajoled Eddie to try again the next week, but counseled him to leave out the booger-related material. "He comes back and the next set is his fart stuff. He comes offstage and he's really proud of himself because he didn't do the booger stuff and he still killed. Silver just looks at him and goes, 'I don't chew my cabbage twice,' and walks away." Keenen tried to convince Eddie to come back a third time, but the younger comedian had had enough of the Improv.

Eddie tried his luck across town at the Comic Strip.

"He was a fucking riot," says Richie Tienken, one of the Strip's co-owners. Eddie became a regular there and, within a few months, asked Tienken to manage him. "I turned him down. What the fuck did I know about managing?"

Eddie asked again. And again. Tienken didn't understand his insistence. Eddie explained that he'd been complaining to his mother that everyone he met was trying to screw him over. She asked if he trusted anyone, and he realized Tienken was the only one. So Tienken relented. "I said, 'So if we fuck this up, we can blame it on your mother?'"

———

Townsend started working as part of an all-black improv comedy group called the Kitchen Table, alongside friends he'd met at the Negro Ensemble Company: Reginald VelJohnson, Angela Scott, Melvin George, and Pam Jones. They'd typically practice sitting around the kitchen table—hence the name—at Scott's fifth-floor walkup on the Lower East Side. According to George, they were the only black comedy team in New York at the time. They'd sometimes get late-night spots at the Improv, Catch, and the Strip, but failing that, they'd set up in Washington Square Park, where they'd often perform alongside legendary street comic Charlie Barnett. ("Not with him, near him," Scott says. "Because Charlie always commanded the biggest crowds.") Their comedy leaned absurdist. They did a musical parody of "Send in the Clowns" called "Send in the Clones." There was a spoof of McDonald's called "McMama's," and send-ups of various television shows and commercials.

"Because we were an African-American group, we were considered a novelty," says VelJohnson, who later starred in *Die Hard*, *Crocodile Dundee*, and as the father on the ABC sitcom *Family Matters*. Still, they were careful not to lean too hard on race. "We happened to be African-Americans who were funny, but we didn't play on the fact that we were African-Americans trying to be funny. We were funny first."

Through Townsend and the Improv, the members of the Kitchen Table met Keenen. When Scott was first introduced to him, Keenen was working the door at the club.

"He wasn't a warm, fuzzy bunny, let's just say that," Scott recalls. "Onstage, he was funny, fun, accessible, animated. Offstage, the opposite."

At least, initially. Keenen was shy, which was sometimes interpreted as standoffish, though as Scott got to know him, he warmed up. Within a few months, Scott, George, VelJohnson, Townsend, and Keenen were hanging out regularly.

"After the Improv closed, we'd all hop into Melvin's car and go on up to M&G's, a soul food restaurant on 125th Street," says Scott. "I'd be on Keenen's lap, and then we'd peel out like clowns at a circus, running inside trying to get fried chicken or the last mac and cheese."

These comics became a support group within the larger New York comedy community. When one of them got a good Friday-night spot, did a good set, got a callback for an audition, they were all buoyed.

"It wasn't a matter of being competitive," says George. "You have to remember this was a time when there were no blacks on television." Once *Good Times* and *What's Happening!!* went off the air in 1979, the only predominantly black major network series left was *The Jeffersons*, until 1984 when *The Cosby Show* premiered. "There was just no black representation on TV, so if somebody got a break, we were happy for them."

George would often visit the Wayanses' apartment, where Keenen's youngest brothers, then just in elementary school, would initiate him into the family's kill-or-be-killed comedy culture.

"Shawn and Marlon used to make fun of me because of the way I dressed," he says. "I always wanted to have a job where I had to wear a

suit. Comedy was my job, so I dressed for it. But it wasn't just your normal suit and tie. I had a tuxedo jacket, a ruffle shirt, bell-bottom slacks.
Shawn and Marlon always made fun of what I was wearing, saying I just
got off the clown shift, and my pants were made from the curtains hanging in the window. Every time I went over there, they lit into me."

By 1979, Townsend was booking a lot of commercials. With the income, he began buying professional-grade video equipment. Soon, he had
cameras, lights, microphones, and converted a part of his one-bedroom
apartment in Woodside, Queens, into a small soundstage. One of the first
things he decided to film was the Kitchen Table. Keenen, who until this
point hadn't been a part of the comedy troupe, came along and suggested
that his younger brother Damon come too.

"Damon was working at Smiley's Deli at the time," Townsend says. "I
remember Keenen saying, 'We gotta get my baby brother involved. He's
really funny and can do characters.'"

There was no grand plan around filming that day. No one was thinking about making a pilot or a "sizzle reel" or sending out the tape to agents
or entertainment executives. The main thought was simply *We've got this
camera equipment, we've got this improv group, wouldn't it be fun to
see ourselves on tape?* The group got together once to rehearse, then met
again at Townsend's apartment and turned on the cameras.

"We were just having fun," says Scott. "We were trying characters
out that we'd later bring to the stage."

Still, even in these relaxed environs, a vague hierarchy emerged.

"Keenen would say, 'Melvin, you're this guy. Angela, you're this girl—
go!'" George explains. "Then we'd improv. Then Bobby would go, 'Okay,
let's do it this way: Melvin, you're this person. Angela, you're this person.
Reggie, you're this person—go!' Then we'd act that scene out.'"

VelJohnson was particularly impressed with Keenen. "He was always the one who had ideas for bigger things," he says. "I was in awe of
his ability to manage and put together comedy bits. I saw him as a leader,
as the great innovator."

Still, the major revelation from the day spent filming in Robert's
apartment was neither Keenen nor Robert. It was Damon.

"He was brilliant," says Scott. "Genius."

"He was so damn funny it made me insecure," says Townsend.

"That's your baby brother!? He's working at a *deli*?" Townsend asked. It wasn't just Damon's first time performing on camera, it was his first time performing anywhere. "He had this hat he stuffed with paper and was a Jamaican dude on the corner acting crazy." He had other characters too: a gay film critic, a neighborhood hustler who, along with his brother— played by Keenen—sold stolen goods from the back of a truck. "All those characters he'd eventually do on *In Living Color*, I saw in my apartment."

The Kitchen Table didn't last much longer. But a seed was planted in that Queens apartment, and even though nobody knew then what it might grow into, there was a feeling that something important had transpired. As Keenen later told an interviewer, "After we did it, we thought, *Damn, we wish we could do this all the time*. In the back of my head, that always stayed with me."

4

"Richard Was a God, So We Were Just Lucky to Be in His Orbit"

New York City was a strange place in the late seventies. Yes, there were blackouts, subway trains covered in graffiti, and a crime spike across the city. Each day seemed to bring a grim new harbinger of doom: *Son of Sam*. Fires rage across the South Bronx. A helicopter crashes into the top of the Pan Am building. A Turkish bathhouse burns to the ground. But it was also a time of reasonably cheap rents and seemingly infinite possibility. Artists, performers, musicians, and comedians could afford to live in parts of Manhattan. It was the era of CBGBs, Martin Scorsese, Max's Kansas City, and Woody Allen. Disco, unfairly dismissed because of its connections to various fringe subcultures—gay, black, drug—was congealing into something harder, less polite.

Keenen recalls walking by a record store in Chelsea around this time and hearing "Rapper's Delight" by the Sugarhill Gang, blaring from speakers inside. The song was simple: three MCs dropping rhymes over the backing track of Chic's "Good Times." But for Keenen, there was more going on. It was as if someone had taken the sounds, the energy, the feel of those summer nights that he'd begun soaking up in parks and parties across Harlem and the Bronx and distilled them onto vinyl. The amazing thing wasn't so much the song itself—even though it would become *the* song that would introduce much of the world to hip-hop—but that some person, some record company thought it was worth preserving this tiny corner of culture for posterity. It had value.

"They were playing it on the turntable," Keenen says. "We were staring at it because it was like, *This is the shit that was in the streets and now it's on a record. This shit is real now.* It was magical."

Damon was even more of a hip-hop diehard. In December 1978, he saw Grandmaster Flash at the Audubon Ballroom in Harlem—incidentally the same ballroom where Malcolm X had been assassinated thirteen years earlier. "I was there when Flash first spun a song called 'Hot Shot,'" Damon said. "Just 'Hot shot, hot shot, hot shot,' for about an hour. But it was the first time we ever saw that, so it was fly."

When *Saturday Night Live* debuted in 1975, it seemed to capture something ineffable about seventies-era New York. *The Tonight Show* had relocated to California three years earlier, leaving the city, once a hub of the entertainment universe, bereft of any real presence on television. Yet, with the Improv and Catch cooking, and the Comic Strip recently opened, New York's comedy scene was thriving. When *SNL* started its first season that fall, it had a scrappy, underdog quality. The studio looked lived-in, the sets like something salvaged from the basement of a local community center. As the show's creator Lorne Michaels explained in Doug Hill and Jeff Weingrad's book *Saturday Night: A Backstage History of* Saturday Night Live, it was all intentional.

"Instead of looking all shiny and Mylar, it looked sort of run-down and beat-up, like New York City did," said Michaels.

The show's cast and writers weren't necessarily plugged in to the New York standup scene—although hosts and guest stars like George Carlin, Robert Klein, Lily Tomlin, and Andy Kaufman were. Much like that scene, *SNL* was overwhelmingly white. The show's lone black cast member, Garrett Morris, had originally been hired as its lone black writer. His participation and impact were laughably minimal. As with the clubs in New York, this isn't to suggest there was a racist conspiracy afoot or that either the show or the scene was populated by small-minded bigots—though, there may have been some. These on-the-ground facts were the legacy of a two-track culture of unequal opportunities that went back generations, if not centuries, and a rather blasé attitude toward remedying them. Lorne Michaels was a Canadian, and when he and the team behind *SNL* started working on the show, they were coming from the worlds of improv, standup, and television variety shows. When it came time to cast or hire writers and crew, the people they knew, the people the casting directors knew were from those same worlds, all of which were—like just about every corner of mainstream entertainment—very white.

There were some efforts to redress this imbalance at *SNL*, most notably enlisting Richard Pryor to host the show during that first season. By December 1975, Pryor was years into his personal reinvention. Since emerging from his woodshedding period in Berkeley around 1972, his standup had begun introducing audiences to the parade of fuckups, assholes, and malcontents that had shaped Pryor's life—Pryor, himself, being the chief fuckup, asshole, and malcontent of all. He rendered them in details vivid enough to be equal parts charming, disturbing, and hilarious. His act read like a satirical commentary on the failures and hypocrisies of post–civil rights America, and as such, rarely seemed all that funny *on paper*. It was only the way Pryor inhabited the characters, the material, and the emotions that made laughter a more natural reaction than tears. His willingness to flout convention and stoke controversy made him widely revered—his 1974 album *That Nigger's Crazy* had won a Grammy and the follow-up, *Is It Something I Said?*, released earlier in 1975, had already sold half a million copies—but also widely feared. Given his popularity and critical acclaim, it made sense that Michaels would want to work with him. But he had a well-earned reputation as an incorrigible drug addict and an unmanageable pain in the ass. When NBC balked at hiring him as a guest host, Michaels resigned.

NBC eventually caved, but that wasn't the end of the story. Michaels flew to Florida and met with Pryor at a jai alai arena. Pryor insisted the only way he'd host is if *SNL* also hired a black actor named Thalmus Rasulala; a black musical guest, Gil Scott-Heron; a black writer, Paul Mooney (a standup comic who wrote with Pryor); Pryor's girlfriend, Kathy McKee; and Pryor's ex-wife, Shelly, for the episode. Michaels agreed to all of it, mumbling to his traveling companions on the way back to New York, "He'd better be funny."

He was. To their credit, neither Pryor nor the *SNL* cast and writers skirted the elephant in the room: race. In one sketch, he plays an author who had whitened his skin in order to experience life as a white man. In another, a father's fears that blacks are taking over the neighborhood are mockingly realized when his children turn black. In a recurring gag, Gilda Radner pops up repeatedly to pick Pryor out of police lineups. Gil Scott-Heron performs his anti-apartheid anthem "Johannesburg." Pryor even manages to name-drop Dick Gregory, a pioneering, politically charged black standup, into one sketch, and get screen time for the ever-marginalized Garrett Morris. But the coup de grâce was a short sketch in which Chevy Chase is interviewing Pryor for a job as a janitor. They play "word association," which starts innocently enough—Chase says "tree," Pryor says "dog," Chase says "fast," Pryor answers "slow," etc.—before devolving into something infinitely more prickly. Chase says "Negro," and Pryor answers with "Whitey, " then comes "Jungle Bunny" and "Honky," and eventually "Nigger" and "Dead Honky."

Mooney, who wrote the sketch—at least according to Mooney; Chase also claims authorship of it—called it the easiest sketch he ever wrote. As a writer and a standup, Mooney was a flamethrower who saw the world in black and white. He didn't believe in sugarcoating the truth, and he'd been a huge influence on Pryor's comedic transformation. Having Chase call Pryor a "nigger" on national television was, in Mooney's view, just vocalizing what white America thought every time they looked at Pryor or Cosby or Gregory or Mooney. In his own memoir, *Black Is the New White*, Mooney is only slightly overstating it when he says the sketch was "like an H-bomb that Richard and I toss into America's consciousness. All that shit going on behind closed doors is now out in the open. There's no putting the genie back in the bottle."

NBC was enamored enough with Pryor's *SNL* appearance that they gave him a prime-time special, which went so well that they then offered him his own ten-episode comedy-variety series in 1977. Pryor's career was near its apex—he'd just starred in *Silver Streak* with Gene Wilder, giving him his first mainstream box office hit and pretty much inventing the modern white guy–black guy buddy comedy formula still beloved in Hollywood today—and NBC was television's lowest-rated network, which led Pryor to believe he'd have a free hand creatively. He didn't, in fact, have the creative freedom he expected, though that might not be why Pryor made only four episodes before the whole thing fell apart.

The story of the rise and fall of *The Richard Pryor Show* is amusing, infuriating, and in many ways, completely predictable. There was trouble from the outset, coming from multiple directions. At the press conference announcing the show, it wasn't clear Pryor even knew what he'd signed up for. He told an NBC publicist he was just doing a few specials, apparently unaware he'd been contracted for a ten-episode series. Pryor was immediately concerned whether he had enough creative juice or the discipline to produce an hour of television every week. According to Mooney, Pryor was indulging mightily in booze and cocaine, which wasn't helping with the discipline part of that equation. He was also concerned that NBC would never let him do the kind of cutting-edge comedy he'd worked so hard to discover in himself. He was tortured by the idea that he might be selling out. As Mooney put it in his book, Pryor's "main stressor, one that he can't resolve, is that whenever he does something popular, he's afraid he's not keeping it real."

But when the show's creative team—which included Mooney, producer Rocco Urbisci, and writer-producer David Banks—initially began meeting at Pryor's home to write the first episode, there was ample reason for optimism. The ideas they were conjuring imagined the sketches Pryor had done on *SNL* as a jumping-off point for the new material, but these would go farther, probe deeper, and be much, much stranger. Mooney recruited a talented young cast that included Robin Williams (in his first television appearance), Sandra Bernhard, Marsha Warfield, John Witherspoon, and Tim Reid. As Warfield recalls, most of the cast were just happy to be asked.

"You have to remember, we were peons and Richard was a god, so we were just lucky to be in his orbit," she says.

For the first episode's opening sketch, Pryor wanted to throw down the gauntlet and make clear how uneasy his alliance with NBC was. An initial idea to show him undergoing a Frankenstein-like operation to be implanted with the brain of an inoffensive white guy was considered but ultimately jettisoned. In its place was Pryor, initially in a tight shot framing just his head and shoulders, introducing the show and addressing very real doubts—including his own—that a comedian as transgressive as he was could possibly work on prime-time network television.

"People say, 'Well how can you have a show? You'll have to compromise. You'll have to give up everything.' Is that a joke or what? Well, look at me: I'm standing here naked." At this point, the camera pulls back to reveal that Pryor is, in fact, naked. "I've given up absolutely nothing!" The full reveal now shows that the completely nude Pryor has been literally neutered—his dick and balls smoothed over to look like the undercarriage of a Ken doll. "So enjoy the show!"

NBC wasn't happy and told Urbisci on the morning the show was to air that they wanted the segment cut. He refused to edit it out and was fired. When Pryor was told, he held a press conference to announce he was quitting. "Everybody will say I'm crazy if I quit, that I'm the crazy nigger who ran off from NBC, but this is stifling my creativity. I can't work under these conditions." (Ironically, the opening sketch was probably more widely seen on newscasts covering the censorship than it would've otherwise been.)

Three episodes were already in the can and a fourth was done filming. The four episodes that aired offered a tantalizing look at what might've been. With the planned cold open pulled, the first episode instead begins with a sketch in which Pryor plays the proprietor of the "Star Wars Bar." Playing off creatures who only speak in unintelligible grunts and moans, Pryor mostly improvises. At one point, he surveys a hulking, troll-like monster in a cloak, shrugs, and says, "You look just like a nigger from Detroit I know." The line got huge laughs in the studio and the control room. According to Urbisci, NBC wasn't comfortable with it but "couldn't cut it because Richard said it. To cut it would've caused more controversy. So the N-word got on TV in prime time." Pryor, it turned out, was so blackout drunk when he filmed the take that he didn't even remember doing it.

Later in the episode, Pryor plays a fictional black president conducting a press conference. He proudly announces that Huey Newton—Pryor's old Berkeley buddy—is being nominated to be FBI director, promises more black quarterbacks in the NFL, and refuses to quit chasing white women. Finally, a white reporter stands and asks, "After your tenure, if your mother goes back to being a maid, will your mama do my house?"

It's a punch line that reiterated the point the "Word Association" sketch had made two years earlier on *SNL*: No matter how African-Americans look, no matter what they achieve, they'll always look the same in the eyes of white people—or at least some of them.

The episode ends with Pryor waving to the audience. "Good night. See you next week," he says, as a jail door closes and it's clear NBC is holding him against his will.

In a sketch in the second episode, Pryor is the lone black man on a team of explorers who find the Book of Life in an Egyptian tomb. As Pryor begins reading from the ancient text, he discovers written proof that civilization was created by black people.

"There ain't nothing here about Whitey!" he declares. "This is ours! Wait till the brothers hear this!" As he grows excited, his white colleagues quietly back out of the tomb and seal it up.

"Get the bulldozers," says the lead explorer. "There's nothing here."

Not everything on the show was even comedy. In the third episode, Pryor is doing a Little Richard impression when suddenly the screen goes fuzzy and black. When it flickers back on, a young woman is sitting, talking to the camera, telling multiple versions of a story of a sexual encounter with another woman. The effect is neither titillating nor comic but still undeniably compelling. The fourth episode features more than fifteen minutes of a raucous roast of Pryor by the cast and producers, as well as a final speech from Pryor as a drunken Santa Claus which is interrupted a dozen times by a buzzing black screen with the word "CENSORED" on it.

And that was that. After four episodes of this bizarre television experiment, Pryor and NBC were happy to be rid of each other. Pryor complained that the network wouldn't let him do what he wanted—which they wouldn't—but, as Sandra Bernhard recalls, there were other problems too.

"Richard didn't like the medium," she says. "He didn't like having to be there every day and having to be creative in that way. He's a very interior person." The show's ratings started off low and kept going down, so NBC wasn't exactly pleading for him to return. Although many in retrospect have called the show a classic, the fact is, very few of them were watching it in 1977. But one of those few was Keenen Ivory Wayans. Echoes of the

Pryor show and its gleefully skewed view of the white world through a black man's eyes would eventually reverberate on *In Living Color* more than a decade later. To Keenen, there was something boundless about Pryor's comedy. Even when it didn't work, when bits fell flat, they fell flat reaching for something.

"Other comedians worked within the confines of their time," said Keenen. "Pryor broke that mold. He redefined what you were able to do." Seeing Pryor embrace the sides of himself that weren't necessarily appealing or commercial or even funny was inspiring. "I was always a weird kid, but I just couldn't figure out what was strange about me. Watching Richard Pryor, I got a sense that it was my humor that made me different."

"There's a New Sheriff in Town"

n 1980, *Saturday Night Live* collapsed. Relations between Lorne Michaels and NBC had been strained, and once contract negotiations with Michaels broke down, it all fell apart. After five seasons, the entire cast left, as did all the writers. NBC pressed on, with a new producer, Jean Doumanian, and a new writing staff. Doumanian hired six white cast members—Charles Rocket, Ann Risley, Gail Matthius, Denny Dillon, Gilbert Gottfried, and Joe Piscopo—but two months before the sixth season was set to premiere, she was still looking for an "ethnic" to fill out the cast.

In September 1980, the show held a special series of auditions that drew a few dozen black actors and comedians. The producers initially seemed to settle on Charlie Barnett, the energetic, charismatic comic known for dazzling crowds in Washington Square Park, but there were reportedly issues with his ability to read cue cards, and he was sent packing. With Barnett no longer in contention, it appeared Robert Townsend had the inside track. There was just one hiccup. Eddie Murphy, who had missed the auditions because he was performing in Florida, kept calling Neil Levy, the show's talent coordinator at the time, asking if he could audition.

"Eddie would call as different people, different characters, and he'd somehow get through my assistant and make me laugh," says Levy. "I'd heard that Jean had already settled on Robert, so I'd tell him we've already got our cast. He wouldn't give up."

He wore Levy down. Eddie was invited to the *SNL* offices on the seventeenth floor at 30 Rockefeller Plaza for an audition. He did some standup and sketch work, which included reading Pryor's part in the five-year-old "Word Association" sketch, opposite Piscopo. Everyone was blown away except Doumanian, who, according to Levy, still wanted Townsend.

"I lost my head," says Levy. "I threatened to quit, and in that moment she said, 'okay.'" Townsend hadn't signed his contract yet, so he was jettisoned and Eddie was hired.

Richie Tienken, Eddie's co-manager at the time, recalls the sequence of events differently. In his telling, Eddie had already auditioned for *SNL* but was passed over in favor of Barnett. After Barnett was let go, Eddie was in Florida with Tienken when *SNL* called asking to see Eddie again. Eddie's initial reaction was, according to Tienken, more along the lines of "Fuck them! They saw me already!" But Tienken convinced Eddie to fly back to New York, and soon enough, the part was his.

Initially Eddie, then nineteen, was only a "featured player," not a full cast member, and was treated as such. In the first two episodes of the season, both of which were viciously panned by critics, Eddie appeared on-screen a grand total of one time, as an extra sitting on a couch with no lines. The show was bleeding viewers, and behind the scenes, Eddie was being ignored by most of the all-white writing staff. But in the third episode, he finally got his chance during a "Weekend Update" bit in which he plays "Raheem Abdul Muhammed," a high school basketball player upset at a recent court ruling in Cleveland that insists that all teams have at least two white players. Eddie's short monologue was not only funny, it was a pointed commentary on race from a series that had generally avoided the subject.

"Anytime we get something going good, y'all move in on it," Eddie's Raheem says. "In the sixties, we wore platform shoes. Then, y'all wore platform shoes. Then in the early seventies, we braided our hair. In the late seventies, y'all braided your hair . . . I don't see no judge saying that every two bathroom attendants have to be white!"

The speech was less than a minute long but made an impact. Eddie's stage time steadily increased after that. His characters and sketches often grew out of improvising with the writers, particularly Barry Blaustein and David Sheffield, who became his favorites. John DeBellis, who'd known Eddie from the New York clubs, got a job writing on the show that same year.

"Eddie was very cocky," says DeBellis. "I got along with him, but I remember how confident he was, how relaxed he was—so relaxed that it gave him that presence."

Still, it was the middle of the season before Eddie was promoted to full cast status, something he held against Doumanian for years afterward. As he put it to *TV Guide*, "She tried to Garrett Morris me—turn me into the little token nigger."

That 1980–81 season is widely considered the low ebb in a series that has seen plenty of peaks and valleys during its forty-plus-year run. Doumanian was ousted midway through the season. Eddie was generally the only reason to watch, and when the season finished, there was a purge of the cast and writers. Among the performers, only Piscopo and Eddie survived.

Eddie's four-year run on *SNL* did more than make him a big star. It injected an often defiantly black voice onto American television in a way that hadn't been consistently seen before. Sure, he was still on a predominantly white show, with predominantly white writers, but Eddie had such force of personality that he quickly became the show's creative center. Even in sketches in which he was a supporting player, his blackness nearly always lent the proceedings another layer, a different viewpoint. Everything bent toward him. And much like Pryor before him, Eddie appeared to delight in skewering his employer. In one of his earliest appearances on the show, he delivers a "Weekend Update commentary" on the military draft, in which he makes the case why he, Eddie Murphy, shouldn't be drafted.

"If I get drafted, who is going to be the token black on *Saturday Night Live*?" he asks, before suggesting someone who could take his place in the military. "This is the man whose very name scares the hell out of me," he says, holding up a photo of Garrett Morris. "I know he's a little over-age, but word has it that he has a lot of free time right now."

When Lou Gossett Jr. hosted the show during season eight, he and Eddie began a sketch playing a father and son, at odds with each other, living in poverty, until they abruptly break character to deconstruct the black stereotypes on display in that very sketch, bringing the white writer to the stage to upbraid him. In a later season, Eddie fronts a reggae band who play their catchy, upbeat tune, "Kill the White People," to a shocked audience at an all-white VFW hall. In a memorable turn on Eddie's final season on the show that seems to directly echo one of Pryor's sketches as guest host nine years earlier, Eddie undergoes elaborate makeup to be transformed into a white man. As "Mr. White," he experiences the joys of living in the white world—impromptu cocktail parties on public transportation; free, no-questions-asked loans from banks—as part of an undercover exposé.

Dick Ebersol, who'd been an NBC executive at the show's creation and ran the show from when Doumanian was fired until Michaels returned in 1985, said, "Eddie is the single most important performer in the history of the show. He literally saved the show."

SNL gave Eddie a weekly dialogue with viewers who, in turn, saw him in a different light than they'd seen Pryor, Cosby, Flip Wilson, or any other black comic before him. Cocksure and charismatic, Eddie was a rock star. This was reflected in the iconic movie roles that helped define his career in the early eighties—*48 Hrs.*, *Trading Places*, and *Beverly Hills Cop*.

"Eddie changed American acting a little bit," said Chris Rock, who hadn't yet begun his standup career back then. "I remember the way black guys used to act in movies before *48 Hrs.* There was a sidekick way of acting that Eddie didn't incorporate. There's the Negro Ensemble way of acting—very earnest: 'I'm representing my race!' Murph was one of the first black actors who acted like a normal person. It's almost like not acting."

Eddie isn't in *48 Hrs.*, *Trading Places*, and *Beverly Hills Cop* to be the wisecracking comic relief. He *is* those films. He is their entire reason for being. He swaggered through every scene, in total control. As he did on *SNL*, he made it impossible to take your eyes off him.

Keenen had met Eddie just before this explosion began, but for the most part, their friendship was forged during Eddie's meteoric rise. He watched his friend go from a guy who couldn't get over doing booger and fart jokes at the Improv to one of the biggest stars in Hollywood, all in a couple of years. None of it surprised him.

"Eddie never felt like because he was black that was going to be an obstacle for him," said Keenen. "Everything about Eddie was organic." Keenen, who'd been such a devotee of Pryor, sensed that Eddie's appeal was different. Lots of white people certainly loved Richard Pryor, but white people wanted to *be* Eddie Murphy. "I remember watching *48 Hrs.*, and the scene when he goes into that bar, when he puts the cowboy hat on and says, 'There's a new sheriff in town.' The audience went crazy. I sat there going, 'He's a superstar.' There *is* a new sheriff in town."

It was more than just a Hollywood moment. In much the same way that blaxploitation films had a decade earlier, *48 Hrs.* laid bare the naked racism that the black community often felt from the white establishment. Consider what was going on in the country at the time: In New York City, increasingly draconian policing and public safety tactics in the seventies had polarized the city. The "War on Graffiti" overwhelmingly targeted black and Latino youth, disingenuously connecting their tagging with high crime rates. By the end of the decade, over a quarter of the white population of the city—more than 1.2 million residents—had departed.

The Civil Rights Movement had done little to alter African-Americans' relationship with the police in the seventies and eighties. At best, that relationship might be described as wary; at worst, it was out-right antagonistic. And hardly without cause. In early 1979, Eulia Love, a thirty-nine-year-old Los Angeles resident, was shot eight times and killed by LAPD officers after a dispute in her home regarding a twenty-two-dollar gas bill. No officers were disciplined, and LAPD police chief Daryl Gates later said one of the officers involved was "just as much a victim of this tragedy as Eulia Love." Later that same year, Arthur McDuffie, a thirty-three-year-old black ex-Marine, was beaten to death by Miami police officers following a high-speed chase. After the officers involved were acquitted by an all-white jury the following year, several days of rioting broke out in Miami's black neighborhoods, resulting in eighteen more deaths, fires, hundreds of injuries and arrests, and more than one hundred million dollars in property damage. These weren't isolated incidents. By 1982, official complaints about police misconduct in New York City were at an all-time high.

Then-president Ronald Reagan had a history of demonizing African-Americans. He'd opposed the Civil Rights Act and the Voting Rights Act. In his 1976 presidential campaign, he told tales of "welfare queens" driving Cadillacs, and "strapping young bucks" using food stamps to indulge in steak dinners. In 1980, he told an audience in Philadelphia, Mississippi—a town where civil rights workers had been murdered in 1964—that he believed in "states' rights," the phrase long used to advocate for segregation. When in 1981 the U.S. Civil Rights Commission released a report on school desegregation critical of the Reagan administration, Reagan dismissed the chairman and vice chairman of the commission that very day. In January 1982, he authorized dropping a federal case against Bob Jones University, which was under threat of losing its tax-exempt status because it prohibited interracial dating. Then there was the one-billion-dollar cut to Medicaid, and massive cuts to the Aid to Families with Dependent Children program—budgeting decisions that disproportionately impacted African-American families.

The message of all this was abundantly clear: Black lives *didn't* matter. Eddie's character in *48 Hrs.*, Reggie Hammond, would certainly have felt that. He opens the film incarcerated and is sprung on a forty-eight-hour leave to help Nick Nolte's character, Jack Cates, with an investigation. Cates's treatment of him would be startling if it wasn't played for laughs: Hammond is physically brutalized and assaulted with racial slurs. That Hammond still swaggers through the story as its hero, winning over Cates in the process, may be a Hollywood fantasy, but the fact that Eddie made Hollywood fantasize about such things feels like a mark of progress in and of itself.

Trading Places boasted a similarly empowering agenda in even balder terms. The film's plot centers around an actual sociology experiment: Can an impoverished, uneducated black man succeed in the business world if granted the same advantages as a wealthy, white Ivy Leaguer? That he can serves as a loud rebuke to Reagan's notion of "welfare queens" and the ongoing political demonization of minorities. That Eddie could sell both these narratives to many of the same people who'd never have endorsed their messages was proof of his potency as a performer.

As Eddie himself once put it, he was "the first black actor to take charge in a white world on-screen. That's why I became as popular as I became. People had never seen that before. Black-exploitation movies, even if you dealt with the Man, that was in your neighborhood, never in their world."

It may be a stretch to say that Eddie's widespread popularity laid the groundwork for civil rights icon Jesse Jackson's announcement in November of 1983 that he'd be seeking the Democratic nomination for president. But Jackson winning five nominating contests and nearly 20 percent of the overall votes for the nomination certainly felt like proof that a bigger cultural shift was under way.

6

"This Is What They Think of Us"

On a busy stretch of highway in Southern California, a police car eased alongside Keenen Ivory Wayans. Keenen hadn't lived in Los Angeles long and hadn't had many run-ins with the LAPD.

"What are you doing?" the cop asked.

Keenen was puzzled. "I'm walking," he said.

The cop shined his flashlight into Keenen's eyes.

Now it was the officer's turn to be puzzled. "But why?"

Keenen's compass had been pointed west for a while, but it had been the encouragement of his old friend and mentor, Chris Albrecht, that convinced him to move to California in 1980. Albrecht had transitioned from club management to a job as an agent at the powerhouse talent agency ICM. His mandate was to sign comics and Keenen was one of his first signings.

Los Angeles is a tough place for an aspiring actor and comedian. Nearly any other place, that ambition, that creative drive, sets you apart, makes you special. In Hollywood, it makes you a cliché. For Keenen, when he arrived, it was even worse. He wasn't just a cliché. He was a cliché without a car.

His years of living in poverty were good training for the life of a struggling actor. He could survive on two dollars a day, no problem. He could stretch a can of corn, a potato, and some chicken into two days' worth of meals. But the lack of transportation was a challenge.

"I walked until I was able to buy a bike," he said. He walked ridiculous distances—from Hollywood to places like Encino and Westwood, five, ten, fifteen miles away—which garnered strange looks from passers-by, and one night, the attention of the cops. "Walking is suspicious behavior in Los Angeles."

In California, Keenen began going on auditions and found his way to the Comedy Store on Sunset Boulevard. If the Improv in New York had invented the comedy club, the Comedy Store refined it. Opened in 1972 by veteran comic Sammy Shore—who ceded control of the club to his ex-wife Mitzi in 1974 to lower his alimony payments—the Store became the West Coast counterpart to the Improv. It was home base for comics like Richard Pryor, Jay Leno, Richard Lewis, Robin Williams, David Letterman, Garry Shandling, Marsha Warfield, and Paul Mooney. Just as at the Improv, comics auditioned to become "regulars," but Mitzi streamlined the rather slapdash clubhouse feel her ex-husband had nurtured at the Store, creating the business model that came to define modern comedy clubs: Two-drink minimums. Opener, middle act, closer. Open-mic nights.

The night Keenen auditioned at the Comedy Store, another young, black comic new to town was auditioning too. Arsenio Hall had packed his clothes and his beanbag chair into a small U-Haul, then driven out from Cleveland on the first day of 1980. He and Keenen began getting spots at the Store's second location, in Westwood, where back then, Mitzi often broke in newer acts.

"The young comics who couldn't work at the main Comedy Store had to go to Westwood," said Arsenio. "You'd see me, Howie Mandel, Sam Kinison. We were all young and most of us sucked."

In 1981, Keenen scored a development deal with NBC, and was subsequently cast as Irene Cara's boyfriend in *Irene*, a television pilot made for the singer that hoped to piggyback on the success of her recent film *Fame*.

"This was a dream come true," said Keenen. He'd had a huge crush on Cara since seeing her in the film *Sparkle* when he was sixteen. Back then, he'd even told a friend that he was going to move to California and marry her one day. He couldn't have known then that he'd actually have a shot. But, alas, the love affair was not meant to be. The *Irene* pilot aired once but wasn't picked up, and Keenen's relationship with Cara never went further than a few on-screen kisses. "I was a young, naïve boy and she was a woman," he said.

Still, Keenen had made his network television debut and felt like the town was starting to open to him. He called Robert Townsend, who was still back in New York, and convinced him to move to Los Angeles.

"I'll fly back and we can drive your stuff out," Keenen told him. "We can write a script in the car." In New York, the two rented a small U-Haul for nineteen dollars a day, packed Townsend's Queens apartment into it, and set off for California. They did, in fact, write their first script together on the ride out—about a basketball team stuck in a haunted house—but the road trip itself might've made better fodder.

"We almost killed each other," says Townsend. "We were like, 'We're best friends! We can write a script! You drive, then I'll drive!'" The trip went off the rails almost immediately. Keenen suggested a route through the South, but the idea of two young black men driving through the rural South in 1980 set off alarms for Townsend.

"Keenen goes, 'Man, I'm in great shape. Anything go down, I'll be handling my business,'" Townsend recalls, laughing. "I was like, 'Okaaay.'" Before they could get down South, Keenen insisted on a stop in Washington, D.C.

"He's like, 'I want to see this girl,'" says Townsend. Problem was this girl had a dog. Keenen was allergic to dogs. Cut to the middle of the night: Keenen's face is swollen, he can't breathe, and Townsend is hustling him out of the apartment and back onto the road. The man who was so confident that he was in such great shape that he could handle his business in the rural South spent the first leg of that journey hopped up on Sudafed, waiting for his face and glands to return to normal size.

Keenen had one other winning idea.

"He wanted to stay at Days Inn because he had the best experience as a kid at a Days Inn. We get to Days Inn, they were so prejudiced!" Townsend laughed at the memory. "They were like, 'Nigger, get out of here!'"

If the New York comedy scene could be an alienating place for a young black man, Los Angeles wasn't exactly rolling out the welcome mat either. In fact, it's almost impossible to overstate what a wasteland Hollywood was for African-Americans in the early eighties.

Television was in its post-*Good Times*, pre-*Cosby Show* drought. Michael Moye, who was a writer on both *Good Times* and *The Jeffersons*, says he was the only African-American writer at the time he joined the staffs of both those ostensibly black shows. Most of the other writers were older white men, contemporaries of the shows' creator, Norman Lear, and thus Moye, in his twenties at the time, was often thrust into the role of being the expert on all things black.

"I was used as a quote 'stamp of approval' for some things," says Moye. "If there was a cultural element of a script, no matter how small, the producers would run it by me. I worked alone at that time, so I did have a tendency to feel like a bit of an outsider, which is ironic [on shows where] the cast is black." (Interestingly, Moye, feeling pigeonholed as a "black writer," broke out of this mold by helping develop *Silver Spoons*—"there was virtually no show whiter than that"—before going on to co-create *Married with Children*. "As you might expect," he says, "I got no questions about culture at *Silver Spoons*.") Moye was one of the lucky ones. He had work.

The prospects for African-Americans in the film world were even drearier. With the blaxploitation era well in the rearview mirror, there weren't really any "black films" being made by Hollywood studios or even larger independent operators. Starring roles for black actors who weren't Eddie Murphy were scant. Richard Pryor had starred in a string of moderately successful films in the late seventies (*Silver Streak*, *Which Way Is Up?*) and one in 1980 (*Stir Crazy*), but after setting himself on fire while freebasing cocaine during the making of 1981's *Bustin' Loose*, his film work grew steadily more depressing: the uneven *Some Kind of Hero*, the borderline offensive *The Toy*, and, well, *Superman III*. And that was, comparatively speaking, a success story for black actors during this period. Bill Cosby's entire early-eighties output was playing Satan in Disney's forgettable and forgotten *The Devil and Max Devlin*. Sidney Poitier had shelved acting at that point to get a chance to direct one decent movie (*Stir Crazy*) and one not-so-decent one (*Hanky Panky*). Besides Murphy and Pryor, arguably the biggest African-American star of the era was James Earl Jones, whose two big starring roles were in a cartoonish fantasy flick (*Conan the Barbarian*) and playing a guy who wears a mask for an entire film until he's replaced on-screen by a white actor when his mask comes off (*Return of the Jedi*). The only black directors besides Poitier who seemed to work at all were Michael Schultz, a Negro Ensemble Company alum who had established a relationship with Pryor, and underground filmmakers like Charles Burnett (*Killer of Sheep*, *My Brother's Wedding*), Julie Dash (*Illusions*), and Jamaa Fanaka (*Penitentiary*), who'd come of age in the so-called L.A. Rebellion movement, and whose films were rarely seen outside film schools and art-house theaters.

This is the Hollywood Keenen, Arsenio, and Townsend were walking into. Keenen split time between standup and going on auditions, an already demoralizing process that was made much more so when the only parts available seemed to be pimps, drug dealers, slaves, and domestic help. The title of Donald Bogle's landmark 1973 history of African-Americans on the big screen, *Toms, Coons, Mulattoes, Mammies and Bucks*, was still sadly apt. As Townsend put it, "You've got this dream, then you get to Hollywood and find yourself on line to play some crack dealer. You're like, 'Wow. This is what they think of us.'"

Keenen and Townsend both found that as well-spoken, educated black men, they didn't fit what casting directors were looking for. As Keenen said, "I'm from a family of ten in the projects and I find out that I'm not 'black enough.'"

Occasionally, this led to unintentional comedy. Like the time a white British director demonstrated to Townsend how to play a black pimp a little "blacker." Or when Keenen read the script for a part he booked as a street thug on a mercifully short-lived TV series called *The Renegades*, which was filled with odd street jargon that he and his fellow black actors didn't even understand.

"We were like, 'What is this? I never heard this word before,'" said Keenen. "So we asked the director. He didn't know. We called the writer to ask what it meant. He said he just made it up. That was just the funniest thing to us: You're making up street slang."

Keenen did score a slightly noteworthy role on a brand-new sitcom set in a Boston bar called *Cheers*, but his face was barely visible. Keenen also had the honor of getting arrested by Erik Estrada on *CHiPs* and booking a part opposite future *Cheers* star Kirstie Alley in a failed pilot called *Highway Honeys*.

In 1983, Keenen's career began to gather a little steam. He played a standup comic in the Bob Fosse–directed film *Star 80*. *For Love and Honor*, a television pilot in which Keenen played an illiterate boxer, actually got ordered to series, managing twelve episodes before petering out. Then, in October of that year, his big break: He was booked on *The Tonight Show*. This was still the era when *The Tonight Show* was pretty much the measure of any standup. Keenen had been doing standup for more than five years and had a pretty polished act, but backstage at *The Tonight Show* before going on, he was wracked with nerves.

"My heart was jumping out of my chest," he said. He'd just seen *Risky Business* and a line from the movie popped into his head. "They were saying my name and I said to myself, 'Sometimes you've just got to say what the fuck,' and I ran out and did my act."

He was equal to the moment. Taking the stage in a slick gray suit and thin striped tie, he looked energetic and at ease. His set was not only funny, it was distinctly black. After opening with a somewhat innocuous bit about the differences between California and New York, he goes into a joke about his brother Dwayne, who, he says, "finds racism in everything." After getting fired from McDonald's, Dwayne rails against the injustice of it all.

"He's like, 'The white man don't want to see you make it! They don't want to see you get ahead. They got a conspiracy out there!' Does he think there's some secret organization sitting around going, 'Now there are too many black people making it in this country. They're making too much progress. Now, let's see . . . We got Malcolm X, we got Martin Luther King . . . Dwayne! He's up for promotion at McDonald's! Stop him!'"

Keenen is animated, jumping between characters, trying out different voices, as he tells stories from his life. One moment he's his dad talking to his teachers at school ("If Keenen does something wrong, you feel free to hit him."), then he's his mom back at school contradicting her husband ("That's *my* child. I laid on my back for thirty-six hours pushing his big head out. Now, when my husband push one out, you go hit that one."), and in the end, there's a lesson ("Rule one in life is you don't hit a black woman's child.").

Another bit is about hitting on white women. "Every time I see a white girl that I think is really pretty and I want to talk to her, I feel like everybody in the room is watching me," he says, before adopting the voice of a gawking white onlooker. "'Look at him. He wants that white woman. That's his slave instinct coming out.' It's like I'm on *Wild Kingdom*."

The crowd loved him and so did Carson, who gave him the ultimate endorsement, waving him over to sit beside him on the couch. As Keenen sits down and the show cuts to commercial, Carson can be heard saying, "That's funny stuff."

"I was having an out-of-body experience," Keenen said. "That moment was the highlight of my career."

When the show returns from commercial, there isn't time for Carson to interview Keenen, but he promises, "Next time you come back we'll have time to talk."

A good set on *The Tonight Show* and the thumbs-up from Carson could change a comic's career back then, and Keenen noticed a few differences right away.

"It put you in a different class of comics and made auditioning easier," he said. More people knew who he was, and even the ones who didn't could see on his résumé that he wasn't a nobody anymore. The idea of a black comic on Carson was still rare enough that it didn't go unnoticed.

"I remember seeing Keenen on *The Tonight Show*," said Chris Rock. "Just seeing a young black guy with a suit on telling jokes with Johnny Carson, I was like, 'Wow. How'd he do that?'"

But Keenen's moment of triumph brought with it a sobering realization. Sure, more people knew who he was, and that gave him a certain cachet at the Comedy Store, but it didn't magically change Hollywood. It didn't suddenly greenlight a slate of black films or create substantive, three-dimensional roles for black actors.

"It was like—you made this big impact, but now what?" said Keenen.

"I Was Young, Black, and Angry"

February 1982. On the sidewalk in front of the Improv on Melrose Avenue in Hollywood, Keenen and Damon are huddled in deep conversation with Arsenio Hall and Eddie Murphy. It's ten months before *48 Hrs.* opens. Eddie still lives in New York, where he's become a star on *Saturday Night Live*. He's in town to tape his second *Tonight Show* appearance ever. His first set was funny, but relatively mild: jokes about catalogue models, kids named after breakfast cereals, and talking cars.

This time Eddie wants to take a bigger risk. That's the problem. His plan is to cut through the unspoken racial tension by engaging the audience in what he calls "some scream therapy." He wants to challenge them to scream "Nigger!" at him at the top of their lungs.

Arsenio was meeting Eddie for the first time on the sidewalk that night and recalled him telling the group that Carson's response was unequivocal. "Johnny was like, 'You're not doing that,'" said Arsenio. It wasn't as if Carson had a moratorium on the word or anything. The conversation on the sidewalk turned to a particular appearance Richard Pryor made on Carson back in 1976. "We were confounded," said Arsenio, "because Johnny used the N-word with Richard." Carson, in fact, had said to Pryor, "You use the word 'nigger.' Does the black community get on you for using that on a show?" As Arsenio remembered, Pryor and Carson "had a great conversation about it."

Maybe it was the changing times or Eddie was simply being held to a different standard, but at any rate, he'd been told no, and wasn't happy about it. "Eddie was like, 'I'm doing my bit,'" said Arsenio. "And he did his bit."

Watching Eddie's routine, even now, feels like watching a masterful high-wire act performed without a net. The first clue that this isn't going to be like his first *Tonight Show* appearance is his outfit: On top, he's wearing a slim-fitting gray blazer, crisp white shirt, and thin tie, but below the waist, it's dark, shiny leather pants. Leather, for Eddie in the eighties, is a pretty reliable measure of his confidence level. (In a *Tonight Show* appearance five months later, he'd be dressed in a white leather suit; in his groundbreaking HBO concert special, *Delirious*, the following year, he'd be head to toe in red leather.)

Eddie swaggers onstage and announces to the audience, "We're going to do some scream therapy, all right? When I count to three, I want the whole audience to scream at the top of their lungs, okay?" One guy in the audience screams, and Eddie ad-libs. "Wait for three!" After some laughs, Eddie re-engages. "Here we go. My count. Everybody scream. We scream"—and here he pauses almost imperceptibly—"'Nigger.'" The laughter turns uncomfortable. *Is he really asking us to scream that at him?*

"It's all right. You've got permission. I ain't gonna hurt nobody. Just wait for me to count to three, okay? Because last time I was out here they screamed it before I asked them." Now, the laughter is harder, edgier. Eddie is essentially calling out the *Tonight Show* studio audience as racists. For the next minute and a half, he teases and toys with them, as he works up to his count of three. He warns against improvising. ("Just scream 'Nigger' . . . I don't want nobody slipping in no 'coons,' no 'Alabama porch monkeys.'") He invites viewers at home to join in too. He orders a drumroll. As he starts to count off, the tension mounts. *Is this roomful of mostly white people about to scream "Nigger!" at a black man on national television? Is this really going to happen?* Eddie gets to a count of two, and notes how excited the audience is—"They got their lips ready," he says, miming someone getting ready to yell—before admonishing them, "I'm not letting y'all scream that."

The tension breaks. It's not clear whether stopping short of the coup de grâce is a concession to Carson or whether it's the entire point of the joke, but it's as dangerous and confrontational a comedy routine as anyone will see on network television in 1982, a sharp knife in the gut delivered with a sly smile. Carson seemed to come around on it too. Once Eddie sat down with him for the interview segment after the performance, Carson commented, "Nothing like a little therapy to set the ground rules before you start work. That's a funny opening." But Carson also claimed to have approved it beforehand. "He asked me about it before. I said, 'Look, go try it. Live dangerously.'"

Over the next eighteen months, as Eddie's career went stratospheric, he grew tighter with comics like Keenen and Robert Townsend, who knew him back in his Comic Strip days. He also grew close to guys like Arsenio and Paul Mooney, all of them bonded together by the cultural dislocation that came with being a black man trying to negotiate the very white world of show business. But the friendship had an unspoken hierarchy. This wasn't a partnership of equals. By 1983, *48 Hrs.* and *Trading Places* had hit, and Eddie was mulling whether to take one million dollars for a week's work on a terrible Dudley Moore film called *Best Defense*. Meanwhile, Keenen and Townsend were praying their latest pilots might make it to air. Nonetheless, the crew would hang out together, go clubbing, and talk comedy. "When we worked together, we never worked. It was just laughing," said Keenen. "We'd be at a club on the dance floor, music blasting, going, 'Yo! You think this is funny?' That's how we'd come up with stuff."

Damon Wayans began visiting his big brother in California shortly after Keenen moved out there, but he still lived back in New York. He'd spent plenty of years doing not much—dropping out of school, working a series of low-wage jobs, nearly going to prison for stealing credit cards while working in the mailroom for a credit card company—but by 1982, buoyed by his brother's success, he seemed to have found some direction in his life and was ready to try standup. For his very first gig, he wrote out his jokes on index cards and shoved them in the pocket of his leather bomber jacket before heading to the club. It was a cold night, so Damon took the stage still wearing his jacket.

"When I got onstage I felt the heat, literally," he said. "I guess it was nerves. I broke out in a sweat. My first joke was, 'I come from a poor family. We were so poor my father drove a 1974 Big Wheel.' The audience cracked up. I felt real hot, so I took my jacket off and threw it." His jokes were still in the pocket. Too embarrassed to retrieve the cards, he stood there, blank. "I had no idea what to say." He ad-libbed a little and ground out a few laughs. "But it was a bad experience. That was the longest five minutes of my life."

Not long after, during Damon's first-ever set at the Improv, Keenen was in the audience watching. So was Angela Scott, who remembers Damon being much more subdued than during his later stage and screen appearances.

"It takes a lot of nerve to get up there and do that, especially if your brother—who's made a name for himself, who's moving forward, who's very funny—is in the audience," she says. "Damon wasn't an extrovert. It was more inward, head down a little bit." But just like when they'd filmed their Kitchen Table improvs, Damon had an arsenal of characters. It wasn't great, but "he delivered a couple of laughs," says Scott.

Damon improved quickly. Around this time, Melvin George was the house emcee at a spot on Union Turnpike in Queens called the Rainy Night House. "He said, 'I'd like to come out there and try some stuff,'" George recalls. Damon and George drove out to Queens in George's battered Mustang and George put Damon on last. "He just brought the house down. Even back then, he was just so sharp."

As Damon's standup progressed, he followed Keenen to California, where he got a job in the Paramount Pictures mailroom and made an important fan: Eddie Murphy.

Damon's comedy was different from Keenen's. Performing came more naturally to him. They both pulled material from their life growing up in poverty, but Damon's perspective on race had a cutting edge. If Keenen seemed bemused by the stupidity of racism and prejudice, Damon seemed angry about it, particularly in his early standup. At any rate, Eddie was impressed and Damon scored a role in *Beverly Hills Cop*, playing an effeminate hotel employee who gives Eddie's character, Axel Foley, some bananas.

"Eddie gave me that role," Damon said. "I didn't have to audition." Eddie's faith was rewarded: It was Damon's first acting job, and he was on-screen for barely twenty seconds, but he made an impact. "That [scene] got a huge laugh. I was working in the mailroom, making twelve dollars an hour, and had to quit my job because everyone wanted me to be the banana guy."

Eddie left *SNL* following the '83–'84 season, and after one interim season with an all-white cast, Damon was hired as a featured player, presumably in hopes of recapturing that Eddie magic at *SNL*. It was quite a moment for Damon. His comedy life seemed charmed. "Eddie came to my celebration party when I got *Saturday Night Live*," says Damon. "He said, 'Don't get integrated into the cast. If you want to stand out, write your own sketches. Even if you only do one sketch, make sure it's centered around you. Otherwise, you get sucked in and become Garrett Morris.'"

Damon took Eddie's advice to heart, but it didn't necessarily serve him well. Lorne Michaels was back helming the show after a five-year absence and hoped to bring Damon along slowly so as to avoid the Eddie comparisons. Damon didn't have the patience for that. He was asked to play a succession of glorified extras. His ideas were routinely dismissed. He felt he was being held back, ignored, or worse, actively marginalized. Frustration set in. He took to walking around 30 Rock wearing dark sunglasses and a scowl. When someone would ask him what was wrong, he'd say, "It's too white in here. It hurts my eyes." He felt on the verge of a nervous breakdown.

"They wanted me to play a slave in the sketch and hold a spear, and I didn't have no lines," he says. "I told Lorne, 'My mother's gonna watch this. I'm not standing there with no spear. Unless I could stab everybody in this scene, I'm not doing it.'" Michaels pleaded with him to be a team player and promised him his time would come. Damon's manager at the time, Brad Grey, told him the same thing. Damon couldn't see it. To him, this wasn't about being a team player, it was about being a slave. Literally.

It all came to a head on-air, during an exceedingly unmemorable sketch called "Mr. Monopoly." Jon Lovitz plays the title character, a lawyer armed with "Get Out of Jail Free" cards. Damon and Randy Quaid play cops with little to do other than push the not particularly funny sketch along. When they ran through it in dress rehearsal, Quaid and

Damon were dressed like *Miami Vice*'s Crockett and Tubbs. Damon thought the sketch stunk but at least he looked kind of cool. Michaels agreed the sketch wasn't working, but zeroed in on the wardrobe—specifically Damon's—as the central problem, telling him, "You look like a pimp." He and Quaid were re-outfitted in plain white shirts, dark pants, and dark ties.

Fuck that. Damon was angry. Angry to be in this unbelievably lame sketch, angry he was being blamed on some level for it being so lame, angry that even the faint glimmer of a silver lining he'd found had been snuffed out, but most of all, angry that this seemingly golden opportunity on *SNL* had curdled so quickly.

When it came time to do the sketch live that night, he decided to give the bland, forgettable character he was being asked to play, well, *something*. He plays the cop with the same swishy brio he'd brought to his *Beverly Hills Cop* cameo, revisiting a version of the character he'd unveiled in his improvs with the Kitchen Table and, even before that, joking around as a teenager in the West Village with Keenen. Of course, in the context of the "Mr. Monopoly" sketch, it made no sense whatsoever. The effect wasn't funny or even particularly anarchic, just supremely odd. At any rate, Michaels lost his shit. He charged backstage and fired Damon on the spot.

"I went berserk," Michaels admitted in James Andrew Miller and Tom Shales's oral history of the show, *Live From New York*. "Damon broke the big rule. The whole business of trust when you're in an ensemble . . . We have live air, we're not just going to go up there and say, 'Fuck fuck fuck fuck.'"

Damon had never seen Michaels lose his cool like that—Michaels hollered some version of "You'll never work in this town again!" among a lot of cursing—but otherwise Damon wasn't too bothered. The situation had been untenable.

"I wanted to get fired," he says. "I was young, black, and angry. I just knew in the moment I was unhappy and not gonna take this shit."

———

By the time Damon was unceremoniously booted from *SNL*, his older brother was facing his own batch of frustrations. Coming off the high of

The Tonight Show, acting work had slowed, and the parade of insulting auditions grew more demoralizing by the day.

Townsend had also reached an early career pinnacle—acting along-side an almost entirely black cast (including Denzel Washington and David Alan Grier) in 1984's Oscar-nominated *A Soldier's Story*—only to be brought down to earth afterward. The stack of scripts waiting for him after that triumph promised the usual array of roles as rapists, muggers, and drug addicts. His agent explained, "Robert, every year they do one black movie and you just did it." Townsend was despondent: "I thought people would be so taken by *A Soldier's Story* that it would be different. It wasn't."

Rather than commit to a future of sitting in audition waiting rooms with the same ten black actors, competing for parts none of them really wanted, in late 1984, Keenen and Townsend began to write.

Sometimes they'd meet at Townsend's house, sometimes at Keenen's. They were a study in contrasts: Townsend sitting calmly with a yellow legal pad, Keenen in constant motion, pacing, doing push-ups and pull-ups, as they'd riff. Even when Keenen finally sat down, the energy was buzzing through him. "His foot is always shaking when he thinks," says Townsend. "We do the different characters, talk it all out. We tussle over the best joke. We just sit in the room for hours, making each other laugh."

It was informal. In some sense, they were just picking up the thread they'd started unspooling with the Kitchen Table, which they'd continued with on their ride out from New York City to Los Angeles. As Keenen recalled, "We didn't know how to write a movie. We just went with the things we did know. We'd lay out pieces of clothing that represented different characters. We'd set up a video camera and then improvise. Whenever we'd switch characters, we'd put a hat on or a scarf or what-ever. Then we'd watch it back. Stuff we thought worked we'd write down. What didn't work, we discarded."

Townsend had about twenty-five thousand dollars he'd saved from acting jobs, which they poured into the project. One of the first things they wrote was adapted from Townsend's standup, a sketch about a black acting school where white instructors teach black actors to speak jive and "walk black." Over a weekend in late 1984, they filmed a vignette of Townsend playing detective Sam Ace in a black-and-white film noir spoof called "Death of a Break Dancer." Keenen played the immaculately coiffed murder suspect, Jheri Curl, and Damon had a small part as a murder witness. The following weekend, they shot a Siskel and Ebert send-up called "Sneakin' in the Movies."

It felt like they had something, and the two began crafting a largely autobiographical story—of a struggling young black actor making his way in Hollywood—that could pull their various sketch ideas together into a coherent film. Then they ran out of money.

It wasn't clear how they might solve this problem. They certainly weren't going to make much money doing standup. Unless you were already a star, the pay on offer at places like the Comedy Store was more cover-your-gas-money than finance-your-independent-film. Keenen and Townsend had made significant inroads in Los Angeles's comedy scene, they had reasonable credits on their résumés, but people weren't yet showing up just to see them.

Beyond that, there was always a sense that they were outsiders. As black comics, it wasn't exactly that they weren't welcome at the Comedy Store, the Laugh Factory, or the Improv, but they were clearly *guests*. The small community of black standups was growing and getting more assertive but didn't really have a room of its own. That was about to change.

8

"Anybody Who Was Anybody Went There"

itting in the darkness of the Comedy Store, Michael Williams wasn't laughing. It was the mideighties, and Williams had been working as a concert promoter and event manager but was disenchanted with that life. He seemed to always be making money for other people, never himself. He needed a night out to clear his head. But at the Comedy Store, he felt out of place—a black man listening to white guys tell jokes for other white guys. Hell, he knew guys funnier than this. In fact, he'd seen one of them, a short, paunchy black comedian named Robin Harris, in this very room a few years earlier. But the audience didn't like Harris back then, didn't get him. Rumor had it the club's owner, Mitzi Shore, told Harris he was "too black" for the Store. So, guys like Harris didn't get much work there, or at any of the other big Los Angeles clubs, like the Improv or the Laugh Factory. If they did, it was only the shitty spots, and they often catered their routines for their audience, which was, like tonight, overwhelmingly, almost oppressively, white. The situation wasn't much different than it had been in New York a decade earlier: Sure, if you were Richard Pryor or Eddie Murphy, the waters parted for you at any comedy club, but what about the younger comics, the guys on the way up, where could they work? Where could they learn? *Not here at the Store*, thought Williams.

He left that night no happier than he'd arrived, but with the seed of an idea. A few months later, on August 5, 1985, that seed was planted at the corner of Crenshaw Boulevard and Vernon Avenue, in the Leimert Park neighborhood of Los Angeles, when Williams opened his own club, the Comedy Act Theater. (Two weeks later, it was uprooted and replanted a few blocks away, on West 43rd Street, after a disagreement with the owner of the original building.) He hired Robin Harris to emcee that first night and brought in seventeen other black comedians, including a tall, light-skinned air force dropout and recent *Star Search* finalist who performed under the name Sinbad. The club filled a void in the landscape of the city's comedy scene almost immediately.

"The very first show, we sold out," says Williams. "The second week wasn't so great. Then I moved to the new location, and it took approximately four weeks before I was sold out every night."

The Comedy Act felt different than places like the Store or the Improv. It was looser, louder, more freewheeling. A DJ, usually comic Ricky Harris, brought comedians to the stage with their own theme music. The audience came to laugh—or, if they weren't laughing, they wrestled the show away from whoever was onstage. Heckling was the norm, and if you couldn't handle it, you weren't going to last at the Comedy Act. Most in the audience thought they were funnier than the comedians onstage, and a few were. Much as in clubs on the infamous chitlin' circuit, or the famed Apollo in Harlem, the vibe was interactive.

A lot of this was down to Robin Harris, who became more than just the club's regular emcee—he was its id. He was thirty years old then, but Harris's approach to comedy was decidedly old school and down home. He was both conversational and confrontational. He roamed freely through the club's tables, subjecting patrons to withering barbs. Anyone foolish enough to head for the bathroom during his set found themselves with the spotlight turned on them, and Harris picking them apart, head to toe. He was quick and cutting, yet somehow charming enough to get away with it.

"Robin would talk about you, your mother, your father, and your baby, and you'd still love him," says Williams. The Comedy Act became known as "Robin's house." During the first month it was open, Damon Wayans and Robert Townsend came in together. Harris brought Damon onstage to do a set, and Damon made the mistake of dissing Harris in his own house, asking the audience, "Doesn't that guy look like a black, ugly Eddie Murphy?" Harris heard the comment and returned to the stage.

"They played 'the Dozens' and Robin destroyed Damon," says Williams. "Damon just stepped into something he couldn't get out of. By the time Robin was finished with him, he was dumbfounded. He didn't know what to do but stand there, hold the mic, and listen."

Harris's legend quickly spread, and the club's spread with it. Because black comics had been so marginalized, just finding enough to fill the lineup each night was a challenge at first. Williams teamed comics up into improv groups and let some go on more than once a night. "A lot of comedians got on every single week whether they were good or not simply because I needed people," he says.

By 1986, the previously strange and unfamiliar smell of opportunity began to waft through the club. The ground was just beginning to shift in Hollywood. *The Cosby Show* had debuted in 1984, and although some dismissed the show's story of an upper-middle-class black family living in a gorgeous Brooklyn brownstone as a fairy tale that mostly served to reinforce the up-by-the-bootstraps laissez-faire economic ideologies of Reagan-era conservatives, that was both a little harsh and perhaps beside the point: It was the number one show on television and would be for the rest of the decade. Meanwhile, Eddie Murphy's first four films had made more than four hundred million dollars at the box office. Arguably, the biggest stars in both television and movies were black comics. No wonder the industry was suddenly curious about whether these successes could be repeated, and if so, with whom. The Comedy Act offered a pool of potential answers. Agents, managers, and bookers started to find their way there. Young black casting agents like Robi Reed, Aleta Chappelle, Eileen Knight, and Jaki Brown were regulars.

"It would be hard to say you're a casting director—especially a black casting director—and not live there," says Chappelle. The club became a magnet for black comedians and ground zero for black entertainment in Los Angeles. On any given night, the crowd might include Wesley Snipes, Denzel Washington, Magic Johnson, or Mike Tyson. Tommy Davidson, who arrived as a young comic from Washington, D.C., in 1988, first met Damon, Keenen, and Townsend there.

"Anybody who was anybody went there," Davidson says. "That was the talent pool." He compared the vibe to Harlem's famed Cotton Club. "It was the hottest black comedy showcase in the country."

Perhaps more important than the high-wattage young black celebrities hanging out at the Comedy Act were the no-wattage struggling comics the club gave stage time to. Some like Davidson, Martin Lawrence, Cedric the Entertainer, D. L. Hughley, Bernie Mac, and Jamie Foxx would become household names, but just as important were those like Don Reed, Ajai Sanders, Rusty Cundieff, John Henton, Michael Colyar, and Myra J, for whom the Comedy Act offered a first step toward a solid career.

Eddie Murphy was so taken with the vibe at the Comedy Act that he essentially tried to recreate it for an HBO standup special called *Uptown Comedy Express* in 1987. (Interestingly, the young HBO executive who bought the special was a guy who'd recently quit his job at ICM: Chris Albrecht.) The *Uptown Comedy Express* lineup included several so-called "friends of Eddie"—Arsenio, Townsend, Chris Rock—along with Marsha Warfield, the former *Richard Pryor Show* cast member who'd recently scored a part on NBC's hit sitcom *Night Court*, and Barry Sobel, a manic club comic who was the show's only white performer. The audience included Magic Johnson, Paul Mooney, and Eddie himself. Eddie's uncle, Ray Murphy, emceed the show in a manner that Robin Harris would've recognized. The set was styled to resemble the Comedy Act too, but the locale had its own significance: The special was filmed at the Ebony Showcase Theatre, which was founded in 1950 by Nick Stewart, best known for playing Lightnin' on the controversial but pioneering TV series *The Amos 'n Andy Show*. The Ebony gave black actors and directors a place to do the kind of work they couldn't do elsewhere, but by 1987 it had fallen on hard financial times. "That production helped shine a light on and preserve that unique history," says Warfield. Eddie staging the special there helped keep the lights on at the Ebony for another five years.

While most of the comics on the *Uptown Comedy Express* special were known quantities, Chris Rock was still a relative newbie. Eddie had seen him performing a late-night set at the Comic Strip earlier in the year and taken an immediate interest. A few days after they met, Eddie invited Rock to come with him to Los Angeles. It was Rock's first time on a plane.

Upon arriving, they went to the Comedy Act. Commercials for *Uptown Comedy Express* tagged Rock as "Eddie Murphy's protégé," but while Eddie was hugely helpful, it was another comic who really mentored him.

"I learned how to do standup from Damon," Rock said. "When I was in the clubs, he was like the only hip black guy doing standup, and he was really nice to me. He took me under his wing, let me eat with him. I was just a kid. I learned more from Damon on how to be a comedian than any other person out there."

Black comedy wasn't taking over the world in the late eighties, but in comparison to the first half of the decade, the playing field was much more open. On the surface, this early blossoming of opportunities seemed sudden. It felt a little like the Comedy Act had created this moment, virtually out of nothing. But that discounts a lot of very deliberate work that had been going on quietly behind the scenes for years.

"It just so happened that at the time, the previous efforts of people like Richard Pryor, Redd Foxx, Flip Wilson, and Bill Cosby to get black people in support positions like agents, managers, hairdressers, whatever, had come into its own, so that the Comedy Act could draw people looking for talent who could *book* talent," says Warfield. When Redd Foxx insisted that "soul food" be brought in to eat on the set of *Sanford and Son*, when Richard Pryor demanded that NBC hire Paul Mooney, inroads were being made. "It's because there was a *Flip Wilson Show* and a *Richard Pryor Show* and Redd Foxx saying 'We need black caterers!' 'I need somebody to do my hair,' 'I want an agent,' 'I want a manager,' 'I want an accountant,' that these kinds of things now became possible for other kids coming up. You had young agents from big agencies who could go find a pool of talent and take it back to Beverly Hills."

The vibe at the Comedy Act was an outgrowth of a long history of black comedy and variety shows, but there was also a new energy afoot. Hip-hop, initially a marginal subculture, had begun to crash into the mainstream. Grandmaster Flash and the Furious Five's "The Message" had been a Top 5 hit on the *Billboard* R&B charts in 1982. The Fat Boys' first two albums had sold nearly a million copies, and the group was featured in one of the earliest promos for MTV. Run-DMC's 1986 album, *Raising Hell*—spurred by their landmark collaboration with Aerosmith, "Walk This Way"—was a massive crossover hit. Six months later, in November of 1986, the Beastie Boys' *Licensed to Ill* became the first rap album to top the *Billboard* charts. Suddenly, the floodgates opened and in poured Public Enemy, Boogie Down Productions, Eric B. & Rakim, Kool G Rap, 2 Live Crew, and Too Short.

A series of rapsploitation films piggybacked on the music's rising popularity. First, there was 1983's *Wild Style*, then came the Harry Belafonte–produced *Beat Street*; *Breakin'*; *Krush Groove*, which was directed by frequent Richard Pryor director Michael Schultz; and the Sidney Poitier–directed *Fast Forward*. The films featured cameos and performances from early rap stars including Afrika Bambaataa, Kool Herc, Busy Bee Starski, Grandmaster Flash, Doug E. Fresh, Run-DMC, Kurtis Blow, LL Cool J, the Fat Boys, and Ice-T.

None of this was happening in a vacuum. Race relations in America have often been categorized as a slow march of progress, but that slow march often seemed to be crawling in the eighties, if not moving backward. In 1985, Philadelphia police dropped two bombs on a house occupied by members of the black liberation sect MOVE, killing eleven people, including five children. No criminal charges were filed against the police. A roll call of deadly violence by NYPD officers against African-Americans—among them, Michael Stewart, Eleanor Bumpurs, Edmund Perry—dominated headlines in the middle of the decade and went consistently unpunished. A group called the Red Guerrilla Defense set off a bomb at the Police Benevolent Association offices in New York, in retaliation for the Stewart and Bumpurs killings. When Bernhard Goetz, a white commuter, shot four black men who'd approached him on the New York City subway brandishing a screwdriver and asking for five dollars in 1984, not only was Goetz acquitted on all but one minor charge, he became a vigilante folk hero in certain circles. Two years later, NYPD officers tried to apprehend a black man named Larry Davis, on murder charges. Davis shot six white police officers and then eluded capture for seventeen days in New York. During the manhunt, Davis became a vessel for the rage of the city's black community. Tenants of the building where he was finally captured could be heard chanting "Lar-ry! Lar-ry!" as he was led away in manacles. The beating death of a black man by a white mob in Howard Beach, Queens, in late 1986, and the (ultimately false) allegations the following year by a fifteen-year-old African-American girl, Tawana Brawley, that she'd been raped by four white men, served to further polarize the city and the country at large.

Of course, listing the most divisive incidents that occurred over a few years is no more an accurate barometer of the country's racial strife than listing the steps forward—Harold Washington became Chicago's first black mayor in 1983; Mike Espy became Mississippi's first black congressman since Reconstruction in 1986; the same year, Martin Luther King's birthday became a national holiday, and the United States imposed sanctions on the apartheid regime in South Africa (although it had to override President Reagan's veto to do it)—is a genuine reflection of growing comity. There were less symbolic, more tangible measures: According to one study, in the mideighties, black poverty was on the rise in the nation's fifty largest cities, and overall poverty rates among African-Americans were roughly 20 percent higher than in the population at large (in 2016, they were about 10 percent higher). Even more alarmingly, incarceration rates for African-Americans in 1986 were 543 percent higher than for whites. Sure, there were signs of progress, but the Melle Mel–voiced chorus of Grandmaster Flash's "The Message" was perpetually apropos: "Don't push me 'cause I'm close to the edge / I'm trying not to lose my head."

"We're the Black Pack, Homey"

*L*incoln Perry was an educated man. He wrote a column for the pioneering black newspaper the *Chicago Defender*. He was a classical music devotee. But in public life, he was Stepin Fetchit, a lazy, ignorant fool, who walked around with his eyes half shut, his mouth half open, speaking in a molasses-thick mumble. Stepin Fetchit was the first black movie star. He earned and lost a fortune playing essentially the same role—often billed as "The Laziest Man in the World"—in dozens of films, mostly during the twenties and thirties. Perry frequently found it useful to inhabit his Fetchit persona off-camera. He let directors think he was illiterate, so they wouldn't bother giving him a script. That meant much of his film work was improvised, which allowed him to build his roles into more than they'd been on the page. Whenever famed studio boss and producer Darryl Zanuck asked him to do something, he'd tell him he had to check with his manager, Mr. Goldberg. There was no Mr. Goldberg. Perry managed himself.

In time, Stepin Fetchit's name became an epithet, synonymous with "sellout." During the Civil Rights Movement, he became an embarrassing symbol of African-Americans' acquiescence to the disparaging image that Hollywood and the white establishment foisted on them.

As Keenen and Robert Townsend had discovered, though, the demonization of Stepin Fetchit hadn't done much to change Hollywood's view of black people. "Black Acting School" was their first real chance to make that point. They'd written the sketch back in 1984, but Townsend's twenty-five thousand dollars in savings had run out before they could film it. After Townsend replenished the coffers with a few acting jobs, he and Keenen filmed the sketch, a broad but devastatingly detailed satire that became the beating heart of the film that grew from it, *Hollywood Shuffle*.

Opening on a scene of slaves escaping their master with the sound of barking dogs behind them, the sketch offers a quick tour of fifty years of demeaning Hollywood stereotypes: the simpering slave, cowering from the white man; the hulking Mandingo, brimming with sexual potency, unable to keep his hands off a white woman; the "house nigger," more comfortable in bondage than freedom; and Townsend, essentially doing a spot-on impersonation of Fetchit, as the slow-witted, malingering butler. It was a sly, piercing denunciation of exactly how far the industry hadn't come in the previous half century.

The big joke in the sketch—and another subtle nod to Fetchit—is that once the director yells "Cut," Townsend jumps out of character: He's actually a classically trained British actor. His fellow slaves are all well-educated thespians too, but also graduates of Hollywood's first black acting school. The infomercial promises to teach its enrollees how to play "TV Pimps," "Movie Muggers," and "Street Punks." It was all of Townsend and Keenen's career frustrations rolled into five minutes. But after filming it, they were, once again, broke. They could never seem to book enough outside acting jobs to fund their film project.

Townsend stumbled on a novel solution. Looking through his mail one day, he found an application for a preapproved credit card with an eight-thousand-dollar credit line. He applied for that one and four more. *Hollywood Shuffle* was financed on credit and ingenuity. Townsend cadged leftover film stock from other acting projects he worked on. He discovered that wearing a UCLA T-shirt could fool merchants into granting him a student discount. For locations, they used the outside of Keenen's house, the inside of Townsend's apartment, or sometimes, random restaurant parking lots. They couldn't afford permits, so they piled their equipment into a van and filmed with one person in charge of looking out for trouble.

"It was crazy but a lot of fun," says Townsend. "A lot of times we had to steal locations, and you can go to jail for that in California." Often, Townsend would station a crew member on the corner as a lookout. If anyone spotted a police car, they'd whistle, all the equipment would quickly disappear back into the van, and they'd drive off, only to return fifteen minutes later to try again. Years later, people would ask Townsend, *Why didn't you hold that shot? Why didn't you zoom for another close-up?* "They don't know that the police were coming!"

In addition to directing, Townsend played the film's lead, Bobby Taylor, a not-at-all-disguised version of himself. Keenen got a producer's credit and played Taylor's workmate at a fast-food joint, as well as Jheri Curl in the "Death of a Break Dancer" sketch. The rest of the cast was drawn mainly from the pair's friends, many of whom, like Rusty Cundieff, Don Reed, Michael Colyar, and Myra J, were regulars at the Comedy Act. Damon was part of the ensemble too, as was Kim Wayans, who'd recently graduated with honors from Wesleyan. Nick Stewart, the former *Amos 'n Andy* star, had a small cameo too. In most cases, Keenen and Robert couldn't afford to pay their actors, so instead they offered to use a credit card to gas up their cars.

"It was really exciting," says Cundieff, who later made his own films (*Fear of a Black Hat*, *Tales from the Hood*) and directed *Chappelle's Show*. "We all felt like we were involved in something special. It was positive in terms of black actors and actresses feeling that they were involved in something that hadn't come before it. It was the beginning of careers of a lot of different people. The theme of the film really supported this idea that we could do some things on our own."

In New York, an NYU film grad named Spike Lee was on a similar, concurrent mission, working on his first film, *She's Gotta Have It*. Keenen recalled flying to New York for the premiere of Lee's film. "We went to the screening and met Spike," he said. "For every great idea, there are a hundred other people with the same idea. While we were in L.A. doing our thing, Spike was in New York doing his. You could feel that something was starting to happen."

When *Hollywood Shuffle* was completed, Townsend used the last of his credit to stage a screening in hopes of securing a distributor. It worked. Samuel Goldwyn picked up the film, paid off Townsend's debts, and when the film was released, it became a modest hit and a big winner with critics. *She's Gotta Have It* had come out nine months earlier, and Lee was already working on his next film, *School Daze*. Townsend didn't see Lee as competition, but as a fellow struggler forging a path where none had existed.

"Before that, there were no black movies," says Townsend. "There was no business model. Then Spike does *She's Gotta Have It*, we start doing *Hollywood Shuffle*. We didn't think, 'The market is saturated.' It only made the door open that much more because Spike had made some money. It was good for everybody."

Among those who knew him well in the mid-to-late eighties, Eddie Murphy was sometimes known as "Money." The name was a term of respect, but also just an acknowledgment of fact: Whatever Eddie did in those days turned to cash, and lots of it. It was also a constant reminder of the pecking order among friends—Eddie made it rain, and the rest of his crew were often positioning themselves to just get wet.

On a late night in early 1987, Money was in his large hotel room at the L'Ermitage in Los Angeles. Arrayed around him were many of his closest friends—Keenen, Arsenio, Paul Mooney. Nights out with these guys were not drug-and-drink-fueled bacchanals. Most of them lived pretty clean. They liked to hit dance clubs, they liked to clown on each other, but their main vice was women, which seemed to always be in plentiful supply. There were a few around that night who had wandered home with them from the clubs. The conversation soon turned to the perpetual state of competition between the friends.

They all felt like they were outsiders storming the gates in Hollywood, but the gatekeepers had always severely restricted how many black men—particularly black comedians—could come through at once. For years, in fact, there had really only been room for one funny black guy at a time: First it was Cosby, then Flip Wilson, then Pryor, and now it was Eddie. But Eddie had already had a great run, and the unspoken question seemed to be, *Who's next?* Whether they'd admit to it or not, that created a natural jockeying for places, for pole position behind Eddie. Sitting in that hotel room, there was a sense that none of them were being well served by this dynamic. Arsenio suggested another way.

"If we'd stop raggin' on each other," he said, "talking about who's best and who ain't shit—instead of this, come together. Why should we bicker when we could chisel a whole lot harder at success through unity?"

Someone commented that none of them were likely to get cast in a John Hughes film anytime soon anyway. Then Mooney, the group's elder statesman, chimed in: "They got the Brat Pack. And we're the Black Pack, homey."

At a press conference for *Beverly Hills Cop II* that August, Eddie made an offhand comment that formalized the crew's existence. "We have a group that I like to call the Black Pack. We hang out together and bounce ideas off each other." He included Arsenio, Keenen, Mooney, and Townsend as the group's charter members, but almost immediately others seemed to get drafted in too, if not by the group themselves then by media speculation and/or proclamation: Chris Rock, Denzel Washington, Damon, Robin Harris, Eddie's brother Charlie, Spike Lee.

"I didn't consider myself part of that group," says Charlie Murphy, who began working for his brother, initially doing security, after getting out of the navy in 1985, but didn't start his own comedy career until decades later. "Those guys were all around the same age, all hitting the clubs around the same time, all had big dreams. They had a camaraderie."

Initially the alliance seemed to pay dividends for the Black Pack. When Arsenio took over hosting *The Late Show* on Fox in the second half of 1987, his Black Pack buddies were there—backstage, watching from the audience, making appearances on the show. An Eddie guest spot meant a sure ratings bump. Arsenio's stature was automatically enhanced.

"We became a bit of a clique," says Townsend. "We were all young artists. When you're young and have healthy egos, you want to take over the world. You look at Hollywood and you're like 'We could do this.'" Close proximity also seemed to keep all the comics at the top of their game. "Steel sharpened steel," says Townsend. "Eddie had done *48 Hrs.*, *Trading Places*, and *Beverly Hills Cop*. He was just killing the game. It couldn't help but inspire. Because when people are really funny, it just makes you go, 'Ooh, I really need to work on my stuff.' It affected Keenen, Damon, everyone."

One night, at Eddie's house, the crew was prepping to go out club-bing. Keenen was in Eddie's closet, rifling through a rack of clothes that fans had sent him. "It was all these bad versions of the *Delirious* out-fit," Keenen said, referring to the red leather getup that Eddie wore in his first HBO special. "I held one up and was like, 'I should wear this tonight.'" A lark quickly grew into something of a dare. He put on what Eddie recalled was the actual *Delirious* one-piece and, to go with it, found a long curly brown wig, large studded Gazelle sunglasses, and a cheap gold chain with an "F" on it, courtesy of a guy who worked for Eddie named Federov.

Keenen declared, "I'm going to be your cousin Frenchy, from Au-gusta, Georgia."

Eddie didn't believe him: "You ain't going out like this."

"I'm doing it."

Before leaving the house, Keenen found a long sausage in Eddie's refrigerator and stuffed it into his skintight pants, giving him what he described as "the hugest schlong in the world."

At the club, Keenen/Frenchy danced, stomped around, and generally made a spectacle of himself. "The sausage is bouncing around while I'm dancing, and women are just like, 'Oh my god.'" Later in the night, Eddie and Keenen ran across their buddy Rick James, the guy whom Frenchy—or at least his fashion sense—was based on. Eddie introduced Keenen as Frenchy, and James was none the wiser.

"Rick has a drink in his hand and I snatch his drink, chug it down," said Keenen. Rick James, being Rick James, was charmed.

"I like this man! You're going to hang out with me!" James told him.

"He takes me and I'm in Rick's limo with Rick and the Mary Jane Girls, dressed as Frenchy," said Keenen. "I stayed in character all night." As it turned out, he didn't have a choice. Keenen had planned on bringing a change of clothes, so he could bow out of the gag once it got old, but Eddie purposely ditched the other outfit back at the house. "It's a good thing I was committed. If not, I would've just been a guy in a high-water, tight leather suit with a sausage in his pants."

Eddie was impressed. "We were out from eleven to six in the morn-ing, and Keenen never came out of character," he said. "The next morning the suit was all fucked up. Keenen's like 6'5" and he was busting all out of the suit." Frenchy would later be revived as one of Keenen's recurring characters on *In Living Color*.

Richie Tienken, Eddie's co-manager at the time, wasn't that amused by his client's friends.

"I felt like, 'Watch out for these guys,'" he says. "'You're surrounding yourself, they're all going to leech on to you.'" Arsenio may have defused some of the group's more cutthroat instincts by suggesting they work together, but they couldn't change the facts: There were limited opportunities for young black comics in Hollywood, and Eddie had the power to anoint. Tienken recalled Keenen and Arsenio, in particular, jostling for Eddie's affections.

"Keenen and Arsenio didn't get along," he says. "It was like watching two broads try to pick up a guy."

There were other cracks in the Black Pack's foundation. Keenen and Townsend had been partners on *Hollywood Shuffle*—they wrote it together, Townsend directed, Keenen produced—but in the wake of the film's success, Townsend became its public face. Not only was he the film's star, his story about financing it with credit cards resonated in the media. He was the one everyone wanted to interview. He was the one who got the invite to go on *The Tonight Show*.

"After the movie came out, most of the credit was given to Robert," Keenen said.

Townsend reaped the spoils of his rising profile. He landed a lead alongside his friend Denzel Washington in *The Mighty Quinn*, a comic caper set in Jamaica. And Chris Albrecht, at HBO, offered him his own comedy-variety show. Keenen was part of that deal, coming along in the same capacity he had on *Shuffle*, as a co-writer, co-producer, and performer. But the title of the series of four specials made it clear the way the two friends' partnership was seen from the outside: *Robert Townsend and His Partners in Crime*.

The *Partners in Crime* specials were formatted like old-school variety shows, with a mixture of sketches, standup, and musical performances. Even more than *Shuffle*, *Partners* drew heavily from the Comedy Act. There were musical performances by Bobby Brown, MC Hammer, and Heavy D. The most memorable stuff tended to be the sketches. One featured Townsend and Keenen playing Michael Jackson and Prince, respectively, as cops. Then there was a send-up of a Jerry Springer–type talk show, a Western spoof called "How the West Was Won . . . Maybe," and a series of recurring sketches called "The Bold, The Black, The Beautiful," which imagined the trials and tribulations of a wealthy black family. The initial *Partners* specials were well received, but Keenen was restless. After working on the first two installments, he stepped away.

"I wanted to do more," he said. "I wanted to direct. I wanted to have more input beyond writing and performing. I needed to spread my wings."

Eddie Murphy rolled up to the Fulton Houses in style. His limousine would've stood out all by itself, but stepping from it wearing tight, cow-skin pants, Eddie wasn't exactly incognito. This was the mideighties, and he was the biggest movie star in the world. He didn't make a lot of house calls. Usually, if you were hanging with Eddie, you were at his place—whether it was his hotel room, his home in New Jersey, his house in California, or the set of his latest movie. But there were exceptions. This was one of them.

The Wayans family still lived in the same four-bedroom apartment in the projects. Keenen had been dutiful about sending money back home from California when he could, but in truth, he hadn't made much. When he was in town, he was sleeping back in his childhood bedroom. Eddie stopped by to pick him up for a night out, but ended up staying a few hours.

It was an event. Shawn, Marlon, and their sister Diedra's son Craig were all there for Eddie's arrival. Keenen had bought a new couch for the occasion because, as Shawn put it, "He didn't want Eddie sitting on the roach-infested couch that my mother still had plastic covers on." Shawn and Marlon were barely teenagers then and certainly knew who Eddie was but treated him no differently than they did any of Keenen's other friends.

"He walked in, he had some cow-skin pants on—ain't too many Negroes in the projects got cow-skin pants," said Marlon. "So while he was there, me, Shawn, and Craig were snapping on Eddie, cracking jokes about his pants. Every time he sat down, we'd go 'Moooo!' We tagged him for hours."

Word spread quickly through the projects that Eddie was afoot, and it became a bit of a scene. "You ever see *The Birds*?" said Shawn, referring to Alfred Hitchcock's classic film. "Where they're trying to escape at the end? It was that with project people. You had to step over them."

Keenen and Eddie had been hanging out a lot around that time. They were working on Eddie's new film project. It was going to be a mix of sketches and standup that Eddie was calling *Pieces of My Mind*. Townsend would direct. They were working out of a Manhattan brownstone just a few miles from the Wayans family's Chelsea apartment. Eventually, the parameters for the film changed. The idea of interspersing Eddie's standup with a series of sketches was pared down to just a single sketch to open the movie. That sketch—which features future *Fresh Prince of Bel-Air* star Tatyana Ali, a then unknown Samuel Jackson, and Keenen's seven-year-old nephew Damien Dante Wayans in small roles—re-creates a scene from Eddie's childhood, standing up in front of a family gathering and telling a wildly inappropriate joke. The rest of the film is Eddie's crackling, gleefully profane standup. The film's title changed to reflect the new reality: *Raw*.

Raw was released in theaters—unheard of for a standup concert film—and grossed over fifty million dollars. Behind the scenes there was some grumbling over Keenen's credits as both a writer and producer. Richie Tienken insists Keenen's work on *Raw* was negligible.

"Eddie was working on his routine and was having a problem with a line," says Tienken. "He talked to Keenen about it and Keenen basically said, 'Well, why don't you say it this way?' And it worked. I said to Eddie, 'That was really nice of Keenen to help you with that.' And he said, 'Yeah, he asked me for a co-writing credit.' I was like, 'What? It was one fucking line. This guy's your friend.'" Tienken points out that comedians are always helping each other out with bits. He's worked with comics such as Jerry Seinfeld, Paul Reiser, and Ray Romano. "They all helped each other. They didn't ask for anything. I think I even went to Keenen and said, 'You've got some pair of fucking balls asking him for that.'"

Chris Rock, who was just getting to know Eddie and Keenen around this time, recalled watching Eddie prepare for the shows on his *Raw* tour, batting around material with friends. Occasionally, Rock and others might help "tag" a joke. "I might have got a line in," Rock told Marc Maron during a 2011 interview, referring to *Raw*. "That's what friends are for, for tags. It's only when they're not your friends when they go, 'I should get a writing credit for that tag.'"

Keenen has always maintained that his writing credit was for his work on the opening sketch. Beyond that, "I was sort of the objective eye. As he'd work out the material, it would be giving notes like, 'Hey, try this.' 'Try that.'" There were rumors that Eddie and Keenen had a falling-out over all this, and one person close to the situation at the time says Arsenio called Keenen afterward and said something to the effect of "You're out and I'm in." For his part, though, Eddie never publicly complained about Keenen's contributions—or lack thereof—to *Raw*.

On the last day of 1987, Eddie threw a party at his mansion in Englewood Cliffs, New Jersey, known as Bubble Hill—"bubble" being a slang term for "party." The New Year's Eve party was lavish: Stoli, Chivas, champagne, a chef fixing made-to-order plates of pasta, shrimp, chicken, and the like, and a well-dressed crowd of the famous (Sugar Ray Leonard, Janet Jackson, Vanessa Williams) and the merely beautiful mixing with Eddie's family and friends.

There was a lot to celebrate. *Hollywood Shuffle*. *Raw*. *Partners in Crime*. The *Beverly Hills Cop* sequel had been one of the year's biggest films. Arsenio was in the middle of shooting *Coming to America* with Eddie. Even Damon, after crashing out of *SNL*, had landed on his feet: He'd had a supporting role in Steve Martin's hit comedy *Roxanne*, had just finished filming a meaty part in the gang drama *Colors*, and was a big draw as a standup. A few minutes into the new year, Townsend gave a toast: "Brothers, let the good times roll."

Keenen had had a busy 1987 too, but it was hard to escape the fact that everything he'd worked on in the past year came to be viewed, rightly or wrongly, as *other* people's projects. He and Townsend were already working on another script, called *The Five Heartbeats*, about the coming-of-age of a fictional R&B group, but Keenen was jonesing to do something everyone would know was *his*. He had an idea what that something might be, but ironically enough, it was something that belonged to Eddie first.

10

"You Can't Kill This Movie"

Tamara Rawitt was running Paramount Pictures' east coast Marketing Department in March of 1985, when Eddie Murphy walked into her office with an offer she couldn't refuse.

"He put first-class tickets on my desk and said, 'Move to L.A. and open my production company,'" she says. Rawitt, a short, sandy brown-haired, no-nonsense New Yorker, had been Eddie's point person in the Paramount Marketing Department during his early-eighties run, from *48 Hrs.* through the first *Beverly Hills Cop*.

"He was the biggest star in the world, on the cover of *Time* and *Newsweek*," she says. "So I moved to L.A. and we started developing projects for him." A few months into the job, she got a call from Eddie. "He said, 'I want you to meet a friend of mine. He's a comedian, he's trying to break into the business, see if you can help him.'" This was her first introduction to Keenen. At the time, Keenen had made some television appearances and had the small part in *Star 80* but was a couple years away from *Hollywood Shuffle*'s release. "When Eddie sent him in, Keenen was a good-looking guy who didn't know he was good-looking," says Rawitt. "He was young, gawky, and kind of insecure."

Rawitt worked with Keenen on a script he'd written for a film he called *Groupie*, but nothing ever happened with it. After two years at Eddie's company Rawitt left to work at United Artists, but stayed in touch with Keenen.

As Robert Townsend rode the post–*Hollywood Shuffle* wave and Eddie prepared *Coming to America* with Arsenio, Keenen was searching for a project he could stamp as his own. He recalled an idea of Eddie's.

"We were all hanging out and he [Eddie] said, 'Wouldn't it be funny to make a parody of black exploitation movies?'" Keenen said. "He actually said, '*I'm Gonna Git You Sucka*.' We all started riffing and throwing out ideas. Then it sat."

Rawitt remembered the idea too and thought it was brilliant. "Coming from marketing, I knew I could sell the shit out of it." She advised Keenen to ask Eddie if he could have the idea. Eddie gave up the rights and the title and asked for nothing in return. Once Keenen had written the first draft of the script, he brought it to Rawitt, because, as Keenen put it, "She was the only film executive I knew."

The script needed work. "I put Keenen through about twenty drafts," Rawitt says. The film got set up at United Artists, and Rawitt was brought in as a co-producer. Keenen hoped to direct it himself. UA was resistant.

"They said, 'You haven't directed a movie before—we gotta find somebody with experience but he has to be black,'" Keenen recalled. Within those parameters, however, options were limited. "They couldn't come up with anybody other than Robert—who I'd just worked with on *Hollywood Shuffle*—and Spike Lee. Both of them had only done one movie. So by default, it was like, 'Why not let the guy who wrote it do it?'" The budget was a relatively measly $2.7 million, so the risk for UA was limited.

During the making of *Hollywood Shuffle*, Keenen had hired a manager named Eric Gold, an ambitious former standup comic from Pittsburgh who worked in the office of Hollywood veteran Ray Katz. According to Gold, getting *I'm Gonna Git You Sucka* greenlit by the studio had as much to do with fortuitous timing as anything else. UA and its parent company, MGM, had a unique deal with 20th Century Fox Video that stipulated Fox would have the home video rights to every other title that MGM released. One film went to MGM/UA, then the next one automatically went to Fox, and so on. At the time Gold and Keenen met with MGM/UA to discuss *Sucka*, the studio already had a film in the pipeline that they figured was a surefire hit, *Rain Man*—and they didn't want to give it to Fox. Keenen and Gold met with UA president Tony Thomopoulos and his team on a Friday. As Gold recalls, they were asked, "'When do you think you could start production?' We said, 'Immediately.' He said, 'Great. Can you start Monday?'" It was perfect. They'd rush it into production ahead of *Rain Man*, thereby keeping the hotly tipped Tom Cruise–Dustin Hoffman project for themselves.

Keenen cast himself as the film's lead, Jack Spade. Most of the other big parts went to actors who'd been blaxploitation stars, including Bernie Casey, Isaac Hayes, Jim Brown, and former Chelsea-Elliott Houses resident Antonio Fargas. Keenen's family, friends, and fellow comics filled out most of the smaller roles. Damon, Kim, Marlon, Shawn, and Nadia Wayans all made appearances, as did David Alan Grier, Anne-Marie Johnson, Robin Harris, and John Witherspoon. Eddie Murphy came to an early screening and offered notes. One of the film's more memorable moments comes courtesy of Chris Rock, who features as an extraordinarily frugal customer in a BBQ joint, bargaining with the proprietors for a single rib and a drink. In 2016, Rock said he gets more comments on his ninety-second part in *Sucka* than he does about almost anything else in his career. The part was based on something he did in his standup.

"I don't want to get punched in the face, but Keenen basically stole a joke of mine," Rock said. "It was in the script. I think Eddie was like, 'Hey, isn't that Chris Rock's thing?' Next thing I know, I got flown from New York to L.A. for a movie that only had a two-million-dollar budget."

According to Gold, "Keenen always planned on using Chris, so that's probably why his line was in the script." That said, Keenen's brother Marlon was under the impression he was in line to play that same role but didn't make it out to California in time.

In the end, the film is an extremely broad satire, at times more goofy than funny, yet also with a definite point of view. In an era when trust between the police and the black community was nearly nonexistent, the cops in *Sucka* are all pretty crooked and incompetent. But the film playfully skewers the black community too. The plot centers around the death of Spade's brother who O.G.-ed—that is, overdosed on gold chains. One scene depicts an inner-city youth gang competition with contestants stripping cars for their parts and racing down the street carrying stolen televisions. *Sucka* toys with blaxploitation's clichés, but the satire feels like a product of affection. The film's conclusion imagines a world where the blaxploitation era never ended, but just kept rolling with the times. As Keenen's Jack Spade walks off into the proverbial sunset, he's got his own updated theme music walking right behind him, performed by South Bronx rappers Boogie Down Productions.

The film almost never got seen. As Gold explains, management at MGM/UA had changed twice since they'd made their deal with Thomopoulos, and the new regime planned to give *Sucka* only a perfunctory release then let Fox Video do with it what they pleased.

"They decided to do the absolute minimum they needed to do to fulfill their commitment," says Gold. "So everything was on the cheap." When Keenen saw the initial marketing plans—or lack thereof—he was furious.

"I felt like they were trying to sabotage the film," he said. He told the head of distribution, "You can't kill this movie. What you don't understand is there hasn't been a black movie like that in twenty years." *Hollywood Shuffle* and Spike Lee's films were great, but those were small, independent features, not studio films. "Imagine there were no white movies and somebody puts one out," Keenen told the UA exec. "You're going to go just because you haven't seen yourself on-screen in twenty years."

Keenen's protestations notwithstanding, the film was initially released in mid-December in only five markets, none of which were New York or Los Angeles. But when box office returns came in, it proved Keenen had been right: *Sucka* had the third-highest debut that week, behind only *Rain Man* and *Dirty Rotten Scoundrels*, two films that had premiered on about ten times more screens. The following week, *Sucka*'s returns improved. Then they stayed steady into early January, despite the fact that UA added no more cities to the release calendar. As Gold, who got an executive producer credit on the film, puts it, "The movie refused to die." Finally, in mid-January, UA doubled the number of theaters *Sucka* was in and the returns shot up more than 300 percent.

Not everyone loved it. In his review for the *Chicago Sun-Times*, Roger Ebert, arguably the country's most influential critic, wrote, "It is the sort of material that makes you wonder why blacks object to the resurrection of Amos and Andy, since '*Sucka*' is incomparably more offensive than anything the Kingfish ever did." The reaction of other critics was mixed, probably more positive than negative, but that particular criticism rankled Keenen.

"Journalists asked me about negative stereotypes and do I think that I'm confirming for white people their ideas of black people," he said. "I said, 'This is a comedy! This is *Airplane!* I grew up watching the Three Stooges and never thought, *Wow! White people are crazy!*'"

Of course, in show business, numbers matter more than words or feelings, and the numbers on *Sucka* didn't lie: The film made about twenty million dollars for UA, a significant return on an investment of less than three million dollars. If Keenen's goal had been to make his own name, to announce his own talent, as an entity distinct from Eddie or Robert Townsend or anyone else, there was no question that mission had been accomplished.

"The Bad Boys of Television"

Keenen didn't really want to make a television show. He was a *film-maker*. He thought he'd just shown the world that. *I'm Gonna Git You Sucka* was the little engine that could, chugging uphill against an indifferent studio and the weight of history. It was in theaters *right now* making *real* money. He wanted to make more *films*. Yet here he was in this meeting talking to *TV* people. And not even real TV people—these guys were from Fox, which was then still a new network and felt distinctly minor-league. He knew enough to be polite and hear them out. And they did sound enthusiastic. "They told me I could do anything that I wanted to do," he says. "That's what set the wheels turning."

The "they" were Garth Ancier and Charles Hirschhorn. Ancier was Fox's president of programming. He was considered something of a "boy wonder" in the television world. He'd been Brandon Tartikoff's protégé at NBC when Fox plucked him, at the tender age of twenty-eight, to help launch what seemed like a fool's gambit—a fourth television network. Hirschhorn was his lieutenant, as well as a friend of Tamara Rawitt's. Rawitt had invited Hirschhorn to a screening of *Sucka*, and Hirschhorn in turn dragged Ancier to the screening room in the basement of 20th Century Fox's old Executive Office Building to see what he'd seen: Keenen was a guy who could make a television show for them.

That's how all four of them ended up in Ancier's third-floor office in early 1989. Joe Davola, Fox's new VP of development, recalls being in that meeting too. Keenen also remembers him there, though Rawitt, Ancier, and Hirschhorn aren't so sure. It's one of many details surrounding the birth of *In Living Color* that few agree on.

Keenen recalls getting a blank check from Fox, "total freedom" as he put it. They were a new network looking to shake things up. He was intrigued. He thought of the characters he and Damon had been making each other laugh with since they were kids. He thought back to those improvs they'd filmed with the Kitchen Table. He thought about *Saturday Night Live*—his brief audition and Damon's disastrous stint as a featured player, as well as Eddie's triumph there—and the way the show seemed to be made by, for, and about white people. He thought about all the black comics and actors he knew, people he'd met at the Comedy Act or on *Hollywood Shuffle* or *Partners in Crime* or *Sucka*. Hollywood had no idea what to do with any of them. But he did.

In a second meeting with Fox, Keenen pitched them sketches and characters—two flamboyantly gay film critics, Louis Farrakhan on the *Starship Enterprise*, two "knucklehead thugs" selling stolen goods from the back of a truck. He pitched them the attitude, the style—the whole show, more or less. He wanted to bring a different voice to sketch comedy. There was an entire rising hip-hop generation that wasn't being spoken for or to. Where were the sketches about Mike Tyson? Where were the Jesse Jackson impressions? Who out there could wring laughs from the way police treated black men? It wasn't just that *Saturday Night Live* was too white. It also wasn't very good. The sketches went on too long. Single-joke premises plodded along for five, six, seven minutes. His show wasn't going to be like that. He knew how to get his laugh and get out. Ancier and Hirschhorn were impressed, and Keenen left the meeting with a greenlight to go make a one-hour pilot.

At least that's the way Keenen recalls it. Rawitt remembers it mostly the same except that she recalls that she was the one who gave Keenen the idea that it was time for them to challenge *Saturday Night Live*'s sketch comedy throne with an African-American sketch show. Ancier says he'd had the idea to do what he called a "black *Laugh-In*" on the bulletin board behind his desk for at least a year and had already reached out to Robert

Townsend to do it, but Townsend wasn't interested. Then *he* suggested the show *to* Keenen. Townsend confirms that Fox approached him about it, but Keenen is adamant that the show wasn't Ancier's idea.

"Garth didn't pitch to me," he says. "It's funny Garth said he had that idea because I used *Laugh-In* as the example of getting in, getting the joke, and getting out."

Jamie Kellner, Fox's first president and Ancier's boss, has a slightly different memory too. He says the concept of a "black *Laugh-In*" actually began as a "black *Hee Haw*." "I said to Garth, 'We should do a black *Hee Haw*,'" says Kellner. "He looked at me with this shocked look." Kellner jokes that Ancier had gone to Princeton and may not have ever seen *Hee Haw*. "He says, 'You mean *Laugh-In*?' I said, 'No, Garth. Think about it: *Laugh-In* was a broad comedy show with a bit of a news bent. *Hee Haw* was, I think, the third-highest-rated show on CBS when it was canceled. It was giving a stage to country people to sing their songs, do their dances, and tell their jokes. We could do the same thing for African-Americans.'"

Hirschhorn recalls pitching his own idea in that meeting with Keenen: a half-hour sitcom based on the guys who owned the rib joint in *Sucka*. "Keenen kind of looked at me and said, 'No. We should do a sketch comedy show and have female dancers between sketches,'" Hirschhorn says. "He pitched me three or four sketches. Each one was funny." The show, he continues, "was one hundred percent fully formed in [Keenen's] head. I just said, 'Yeah, forget everything I said. We're going to do exactly what you say.'" (Interestingly, there actually was a *Sucka* spinoff pilot in the works, called *Hammer, Slammer & Slade*, which aired once on ABC but wasn't ordered as a series.)

It's possible to read all sorts of nefarious things into this web of contradictory memories. It wouldn't be the first time in Hollywood that multiple people tried to take credit for a good idea, and any self-serving anecdotes should always be viewed skeptically. That said, in a job where nearly every day is filled with meetings, most of which are completely unmemorable, misremembering the details of one or two meetings that took place more than twenty-five years ago seems a pardonable sin.

There's one more interesting tidbit about *In Living Color*'s conceptual origins: Ancier's idea for a "black *Laugh-In*" had a history of its own. There had already *been* a black version of *Laugh-In*, created

way back in 1968 by original *Laugh-In* producer George Schlatter. The
show, titled *Soul*, was an hour-long pilot made for NBC and featured a
who's who of black comics at the time: Slappy White, Nipsey Russell,
George Kirby, Gregory Hines, and—in his first television appearance
ever—Redd Foxx. The pilot aired once but wasn't picked up. To watch
it now is revelatory.

In the late fifties and sixties, NBC's slogan was "brought to you
in living color on NBC," and *Soul* opens with a shot of the iconic NBC
peacock, followed by one actress promising viewers, "You never saw
such *living*," and another following her, "And you never saw such
color." The show is almost shockingly progressive for the era. In between dance numbers and musical performances by Lou Rawls, Joe
Tex, and Martha Reeves and the Vandellas, most of the humor is racially charged. There are jokes about police violence against black
men, the KKK, and white ignorance of black culture. Most of the jokes
are quick interstitials. One actress asks another, "Do you know how
many black brothers are fighting for freedom in Vietnam?" Another
answers, "Yeah, almost as many as here." Redd Foxx and Slappy White
do a short bit about segregationist Alabama governor George Wallace's
potential presidential bid.

> Foxx: "You think Wallace should run again?"
> White: "Yeah, and the next time I hope they catch him."
> Foxx: "In Harlem."
> White: "At night."
> Foxx: "On a rooftop."
> White: "With dark glasses on."
> Foxx: "Eating a pig's foot."

Schlatter says the studio audience's reaction to the show was huge,
but NBC was afraid that if they bought it, "they could never cancel it,"
without it being a PR mess. But *Soul* wasn't completely lost to history. "I
sent a copy to Keenen Wayans," says Schlatter. This was during the time
Keenen and Fox were first developing *In Living Color*. "*Soul*," Schlatter
says, "was kind of the prototype."

In early 1989, when Keenen was first meeting with Fox, the company's future was still very iffy. Rupert Murdoch had launched the network in 1986 with a small team of executives that included Barry Diller, Kellner, and Ancier. At the time, the idea of a fourth television network seemed like a moon shot. ABC, NBC, and CBS had monopolized the airwaves for more than a generation. And Fox's early returns weren't impressive.

When the network launched in October 1986, their inaugural program was *The Late Show* with Joan Rivers, which quickly became a wrenching, expensive, complicated failure. Once Rivers was fired, less than a year after the show debuted, Fox rotated in a series of guest hosts that included Suzanne Somers, Frank Zappa, and Arsenio Hall. Arsenio, then just a middling standup, looked the most promising and was given a thirteen-week contract. Although Arsenio's tenure saw a spike in ratings, he was just a placeholder. Fox was already in preproduction on a new late-night satirical news magazine, *The Wilton North Report*, which hijacked the *Late Show* time slot in December then lasted a grand total of four weeks before being axed.

In prime time, Fox was only programming two nights a week—Saturday and Sunday—in early 1989. Their quality control wasn't necessarily that much worse than other networks, but Fox was hampered by the fact that, particularly during its first couple of years, it wasn't even on the dial in every market. Even when it was, Fox was often slotted deep in recesses of the UHF band, with spotty reception. For ill-conceived projects like *Mr. President*, *Karen's Song*, and *The New Adventures of Beans Baxter*, it probably wouldn't have made a difference. But for shows like *Married with Children* and *The Tracey Ullman Show*—often regarded now as classics—the struggle to garner respectable ratings felt like fighting with one hand tied behind your back. Meanwhile, the network was bleeding money. Sandy Grushow was VP of creative advertising in Fox's film division when he was tapped by Diller to lead the Marketing Department at the network in 1988.

"I remember walking in my first day on the job," says Grushow. "The day before there was a story on the front page of *Variety* that said, 'Fox loses $99 million, News Corp considers shuttering the network.' It was that into which I walked."

Still, there were successes: *21 Jump Street*, a slick drama about young cops working undercover at high schools, starring a youthful Johnny Depp, was a hit, particularly among younger viewers; *America's Most Wanted*, a proto-reality show made on the cheap, had debuted in 1988 and built surprising buzz. By 1989, *Married with Children* was consistently drawing more than ten million viewers a show. The outlines of an overall programming strategy were taking shape. If Fox wanted to compete with the "Big Three" networks, they couldn't simply imitate them. Ancier admits that coming from NBC, he made that mistake. "You can't put a show on an alternative network like Fox and expect people to come to it," he says. "Barry Diller actually had this expression which was, in retrospect, absolutely correct. 'When you're an alternative network, you have to grab people by the collar and drag them to your station.' You're not going to drag them over if the shows you're making are ABC-lite."

Fox executives took note of what was working for them. What *Married with Children*, *Tracey Ullman*, *21 Jump Street*, and *America's Most Wanted* had in common was that they didn't feel like network television. "A bunch of the shows had this edge that you wouldn't have seen on the Big Three networks back in those days," says Kellner. "That's the thing the audience responded to. It brought us demographics that differentiated us from the Big Three. We were younger and more male. A lot of advertisers were interested in that and obviously we needed money because we were losing a hundred million dollars a year."

One event catalyzed this emerging programming strategy. In January of 1989, a suburban Detroit mother named Terry Rakolta stumbled upon an episode of *Married with Children* and was so appalled by the raunchy "anti-family attitudes" on display that she began a letter-writing campaign and pressed advertisers to boycott the show. Initially, she was successful: Several advertisers pulled commercials, but in doing so, the boycott made the show's creators—and Fox, by extension—into unlikely First Amendment martyrs. The subsequent media firestorm only focused more attention on the show and on the upstart network in general. This was the "aha!" moment. In time, Fox would begin branding themselves "The Bad Boys of Television."

Michael Moye, *Married with Children*'s co-creator and showrunner, says that although the Rakolta boycott helped his show in the long run, he was initially dismayed at how much fear Rakolta stoked at Fox. "Executives were diving under their desks," he says. "She had become a bit of a celebrity, doing morning shows, and I always thought there should be some sort of rebuttal. But they were scared." To Moye, at least initially, the "Bad Boys of Television" concept was as much bluster and marketing as it was actual strategy.

"That was their motto," he says. "How much they really believed, how far they were going to go with it, is still a bit of a mystery. Because it seemed, particularly in the early years, their motto should've been amended: 'We're the Bad Boys of Network Television . . . if you guys are okay with that.'"

The Rakolta incident kicked off right around the time Keenen came in for that first meeting with Ancier, and while it's certainly debatable how committed Fox was to the idea of edgier programming, what Keenen was proposing definitely fell in line with it. It also fit with some broader changes in television viewership. Cable TV—then still in its infancy—had begun to lure viewers away from the traditional networks. Specifically, it had begun to lure wealthier white viewers. The demographics for network television's viewing audience were shifting. By the end of the 1980s, African-Americans were watching 44 percent more network TV than other households. NBC was the only network that seemed to have noticed. Their lineup at least nodded toward the existence of African-Americans, with shows like *The Cosby Show*, *A Different World*, *227*, and *Amen*.

After the *Wilton North Report* had quickly petered out, Fox hoped to revive *The Late Show* with a permanent host. Arsenio was the obvious choice. He said he asked Fox for an "escalating scale": He'd take less money up front, but if the show did well, if its ratings went up, his pay would increase along with the ratings.

"I went in and pitched that," Arsenio told Neal Brennan and Moshe Kasher during a 2014 podcast. "They were like, 'Just get the fuck out of here. You're lucky to even be in a room indoors.'" An executive at Paramount Television named Lucie Salhany caught wind of that meeting and staked out a parking lot outside Eddie Murphy's office. When Arsenio pulled up in his car, she introduced herself. She wanted to do a late-night syndicated talk show with Arsenio. "She gave me points based on my execution," Arsenio said. "The better the show did, the better I personally did."

The *Arsenio Hall Show* debuted on January 3, 1989. Coming on the heels of his appearance in *Coming to America*, the show quickly found its feet, proving popular particularly with young, urban audiences. Fox, no doubt, rued Arsenio as the one that got away. It was not long after his debut that Keenen walked into Garth Ancier's office for the first time.

Ancier says the original working title for *In Living Color* was *Blackout*, but Ancier himself left Fox in March 1989, and Hirschhorn followed him out the door a few months later. Peter Chernin, who'd previously been at Showtime, came in as Fox's president of entertainment, but the two executives who'd been most instrumental in bringing Keenen to Fox—Ancier and Hirschhorn—were now gone. The project was suddenly an orphan. The first person to step into the breach was Joe Davola.

"This project was still being put together so, not knowing any better, I call up the network president and say, 'I want to run this project,'" says Davola. "He said, 'Okay.'"

Davola was a brash New Yorker who'd recently come to Fox from MTV, where he was a producer. Even though he was an executive now, he still thought of himself as a producer and felt a kinship with the Wayans siblings. "My wife had gone to junior high school with Damon, Keenen, and Diedra. I think she was in Diedra's class." At an early meeting, Davola whipped out his wife's old school yearbook to show to Keenen. "It was a weird connection. He grew up not far from my apartment in New York City, so we had a bond. I wasn't a suit and tie–wearing executive. All that stuff just gave us a little bit of an ease."

Although he got the commitment from the network, Keenen still needed a production studio to underwrite the development of the pilot. At the time, the FCC had placed restrictions on networks producing and owning their own shows, so it wasn't unusual that Fox's own studio arm, then called Twentieth Television, passed on producing the pilot themselves. Keenen turned to an old friend, Chris Albrecht, who had become a senior VP at HBO.

HBO was known then mostly as outlet for second-run theatrical films, but Albrecht's job was to develop original programs, which at the time mostly meant standup and music specials. Albrecht had been pushing HBO to develop new sitcoms and dramas, but the network's previous efforts in that direction—occasionally amusing but generally forgettable fare like *The Hitchhiker* and *1st & Ten*—hadn't generated much enthusiasm. When Keenen came to Albrecht asking if HBO could produce Keenen's pilot for Fox, Albrecht was in the process of trying to convince HBO chairman Michael Fuchs that HBO could make money packaging and selling shows to other networks. This made a good test case. Carmi Zlotnik, who worked in original programming production at HBO, was one of Albrecht's like-minded allies within the company.

"Chris and I bonded on this idea of 'Let's own more, let's do more,'" says Zlotnik. He felt like he had the perfect guy in mind to work with Keenen on the pilot. "My biggest contribution was hiring Kevin Bright."

Bright was another New Yorker. In fact, he'd graduated from the same high school as Keenen, Seward Park, a few years before him. Bright had been a producer for HBO, and worked on specials for Martin Mull, Harry Shearer, and David Copperfield. At the time he first met with Keenen about possibly working on the pilot, he says, "it was absolutely the worst year of my career. I hadn't worked in six months and my twin boys were about to be born, so I was pretty desperate." On the HBO specials he'd done, Bright had been very involved in the creative process. In his meeting with Keenen and Tamara Rawitt, Keenen made clear that's not what he wanted. "He said, 'I just want somebody to handle the budget, the hiring, and the line producer stuff.' He didn't want me getting involved creatively at all. I would've said anything at that point to get the job, so I said, 'Sure.'"

When Bright came aboard, he recalls the project was going by the title *Urban Renewal*, which he thought "horrible." It didn't last long. Keenen recalls that he wanted to use the name *Live in Color*, "based on the old NBC [slogan]." But *Saturday Night Live* already used the word "live." "So we decided to change it to *In Living Color*."

Bright says it wasn't quite that simple.

"The band Living Colour had just come out with their first record right when we were starting to really hire everybody and get the show together," he says. The funk-rock band's debut album, *Vivid*, had come out in mid-1988, but hadn't begun gaining momentum until later that year, when MTV started playing the single "Cult of Personality." One of the songs on the album, "What's Your Favorite Color?" sported a catchy chorus, "What's your favorite color, baby?/Living Colour!"

Bright heard the song and brought it to Keenen and Rawitt. "I said, 'The name of the show should be *Living Color* and this should be our theme song.'"

"Won't they sue us?" Keenen asked.

"No," Bright answered. "They can't own the words 'Living Color.' And besides they spell it funny with a 'u' in it, so they can't sue us if we don't spell it that way. If anybody owns the term 'Living Color,' it's NBC because they used the motto, 'brought to you *in living color* by NBC.'"

"*That's* what I want to call the show," Keenen said. "*In Living Color.* I like that."

Bright says they tried to license the song "What's Your Favorite Color?" but the band turned them down. In fact, that's the song behind the opening credits in the original one-hour pilot. (Once the show was on the air, the band Living Colour did in fact sue over the show's title and its logo, which the band claimed was similar to the one they'd used on their album. The suit was settled.)

Zlotnik recalls Bright bringing Living Colour's CD to him, explaining that the song and the band had the same kind of attitude the show was aiming for. Rawitt similarly remembers Bright suggesting the song but says she was the one who coined the title *In Living Color.* "I said, 'You should call the show *In Living Color* because now finally a show *is* in living color."

12

"The Running Joke Was If Your Last Name's Not Wayans, You Didn't Have a Shot"

Everyone told Rob Edwards that working on the *In Living Color* pilot was a bad idea. He'd just come off a stint writing for the success-ful *Cosby Show* spinoff, *A Different World*. If he wasn't careful, he could get stuck in the sketch world, where writers got paid a fraction of what they did for sitcoms. But when Tamara Rawitt—who'd been tasked with finding writers for the pilot—asked Edwards to come pitch ideas to Keenen, he didn't hesitate.

"I think I was the first person Keenen interviewed," says Edwards. "I'm sitting there with him and Keenen says, 'Frankly, I have no idea what I'm going to do with this.' We just start spitballing: We can hit Arsenio, Mike Tyson, Michael Jordan, whoever out there in the world hasn't been made fun of. No sacred cows." One idea Edwards remembers tossing out was "Great Moments in Black History," which became a recurring sketch on the show.

As a young black writer with sitcom experience, Edwards seemed the perfect prototype for the writing staff, but there weren't many with the same profile. Another early hire looked, superficially, like Edwards's antithesis: Buddy Sheffield was a baby-faced white guy from rural Mis-sissippi, whose credits included a short-lived Dolly Parton variety series, an attempted revival of *The Smothers Brothers Comedy Hour*, and a syndicated sketch show called *Comedy Break*, which featured Kevin Pollak and Jan Hooks. Sheffield's brother David had been one of Eddie Murphy's favorite writers during his *SNL* run and had co-written *Coming to America*.

"I had an interview with Keenen and Tamara and just pitched some ideas," Sheffield says. "This was around the time of the *Exxon Valdez* oil spill. I pitched a sketch about a slave ship running aground and causing a big slave spill. It never got written, never aired, but they thought that was funny."

Sheffield recommended a writer he knew from *The Smothers Brothers* named Howard Kuperberg. A black standup named Jeff Joseph and a former *Late Night with David Letterman* writer named Sandy Frank rounded out the relatively skeletal staff for the pilot.

It was easy shorthand for Keenen to define his vision for *In Living Color* as a "black *SNL*," and one of the most important people he'd hire for the pilot was director Paul Miller, who'd just spent three years working on *SNL*. But Keenen also wanted to do things differently than *SNL*. He wanted shorter, tighter sketches. Because *SNL* was broadcast live and because it took time to construct and deconstruct the sets, he felt the show was compelled to let sketches run longer than they should. For his show, Keenen didn't want meandering character studies—he wanted jokes. "A sketch wasn't gonna be more than four minutes," he says. "If it was a one-joke premise, it wasn't gonna be more than two minutes, preferably thirty seconds to a minute."

Another thing Keenen noticed: *SNL* was a writers' show. Cast members could be filtered in and out, but the writers were the engine that made it all go. The show had been on for almost fifteen years and writers like Jim Downey, Herb Sargent, Al Franken, Tom Davis, Robert Smigel, and Marilyn Suzanne Miller had been there for large swaths of that time. They knew how the show ran, and in some ways dictated to the incoming cast the way it would continue to run. That didn't always serve the show. "A lot of times," Keenen says, "people were in sketches that weren't built for them."

Keenen wanted to invert this relationship. He saw the writing staff as being there primarily to service the cast, not the other way around.

His show would be built around its cast. Which is to say, it would be built around his family, starting with Damon.

"Damon was at a point comedically where he was the most brilliant guy on the planet," Keenen said. "The way he thought, the way his point of view was completely different than mine or anybody else's. He was really on the edge."

Kim was still a relative Hollywood neophyte, but since their days in the Fulton Houses, nobody in the family had been more intensely focused on breaking into show business. After graduating from Wesleyan, she'd moved to Los Angeles and gotten a job as an assistant at CAA, one of the biggest Hollywood talent agencies. She'd had small parts on *A Different World* and the Vietnam War drama *China Beach*. Keenen wanted both Damon and Kim in the cast, but as he puts it, "Fox didn't think I was being objective." Damon had a résumé and a reputation to convince them, but Kim had to audition.

"It was very exciting but also nerve-wracking," she says. "The last thing I wanted to do was embarrass my brother."

Shawn had just started doing standup and was still very green. Keenen hired him as a production assistant on the pilot. Marlon had plans to go to Howard University the following fall, but as preproduction got under way, he was frequently hanging around.

"The Wayanses are kind of a comedy troupe in and of themselves," says Edwards. "They'd go out to dinner—they eat as a family all the time—and try to crack each other up." The next day, they'd recount the highlights of the previous night's meal for the writers' benefit. "The writers would take as much of this down as humanly possible. They have incredible characters, timing, and a great sense of what's funny." Kim seemed to have Keenen's ear and exerted a subtle influence over a lot of creative choices. And Marlon really impressed despite still being a teenager. "We all instantly thought he was in a league with Damon and Keenen."

Several people said Keenen's original plan was to cast the entire show with African-Americans, but Aleta Chappelle, Fox's head of casting at the time, says that by the time casting began in earnest they were looking for a white man and a white woman to augment a largely black cast. Rawitt says that they were searching for comics who were versatile, "that had characters, could do accents, were physical, could do anything.

It was like casting Noah's Ark: We had to find two of each who could do everything because we were going to have a small cast."

Initially, the search centered around three cities: New York, Chicago, and Los Angeles. Among those who auditioned were Comedy Act Theater mainstay Robin Harris, Keenen's old friend from the Improv Melvin George, and two comics who'd later come to prominence on *Curb Your Enthusiasm*, Susie Essman and J.B. Smoove.

Damon recommended a friend of his: a tall, lanky, rubber-faced Canadian named Jim Carrey. Carrey had been doing impressions since he was a kid growing up outside of Toronto, and started standup as a teenager. When Damon first got to know him, Carrey was a recovering impressionist. He'd had fans, bookings in Vegas—many had tipped him as the next Rich Little. Carrey found the prospect mildly horrifying. Instead, he began going on late-night at the Comedy Store, trying to come up with a new act. Damon was one of the other late-night misfits at the club, doing comedy that was too edgy for prime time. The two struck up a mutual admiration society.

"I remember loving Damon's standup because he took such huge chances and wasn't afraid to say anything on his mind," says Carrey. "He had one really sick bit where he talked about his sister being beaten senseless by her husband. He said, 'Why are you with this guy?' And then, imitating her swollen lips and half-shut eye, he'd answer, 'I dooownn't knooow. D'ere's jooust somefin' abou' 'im.' It was *so* wrong. I remember thinking, *This is one of the angriest comedians I've ever seen*. One day he came up to me after seeing me experimenting onstage and said, 'Man, you're one of the angriest comedians I've ever seen in my life!' We became friends."

Carrey was an undeniable talent but had the stink on him of a guy Hollywood didn't know what to do with. He'd been in Los Angeles for nearly a decade. He'd starred in a short-lived NBC sitcom (*The Duck Factory*), a high-school-vampire flick (*Once Bitten*), a Francis Ford Coppola film (*Peggy Sue Got Married*), and with Damon in a goofy comedy (*Earth Girls Are Easy*). He'd auditioned for *SNL* multiple times. Nothing seemed to be working.

"I was slated to go on *The Tonight Show* and they saw me do a bad show one night and canceled me," he says. "I went to audition for *SNL* and there was a guy attempting to commit suicide off the roof of NBC, standing on the letter 'N,' trying to get the nerve to jump. I didn't think that was a very good omen. But Keenen actually saw the tape of my *SNL* audition, in which I played this really racist guy who said the N-word. He thought I was an outlandish guy."

"His standup was very alternative," says Keenen. "He'd do all these crazy characters." One bit was about a guy who'd survived a nuclear attack. It was all very dark, closer to performance art than traditional standup. Keenen liked him as an impressionist but wasn't sure about him beyond that. Damon pressed his older brother into giving Carrey a shot.

At an initial audition in Los Angeles, Carrey was one of 150 or so hopefuls. He needed to do something to stand out. "I felt like the most important thing was to show them that I don't give a damn," Carrey says. He didn't come with any prepared characters, but when they began doing improvs, something clicked. "Suddenly I'd be a Scotsman and suddenly I'd be a pirate," he says. "I'd make really quick choices. I remember pulling out an impression of Nipsey Russell in the middle of one sketch. They were just falling on the ground."

"At that point," says Keenen, "Jim became an obvious choice."

But Carrey was pretty much the first white guy they'd auditioned and they weren't ready to call off the search. They auditioned countless others. One night, Keenen, Eric Gold, and several others went to the Westwood Comedy Store. The showcase they'd arranged started at nine, and as they arrived, a young comedian onstage was doing a wrenching, sad-sack bit about his own sexual inadequacies. Later, after the entire showcase was finished, and a gaggle of comedians had done their short sets, Gold turned to Keenen and asked, "Well, who did you like best?"

"I liked that first kid," Keenen answered.

Gold tried to pin him down. "The tall, thin guy?"

"No, that wasn't him," Keenen said.

"The fat guy?"

"No, not him. The first kid, who did the bit about how he prematurely ejaculates all the time, but he's really great for about two minutes. The two-minute wonder. That kid."

That kid wasn't part of the showcase, Gold told him. He was the last comic to go on before the showcase started.

"Well, I like him," Keenen said. "Who's that?"

"Adam Sandler," Gold said. At the time, however, Sandler wasn't available. The following year he started on *Saturday Night Live*.

Sandler wasn't the only future *SNL* cast member to get a look. Rob Schneider auditioned, as did David Spade. Spade made it through a few rounds. When a callback conflicted with a two-week standup gig he'd booked in Hawaii, he canceled the gig to go to the audition, where they split up into groups to do improvs.

"I'm not a great improv-er but they did need a white guy," Spade said. "I didn't know I was against Jim Carrey. If I [had] known, I would've skipped it. I wasn't very good. I don't do characters. He was so perfect. I was like, 'Why did you waste all of our time?'"

———

Survivors of the regional casting sessions were invited to a final showcase at the Laugh Factory in Los Angeles. About thirty hopefuls, including such future notables as Martin Lawrence, Thomas Haden Church, and Bonnie Hunt, gathered upstairs at the club, eying each other like prizefighters, waiting for their turn onstage. Although most were struggling young actors or comics, quite a few were initially lukewarm about the project.

Tommy Davidson was one of those. Since arriving in Los Angeles the year before, he'd already been a hot standup, opening for Eddie Murphy and Richard Pryor. He'd starred in a pilot for Murphy's production company and was being offered a deal to be written into Candice Bergen's hit sitcom, *Murphy Brown*. In his short time in show business, Davidson was already jaded.

"I actually turned *In Living Color* down," he says. "I'd been through the mill of a lot of top offers. My agent said, 'Why don't you just go audition?' Good agent." Nonetheless, Davidson was convinced that he'd blown the first day of auditions. "I wasn't really used to sketch and improv. They say, 'Okay, you're in a cab and you're a Latin guy—go!' I hadn't yet put together the ability to channel something in an instant. I did terrible." Apparently, not everyone agreed, and he was invited to the final Laugh Factory showcase. "I was thirtieth out of thirty comics and I killed everybody. That got me the show."

Kelly Coffield showed up to the Chicago casting session on a lark. She was a graduate student, studying theater and performing in a "very dramatic" play at the time. Her agent convinced her to audition, but Coffield was certain she was wrong for it. She wasn't a standup, didn't do much improv, and had no idea who Keenen was. Also, she was white. Nonetheless, several weeks after the audition, Rawitt called her and told her to come to Los Angeles ready to do five to ten minutes of her best material. There was only one problem: She didn't have any material. She was an actress, not a comic.

"You did a lot of characters at the audition," Rawitt told her. "Can't you do that?"

"But how? Do I just come in with a bunch of monologues?"

"Oh, you'll figure it out."

Coffield (whose married name is now Kelly Coffield Park) boarded the plane to Los Angeles with no clue what she was going to do onstage. Sitting in her airplane seat, she came up with the idea of playing all the parts in a women's support group where the main character is Sleeping Beauty. She began scribbling it all down furiously on cocktail napkins.

At the Laugh Factory, armed with her pile of cocktail napkins, Coffield felt intimidated immediately. Most of her competition were standups used to commanding stages like this. "I'm sure everyone can relate to being in a situation where you're positive you don't belong," she says. "You know, like, *Maybe they remembered the wrong girl from the auditions*. I really did feel like an imposter. I was getting more and more terrified as it came closer to me going up there. Nobody was doing anything like what I was doing."

When Coffield finally got onstage, she was initially met with confused stares. "Part of my thing was I was going to make everybody in the audience part of this meeting," she says. "So it was just weird. There was absolute, utter silence. Then somebody started laughing, and then there was a lot of laughter. I thought, *Either they're being really nice or they're making fun of me, but in any case, I'm almost done*."

When she finished her set, she strode offstage and straight out of the club. She kept walking all the way down Sunset Boulevard back to her hotel. "I was physically shaking," she says. "Just wringing my hands, like, *What the hell just happened?* It was horrible." She flew back to Chicago the next day. She was satisfied to have survived the ordeal, and expected to never hear about it again. A few weeks later, she was cast.

T'Keyah Crystal Keymáh was another product of the Chicago auditions who felt ill-fit for the show. Keymáh thought of herself as an actress, not a comedian. She hadn't liked *I'm Gonna Git You Sucka*. Nonetheless, she showed up to an open call at the Regal Theater in Chicago with two friends, Ali LeRoi and Lance Crouther.

"There were some other actors there who were really horrible," she said. "They were doing comedy monologues from staged shows that weren't at all appropriate in the same room with standup comedians. I thought, *God, if I'm going to look like that, strike me dead right before I go on.*"

At the Laugh Factory, Keymáh, a former Miss Black America runner-up, performed a piece she'd written called "Blackworld." In it, she acted the part of a young girl, playing make-believe in her basement. She imagined, through the eyes of a child, a world where the nation's ugly racial history had been erased, her family had money, black people owned businesses, Jesse Jackson was the king, Nelson Mandela and James Brown were free men, and she had real black dolls with "real black people hair." It was funny, but also sentimental and heartbreaking. Keenen loved it.

"I thought, *Wow*," he says. "That's poignant, it's cute, it's well performed, and it says something." Keymáh was in.

David Alan Grier had been a part of Keenen and Robert Townsend's circle for a few years—he'd had a small part in *Sucka* and a slightly larger one, alongside Townsend, in *A Soldier's Story*—but like Coffield and Keymáh, he wasn't really a comedian. He was a graduate of the Yale School of Drama. He'd been nominated for a Tony Award for his lead role in a musical about Jackie Robinson. He'd grown up a serious young man too. His father, William Grier, was a psychiatrist who co-authored the seminal 1968 book *Black Rage*, a study of the historical and psychological roots of racial animus in America. Grier was from Detroit, and had marched with his family alongside with Martin Luther King Jr. through the streets there in 1968 as part of the Poor People's Campaign. Grier had even flirted with becoming a Black Panther in his teenage years. When the *ILC* audition came along, he was still reconciling these different sides of himself.

As he puts it in his memoir, *Barack Like Me*, "Even though . . . I know

I can be funny and I was voted class clown in elementary, middle and high school, I still see myself as a serious actor. I don't have a standup act, I don't have a bunch of characters I do." Keenen pressed Grier to give it a shot. When he was eventually offered a spot in the cast, Grier says he turned it down before Kim Wayans eventually helped change his mind.

Kim Coles, who'd first been asked to audition after Keenen met her at a party and recognized her from her standup on the syndicated series *Showtime at the Apollo*, was plucked from the New York casting sessions. "My understanding was they wanted standups who could do characters," says Coles. "Luckily for me, I had a bit where I did all the contestants in a Miss America pageant from all over the world, so I did all these different accents."

T.J. McGee was a popular comic and impressionist who'd met Keenen at the Comedy Act Theater. He hadn't taken the audition that seriously until he'd shown up at the Laugh Factory that night and seen the talent assembled—both the hopefuls upstairs and the Hollywood heavy hitters in the audience. Still, his expectations were tempered. "The running joke," he says, "was if your last name's not Wayans, you didn't have a shot."

Following the Laugh Factory auditions, the pilot's cast took shape. Joining Keenen, Damon, and Kim would be Carrey, Coffield, Keymáh, Davidson, Grier, Coles, McGee, and Toney Riley, another comedian/actor Keenen had first discovered at the Comedy Act. Jeff Joseph, a talented standup, would do double duty as both a writer and cast member.

Chris Rock had been in the mix for a role too. In a 1989 interview with journalist David Mills, he sounded confident a job on the show was his. "I'll be a writer and a performer," he said. "Nothing's been inked out yet. They're just negotiating the contracts and stuff." However, Rock wasn't even at the Laugh Factory showcase. A year later, he told Mills he didn't know what happened. "It's a whole L.A. thing. I'm in New York. Things just happened, man. I'm not out there. It was more of an image thing. I don't want to dis anybody, but it was a Fox decision more or less."

Keenen says that guys like Rock and Martin Lawrence were funny, they just weren't ready. "At that moment in time, they were one step behind the other guys." Aleta Chappelle says Rock was "somebody we thought about for a while," but he was "very nervous." According to Rawitt, the main problem with Rock was that he just wasn't really what the show needed.

"Chris was a genius writer and great at being Chris, but the show needed people who could do a myriad of characters and accents," she says. That's not what he did. "If we had our own 'News Update' desk, he could've owned that space."

Contract negotiations took longer than expected. All the cast's contracts were standard five-year deals and had a "favored nations" clause in them that stated, essentially, that all the actors would get paid equally. The clause was common for new shows with an ensemble cast. Carrey, though, had a thicker résumé than most of his castmates and had a higher standard "quote," which is to say he wanted more money. But giving Carrey more money would break the "favored nations" deals. For a while, it looked like Carrey might drop out over it.

"We probably saw two thousand other white guys," says Gold. "All Keenen said was, 'I want Jim Carrey. I want Jim Carrey.' Every goddamn day it was 'Get me Jim Carrey.' And Jim didn't want to do the show. He kept saying, 'No.'"

Carrey says he was just evaluating other offers, and laughs off the notion forwarded by some that being the token white guy on a black show was giving him pause.

"No, to me, I knew Keenen and Damon and knew they were really creative, talented guys," he says. "The racial shit didn't concern me."

Regardless, the negotiations dragged on. Thomas Haden Church, who'd later go on to get an Oscar nomination for the film *Sideways*, was the show's backup option. In the end, though, Gold crafted a solution that got Carrey more money without breaking the "favored nations" deal. Carrey signed the same deal as his new castmates, but also got a separate deal from the studio for "non-series television." That second deal led to him being cast in a dramatic role as an alcoholic in a 1992 television movie called *Doing Time on Maple Drive*, which was nominated for three Emmys.

The other tricky contract was Damon's. Gold, who already managed Keenen and would soon be co-managing Carrey, had started managing Damon too. But as the pilot came together, Damon hired a new agent who got in his ear and suggested Gold could be doing more for him. Damon subsequently fired Gold. His new agent tried to play hardball with Fox to get Damon a better deal. Fox wasn't having it. Damon, they decided, was more trouble than he was worth. As Gold puts it, "Damon was out."

Damon had plenty going on in his career at the time, and several people suggested he was hedging on whether he wanted to be tied down to a weekly show for five years. Damon, though, has said that after getting fired off *SNL* he "needed redemption." Regardless, Keenen was upset. Damon was integral to his plans. Plus, he was worried about his younger brother.

"Damon had blown several career opportunities because of his emotionality," says Gold. "He'd already self-destructed on *SNL*. Damon also thought Keenen should've made him an executive producer. Keenen was adamant that we had to figure out something."

The solution was to hire Damon as a "guest star" for the pilot. "Basically Fox punted and figured they could deal with him later when they knew whether the pilot would go to series," says Gold. "If Damon was anyone else besides Keenen's younger brother, he never would've been allowed to do the pilot."

Damon soon rehired Gold (and then fired and rehired him several more times over the next decade and a half) and, after the pilot, signed a separate one-year contract. Gold believes this was a good deal for Damon, because it gave him more leverage later on. Damon, however, felt disrespected by the whole turn of events.

"When I walked into *In Living Color*, they treated me like Keenen's little brother," he says. "I had a one-year deal. They didn't even respect me enough to make me a regular. I was a recurring character." That first contract, he says, paid him only fifteen hundred dollars per episode. "I don't think Fox knew what I could do."

———

A.J. Johnson had just moved to Los Angeles when she first met Keenen in a club on Melrose Avenue. Johnson had been a Miss Collegiate Black America, as well as a sorority step captain at Spelman College in Atlanta, and had had a small role in Spike Lee's *School Daze* before graduating. She was making her living as a dancer and was with friends at the club the night Keenen spotted her on the dance floor. It was something to see.

"My dance style was grabbing a girl standing on the side of the dance floor, grabbing another girl, teaching them a quick count of eight, and now, we're grooving to this count of eight and everybody's putting their own style on it," says Johnson. Slowly, more people joined in until the floor was jammed with dancers all working off the same theme. "It was almost like the beginning of line dancing."

Keenen liked what he saw and came over to talk to her. He wanted dancers on *In Living Color*, but was trying to figure out what exactly that was going to look like. *Laugh-In* had used quick dance "bumpers" between segments, and he also remembered that Jackie Gleason's various variety shows had featured the June Taylor Dancers.

"All these are pieces of my childhood," he says. But he wanted to put his own spin on it. His dancers wouldn't be old-school chorus line girls, they'd be the cool, stylish chicks people gawked at in clubs. Girls like Johnson. *Fly* Girls.

"I really like this freestyle thing you do," Keenen told Johnson at the side of the dance floor. He explained that he had a project he was working on that he wanted to talk to her about. "Can we do lunch tomorrow?"

Johnson wasn't entirely sure whether this was really about work or if he was trying to pick her up, but she didn't really care.

"He was hot!" she says. "Physically, as a man, as well as in his career. So I had no reason not to meet him for lunch. Either way, personally or professionally, I'm winning!"

Keenen did want to talk about work at lunch the next day, though it's also worth mentioning that he and Johnson ended up dating—"for a minute," as Johnson, puts it—not too long after that too. At lunch, he explained his vision for the Fly Girls.

"He showed me some clips of *Laugh-In*," Johnson says. That was the template, but of course, hipper. It was a fairly radical idea. "You have to remember this was the end of the eighties. There was nothing on TV like it."

He wanted her to replicate the energy that he saw on the dance floor at the club, but in thirty-second snippets. He asked her to put together a small troupe and show him what it might look like.

Johnson already had a few dancers in mind. She'd recently worked with two of them, Lisa Marie Todd and Deidre Lang, on a video for a song called "Just Coolin'," a collaboration between the R&B group LeVert and rapper—and Keenen's friend—Heavy D. "If you look at the 'Just Coolin' video, you'll see where the Fly Girls concept came from," says Johnson. "It's me, Deidre, Lisa, and two or three other girls. That video—girls on the street, hip-hop clothes, offering up dance battles when they run into guys on the street—that whole concept is what we transferred to *In Living Color*."

The pilot's budget was tight, so there was only one small audition, and afterward Johnson chose who she knew she wanted from the beginning—all young dancers, all friends of hers, all black. Another friend, an actress and dancer named Tisha Campbell, who'd been one of the leads in *School Daze*, was frequently around to lend a hand with the choreography. Johnson admits that she didn't totally see Keenen's vision for the Fly Girls. As he watched them work on routines, she told him so.

"I don't get why you want dancers coming out in the middle of a comedy show," she said.

"I'm telling you," Keenen insisted, "it's going to be one of the hottest parts of the show. It's gonna be crazy!"

"I still don't get it. You're going to have some dancers out there for a couple of seconds. Big deal."

"When I saw you dance in the club that night, that's when the vision hit," Keenen said. "Everybody in America's gonna wanna do these dances. Everybody in America's gonna wanna dress like these girls. Trust me!"

"Well," Johnson said, "I'm gonna have to."

13

"Is This Okay to Say?"

Kim Coles was exhausted. She'd had a standup gig in London, and had flown to New York then taken a red-eye into LAX so she could be there for the cast's first day of work in the spring of 1989. After landing around three in the morning, she found a place to stay near the airport, slept for a few hours, showered, and then arrived at the Fox lot, on the corner of Wilton and Sunset. She was buzzing with nervous energy—and lack of sleep—as she met her castmates. "We were just sort of sizing each other up, looking to see who'd gotten the job," she says.

Many of the other cast members knew each other already, and not just the ones who were related. Damon and Jim Carrey were close friends. David Alan Grier had appeared in *I'm Gonna Git You Sucka* and *Partners in Crime* and was close with the Wayans siblings. Tommy Davidson had been a regular at the Comedy Act Theater and knew Keenen, Damon, T.J. McGee, and Toney Riley. Coles only knew Davidson, from doing standup gigs with him. Kelly Coffield and T'Keyah Crystal Keymáh, who were moving from Chicago, were relative outsiders too. Coles and Coffield decided to sublet a house together in West Hollywood.

"We were all just excited to be with one another," says Coffield. "There hadn't been a show like this before. There was great camaraderie.

We used to say, 'This must be what it was like to be on the *Mickey Mouse Club*.'"

The writing staff cranked out sketches every day. The ones Keenen liked got written up on notecards and tacked to the big bulletin board in Tamara Rawitt's office. The ones he didn't, went in the trash can. There was a feeling, at times, that the writing of sketches was an end in and of itself.

"I thought I'd written more than half of the show," says Rob Edwards, "then the next day you'd see the board again and everything I'd written was gone. I'd write a bunch of new stuff that would go up, then a couple days later, the board would shift." Material that seemed funny at first would naturally grow stale with repeated exposure. Edwards says the smarter, more experienced sketch writers—"which I was not"—held their best material until the end of the writing process. In a few weeks of writing, a mountain of sketches was generated. The pilot was slated to be an hour long, and Keenen wanted to produce at least an hour and a half of solid material to edit down. Extra sketches could always be banked for future shows. When the cast, producers, and writers got together to read through the initial cache of scripts, director Paul Miller, the *SNL* vet, was floored.

"I'd been through that with *Saturday Night Live*, but I had never been through anything like this," he says. "There must've been a hundred sketches read in one day. It was kind of numbing."

Interesting ideas got lost in the shuffle. Howard Kuperberg recalls a piece he wrote called "Picasso's Black Period," with Carrey as Picasso, that was discarded. Edwards wrote a sketch imagining the 1934 NAACP Image Awards. Trophies would be awarded to the likes of Stepin Fetchit and Hattie McDaniel, who played a series of infamous "mammy" roles, most famously in *Gone with the Wind*.

"The joke is the idiotically stereotypical characters that were accepted as mainstream entertainment back in the day," says Edwards. "I wrote it and everybody was high-fiving, but we wound up not shooting it. That broke my heart."

Some of the sketches that survived had a history that dated back years or even decades. Keenen and Damon had been playing some version of Wiz and Ice since they were teenagers. Kuperberg and Buddy

Sheffield helped turn them into the first "Homeboy Shopping Network" sketch. "Men on Film" dated back to Damon and Keenen's youthful masquerading as a gay couple around the West Village, and as movie critic siblings Dickie and Donald Davis. Sandy Frank reimagined them as Blaine Edwards and Antoine Merriweather. Initially, Damon and Keenen were set to play Blaine and Antoine. As Damon recalls it, Keenen gave his part away to Grier simply because he had too much other stuff to do, and Grier didn't. Grier says he was originally slated to play the father in another sketch called "Hey Mon" about a family of Jamaican immigrants, but couldn't muster a passable Jamaican accent, so Damon—who had a Jamaican character in his arsenal as far back as those Kitchen Table improvs—took that part, and Keenen gave Grier the part of Antoine.

Edwards recalls a related bit of horse-trading between Damon and Keenen. Both did pretty good Mike Tyson impressions, and either could've played the boxer in a sketch that imagined Tyson and then wife Robin Givens on an episode of the dating show *Love Connection*. Both were also capable of playing Blaine in "Men on Film."

"Whoever did the film critic was going to get a lot of really creepy mail," says Edwards, "but whoever did Tyson was going to get punched in the face at a party when they least expected it. Tyson was notoriously thin-skinned and self-conscious about his voice. They kind of went rock-paper-scissors: Keenen got Tyson and Damon wound up doing the film critic."

Grier says the initial "Men on Film" script had fictional movie titles in it, but after read-throughs and rehearsals, he and Damon began improvising. "We started using real movies that had no gay connotation—like *Top Gun*, or whatever—which really upped the ante. The straighter the movie, the funnier it got that we would put this gay inference in it."

Blaine and Antoine are very much a product of a pre–politically correct era. Even back then, it raised the hackles of more than a few people. Don Bay, a gentlemanly lawyer who had been hired by Fox to run its Broadcast Standards and Practices Department, recalls meeting Keenen for the first time in the office of the VP of programming. Keenen outlined the show and mentioned "Men on Film."

"I was concerned about how gays would be treated since the subject was a sensitive one at that time, and I'd met with reps of the gay commu-

nity before," says Bay. Fox Chairman Barry Diller was also uncomfortable with the sketch.

Back in 1989, Diller was already a legendary Hollywood executive,
known as one of the smartest, toughest, most ambitious guys in the industry. He'd started in the mailroom at the William Morris Agency
(now known as William Morris Endeavor), worked his way up to head
of prime-time programming at ABC and eventually chairman of Paramount Pictures, where he reigned for a decade before being lured to Fox.
He was short and stocky, with a clean, shiny bald head that only seemed
to add to his intimidating mien. Diller read the "Men on Film" script, and
according to Keenen, he raged to Fox president Peter Chernin about it.

"He ripped Peter a new ass and was like, 'We can't do this,'" says
Keenen. "He called me and was like, 'This might be going too far.' I said,
'I'll tell you what: Come to the rehearsal. Come see it and if you have an
issue with it after that, let's talk.'" Diller came to the dress rehearsal in
front of a live audience. "It sounded like somebody put a bomb in the
building," Keenen says. "That's how big the laughs were. People were
stomping their feet. No one had ever seen anything like this. Barry
watched the whole thing and that was it." Diller was convinced.

As the dates for filming the pilot loomed, there was no real sense
among the writers and cast which sketches were in and which were out.
Of those one hundred or so that had been read through initially, many
had been discarded but many remained and new ones popped up all the
time.

"There would be six sketches up on the wall and we'd be prepping
them with costumes and casting," says Edwards, "and the next day, you'd
go in and six new sketches were up. Three days later, there would be
three new sketches up. We never really knew what the rundown of the
show would be."

This was a nice problem to have. There was so much good material
that they were spoiled for choice. But the longer Keenen put off making a
final call on the pilot's rundown, the more it created a logjam in the production cycle. People were waiting on him to do their jobs.

"We were about two weeks away from shooting and Keenen had not
locked into a show yet," says producer Kevin Bright. "He just kept the
writers writing and writing and didn't want to commit. Paul Miller and

I were really concerned. We had to get scenery built. We thought maybe if we initiated a rundown based on the material we had, it would pin him down, get him to think about it and then work with us to commit to a show. So we did and showed it to him. He liked it and we were going to go with that." But Bright had broken the rule Keenen had asked him to commit to when he first started: He wasn't supposed to be involved with creative decisions. "Tamara came into my office and told me Keenen was angry. I was out of my lane."

Miller says they ended up producing "many more sketches than we could ever use in one episode." In addition to "The Homeboy Shopping Network," "Men on Film," and the Mike Tyson "Love Connection" sketch, the final rundown included Keymáh's "Blackworld" piece that she'd auditioned with, as well as a few short "Great Moments in Black History" bits that Edwards had proposed at his first meeting with Keenen. There was also a sketch with Keymáh hosting a female empowerment cable access show called "Go On Girl." Damon had a short commercial parody for the United Negro College Fund, in which he played a malapropism-spouting prison inmate named Oswald Bates. The character was based on an impression Marlon used to do of a guy from the family's old neighborhood who'd gone to prison and returned spewing all sorts of half-cocked wisdom. Damon had also written a funny Calvin Klein commercial parody called "Oppression." In addition, the final rundown included a sketch Sheffield and Kuperberg had penned, a commercial for a Broadway show featuring Sammy Davis Jr.—as played by Tommy Davidson—starring as South African freedom fighter Nelson Mandela, that was universally beloved among the cast and writing staff.

But arguably the sketch that both set the template and the bar for *In Living Color* was a *Star Trek* spoof called "The Wrath of Farrakhan." In it, Damon plays the militant Nation of Islam leader Louis Farrakhan aboard the *Starship Enterprise*. Farrakhan, as David Alan Grier's Spock helpfully tells Carrey's Captain Kirk (and viewers), "is a former calypso singer who later became leader of a twentieth-century African-American religious sect." At the time, Farrakhan was known mostly for controversial statements that some construed to be anti-white and anti-Semitic. In the sketch, Farrakhan proclaims, "I've come to warn your crew of their enslavement on this vessel." Everywhere he looks on the *Enterprise*, he sees oppression. Uhura, played by Kim Wayans, is a glorified secretary who hasn't gotten a raise in fifteen years. Grier's Spock is the crew's strongest and smartest yet only second in command. Soon, Farrakhan, ever the rabble-rouser, has fomented an insurrection.

Kim Wayans calls the sketch "quintessential *In Living Color.*" It's one of Keenen's favorites too. It's pop-culture silliness spiked with sharp sociopolitical barbs. It makes fun of Farrakhan but also suggests that despite his occasional flights into the absurd, he often has a valid point. As Keenen put it, "It was just the right mix of everything."

The executives at Fox weren't thrilled with it, though. As Rawitt recalls, "Everybody at Fox said, 'Nobody knows who Louis Farrakhan is! Nobody is going to care!' The point is you let us create a show for black culture. Everyone in black culture knows who Farrakhan is."

Fox figured anything about Farrakhan was likely to stir up problems either from the Anti-Defamation League or the Nation of Islam itself. Probably both. Keenen believed Farrakhan himself deserved a fairer hearing than he'd gotten in the culture at large.

"Farrakhan is a brother that when white people hear his name, they start shaking in their boots," he told journalist Nelson George in the early nineties. "Farrakhan isn't the hatemonger he's painted out to be. If people would listen to him they'd realize that he may have a different opinion but he's not Adolf Hitler."

There was a part of Damon that simply got a kick out of Farrakhan. Here was a guy who wasn't trying to mend fences and promote racial healing. He was unapologetically angry. Farrakhan was himself, apparently, a fan of "The Wrath of Farrakhan."

"Thankfully, he found it funny, " says Damon. "His son told me, 'Man, Pops loves that. He thinks it's really hilarious.' It's nice to know he has a sense of humor because there's a nation of people who love him and if you make fun of him it could be very painful."

Keenen was steering the show without a road map. He was making people nervous. Even the show's own writers and producers didn't always agree with him.

"Most of the time, the joke is on the media, on white people, on white fear," says Edwards. "'Homeboy Shopping Network' divided the staff. That one seemed to come from a different point of view where the people being made fun of were poor black people." It was certainly possible to see Wiz and Ice as just a new version of the same Stepin Fetchit stereotypes Edwards had skewered in his 1934 NAACP Image Awards sketch. "For us black writers, it seemed like it was punching down, which you're not supposed to do in comedy. It seemed like making fun of people who didn't need to be made fun of." The same, he says, applied to "Men on Film." In both cases though, political righteousness proved less important than comedic effectiveness. "Sometimes when you take something to the stage and it gets a laugh, the laugh wins out," he says. "Ultimately, we lost the battle."

It was the first battle in a war that would last as long as the show itself.

———

Keenen had to be convinced to host *In Living Color*. He had no real interest in getting onstage to welcome the audience and introduce everyone. But there was a pervading feeling that not only would Keenen's presence give the show a sense of cohesion—as opposed to being a bunch of disconnected sketches—Fox felt it would make it clear that the creative force behind these racially charged sketches was a black man.

For the pilot, the plan was to run through the show on two consecutive nights, in front of two different audiences. That way, they'd have two takes of every sketch. If necessary, they could do "pickups"—filming extra bits that didn't work in the original takes—after the audience left.

The first night, after Tommy Davidson warmed up the crowd with some standup, Keenen opened the show by introducing the Fly Girls and the show's DJ, a guy known as DJ Daddy Mack, who was dressed in a tall black top hat with a big Africa emblem on the front of it. Keenen then wandered backstage to introduce the cast and crew.

"I'll tell you what I'm most proud of," he says to the camera. "Unlike other shows, I've got nothing but qualified black people backstage making decisions." With that, he opens the writers' room door and a bunch of white writers scurry out. He claims they're the cleaning staff. He introduces a black cleaning lady as the head writer.

"Now I'm going to introduce you to our cast," he continues. "We went nationwide to find the most talented people in the country." He then introduces "Damon Wayans," "Kim Wayans," "Crystal Wayans," "TJ Wayans," "Toney Wayans," "Tommy Wayans," and so on. Next, Keenen boasts about how integrated the show is. "People of all races working together as one big happy family," he says as he opens a door marked, "White Cast Members Only." Behind it are Carrey and Coffield. He's shining shoes. She's ironing. They're both grinning broadly and singing, "Camp Town Ladies." Keenen smiles. "Oh, those people. Always singing, always happy." It was a whip-smart, playfully barbed reversal of the racial dynamics that had ruled television since the medium's invention.

Back in front of the audience, Keenen is confronted by the network's "censors," who make it clear that most of what Keenen had been planning for the pilot is unacceptable. Keenen makes a show of defiance. "I refuse to be silenced," he tells the audience. "We had this really great sketch that I wanted to do for you anyway. It started off like this: See, Ronald Reagan in 1975 . . ." At this point, Keenen is rendered inaudible by the sound of a loud, long beep. He continues ranting, but can't be heard. The bit is a direct homage to—or, less charitably, a rip-off of—a routine from *The Richard Pryor Show* more than a decade earlier.

The first set-piece is the "Love Connection" sketch with Coles as a gold-digging Robin Givens, Keenen as Tyson, and Carrey as the show's host, Chuck Woolery. Later in the show, Davidson does his Sammy Davis Jr. as Mandela. Dressed in a Star of David necklace, pinkie rings, and an African dashiki, Davidson turns the song "Candy Man" into "Mandy Man": "Who can take apartheid/Turn it inside out/Show those Afrikaans what this freedom gig's about?/The Mandy Man can . . . The Mandy Man can but they locked me in the can and threw the key away."

Coffield pops up twice as part of a recurring meta-routine, playing an uptight white woman writing a letter to the network to complain about the show. "I realize in the past blacks have suffered some . . . unpleasantness," she dictates aloud, "with that whole slavery thing and all, and that some resentment may be justified. Maybe it would help you if I shared with you a little secret I know. Just take a deep breath and say to yourselves, 'Sticks and stones may break my bones, but hundreds of years of oppression may never harm me.'"

There are other short interludes. The two "Great Moments in Black

History" sketches—one with Toney Riley as a lazy gas station attendant who "invents" self-serve gas stations by telling a customer to "Get it your damn self!"; the other with Jeff Joseph as Slick Johnson, the first black man on the moon, left behind by the crew (and subsequently erased from history) when the mission needs to jettison weight for the return to Earth—are in and out in about a minute. A spoof of the show *227*, called "Too-Too Ethnic," is less than thirty seconds.

Keenen's instincts seemed to be spot-on. For "The Homeboy Shopping Network," a truck full of electronics and other "stolen" goods was driven onto the soundstage as a prop.

"When we did a rehearsal," says Bright, "there was one of those smaller satellite dishes in the truck and Keenen said, 'No, I want one of those big, giant satellite dishes.'" Bright wasn't sure it was worth the trouble.

"It's going to be awkward and hard to get that out of the truck," he told Keenen.

"No, man, I want the big one," Keenen insisted.

For the pilot taping, Bright got a huge dish with the words "Property of NASA" on it. Bright laughs. "Keenen was right. I remember him lugging that satellite dish out of the truck the first time. The big one was so much funnier."

As the sketch was being filmed, Paul Miller was in the control booth. The technical staff was laughing uncontrollably. The show's lighting director, an older white man, turned to Miller, a little sheepishly.

"I can't believe we're doing this," he said about the "Homeboy" sketch. "Is this okay to say?"

Miller nodded. "Yeah, because Keenen is saying it. It wouldn't be okay for you or me to say, but it's okay for Keenen."

The pilot's tone was consistently cutting without ever falling into outright nastiness. It had a clear point of view. Edwards recalls that it took the crowd a sketch or two to get the rhythm of the show. Then, he says, the place went nuts.

"Black audiences don't just laugh at stuff, we stomp our feet, we high-five," he says. "People were literally running up and down the aisles during the taping, high-fiving each other. One of the executives turned to me and said, 'Did you pay these guys to do that?'"

The second show, the next night, went just as well, if not better.

"I've never done a show that felt that way in front of an audience," says Bright, who later became the co-creator of *Friends*. "At *Friends*, I'd never seen a first taping of anything where the audience was that crazy. They were on fire, both audiences. It was like the show had been on forever." After the second show, Bright encountered Keenen backstage. "Keenen wasn't an emotional, touchy-feely guy, and when we finished the second show, he physically lifted me up in the air and gave me this big bear hug. It can't go better than that."

Kim Wayans, who, in addition to her part in "The Wrath of Farrakhan," also appeared in "Go On Girl" and "Too-Too Ethnic," says the energy in the air was palpable. "You could feel something new, exciting, and fresh happening," she says. "After the pilot, we all knew we had something special."

14

"If He Ain't Got No Jokes, I Don't Need Him"

Keenen walked toward the conference room at Fox's Executive Office Building not knowing what to expect. The pilot had gone great, but since then he'd heard a lot of nothing from the network. *There was research to be done. They were testing it.* Today's meeting was with something called "The Research Group." Both Barry Diller and Peter Chernin were going to be there too.

Keenen liked Diller and Chernin and he thought they liked the show. Yet months had gone by since the pilot with no word of whether it would get ordered as a series. The cast members were under holding deals but had scattered to the wind. Damon, Jim, and Tommy were doing standup. Kim Wayans got a temp job as a secretary at an oil company in downtown Los Angeles. Coffield and Coles went to New York. All would occasionally call Keenen to check in. He wished he had more to tell them. Some began to assume the worst. A recent call from Coffield was typical.

"I just got offered a play in New York," she told him.

"What are you asking?"

"I'm asking if you have any idea if this thing's going to get picked up."

"No idea," he told her. "Just do the play."

Keenen hoped this meeting would start to clear things up, though he wasn't expecting much. When he sat down, he saw who The Research Group was: five stiff-looking white guys in dark suits and starched shirts. "I felt like I was sitting with the NSA," he says. "Not a funny bone in their bodies."

They told him about the work they'd been doing. They'd been showing the pilot to focus groups and asking people how it made them *feel*.

"Wow," Keenen said, a little taken aback. "That's deep."

"Tell me what your vision is for the show," said one of the suits.

Keenen told them it was going to be fresh and new. "It's going to be revolutionary!" he said excitedly.

There was silence in the room. Keenen quickly divined that to these five men in dark suits, "revolutionary" wasn't a good thing. It conjured visions of Black Panthers and Molotov cocktails. Of Malcolm X's demand for freedom, justice, and equality "by any means necessary." He tried to assuage their fears.

"No, not *take-over-the-world* revolutionary. Revolutionary in terms of funny."

The room exhaled. The Research Group seemed satisfied. He'd never seen any of the men before that day, and once the meeting was over, he never saw any of them again.

Far from being an odd aberration, the meeting was a pretty good indicator of what went on for about nine months following the making of the pilot. Fox said they wanted edgy programming, but now that they had it in their hands, they weren't sure what to do with it. It's not that they didn't like the show. They just didn't know how everyone else would react to it.

"It was really, really funny but people were nervous to put the pilot on," says Joe Davola, the VP of development who oversaw the show. "You're talking about a Fox network that's run by white executives. Everybody was oversensitive. We didn't want to offend too many people."

Diller, in particular, was very worried about being perceived as racist. The solution, Diller and others at Fox thought, was to get buy-in from prominent African-American groups. The pilot was screened for members of the NAACP and the Urban League. Fox reached out to C. Delores Tucker, a civil rights activist who later became a prominent crusader against rap music, and Alvin Poussaint, another activist who was a consultant on *The Cosby Show*. Meetings were arranged with various interest groups. Keenen was appalled and refused to attend.

"A couple of groups wanted to be brought on as consultants which Keenen thought was a bribe," says Eric Gold. The quid pro quo was unstated but understood: If Fox paid a consulting fee, the groups wouldn't make a fuss. "Keenen didn't like it and wouldn't even meet with them."

As one story goes, at one point the NAACP tried to pressure Keenen by asking how many black writers and producers he'd hired. He challenged them to send over a list of all the black writers and producers they knew. They didn't have any such list and that was the end of that. Keenen found the whole idea of checking his work with other black people galling. Did Woody Allen need a thumbs-up from the Anti-Defamation League before he released a film? Did studios clear every John Hughes movie with suburban white people?

"At one point, Fox brought this old black man that they wanted to hire as a consultant to the show," says Keenen. "They told me how he'd marched with Dr. King and had a lump on the side of his head from when he got beat up. I said, 'I respect all he has done, but if he ain't got no jokes, I don't need him. He's no blacker than me. I don't need him to validate me.'"

Gold was impressed. "His show's future was on the line when it was sitting on the shelf. He stood up, erect, and said, 'I'm not doing it that way.' Can you imagine this? Where did this guy learn this kind of backbone?"

Fox had reasons to be optimistic about *In Living Color*. All around, the seeds planted in the earlier parts of the decade were beginning to flower. Arsenio's talk show was becoming a cultural phenomenon. *The Cosby Show* was the top-rated show on television. Its spinoff, *A Different World*, was also a hit. Spike Lee's *Do the Right Thing*, a vivid, funny, complex, and disturbing film that presented a slice of black life in Brooklyn that seemed a million miles away from the Huxtables' home address, had been nominated for the Palme d'Or at Cannes. *Harlem Nights*, Eddie Murphy's directorial debut, which he starred in alongside his idols (Richard Pryor, Redd Foxx), his friends (Arsenio, Robin Harris), and his family (Charlie Murphy, Ray Murphy), was released in late 1989 to middling reviews but strong box office returns, eventually earning nearly one hundred million dollars. And in January 1990, Fox spun off a strange little cartoon family sitcom called *The Simpsons* from *The Tracey Ullman Show*. The early reviews were glowing.

Still, it wasn't clear what might prod the network's top brass into making a decision about *ILC*. Time dragged on. Nearly nine months had passed since they turned in the pilot and still no word. Tamara Rawitt tried to force their hand. She slipped videotape copies of the pilot to everyone she knew in the industry. The tapes got passed around. Davola gave out copies too.

Martha Frankel, a writer for *Details* magazine, went to dinner one night in Los Angeles with Rawitt and another friend. At dinner, Rawitt bemoaned the situation. She'd helped build this show from the ground up, they'd made this amazing pilot, everyone loved it, but Fox wouldn't put it on.

Rawitt handed her a videotape, and when Frankel got back to her hotel, she popped it in the VCR. "It was truly the funniest thing I'd ever seen," Frankel says. The following night, she invited several friends to her room and showed it to them. "We were screaming with laughter." She called Rawitt and asked if she could write a story about the pilot. Rawitt encouraged her to.

Frankel wrote a page-long rave about the pilot, asking pointedly why Fox was sitting on it. When the issue hit newsstands, Rawitt ripped the article out and sent it to Diller's office.

"I said, 'Now what are you afraid of?' The next day we got a pickup for eight episodes."

———

Changes had to be made before the first episode aired. An hour of sketches every week was too much. Too much for the audience and too much for the creators. *ILC* was going to work better as a half-hour show, something Rawitt says she figured from the outset. Leave the audience wanting more.

Much to the chagrin of Chris Albrecht and Carmi Zlotnik, HBO, who produced the pilot, didn't have the stomach to hang in there for the series. This wasn't a reflection of the controversies the show might engender, it was a money issue. Michael Fuchs, the head of HBO, wasn't prepared to "deficit finance" *ILC*—essentially, lose money in the short run in the hopes of turning a big profit if and when the series went into syndication.

"HBO really didn't understand what [deficit financing] meant," says Zlotnik. "When the full recognition of the financial responsibility dawned on them, they said, 'No.'"

Without HBO, the project got passed to Fox's own studio arm, Twentieth Television, in what was, at the time, an unusual arrangement. In 1970, the FCC had put in place a set of financial interest and syndication rules—or fin-syn rules—that prevented networks from owning most of the prime-time programs they aired or airing syndicated programming in which they had a financial stake. This led to the rise of powerful independent production studios like Carsey-Werner, which produced and owned *The Cosby Show*, *A Different World*, and *Roseanne*, as well as Norman Lear's Tandem Productions, which had a stable of shows that included *All in the Family*, *Good Times*, *Sanford and Son*, and *Diff'rent Strokes*. However, throughout the eighties, the fin-syn rules were relaxed, which allowed Fox to do the exact thing the rules had originally set out to forbid: both own and air a show, in this case *In Living Color*. It was an arrangement that would eventually have far-reaching consequences for the show and its creators. (The fin-syn rules would be eliminated completely in 1993, making *ILC*'s situation commonplace in the decades to follow.)

Although Zlotnik and Albrecht were disappointed to no longer be involved, Zlotnik says the experience sparked HBO to turn its attention toward original programming, a development that in the next two decades changed the face of television completely.

"The reason we were able to build everything that we did at HBO in some ways goes back to *In Living Color*," says Zlotnik. Original programming had been something of a redheaded stepchild at HBO, with a relatively small budget and a similarly scaled ambition among the top executives. Now they'd produced the *ILC* pilot but handed the show to Fox because of that lack of ambition. Once the show became a hit, says Zlotnik, "Chris [Albrecht] used that as leverage to say, 'I was able to develop a big hit that's become good business for Fox. It could've been for HBO. I can do this more than once.'" By 1990, he'd convinced the network to start HBO Independent Productions, which produced shows like *Martin* and *Everybody Loves Raymond*. The next step was to convince HBO he could make shows for their network too. Once Albrecht was installed as head of programming, shows like *Sex and the City*, *Band of Brothers*, and *The Sopranos* ushered in the next so-called Golden Age of Television. Albrecht subsequently became the company's CEO. "I trace that all back to the inflection point of *In Living Color*," says Zlotnik, "which proved Chris had an acumen for relationships with talent and producing shows that can make money."

With Albrecht and Zlotnik gone, the producer they'd brought in for the pilot, Kevin Bright, was out too, though not by choice. He'd already run afoul of Keenen by creating the initial rundown for the pilot, and in other places seemed to be straining against the strictures of his mandate to keep his nose out of the creative side of the show. Davola says that there was also a feeling that he was too close to the production people on their way out. According to Gold though, there was a more immediate, more personal reason for his dismissal: He had Shawn Wayans's car towed.

"Kevin Bright ended up getting fired off the show for the worst possible reason," says Gold.

Shawn was working as a production assistant on the pilot, and by his own admission, had very little idea how a television production worked. Among the things he didn't know was where to park his car. "I remember not understanding that I was parking in the producer's parking spot," Shawn says. "I had no idea. I was just looking at it like, *My brother Keenen parks here, and Damon parks here. I want to be close to their cars, so I'm gonna park here.*"

But to some, this was a sign of unearned and unwelcome entitlement on the part of the show creator's little brother. It crystalized a lot of anxieties about Keenen possibly playing favorites with his family members. At any rate, Bright had his car towed. The incident was the culmination of several things that put some distance between Bright and the show. "It was after a lot of *Maybe Kevin doesn't get us*," says Gold.

Bright was hugely disappointed to be out, but things worked out okay for him. He had already started developing the show *Dream On*, with Marta Kauffman and David Crane, for HBO, which eventually ran for six seasons. In 1993 he formed Bright/Kauffman/Crane Productions, and produced a sitcom about six young New Yorkers called *Friends*, which became one of the most popular sitcoms in television history.

The *ILC* writing staff also went through a shakeup. After the long lag time between pilot and the pickup, only Sheffield and Frank returned for the series. Rawitt had to re-staff almost completely. Her initial haul netted two more ex–*David Letterman* writers, Matt Wickline and Joe Toplyn; a writing team of two women, Mimi Friedman and Jeanette Collins, who'd never worked in television before; and two seasoned black stand-ups, Franklyn Ajaye and Barry "Berry" Douglas.

With the show running at thirty minutes instead of an hour, the cast needed trimming. Jeff Joseph left with Bright to work on *Dream On*. Toney Riley and T.J. McGee were deemed surplus to requirements. McGee was surprised by his dismissal. So surprised, in fact, that he showed up back at the Fox lot, thinking he still had a job.

"They were going, 'Didn't somebody tell you?'" McGee says. "I'm like, 'Tell me what?'" Eventually the show's casting director, Robi Reed, whom McGee knew from the Comedy Act, told him that they'd contacted his manager about it, but apparently she hadn't passed on word. At the time, McGee had a part in another pilot for ABC that his manager was more keen on anyway. He later heard through the grapevine that she'd been working to get him out of his holding deal with Fox so he could do the ABC show.

"She kind of destroyed my relationship with Keenen," he says. "I'm embarrassed to say it, but she told Keenen, 'T.J. shouldn't be a part of this nigger shit.' They thought I wanted off the show. I didn't. I loved the show."

The Fly Girls underwent personnel changes too. A.J. Johnson was offered a part in *House Party*, a low-budget film that a pair of brothers named Reggie and Warrington Hudlin were making with rappers Kid 'n Play. Keenen told her she had to make a choice: the show or the movie. Johnson wanted to do both. "I can choreograph a thirty-second dance number in my sleep," she told him.

It was a sticky situation made slightly stickier by the fact that Johnson and Keenen were, in her words, "kind of dating." "I remember us arguing about it, professionally and personally," she says. "Like, 'Why are you holding me back from going away to do a movie over a thirty-second dance bumper?' We had a hard time in our friendship over that."

In the end, she chose *House Party* but didn't want to leave Keenen hanging. She recommended her own replacement, another young actress/dancer who, like her, had gotten her start in a Spike Lee movie: Rosie Perez.

Keenen had met Perez at one of Eddie Murphy's Bubble Hill parties, but didn't really know her. Robi Reed, though, had cast her in *Do the Right Thing* and arranged for the two to meet. They hit it off. Keenen told her to expect a call from one of the show's producers in the coming days to work out a contract. The call never came. Perez finally called the production offices herself and a producer told her they'd hired someone else.

"I couldn't believe it," says Perez. "I didn't have Keenen's number. I didn't know Keenen like that, so I said, 'Will you leave a message with Keenen?' He didn't call me back." Perez had an offer to choreograph LL Cool J's concert tour, so she took it.

Keenen maintains it was all a miscommunication. Regardless, instead of Perez, a seasoned choreographer named Carla Earle was hired. The decision was made to cast a wider net for dancers, so Earle arranged new auditions and saw more than two thousand of them during a three-day stretch.

Deidre Lang, a dancer from the pilot, says there was a clear imperative with the new auditions. On the pilot, she explains, all four dancers were African-American. "Once the show got picked up, they were like, 'We need this to be more of a melting pot. We need to have each race.' So there was somebody for everybody.'"

One of the dancers who auditioned was a young, striking Asian-American named Carrie Ann Inaba. It was one of Inaba's first casting calls and she fretted over what to wear. "I chose this super-lacy bra I bought from this really expensive lingerie store, black leggings, motorcycle boots, and a black jacket." Keenen later told her that the outfit got her the gig.

"He was like, 'Your outfit was so strange but you looked like you thought it was the best,'" she says. "'You walked in with so much confidence I pretty much gave you the job the moment I saw you.'"

Along with Inaba, two other women were hired from the auditions: Michelle Whitney-Morrison, a raven-haired beauty who'd been on the television show *Fame* and had a minor role in *School Daze*, and a tall blonde named Cari French. Lang stayed on from the pilot, as did Lisa Marie Todd. The final troupe fit the United Colors of Benetton ideal. "We had an Asian girl, a dark-skinned sister, a light-skinned sister, an Italian girl, and a white girl," says Earle.

The DJ from the pilot, DJ Daddy Mack, was replaced for the series with a new DJ, SW1, better known as Shawn Wayans. Keenen knew Shawn wanted to be a part of the show, but also knew that as a writer, standup, or actor, he simply wasn't ready. Bringing him in as the DJ, introducing him to audiences on-screen while he worked on his comedy chops, made sense, though Shawn maintains that wasn't the original impetus for the change.

"They tested the show and the DJ they had was good but didn't feel like he fit the look and the feel of what they were doing," says Shawn. "They wanted someone with a bit more swag. I had a little swag so one of the producers suggested me."

The not particularly well-kept secret was that Shawn, unlike the man he replaced, wasn't a real DJ. Up in the booth at *ILC*, his job was to merely *act* like a DJ. None of his equipment was connected to anything. "I'd listen to the tracks and make sure I was on cue when the camera cut to me, to look like I was mixing," he admits.

As Keenen puts it, "It didn't matter whether he was a DJ or not because it wasn't live. He was a cute kid and he wanted to be around his brothers while he was working on his standup, so I put him up there."

Perhaps Shawn's biggest musical contribution was helping to recruit rapper Heavy D to do the show's theme song. As Keenen recalls, "Heavy grew up with my cousin in Mount Vernon, and him and Shawn were friends. So I sat with him and told him what the show was and he went off and put it together." Heavy D, who died in 2011, was already a star in hip-hop, and his association with the show helped build the show's credibility and recognition in that world. For Keenen, the song, with its energetic verses, rhythmic turntable scratches, and singsongy chorus—"You can do what you want to do/*In Living Color*"—was "perfect" for what he was trying to get across. "I couldn't ask for anything more."

In trimming the show down to a half hour, cuts needed to be made to the pilot. Sammy Davis Jr. was undergoing a very public battle with throat cancer in late 1989 and early 1990—one that he'd eventually succumb to in May 1990—so the decision was made to shelve Tommy Davidson's Sammy-as-Mandela sketch. At the time, it was a perhaps understandable—reportedly, a test audience reacted negatively to it—though with the release of Mandela from prison in South Africa that February, a counterargument could easily be made that the sketch would never have been timelier. The fact that it was permanently shelved and has never publicly surfaced leaves Davidson still smarting all these years later.

"I don't know why they didn't air it because somebody being sick is not enough to me," he says. Far from being a takedown of Sammy, the sketch "was an ode to him. Personally it would've established me as one of the front-runners of the whole damn show." Instead, Davidson was barely in the show's first episode. Some have suggested Keenen was trying to ensure Damon would be the breakout star of the ensemble. As Davidson sees it, "There wasn't a lot of Tommy Davidson–centric energy at the show."

Other choices had to be made about Episode 1, and everyone, it seemed, had an opinion, including Barry Diller and Peter Chernin. If Diller was known as bullish and intimidating, Chernin was prized for his bedside manner. A former English literature major at Cal-Berkeley, he had softer, doughier features and a kind, fatherly countenance. Chernin had worked in publishing before moving over to television at Showtime, where, like Albrecht at HBO, he pushed the network toward original programming. By the time he came to Fox in 1989, he was an executive known for building bridges not burning them, a guy with a knack for dealing with talent. He was the one you sent in to ease your show creator off a ledge. Chernin had asked Joe Davola to talk to Keenen about toning down the first episode, but Davola balked. Davola had spent a lot of time building trust with Keenen, and didn't want to ruin their relationship. Besides, he didn't want to be the messenger for a message he didn't agree with anyway. About a week before *ILC* was set to debut, Chernin came to see Keenen himself.

"Peter said, 'We want to make some changes to the pilot,'" Keenen recalls. "'We want to take out "The Homeboy Shopping Network," "Men on Film," and "The Wrath of Farrakhan," come in with some tamer stuff, and slowly build this audience. Then we can really push the envelope.'"

It wasn't a totally unreasonable suggestion. Why scare away potential viewers right out of the gate? Why not warm them up a little, build a relationship with them, so they'll be open to the more radical sketches later? Fox wasn't in an unassailable position. The network was limping along, still only broadcasting three nights a week, with a couple of modest hits to its name. Upsetting viewers and advertisers wasn't in its best interest. Chernin and Diller weren't big, bad, clueless executives stomping out creativity they didn't understand. They liked the show. They liked Keenen. They wanted to help him succeed. Chernin wasn't trying to sand down the show's jagged points, just rearrange them a little.

Keenen wasn't interested: "I said to him, 'Peter, I wanna kick the door in, guns blazing. Whatever happens, happens. If we fail, we fail big. If we win, we win big. I don't wanna spoon-feed the audience. I want them to know exactly what time it is. I'm willing to take that risk. Whatever heat comes, send it my way.'"

It was an impassioned defense and Chernin took it in for a minute. He told Keenen he'd talk to Diller and get back to him. It was a high-stakes staring contest. Fox blinked first.

"They were like, 'Okaaaay,'" says Keenen, letting out a theatrical sigh. "'If you'll take the heat and you're okay that this could be the worst thing that ever happened in the history of television, we'll support you.'"

With that less-than-unqualified vote of confidence, *In Living Color* debuted on April 15, 1990.

15

"It Was Just This Overnight Sensation"

Five days before *In Living Color* debuted, Public Enemy released *Fear of a Black Planet*. That a fiercely militant, unabashedly angry and not particularly radio-friendly album of Afrocentric hip-hop managed to hit the Top 10 on the *Billboard* chart and sell more than a million copies in its first two months on record store shelves is a pretty decent indicator of the tenor of the moment. The group's outspoken frontman Chuck D had begun telling journalists a couple years earlier that rap was black America's CNN. N.W.A.'s *Straight Outta Compton* certainly offered a better sense of what was going on in the streets of Los Angeles than the nightly news could. But while rap may have been delivering black America's news, most of the reports from the front were harrowing.

African-American communities were being decimated by crack cocaine in the late eighties and early nineties. The percentage of black children in foster care doubled during this period, fetal death rates and weapons arrests rose 25 percent. In 1989, the per capita income for black families was roughly half that of white families. The unemployment rate was more than double. An astonishing 33 percent of black families were living in poverty, as compared with 10 percent of white families. Perhaps most alarmingly, the homicide rate for black men under twenty-five doubled between 1984 and 1994. A generation was on the verge of being lost.

This grim tale had a flip side, however. College attendance rates for African-Americans rose during the second half of the eighties, and although black household incomes remained stubbornly below white households', they weren't stagnant, rising 84 percent over the course of the decade. This *was* progress.

This complex narrative played out in ways big and small across the nation. In New York, in August of 1989, a black teenager was shot and killed after being set upon by a white mob in Bensonhurst, Brooklyn. Al Sharpton called the city, "America's capital of racial violence." Then in November, the city elected its first black mayor, David Dinkins. In Washington, D.C., Marion Barry, a former civil rights activist, had become so-called "mayor for life," serving three terms between 1979 and 1991. He was denied a fourth term after being arrested for crack possession in January 1990. He claimed he was framed by the FBI.

With *Fear of a Black Planet*, Public Enemy was wrapping its arms around this entire messy dynamic. The album's title—particularly viewed in conjunction with PE's previous album title, *It Takes a Nation of Millions to Hold Us Back*—could be taken in many ways: a lamentation, a rallying cry, a warning. And the album itself was filled with songs that fell into all three of those categories, sometimes all at once—"Brothers Gonna Work It Out," "911 Is a Joke," "Welcome to the Terrordome," and of course, "Fight the Power," a call to arms that had been the score and the subtext of Spike Lee's *Do the Right Thing*. "Burn Hollywood Burn" took the film industry to task for its demeaning depictions of African-Americans, singling out *Driving Miss Daisy*, featuring Morgan Freeman as a contented, subservient chauffeur. (The film had just won a Best Picture Oscar, much to the vocal dismay of Lee, whose *Do the Right Thing* was shut out at the Oscars.)

Chuck D, coincidentally, grew up down the street from Eddie Murphy in Roosevelt, New York. He knew him well enough that when Eddie showed up at the door of Chuck's house hoping to take Chuck's sister out, he lied and told Eddie she wasn't home. In their teens, Chuck and Eddie had attended a seminar together called "The Afro-American Experience," led by Black Panthers and black Muslims. He felt a kinship with Eddie, with Spike, and even with guys like Keenen and Arsenio though he didn't really know them. They'd all come of age as ambitious, artistic black men in the generation after the Civil Rights Movement, and all seemed to be hitting their stride around the same time, introducing white America to art, comedy, music, and ideas that had previously had little airing outside black enclaves. "There was something special going on at that time," Chuck says.

All around them was the evidence. One month before *In Living Color*'s debut, the Hudlins' film, *House Party*—which co-starred Comedy Act alums Martin Lawrence and Robin Harris—premiered. The film's reception certainly felt like a good omen for *ILC*: *House Party* opened at number three at the box office, despite a production budget one-tenth the size of the two films that grossed more that weekend. The film, like *Sucka* before it, was proof of a wildly underserved market. Tragically, Harris, who was being tipped as the next big breakout black comedy star, died of a heart attack nine days after the film's release.

———

The first episode of *In Living Color*, which aired at 9:30 p.m. ET on Sunday, April 15, mixed material from the pilot—including "The Homeboy Shopping Network," "Men on Film," and the "Love Connection" sketch—with stuff that had been written and produced in the weeks after the show got its pickup order. One of the new sketches, a commercial parody for a credit card called "Equity Express," in which David Alan Grier is harassed and ultimately arrested because a store owner suspects he's "not the sort of person to be carrying a gold card, *if you know what I mean.*" Keenen was justifiably pleased with the debut.

"Everything lined up right," he says. "All the stuff I wanted to try worked. The sketches were funny and we were making fun of people no one had made fun of before. The dancers didn't look weird in the context of a sketch show. The hip-hop music didn't throw you off. It was different than anything you'd seen on TV."

Slotting in after Fox's two hit comedies, *The Simpsons* and *Married with Children*, the episode was seen by nearly twenty-three million viewers, a gargantuan premiere that outstripped the network's most optimistic projections.

"We were very fortunate," says Sandy Grushow, the senior VP of advertising and promotion at Fox. "We were playing a hot hand which got significantly hotter when we launched the show. We had the right audience already in our grip. Young people who'd been disenfranchised by the Big Three had already discovered *The Simpsons* and *Married with Children* and made them huge hits. Launching *In Living Color* helped supercharge the night."

Director Paul Miller was astounded at the reaction to the show. "They had it on on a Sunday night and by Monday, everybody was talking about it," he says. "I've never had an experience like that. It was just this overnight sensation."

In fact, the months of hemming and hawing Fox had done about the pilot had an unintended positive consequence: By the time the show finally aired, it had serious buzz around it. Copies of the pilot were being sold on street corners in New York long before the premiere. As Kim Wayans recalls, "In those months it took Fox to finally move on *In Living Color*, a few people had slipped tapes underground in the industry."

One of the twenty-three million people who saw that first episode was Mike Tyson. Tyson was going through a tough spell. He'd looked terrifying and invincible, winning his first thirty-seven fights without a blemish on his record, before being knocked out by Buster Douglas in a stunning upset that February. The "Love Connection" sketch was written and produced months before Tyson's loss to Douglas, but that probably didn't lessen the feeling for Tyson that he was being kicked while he was already down. Arguably, his ex-wife Robin Givens comes off worse, but Keenen's portrayal of Tyson as henpecked, high-pitched, and feebleminded—a portrayal he'd revive later in the season during a sketch called "Three Champs and a Baby"—left a mark, and Tyson wasn't initially prepared to just let it go. He saw Keenen at a club one night and approached him.

"That was the scariest moment of my life," says Keenen. "All I feel is this paw land on my shoulder. I turn around and it's the heavyweight champ of the world. He stepped to me. He goes, 'What? I kill your mother or something?'" Tyson told him he'd seen Keenen's impression of him. He wasn't amused. "He was like, 'Yo, you gotta freeze that.'"

Keenen had practiced martial arts for years. Since he was a kid, he'd been taught to stand up for himself, even if it meant taking a beat-down.

He knew he couldn't let the targets of his satire bully him into pulling punches. On the other hand, this was Mike *Fucking* Tyson. "In my mind, I was like, *I'm going to have to take this. Ain't nothing I can do right now.* He shut me down." A few months later, Keenen ran into Tyson again, but this time, the ex-champ had mellowed. "He was actually really cool. He was like, 'Yo, I was just going through some things. You do your thing.' He gave me the green light to go ahead and get back to it."

Kim Coles, who played Givens in the sketch, ran into Tyson herself, while touring as an opening act for Luther Vandross the summer after the first season ended. "He pretended like he was mad," she says. "Like, 'I don't appreciate you making jokes about me on the show!' But he had a good sense of humor about it. Then he invited me to his hotel room and I promptly got on the tour bus. He was like, 'I'm having a party back at my room.' I was like, 'I gotta be on the tour bus. Sorry. Bye!'"

Fox's reaction to the first episode's big ratings was rather curious. After scoring in that time slot on Sunday night at 9:30, the show was immediately moved to Saturday at 9. Saturday was traditionally not a big television viewing night, and without the lead-in of *The Simpsons* and *Married with Children*, the ratings for the second episode nosedived to less than half of the debut. Eric Gold was befuddled.

"What's the first thing they do once it's almost a hit? They move it. It almost killed it. We were hot but we plateaued and started to come down. People couldn't find it."

Jamie Kellner, the network president, says, "Originally the conceit was to drive the audience from *Married with Children* into the premiere. Then our strategy was every network's strategy: You take your anchor show and move it around to stack a bunch of other shows behind it." To be fair, even after the move, the ratings were still strong. They ticked back up in the coming weeks, though never reached anywhere near as high as the debut—that is, until the show was moved back to Sunday night halfway through the first season.

———

The show's offices occupied the fifth floor of an office building on a lot that had been called Metromedia Square until Fox took it over in 1986.

The building dated back to the forties, and was showing wear. The numbers had faded off the elevator buttons and very few windows in the show's offices opened. The "*In Living Color*" sign adorning the entrance to the offices was marked in brightly colored crayons, but the suite itself was rather drab and generic, with the writers' and producers' individual offices in a U-shape surrounding some communal space and a kitchen in the middle. The one nod toward modernity was a state-of-the-art gym facility that Keenen negotiated into his contract, and which Fox built for him as part of the office suite. Downstairs were dressing rooms for the cast members and dancers, rehearsal space, and the soundstage where filming took place. On the wall of Keenen's fifth-floor office, tacked up next to his desk, were four-by-six index cards with the titles of sketches in the works. From the office window, he could see the iconic Hollywood sign, five miles away in the hills to the north.

Once the series was up and running, it settled into a punishing bi-weekly routine. The writers showed up Monday morning, and each was expected to pitch five sketch ideas to Keenen and Tamara. If they liked a pitch, the writer was asked to write it up into a full sketch for the week's "packet." Those sketches were then read at a table read the following Monday. But if a writer didn't get any pitches selected, he or she often had to pitch again and again until something scored. Following the table read, the sketches were narrowed down further. After rehearsals on Tuesday and Wednesday, there were notes and rewrites on Thursday. Rewrites were sometimes done by a different writer than had written the original sketch, and there were opportunities for most anyone to toss in jokes. The show was filmed in front of a live audience on Friday. Usually, two to three times as much material was shot as ever aired. The normal cycle was two weeks from when an idea was first pitched until it was filmed, but there were always two shows being worked on at any one time. So every Monday, for example, writers were pitching for the following Monday's packet, as well as sitting at that day's table read.

"There was a lot of pressure," says Franklyn Ajaye. "Keenen was a demanding boss. People didn't really look forward to a pitch meeting after a while." Ajaye had been a standup for years, had appeared on *The Tonight Show* and Flip Wilson's show, had a small part in *Car Wash*, and even worked briefly with Richard Pryor on an ill-fated, coke-addled film project called *Uncle Tom's Fairy Tales* in the late sixties. His comedy was cerebral—he was sometimes known as "the Jazz Comedian"—and faced with the overwhelming workload, he paired up with another veteran black standup, Barry "Berry" Douglas. "It was easier to come up with ideas with a partner," says Ajaye. "Barry was a little more bawdy than I was but we seemed to complement each other well."

Rawitt had brought in Ajaye and Douglas as something of a cultural counterbalance to the white, Harvard types that typically dominated comedy writing. Finding black comedy writers had been challenging. Very few shows had ever hired them before. It wasn't easy to know where to look.

The writing staff was generally two to an office and only gathered together for pitch meetings, table reads, and the like. Mimi Friedman and Jeanette Collins were white improv performers who'd written some commercials. "When we were hired, we were told the demographic was eighteen-to-twenty-four-year-old inner-city black males," says Collins with a wry laugh. "So we're the *perfect* people to write that." In fact, one of the sketches they pitched in their initial job interview was called "Leave It to Cleaver," a send-up of the classic, white-bread television series but with radical ex–Black Panther leader Eldridge Cleaver in the title role. "It didn't get used," says Friedman, "but it got us the job."

The pitch was indicative of the pair's work. Friedman and Collins wrote "Della Reese's Pieces," which was, in Friedman's words, "merely a play on words that became a sketch," and "Mitzvah Train," an over-the-top commercial for what was billed as "the city's premier Afro-Judeo video dating service." Probably their most lasting contribution was "Snackin' Shack," a sketch set in a health code–flouting soul food dive. "That was based on a restaurant we'd gone to many times in New York, the Pink Peacock," says Friedman. "Snackin' Shack" would become a recurring set-piece on the show.

Their philosophy as white women writing black sketches was simple. "We wouldn't write *black*," says Friedman. "We're not going to write Ebonics. We'd just give the architecture of the sketch in our words and let the actors take off from there."

When filming in front of a live audience, the cast typically ran through a sketch at least twice. The first time, they mostly stuck to the script, but the second time there was license to improvise. Keenen estimates that close to 90 percent of the sketches that aired had moments of improv in them.

"I'd tell everybody before the first take to put something in your back pocket," he says. "Then I'd just let it go and whatever happened, happened. Everybody would be improvising. You can see it on somebody's face when they got caught off guard but didn't break character. A lot of great moments came from that." Damon and Jim, in particular, seemed to thrive in these second takes. In one early sketch, Jim plays an overenthusiastic, underprepared karate instructor teaching a self-defense class for women. Kelly Coffield is one of his students.

"Jim made everybody work because he was so insane," says Keenen. "If you didn't keep up, he was gonna blow you off the screen. At rehearsals, I kept encouraging Kelly to go for it. In that scene, when Jim starts to whoop on her, she goes for it and gets this huge laugh."

Coffield, who stabs Carrey's karate instructor multiple times in the sketch and then tosses herself airborne when she's punched in the face, says that sketch was an "epiphany": "I realized you have a role, you play that role, but if you've got a better joke, definitely do it in take two."

The nature of the show meant Carrey and Coffield were frequently cast as uptight white people, or merely as foils to the other actors. But the cast's token Caucasians didn't feel like outcasts. In fact, both arguably integrated into the show more easily than some of the African-American cast members.

"Obviously, we were going to be poked fun at," says Coffield. "But I didn't feel like we were separated out for any kind of awful treatment. I was never made to feel I was being ganged up on or picked on. People used to say, 'Now you know what Garrett Morris felt like on *Saturday Night Live*.' But that's not at all what Jim and I were on the show."

Carrey seemed temperamentally incapable of fading into the background of a sketch. Even in parts where his main job was just to set up someone else's jokes, he'd find a way to wring a laugh from it. The "Love Connection" sketch is a good example. He's not the focus and could've played Chuck Woolery straight. Instead, his voice, his physicality, every part of his impression is wildly over-the-top.

"I used to cite him to all the other cast members," Keenen said. "He's an example of 'There are no small parts.' That's just how Jim always approached his work. He doesn't walk through anything."

Although some may have quietly resented Carrey's unabashed hamming, ultimately the show was better for it.

"You don't want to upstage what the point of the sketch is, but if you can get a laugh without doing that then absolutely you should," says Carrey. "I was always working hard to try to make everything as interesting as possible. Some of my favorite things on the show are incidental characters."

It would take Carrey longer than most remember to establish himself as one of the show's main draws. Through much of the first season he's making the most of secondary roles. Toward the tail end, though, he conjured Vera De Milo, a deep-voiced, muscle-bound, comically mannish woman.

"I was working out at Gold's Gym and went to the counter to get a smoothie and there was a woman bodybuilder who came up beside me and said, 'I'll have a protein smoothie,'" Carrey recalls. "She had that voice and I just went *Click! I don't know what that is but there's something there*. That was the birth of Vera De Milo." The character was unabashedly silly, but there was also something very of-the moment about her. "It was what was happening in the gyms—steroids. It was female empowerment at the same time as it was making fun of the fact that we're all using drugs to get to that place."

When it came time to film the first Vera sketch, Carrey walked onstage clad in a skimpy leopard-print bikini, his hair in pigtails. He could tell by the audience's reaction that the character was going to work before he even opened his mouth to speak. "It was enormous," he says. "When you scored with a character on that show and felt like the character is going to be able to come back because it got such a huge response, it's like heaven. It's a feeling of total acceptance. Then you build on that. Once Vera happened, everything else started to fall into place."

16

"Until It's Funny, I Can't Care"

Two weeks after the show premiered, Tamara Rawitt went to the Beverly Center, a large upscale mall in Los Angeles, to do some shopping. She was wearing an *In Living Color* T-shirt that the production staff printed up for the cast and crew while they were making the pilot. When shoppers saw her T-shirt, they went bat-shit crazy for it.

"I got bum-rushed," she says. "People were handing me twenty-dollar bills to buy the shirt from me. This is before the Internet. Having grown up in marketing, I knew the show was going to be a huge hit based on just that reaction at the Beverly Center."

Despite the time slot move and the ratings dip, Fox was happy with their newest show and, in early May, added five episodes to the original eight-episode order. There was some backlash from the NAACP over "The Homeboy Shopping Network" and others cried foul at the "Men on . . ." characters, Antoine Merriweather and Blaine Edwards, who appeared in three of the first seven episodes, with the *Detroit Free Press* critic calling them "a gay *Amos 'n Andy.*" But even criticism of the show fed the sense that people were talking about *ILC*. Michael Hill, writing in the *Baltimore Sun*, called it, "the hottest, hippest comedy show on television. It's got the same sort of buzz that accompanied early *Saturday*

Night Live, the same sort of feeling that these are people you haven't been allowed to see on TV before." The *St. Louis Post-Dispatch*'s television critic, Eric Mink, wrote, "*In Living Color* is outrageous, sexy, occasionally raunchy and often hilarious, sometimes uncomfortably so. It also can be self-indulgent, simplistic, tiresome and offensive—although the latter quality is inevitably in the eye of the beholder. All that said, in less than four weeks, Fox Broadcasting's '*In Living Color*' has become must-watch-or-tape television on Saturday nights, the new standard-bearer for slashing, squirming-in-your-seat satire."

The racially charged tone of the pilot notwithstanding, Keenen was wary about making *ILC* a vehicle for him and the writers to simply make political points. As Keenen told comedian David Steinberg in 2013, "I knew I couldn't be too political because my politics would come across as angry." Early in the show's first season, it became clear that while the show would have its share of biting political satire, often it would just go for big laughs or goofy celebrity impressions. Keenen portrayed his old friend Arsenio as an obsequious dimwit with a big butt, and Marion Barry merely played straight man to Arsenio's buffoon. *Driving Miss Daisy* wasn't lampooned for its retrograde depiction of black men, but rather used as an opportunity to make an easy sex joke in "Riding Miss Daisy." Funny perhaps, but not exactly high-minded social criticism.

Franklyn Ajaye and Barry Douglas struggled to find their place in this mix. They rarely got material on the show, and even when they did, it was a wrestling match. Case in point was "Endangered Species." Kelly Coffield plays an anthropologist who is a guest on *The Tonight Show* and brings with her an exotic, endangered species: a young, streetwise black man—"or b-boy," as Coffield's character puts it—played by Tommy Davidson. When Jim Carrey, hosting the show as Alan Thicke, asks Coffield, "Is he dangerous?" Coffield answers, "Well, Alan, like any of God's creations, without love, a proper diet, a decent education, and equal opportunities, he could be extremely dangerous." The politics here are overt, and for Ajaye and Douglas, who'd pitched the sketch, that was the point. But Keenen was skeptical.

"It was a brilliant premise and definitely had something to say," said Keenen. But he objected to a line about the reason why this species was, in fact, endangered: They were being killed for their sneakers—a reference to a rash of such crimes in the previous few years. The line was cut from the sketch because, according to Ajaye, "he felt it was a downer."

For his part, Keenen explained, "The fight between me and Franklyn was that it had to be funny first. I think we accomplished both, but it was definitely a back-and-forth because he was like, 'Why do we have to be funny?' I knew anything we had to say had to have humor or people are just going to tune out. That's one of my favorite sketches but that's one of the biggest battles."

Ajaye and Douglas pitched other stuff in the vein of "Endangered Species," including "Save the Children," an infomercial focused on two kids living in a gang-infested neighborhood, but nothing came of it. "I was very disappointed," says Ajaye. "But that wasn't the direction Keenen wanted to go."

A version of this argument would repeat itself again and again throughout Keenen's stewardship of the show, but his vision rarely wavered. It wasn't that he didn't want sketches to take bold stances. But that was *always* secondary. "It was about being funny," he says. "It wasn't about trying to be important. That was a battle I'd have at times with writers. They wanted to have a message but it wasn't funny. If you can get something in there, go for it. But until it's funny, I can't care."

John Bowman, a handsome, ex-*Harvard Lampoon* editor who'd written for *Saturday Night Live* and *It's Garry Shandling's Show*, joined the writing staff a few episodes into the first season and seemed to grasp Keenen's perspective immediately. "Keenen always insisted that you not come across with a political or racial point of view," he says. "Sometimes the white writers would come up with a hard-hitting thing that took a racial attitude and Keenen would say, 'No, no. That may be politically correct but it's not funny. All you're doing is trying to incite people, you're not trying to make them laugh.'"

Keenen was smart, educated, and engaged with the world, but as a comedian, he was an unrestrained populist. Big laughs weren't dismissed because they were broad. Clever wasn't always funny. "My philosophy has always been the audience will decide," he says. "I'll do something and if the audience doesn't laugh, I don't keep it because I'm not making stuff for myself. I'm not trying to be self-indulgent. The overall intent was always to be funny, and not just *inside* funny."

Ajaye and Douglas were dismissed halfway through the season without acrimony. "We were let go with a good recommendation," says Ajaye. "We weren't really writing to the sensibility he wanted, we weren't getting a lot of stuff on, so why should he keep us?"

Mimi Friedman and Jeanette Collins were also let go midway through the season, for similar reasons. The duo consistently struggled to strike the right tone in their writing.

"We were the only women on staff," says Friedman. "We wrote a couple things that were more, I don't know, *post-feminist*, but it was not the right forum for it."

The writing staff was in constant churn. After Bowman joined, another *Harvard Lampoon* alumnus, Steve Tompkins, followed. Tompkins had submitted three sketches to the show, two of which were eventually produced.

"The sketch that got me the job was called 'The Michael Jackson Mr. Potato Head Toy,'" says Tompkins. It was a commercial parody for a Mr. Potato Head featuring different noses, chins, and lips to construct Jackson at different stages of his career. "The joke that got me hired was after you assemble Michael exactly the way you want, the guy in the commercial goes, 'Hmm, something's not right,' then grabs the potato peeler and peels it white."

He also submitted a *Cosby Show* parody in which the Fat Albert gang shows up at the Huxtable house and shakes down Dr. Huxtable for money. When he arrived at the Fox lot for his first day of work, the crew had already built the set for the sketch. It was ultimately aborted. "The reaction to *In Living Color* had been so overwhelmingly positive that I think Keenen got cold feet about taking down Cosby because we never did," says Tompkins. "In the first season, we talked about it a lot but nothing ever seemed to push the right button for Keenen. All we ended up doing was a Pudding Pop commercial parody [in Season 3]. We never really targeted Cosby at all."

Writers who worked on the show in later seasons also recall a hands-off policy—or at least a kid-glove policy—regarding Cosby. One says that there were three public figures explicitly off-limits: Martin Luther King Jr., Sammy Davis Jr., and Cosby. Another recalls Cosby calling Keenen to ask him not to do a sketch about a well-traveled rumor that

Cosby had gotten caught getting a hand job under a table. Keenen insists he never went easy on Cosby. As hard as it is to believe now, back then, he says, there wasn't much ammunition. "Cosby didn't get a pass," he says. "Most everybody had some scandal or some way they put their foot in their mouth. There wasn't anything on Cosby."

Whatever the reasons, Keenen's decisions were, for the most part, the final word on the show's creative direction. People's impressions of him seemed to fall at opposite ends of a spectrum. Some found him funny, thoughtful, and self-confident. To others, he was arrogant, standoffish, and sophomoric. Most, though, ultimately respected his vision for the show. He wasn't a screamer or a tantrum-thrower, but he could be a tall, quiet, intimidating force. He felt he knew how to best run the show and took others' input to a point then didn't brook dissent much past that.

"It was a dictatorship," Keenen admits.

As Eric Gold puts it, "Keenen was a benevolent dictator. He wore his authority pretty well. You have to be a benevolent dictator because you can't do these shows by committee. He was the final word and sometimes people liked the final word and sometimes they didn't."

Joe Davola was in the slightly uncomfortable position of having to deliver the network's notes to Keenen on each week's episode during that first season. Delivering notes is always delicate—few showrunners really want the creative input of the "suits"—but in this case, Davola sensed an extra layer of discomfort.

"The first time I had to deliver notes, Keenen was ready for war," says Davola. "So the way I did it was I hiked my pants up to my stomach, walked in, and went, 'Whitey's here!' Damon and Keenen were on the floor cracking up. I defused the situation."

One thing few questioned was Keenen's understanding of the mechanics of comedy. Some might say he understood it more as an engineer than an artist, but the fact is to run a show like this, an engineer may be more useful than an artist.

"Keenen is one of the true geniuses of sketch comedy," says David Alan Grier. "Meaning, you do a scene, it's all flat, and Keenen says, 'If you pick up your pencil, look to the right and say the same joke, it's gonna work.' You trust him, you do it, and it kills. Most people don't know comedy. They can't fix it. You stumble on a great joke, you don't know why it's great. But Keenen had that ability. I've been acting over thirty years, there's maybe two or three people like that."

———

The near-constant search for new writers—particularly new black writers—led Keenen to bring in Paul Mooney midway through Season 1. Mooney had been Richard Pryor's writing partner, he'd had a small part in *Hollywood Shuffle*, and was a bona fide comedy legend, as he'd almost certainly be the first to tell anyone within earshot. A tall, undeniably handsome man, he carried himself with an almost regal air, and had an indignant, withering, unapologetic take on race relations that informed not only his comedy, but his entire worldview. White people had "the complexion for the protection," and black people had every right to be pissed off about it. His jokes were less jokes than provocations. "Being a black man in America is like being the fucking boogeyman," he said in one of his bits around that time. "And frankly I'm tired of being the goddamn boogeyman. I get on the elevator, white people hop off. I walk down the street, white women grab their fucking purse automatically. Makes me feel guilty I didn't snatch the shit." He was famous for his confrontational late-night sets at the Comedy Store. He relished audience members walking out. He was completely unfiltered.

"Mooney was brought in as a grenade," says Rawitt. "He's sort of bulletproof when it comes to wearing it out loud and saying anything. I think it was Keenen's own amusement and perversion that had Mooney around just saying incendiary, racist things."

According to T'Keyah Crystal Keymáh, "When word got out that he was coming to the show, there was panic among the white writers."

Buddy Sheffield, who was one of those white writers, says Mooney was "hardly ever there. He'd come in and out. He'd come to the table sessions. About all I remember him doing is sometimes somebody—or me, in particular—would pitch an idea and he'd say, 'Oh, no, homey!'"

Kim Bass, a black writer who joined the show's staff around the same time as Mooney, says that "when Paul was at the writer's table, we'd be discussing a topic, and when it got in his wheelhouse, everybody waited to see what Paul was going to say. He had that booming voice: 'Oh, I'm gonna go there, homey!'"

Mooney was definitely not just another staff writer, and from the moment he got there, Keenen gave him special treatment, although not necessarily the kind anyone else would've envied. He told Eric Gold to put Mooney in the "worst office we have."

"There's a shitty office underneath the stairwell," Gold told him.

"Put him there."

When it was lunchtime, Keenen made sure no one took Mooney's lunch order. The idea was to keep him agitated.

"Paul is funniest when he's angry," says Keenen. "If you look at his act, whenever Paul would do TV, he'd never be funny because he'd have to try to be nice. When you'd see him in the club and he was pissed, he was brilliant. I wanted that energy out of him."

Therefore, as Gold recalls, "Keenen kept having everybody fuck with Paul Mooney." Mooney's frequent response to all this would stand as his most significant contribution to the show: "Oh, homey don't play that!"

Although Mooney never wrote any sketches, in a roundabout way, he was responsible for the creation of one of *ILC*'s most enduring characters, Homey the Clown.

"It's funny because people will attribute Homey to Paul but in the wrong way," Keenen explains. "Paul didn't come up with Homey. Paul was the inspiration for Homey. Homey *is* Paul Mooney. Instead of an angry comedian, he's an angry clown. He's a guy whose job is to be funny but he's the antithesis of that."

Matt Wickline, one of the show's writers, conjured the idea for Homey after watching Mooney around the office. Damon, who played Homey, added elements of a character called the Angry Comic that he'd been doing in his standup.

"The voice of Homey is from the Angry Comic," says Damon. "Basically, he comes out and goes, 'Good evening, Whitey. Or would you prefer Ofay white devil cracker honky trash? A very funny thing happened on my way down here tonight: I killed three white people. I guess you had to be there. You would've been dying.' That was Homey's voice."

In the first Homey sketch, he's performing at a children's birthday party, but when a little girl asks him to "Do a silly clown dance," he refuses to "degrade" himself. "I don't think so. Homey don't play that," he says, smacking the child with a weighted sock, and coining a catchphrase in the process. For a magic trick, he takes a dollar from one kid, folds it up, and puts it in his pocket. "Let's get something straight, kids: Homey may be a clown but he don't make a fool out of himself."

"Homey," like "The Wrath of Farrakhan" before it, was a sketch that ticked all the boxes for *ILC*. It's undeniably silly, but Homey's sense that the white world is against him, however exaggerated, is funny because of the nugget of truth at its core. As the character developed over the course of the coming seasons, Homey often felt like an alternate mouthpiece for Keenen and Damon to express their frustrations with the show, with Fox, with their own careers, and with the wider world. Homey the Clown was, in some sense, *In Living Color*'s aggrieved, outspoken id.

In the second Homey sketch, later that first season, Homey is entertaining carnival-goers with a well-dressed, blond-haired ventriloquist dummy he calls "Mr. Establishment."

"Now tell the nice people how you've tried to keep Homey down," he says.

The dummy answers: "Well, I've structured society in such a way that men like Homey face nearly impossible odds of achieving any sort of educational opportunity. Therefore, they're unable to obtain gainful employment, thus forcing them to resort to an alternate source of income. Sooner or later, they just end up in jail, just like Homey!"

"Now let's show the nice people how Homey gets back at Mr. Establishment." With that, Homey thrashes the doll, bashing it repeatedly into a table.

Much like Mooney's humor, the joke here is less a joke than a truth packaged as an incitement. Underneath the grown man in a clown costume holding a dummy is a historical grievance answered with furious violence. To play that for laughs takes some insidious genius. Keenen may have known, as he'd told David Steinberg, that if he aired his politics too nakedly they'd "come across as angry," but here, he figured out how to dress them up in a bright red wig and floppy clown shoes, and slip them onto prime-time television.

"The Brothers Brothers Comedy Hour" pulls off a similar trick. As the sketch's intro tells viewers, the Brothers Brothers, played by Keenen and Damon, are "the most nonthreatening black men on television." It's a Smothers Brothers spoof, but both brothers here are named Tom ("We're both named after our uncle," Keenen crows), and their deceptively upbeat songs and banter offer a harsh commentary on the entertainment industry's regressive racial mores.

"The networks want blacks but they don't want them real," the pair sing, "so Oreos like us get a hell of a deal." The song echoed *Hollywood Shuffle*'s central conceit. "It's hidey ho, as I pick out my 'fro/We all play the same parts, no matter the show/The guys are all pimps and each chick is a ho/If we just sell out we'll be rolling in dough."

Later Brothers Brothers sketches were even more vicious, often calling out offenders by name. Interestingly, just as Homey the Clown was conceived by a white guy, Matt Wickline, the main writer behind the Brothers Brothers was also a white guy, Buddy Sheffield, who'd worked with the actual Smothers Brothers on a short-lived reboot of their *Comedy Hour* in the late eighties. Even though he wrote the sketches, Sheffield says he was also just responding to what his boss wanted. "Keenen," Sheffield recalls, "loved to make fun of what black people call Uncle Toms." (Sheffield, whose brother David wrote for Eddie Murphy on *Saturday Night Live* and co-wrote *Coming to America*, jokes that he and his brother may be the only "two white guys from Mississippi who have NAACP Image Awards.")

Neither Keenen nor Damon actually sings in the Brothers Brothers sketches, they lip-sync to prerecorded tracks. A rumor persists that the voices on the recordings belong to the actual Tom and Dick Smothers. But Tom Rizzo, *ILC*'s longtime music coordinator, says he had only forty-five minutes to record the music for the first sketch, and "there was no time to find a singer." Both voices, he says, are his.

Although not every sketch was a searing deconstruction of contemporary ideas on race and culture, it was these sketches that seemed to cement the show's subversive reputation. "*In Living Color*," wrote Joyce Millman in the *San Francisco Examiner*, "is the most politically aware show in prime-time. With its scathing social satire, it plays like a *Smothers Brothers Comedy Hour* for the 90s . . . *In Living Color* is so frank about racial issues that it's often downright anarchic."

A big part of making the show each week was the delicate dance with

Fox's Standards and Practices personnel. Though, according to Don Bay, who ran the Standards and Practices Department for Fox, officially Fox didn't even have a Standards and Practices Department at that point.

"I was, at that time, a behind-the-scenes consultant," says Bay. "Fox management wanted to establish Fox as an edgy broadcaster compared with the older, more staid networks. They didn't want to admit a Standards person was employed."

To Keenen, Tamara Rawitt, and the rest of the show's creative staff, that was a distinction that held little significance. Scripts needed the approval of the Standards department, and one of their reps was always in the booth during tapings. "It's literally somebody standing backstage," says Keenen, "coming to you saying, 'You gotta do it again. You can't say that.'"

It was a daily frustration but particularly, in the wake of the Terry Rakolta/*Married with Children* imbroglio, the higher-ups at Fox took the Standards Department seriously.

"Standards and Practices reported directly to me," says Jamie Kellner, Fox's president. "They have to get every sketch and tell us whether we can put it on the air. There have been stations that lost their licenses because they put content on that was deemed inappropriate. This is not an issue you take lightly. This is a red-hot line into your office."

In some cases, this led to pretty comic horse-trading—"Take out two 'bitches' and put in one 'ass,'" as Damon puts it—but at times, as Buddy Sheffield notes, the negotiating was less reasonable.

"Sometimes Damon would have a certain line and the censor would say, 'Oh, no. You can't do that,'" says Sheffield. "So Damon would then come up with something worse than what he said the first time. Then they'd do a third take, and by that time, it would be absolutely vile and the guy would say, 'Let's just go back to the first one,' which is exactly what Damon wanted."

One sketch that became a flashpoint during Season 1 was "Bolt 45," a commercial parody of Billy Dee Williams's Colt 45 malt liquor commercial. In it, Keenen, as Williams, plies his date, played by Kim Coles, with Bolt 45, which he tells viewers has "five times the alcohol content of your average stout beer, so it gets any lady in the mood for what I'm after." Once Coles's character passes out, the commercial ends with Williams swinging her legs open, about to take advantage of her. It's not hard to imagine the Standards Department would've found this casual depiction of date rape objectionable. Coles herself wasn't particularly happy with it.

"I remember being very uncomfortable because he had to pick me up, open my legs, and climb in between," she says. "I'm married and knew it would make my husband uncomfortable too."

The Standards Department insisted on several cuts and Keenen obliged, but as he explains, "the person responsible for actually putting the tape on air put the wrong one on, so it aired in its entirety. [Fox] got really pissed."

The incident has always been chalked up to an innocent mistake, but it may not have been. Kris Trexler, the show's longtime editor, was often tasked with making last-minute edits to sketches on extremely tight deadlines, so it wasn't uncommon for him to create multiple edits anticipating the Standards Department's objections. But his loyalty was to Keenen. With the "Bolt 45" sketch, he hints that he may have taken the opportunity to prove it.

"People make mistakes and *somehow* a mistake got made that *somehow* was more along the lines of what the show creator would've been happy with," says Trexler. "I'm not going any further than that."

Far from being chastened by the battles with Standards or complaints from special interests and viewers, the writers and cast seemed to thrive on stirring shit up.

"Occasionally, there would be group readings of letters that we'd gotten, because they were so insanely full of hate and upset [over stuff] we thought was so innocuous," says Coffield.

It was easy to laugh that stuff off when you were a hit. After the initial scheduling changes and subsequent ratings wobble, the show regained its footing. Each week, eighteen to twenty million viewers were tuning in. Even the show's reruns managed to consistently draw close to eighteen million viewers. Through the late spring and early summer, *ILC* won its time slot nearly every week. And the show, along with *The Simpsons* and *Married with Children*, was making a huge splash with eighteen- to thirty-four-year-old viewers.

"People didn't talk about demographics up until that point," says Sandy Grushow. "Up until Fox, it was all about 'households.' Fox trained the press to report on demographics. Advertisers very much wanted to reach that young audience."

Rose Catherine Pinkney was a new executive at Fox's studio arm, Twentieth Television, when *ILC* launched and, notably, the only African-American executive working on the show. That gave her a slightly different perspective on the show. "If you were a person of color, you had more of the inside track," she says. "Keenen didn't care if white America got the joke."

Of course, the network surely did. From the beginning, Fox pushed to broaden the show's audience. "Once you get something to work, that's when a lot of the work begins because you have to exploit the success," says Kellner. "If it's a hit every advertiser wants to buy into, you drive your CPMs [cost per mille, or per thousand people seeing a commercial]. You have to be able to exploit the show to the advertisers and get the affiliates excited. It's not hard to get the guy in New York or Atlanta excited, because there's a large black population you know is going to love the show, but in the network business, you've got to get *all* the affiliates excited, even the guy in Portland, Oregon, where you have a black population of 3 percent."

Increasingly, even the guy in Portland was excited. *ILC* had become the white-hot center of the pop culture world. "It was bubbling," says Kim Coles. "You could absolutely feel the heat. We had rappers and singers visit the set. You could feel the energy of the audiences that came to see us."

The show had also earned respect within comedy circles, even at the institution that in many ways it was created to supplant, *Saturday Night Live*. "I remember one day sitting in the booth at midnight while we were shooting and I get a tap on my shoulder," says director Paul Miller. "It was Al Franken, who'd been one of the writers at *Saturday Night Live* when I was there. I turned around and he says, 'I just came to congratulate you. You guys are doing a great job.'"

17

"What They Thought Was Hip-Hop, Wasn't Hip-Hop"

When LL Cool J's 1990 tour made a stop at the Universal Amphitheater in Studio City, California, Keenen made a point of getting himself backstage. He wanted to see Rosie Perez. Carla Earle, the choreographer hired to replace A.J. Johnson, wasn't working out. He still didn't understand how things had fallen apart with Perez and was anxious to see if he could remedy the situation. When he found her after the concert, he asked why she didn't take the job he'd offered her. She explained that a producer told her they'd hired someone else. He insisted he always wanted her for the job and, in fact, still did.

"What are you getting here?" Keenen asked. "I'll double it."

Perez wasn't convinced.

"All right," Keenen said. "I'll give you another fifteen hundred more a week."

She said she had to ask LL.

The rapper was supportive, telling her, "Go get that TV money."

Why Keenen dumped Earle isn't totally clear. Earle says she was pregnant when she got hired but nobody at the show knew. She didn't gain much weight during the pregnancy and even though she was approaching her due date during the six weeks she worked with the Fly Girls, she wasn't showing.

"They didn't find out I was pregnant until I was going into labor," she says. Her pregnancy, she believes, "was uncomfortable for Keenen." *ILC*, she says, "was a boys' club. At the time, I was in my early thirties, fit—I was his type, let me put it like that. However, I wasn't about to start sleeping on anybody's couch to progress or keep my position. I earned everything I got." When her son was two weeks old, she says, she was released from her contract without explanation. "A few people advised legal action. I just wasn't going that route."

Others have cast Earle's dismissal as a creative one, unrelated to a pregnancy or any personal issues. Whatever the reason, her abrupt departure didn't exactly smooth the way for Perez's arrival. When the new choreographer arrived at *ILC*, Keenen gave her two specific instructions regarding the Fly Girls. One was that they had to look good—their hair, their bodies, their clothes, the whole package. "No fat, busted chicks," was the phrase Perez recalled Keenen using. She was charged with ensuring they kept themselves up. The second instruction was that he wanted the Fly Girls to dance like MC Hammer. Hammer's "U Can't Touch This," a toxically catchy dance-rap confection that sampled Rick James's "Super Freak," had hit the Top 40 the month *ILC* debuted and was rocketing farther up the charts fueled by a video featuring Hammer's hyper-athletic, baggy-pants-ed dance moves.

"Then you should hire his choreographer," Perez told him. That made Keenen laugh. "I don't do Hammer," she said. "I do me."

Perez's early days were rocky. Earle was a professionally trained dancer and choreographer, well versed in jazz, tap, classical, and African dance. So were the dancers she'd hired. Perez was not.

"Rosie was a non-trained dancer," says Carrie Ann Inaba. "She got her start from that dance she did in *Do the Right Thing*. She had no background at all. We were speaking two completely different languages."

Deidre Lang, who'd been on the show since the pilot, says that sometimes this communication gap begat unintentional comedy. "She would say, 'Yeah, Deidre, do that step, you know that step, that pirouette-y,'" says Lang, imitating Perez's heavy Nuyorican accent.

Perez was as skeptical of the Fly Girls as they were of her.

"They were so technically trained, but Carrie Ann was the only one that had a little hip-hop dance experience," says Perez. "The rest, what they thought was hip-hop, wasn't hip-hop." Perez drilled them hard to get them up to speed, often eight hours a day or more, five days a week, which didn't necessarily endear her to her new charges.

"She was stern and hard," says Lang. "Some girls didn't really like that too much. She butted heads with some of them."

This professional disconnect may have been the root of the problems, but it wasn't the extent of it.

"We all didn't get along right away," says Inaba. "Rosie's a strong personality and we were all cast because we were strong personalities." Beyond that, there was just the natural friction that comes with spending all day, every day working closely with people. "Women in a room together," says Inaba, "is not always easy."

Perez admits, "It was tense when I came in. They'd bonded with the previous choreographer. I mean there wasn't any fighting or anything like that, but it was emotional for them, which is completely understandable. But I was very young, so it took me a minute to digest it." At one point, Perez's frustrations got so bad that she walked into Keenen's office and unloaded.

"They hate me!" she told him, almost in tears.

Keenen was unmoved. "You just have to do your job," he said.

The Fly Girls worked out the kinks. One night, watching Ann-Margret dance alongside Elvis Presley in *Viva Las Vegas*, Perez had a revelation: She quit trying to make the Fly Girls dance exactly as she wanted. "I combined what they had and what I had, then we started to gel."

Perez took charge of choosing their music too, which, in that first season, leaned heavily on New York rap. Songs by Public Enemy, Eric B. & Rakim, Queen Latifah, and 3rd Bass all soundtracked Fly Girls dance numbers. Simply airing hip-hop back then was revolutionary. This was long before every city had a big hip-hop radio powerhouse on the dial. Rap was often relegated to late-night specialty shows or college radio. *Yo! MTV Raps* debuted on MTV in 1988, and Arsenio occasionally had rappers on his late-night show, but *ILC* was prime-time network television. These songs were being heard by anywhere between ten and twenty million people.

Perez frequently flew home to New York on weekends to hear what DJs were spinning in clubs, in order to keep her finger on the pulse of what was coming *next*. She'd return with armloads of CDs and tapes, then sit in her office playing them. Initially, her office was on the same floor as the writers' and producers', but "one of the executive producers couldn't stand all the music I was playing, so he put me down in the basement. It was all cinder block."

The Fly Girls often rehearsed for more than forty hours a week in order to dance on the show each week for between two and three minutes. But Perez's work paid off.

"When Rosie came on, she helped to shape the look and the whole style," says Keenen. "She was connected to underground hip-hop, so all the dance moves were stuff people hadn't seen yet. They were coming straight out of the clubs. A lot of the credit for the Fly Girls goes to her."

The troupe became a phenomenon. "I remember being on the elevator one day and someone asking us if we had gotten our letters," says Michelle Whitney-Morrison. "We didn't know what they were talking about. They said that we received fan mail. That's when I thought, *Huh, people really do know who we are.*"

As Inaba puts it, "The Fly Girls were something of their own. They had their own following, their own identity. There weren't many shows that featured five girls with different ethnic backgrounds, doing this new style of dancing that they really hadn't seen on TV. We weren't five-foot-seven, stick-figure girls. We were regular girls who could shake. People were hungry for it."

———

Many of the first season's breakout sketches and characters—"The Wrath of Farrakhan," "Men on Film," "The Homeboy Shopping Network," Oswald Bates, Homey the Clown, "Hey Mon," the Brothers Brothers—had one thing in common: Damon Wayans. More than any other cast member, Damon seemed on a trajectory for stardom within weeks of *ILC*'s debut. Some might've grumbled that his near ubiquity on-screen that season and the frequency with which his characters recurred had the whiff of nepotism about it, but it was impossible to deny the electricity he exuded.

Unlike a lot of the cast members, Damon also was a writer on the show, which gave him certain advantages. He wasn't constantly hoping the writing staff would craft something that worked for him, or nudging them to. Many of his characters were adapted from bits he'd been honing for years. Off-camera, Damon could be quiet and withdrawn. In pitch meetings and at table reads, he was sometimes off to the side, but it was clear that, on the subject of funny, Keenen trusted Damon's opinion above all others.

"Keenen was executive producer and would say, 'I want things done this way,' and then Damon would sometimes quietly either nod his approval or shake his head no," says Kim Bass, who'd known and worked with Damon before getting hired as a writer.

Bowman, who would become the show's co-head writer in Season 2, says Keenen "really liked high performance energy. Things I might've written for *Saturday Night Live* that might've been more writerly conceits wouldn't have made it on *In Living Color*. Keenen really responded to character-based stuff." Anton Jackson, a homeless character Damon had first started doing in his standup, was a good example. "If you saw the written material for that character, you probably wouldn't respond to it. That whole sketch was about Damon's performance."

Anton could've easily just been a pathetic drunk—and at times he was. But often, as with Richard Pryor's famous wino character, which no doubt had been an influence on Damon, Anton was more a court jester, slipping in sly jabs at the criminal justice system, social welfare programs, bourgeois values, or the entertainment industry. His first appearance on the show was a good primer for what followed. "My name is Anton," he announces to a subway car full of commuters after staggering forward and picking his nose. "I'm a victim of society and an entertainer."

A lot of material was scavenged from the Wayans family's past. Kim based her neighborhood gossip, Benita Butrell, on "a couple of women in our neighborhood in the projects that used to just sit on the bench and talk about everybody's kids," she says. "They'd smile in your face, but the second you walked away, they had something negative to say." Keenen has said that another inspiration for Benita was their mother.

Even as Damon was primed to be the show's breakout star, the cast as a whole was still mostly in thrall of simply being a part of this unlikely success story. No one was rich yet. Even Keenen himself was still driving around in a beat-up Toyota. The cast competed with each other for screen time and the biggest laughs, but outright envy and jealousy—for the most part—were kept in check. The cast felt bonded through the long hours together. Many nights they'd be at work from eight in the morning until ten at night. Most of them went to lunch together at places like the Living Room or Kate Mantilini on Wilshire Boulevard.

"We would just all shove ourselves into somebody's car and go out to lunch every day," says Coffield. "One time we were all having lunch together and Damon brought up this idea, 'Wouldn't it be awesome if we could all rent an apartment together? We could use it as an office in which we could develop stuff.' We never did, but it was something we were considering because we couldn't imagine not wanting to hang out with each other more."

Their chemistry didn't go unrewarded. In August, when the Emmy nominations were announced, *ILC* got three: Episode 1 was nominated for Outstanding Writing in a Variety or Music Program, Episode 5 for Outstanding Choreography, and the show overall got a nod for Outstanding Variety, Music or Comedy Series. That summer, Keenen signed a production deal with Universal and began developing a film to write, direct, and star in, called *Lloyd of London*. But now, finally out of the shadow of his more famous friends, there was almost no time to enjoy all the good fortune. With Season 1 drawing to a close, Keenen had only one thing on his mind.

"'I need a break,'" he says, laughing. "That was it. I was so exhausted. We all needed a break."

18

"That's the Beauty of It: It's Dangerous and We Shouldn't Be Doing It"

Kim Coles hadn't had a great first season. She wasn't on-screen that much, and some of the time she was on-screen, she was, by her own admission, "pretty uncomfortable." Just before she'd landed the *ILC* role, she'd shed fifty pounds, and many of her parts—as Robin Givens in the "Love Connection" sketch, as a drunken floozy in the "Bolt 45" sketch, wearing a bathing suit in a tampon commercial parody—required her to flaunt a new body with which she wasn't yet at ease. She may have eventually overcome those issues, but there were other bad signs for her right from the start.

On the pilot, she and Kim Wayans were slated to be in a sketch together called "Too-Too Ethnic," a spoof of *227*, the Marla Gibbs–Jackée Harry comedy on NBC. Jackée played a broad character who looked a little like Coles, so it seemed a no-brainer to Coles that she should play her. Keenen disagreed.

"He let me know that Kim does Jackée in her act, so she's going to play her," says Coles. "I remember fighting that one. I was like, 'I look like Jackée and she looks more like Marla, so let me have a stab at it.' He said, 'No.'" For Coles, it was an early lesson in the show's dynamics. "What he says goes. That's how some bosses run their ship."

It was the first of many times Coles felt Keenen favored his sister over her. She says she was frequently cut from sketches. More often, she wasn't in them at all. "It became evident that it was Keenen's job to make his sister a star," she told the *Dallas Morning News* in 1993. "Keenen would take things right out of my hands and give it to her."

Keenen doesn't recall it that way. "That was her perception," he says. "The truth was Kim [Wayans] used to write. Kim Coles didn't. So, as the cast came with their ideas, their ideas got written into the show. The ones who didn't write were auxiliary players. Her perception was that she wasn't being given the sketches. You can't be given somebody else's sketches. She didn't step up."

Others at the show, however, agree some of Coles's problems could be traced back to the fact that she was often competing with Keenen's sister for roles. But Kim Wayans takes issue with the idea that she, or any of her siblings, were somehow gifted something they didn't earn. "Keenen really tried to be very fair," she says. "His thing was you had to produce, you had to create. If you wanted more airtime, come up with some funny shit. Some people were able to step to the plate more than others. But there wasn't a favoritism thing going on where he was just giving me hilarious stuff. Ninety percent of the things you see me do on *In Living Color* are things I created on my own, characters I wrote myself, developed myself. Now, if you didn't have the skills to write sketches or create characters, maybe you did find yourself a little stuck and feeling resentful. And who knows how you twist that in your head, how you make it 'family favoritism' as opposed to 'I'm not able to write my own sketches or come up with characters.'"

Coles says she put together an extensive list of characters that she could do and gave it to the producers, but that didn't get her more airtime. As the season wore on, she grew more withdrawn.

"There were some episodes that were very hard to watch because the only thing I was in was the final credits," she says. "You have to sit there all week long, go to the makeup chair, and then be available to stand onstage and wave to the audience. I'll never forget, one time, Tommy grabbed me and tried to make me dance a little bit. I was just so broken. You break a performer's spirit if you don't let them perform."

Coles admits she never really tried to address the festering problems between her, Keenen, and Kim, never tried to clear the air, but she's sure it wouldn't have made a difference. She'd tried to assert herself with "Too-Too Ethnic" and was shut down. "I saw what happened when you fought, when you pushed back. It didn't work so I stopped." After a while, she says, "I sat in my dressing room and cried. I'm not a fighter."

A persistent rumor also floated that something romantic had developed briefly between Keenen and Coles and when that soured, it further poisoned her experience. Both Keenen and Coles deny anything ever happened, but the mere existence of the rumor likely didn't help. Another story had it that Coles had been approached by Keenen's old friend and rival Arsenio Hall about doing her own show for his production company and that in even entertaining the idea, Coles appeared disloyal. At the time, Coles said, "I was under contract to Keenen. I respect him too much to ever pursue any work in conflict with *In Living Color*."

At the end of the first season, Keenen told Coles she wasn't living up to her potential and explained what he expected of her going forward. But shortly after production began on Season 2, Coles was fired.

"I remember getting a call either after the first or second week saying don't come to work on Monday," she says.

As Keenen explains it, "I didn't want any dissension. I didn't want negative voices. So, when I saw that kind of behavior I just nipped it in the bud." He says her anger and disappointment "started to really affect her, and when it started to affect other cast members, that's when she had to go."

Coles agrees that by that time, she felt defeated and had completely shut down. But initially she wasn't even told why she'd been axed.

"It took me two weeks to get him on the phone to say, 'You didn't look happy. You weren't bringing your 'A' game,'" she recalls him explaining. "I said, 'You didn't let me do anything.' He even said to me, 'Why didn't you fight? Why didn't you do what some of the others did?' People began to dance for him in that way. I never did. That was my downfall. I never kissed the ring. I didn't know I had to."

A couple years after she was fired, Coles was cast as one of the leads, alongside Queen Latifah, in the hit sitcom *Living Single*, a part she admits likely wouldn't have happened if not for *ILC*. That, to her, felt like the silver lining on the storm clouds that engulfed her days on the show.

"I have since seen Kim Wayans and she has apologized to me for the way I was treated, so that was powerful for me," she says. Coles has also had a reconciliation, of sorts, with Keenen. "When faced with it, years later, he said, 'I had to let you go. I knew you were going to be fine.' That might be a line or that might be the most gracious thing he has ever done or said to me. I'm grateful for it."

———

A week before Season 2 premiered, the show won the Emmy for Outstanding Variety, Music or Comedy Series, beating out *The Arsenio Hall Show*, *Saturday Night Live*, and *Late Night with David Letterman* in the process. The award seemed particularly significant: The show was new, and Fox was barely hanging on as a fourth network. *ILC* had been a hit relative to expectations, but wasn't even one of the top twenty most watched shows in prime time.

"The Emmy was validation of everything the show was trying to do," says John Bowman, who along with Buddy Sheffield was promoted to head writer at the beginning of the new season. For Keenen, that they'd beaten out *SNL* and *Arsenio* offered a little extra relish.

The show returned with a bigger budget, which meant expanding the offices a little, and more money to shoot more complicated sketches, often away from the studio, on location. Fox also moved the show's time slot again, this time to eight o'clock on Sunday night. This could have certainly been viewed as a vote of confidence, as the network clearly saw *ILC* as a show that could anchor the whole night. But eight was also considered "family hour," which meant even stricter scrutiny from Standards.

Despite efforts to keep the writing staff from the first season intact, many left, including key contributors like Matt Wickline, who'd helped create Homey the Clown, and Sandy Frank, who left to work on a new show called *The Fresh Prince of Bel-Air*, featuring a lanky rapper named Will Smith. The burnout rate among writers was high.

"Keenen was a difficult guy to please," says Steve Tompkins, one of the Season 1 writers who stuck around. "It was hard to predict exactly what would push the right button for him, and it changed over time.

Something that worked one week might not work the next week. You went through periods where you were either in his favor or not."

Bowman liked working for Keenen, but "if things weren't getting laughs he was like any other comedy boss—he doesn't like it. He gets mad. The writers who tended to survive and thrive were thick-skinned and didn't take Keenen's criticisms to heart."

Sometimes worse than Keenen's scorn was his abject disinterest. He wasn't necessarily the kind of boss who nurtured writers or developed personal relationships with them. You either could do the job and were useful or you couldn't and you weren't.

"Writers were fired if they didn't produce," says Bowman. "You were always aware of that." There was something to be said though for his honesty. "Even though Keenen could be distant and aloof, he consistently rewarded talent."

Sheffield says that although he and Bowman were head writers, "Keenen never really ceded the responsibility completely. The head writers would run the table, then we'd put together the best script and give it to Keenen and Tamara, and they'd make the ultimate decisions."

As Bowman puts it, "Keenen's hand is in almost every sketch those first couple years. He was involved with everything."

Of the five new writers hired for Season 2, only one—Pam Veasey—was black. Along with two holdovers from Season 1, Kim Bass and Paul Mooney—plus Keenen and Damon—that made for a decent contingent, but they were still far outnumbered by the white writers. One new writer, Les Firestein, had grown up on the edge of Harlem and felt at home with black culture.

"A lot of stuff that would become grist for sketches was just kind of in the air," he says. By 1990, hip-hop was everywhere. *Newsweek* put Tone Lōc on its cover under the headline, "Rap Rage." 2 Live Crew were on the front page of the *New York Times* after their album *As Nasty As They Wanna Be* was declared legally obscene. *The Fresh Prince of Bel-Air* debuted on NBC. Vanilla Ice—who may have struggled for credibility but was as good an example as there was of hip-hop's expanding borders—topped the *Billboard* charts, the first rapper ever to do so, with "Ice Ice Baby."

Even the venerable *Saturday Night Live* seemed to be acknowledging the shifting sands by introducing two new black cast members, Chris Rock and Tim Meadows, that fall. Hip-hop was seeping into everything. In early 1991, *New Jack City*, a violent, modern-day blaxploitation flick that starred Ice-T alongside Rock and Wesley Snipes, was a surprise box office hit that opened the door over the next few years to films like *Boyz n the Hood*, *Menace II Society*, and *Juice*. The week of *New Jack City*'s release coincided with the release of an even more influential bit of film: a video of LAPD officers viciously beating a motorist named Rodney King. Two weeks after the King beating, Latasha Harlins, a fifteen-year-old African-American girl, was shot in the back of the head and killed by a Korean grocery store owner. Los Angeles felt like a powder keg. Relations on the *ILC* set though stayed mostly insulated from the outside world.

As Tompkins recalls, "That idea of it being white and black in the writers' room wasn't really an issue." Well, not a *major* issue. "Anybody was entitled to pitch anything," he says. "There were times when somebody would pitch something and Keenen would cock an eyebrow because it came down slightly on the wrong side of what was funny about something." At those moments, he'd often mime playing a banjo in the middle of someone's pitch, a nod to the classic redneck-sploitation flick *Deliverance*.

Adam Small was a new writer hired as part of a writing team with Fax Bahr. The two had been sketch performers together, and were known around the office by the collective sobriquet "FaxandAdam," but during Small's first week, his other half was honeymooning in Africa. Small, undeterred, was determined to make his mark and show off just how dark and brutal his humor could be.

"I came in the first day, the first thing I pitched was 'Ghetto Children Action Figures,'" Small says. "They were little dolls but it was a thirteen-year-old gangbanger, a bullet-riddled Cadillac, a Korean liquor store owner dead, lying in his own pool of blood, a twelve-year-old pregnant gang sister."

As Small's pitch went on, the room got very quiet. Bass, one of the room's black writers, winced. "But he didn't give up on the idea," says Bass. At least not yet.

"All of a sudden," says Small, "everyone in the room started playing the *Deliverance* banjo. Keenen looks at me and goes, 'Homey, we don't go there.' It was too race inflammatory on the first day. They didn't know me. They didn't trust me."

On Les Firestein's first day at *In Living Color*, Bowman took him aside to offer some advice. Firestein was a tall Stanford grad, with dark, curly hair and a warped sense of humor. He'd been an editor at the *National Lampoon*, but *ILC* was his first television job. Bowman, with his credits on *SNL* and Garry Shandling's show, seemed like an old sage.

"If you're an okay writer," Bowman told him, "you should make half a million dollars a year. If you're a good writer, you'll make anywhere from three-quarters of a million to two million dollars a year."

"What if you're a great writer?" Firestein asked.

"Hmmm. Fifty thousand."

Firestein quickly established himself as a force on the writing staff. He had a hand in many sketches and seemed to not only fit seamlessly into the behind-the-scenes culture of the show but reshape it in his own image.

"Weirdly, the show was my sensibility," he says. "Obviously, I'm not black, but they'd really go for it with anything, which was my sensibility coming out of *National Lampoon*." Virtually nothing, as Firestein sees it, should be off-limits as subject matter, and he offers what he calls a "horrible story," to illustrate his point.

At the time, there was a popular series on ABC called *Life Goes On* that featured a main character with Down syndrome, played by Chris Burke, an actor with Down syndrome. "I'd written a sketch, I think called 'Mongoloid Mobster,' where the kid wanted to break out of being typecast and play a gangster. Keenen's attitude was 'We'll do that sketch if he'll be in it.'" The sketch never happened, but Firestein appreciated Keenen's openness to something so seemingly beyond the pale.

Firestein brought that same no-holds-barred spirit to the show's offices. Kim Bass recalls him bringing a bicycle in one day and organizing races around the office.

"You have to understand," says Bass, "every corner is a blind corner, and you're riding this bike as fast as you can. You don't know if you're going to run into Tamara or Keenen or one of the suits from Fox and break an arm. Someone said, 'Les, somebody is going to get hurt.' He said, 'Yeah, that's the beauty of it: It's dangerous and we shouldn't be doing it.'" He was talking about the biking, but it seemed to sum up Firestein's attitude toward comedy too.

Other office hijinks included the procurement of wildly inappropriate exotic dancers to celebrate staff members' birthdays.

"It started with my birthday," says Bahr. "Les and Adam hired a stripper to come in during a pitch meeting."

As Bass remembers it, this particular stripper "was very elderly. Maybe eighty years old with a feather boa, high heels, and everything. People were against the wall, either cringing or laughing. Poor Fax had no idea. He was completely ambushed."

"It was incredibly embarrassing, weird and just horrible," says Bahr. "Everyone felt terrible for this poor woman. She didn't really strip, she got into a bikini and tried to give me a lap dance."

The event was such a success that it became a tradition, albeit with a different kind of offbeat stripper every time: a three-hundred-pound drunken woman; a gay man in his midsixties, also inebriated; and for Keenen's thirty-second birthday, two drag queens. "It was scary," said Keenen.

This was the prevailing atmosphere. Not everyone enjoyed it with the same fervor. Pam Veasey, a petite, attractive black woman who'd worked briefly on the Nell Carter sitcom, *Gimme a Break*, had been so gung-ho to write for *ILC* that she'd camped out in the offices for hours without an appointment during the first season, begging for a chance. At the time, there weren't any openings. When staffing began for Season 2, she was hired. That was the easy part.

"It was hard for the women cast members as well as the women writers," she says. "You gotta hang with the guys and they didn't pull any punches. When you got in that room, they let you know right from the start that this was a *guys'* room. If you were too sensitive, take your purse and go. You had to be aggressive, you had to really try to fit in a room where a lot of crazy stuff happened."

Veasey found a natural ally in the staff's other female writer, Becky Hartman (now Becky Hartman Edwards). The two shared an office together and an outlook.

"Pam and I are pretty strong women," says Hartman. "I was always a tomboy. I originally aspired to be a sportswriter so was used to being one of the only women. That being said, there certainly was an under-current of sexism or that sort of frat mentality a little bit. Pam and I would turn to each other for a sanity check or to vent." Survival and acceptance in the writers' room required an ability to give as good as you could get. "If you were a woman who could tell a really good dirty joke or defuse with humor if someone was being an asshole, that could help you survive."

As Keenen himself has pointed out, "This was pre-sexual harass-ment and all that, so if you were a female writer, you had to be able to hold your own. It was a male-dominated business. The female writers put up with a lot of shit and got very tough very quick."

The writers worked on thirteen-week contracts, which meant during a twenty-six-week season, there was an opportunity in the middle to make changes. Two new writers, Greg Fields and J.J. Paulsen, were added half-way through the second season. They'd have very different trajectories on the show and beyond.

When Fields came to *ILC*, he was already a veteran comedy writer with an impressive résumé. He'd written for Johnny Carson on *The To-night Show*, with Sheffield on the reboot of *The Smothers Brothers Com-edy Hour*, and had co-written the hit Rodney Dangerfield movie *Back to School*. Fields grew up in Kentucky, where he was a star athlete, then worked as a standup for a while before getting his writing career on track. By the time he was hired for *ILC*, he was a little older than most of the rest of the writers, a little pudgy, and wore sweatpants and a baseball hat to work nearly every day.

"He was a very, very nice guy and a joke machine," says Bahr. Fields, who died of a heart attack in 2002, was a laid-back, well-liked level head in the office who never seemed ruffled by the roller coaster of emotions that came with making the show.

"Greg had a really high-pitched voice and kind of seemed like a hill-billy," says Firestein. "Unlike a lot of people on the staff, he had a family, so Greg's attitude was different than a lot of people's. He'd be like, 'Can't we just get this done?'"

Paulsen was a young comedy writer whose only prior credit was on *The Sweet Life*, a vehicle for singer-turned-actress Rachel Sweet that aired on what was then called the Comedy Channel and later became Comedy Central. (Also on the *Sweet Life* writing staff: Jon Stewart, future *Sex and the City* producer/writer/director Michael Patrick King, and *ILC* writer Becky Hartman.) Firestein recalls that Paulsen's introduction to *ILC* was rough.

"J.J.'s first day on the show was an all-nighter," he says. "Like, you showed up at nine in the morning and left at eleven at night the next day." The rest of Paulsen's tenure wasn't particularly noteworthy, and he lasted only the length of his thirteen-week contract. He continued to work in comedy for the next decade and a half, but his story has a grim coda: In 2009, he was convicted of beating his wife to death and sentenced to twenty-six years in prison. He was released in 2016, after serving seven years.

Firestein says Paulsen was "workmanlike" on the show but not overly productive. There were odd, colorful stories about him whispered on the set, some with a bit of a dark tinge to them. "You're always surprised when someone murders someone, but this was the least surprised you could be in terms of all the people who were there," says Firestein, who can't help finding a twisted, off-color joke in all this. "It's good that to the best of my knowledge the first and only murderer to come out of that show was a white guy. J.J. was the Jackie Robinson of that show."

Several writers recall that, starting in Season 2, there was a concerted effort to create franchise-able characters. This wasn't just marketing—it was survival. Starting with a completely blank slate each week wasn't sustainable for a writing staff already working insanely long hours.

"You get to a point," says Sheffield, "where you're spending so much time on the show, you're there late at night, you don't have dinner with people and talk to them, you don't watch other TV, you don't go to movies, and you don't do any of the things that trigger sketch ideas. If you're not careful, you end up writing sketches about your own sketches because that's all you ever see."

Just as the first season's writers had discovered, Keenen wasn't enamored with the idea of using *In Living Color* as a platform to expound on the evils of racism and the problems with American society *unless* it was going to be funny. Tompkins says it was usually the white writers "chomping at the bit to write sketches that were really edgy and controversial and kicked up some dust. But Keenen, Damon, and Kim, they *lived* the black experience. They didn't need to spend one more day fighting that battle."

For Tompkins, his experience at the show improved considerably once he came around to this realization. "Keenen wasn't out to make the most biting satire or the most insightful condemnation of the black experience in America. He wanted to do big, goofy, fun characters, like Carol Burnett."

Many of the recurring characters that debuted in Season 2 reflect that reality: David Alan Grier's Al MacAfee is a dimwitted high school teacher; Jim Carrey's Dickie Peterson is an adolescent social outcast masquerading as vigilante law enforcement; Keenen's Frenchy is an unfiltered Rick James wannabe based on the character Keenen had created years earlier when he raided Eddie Murphy's wardrobe; Kim Wayans's Lil' Magic is a desperately ambitious, wildly ungifted child actress based on her younger self; Damon's Head Detective is a sight gag—he's literally just a head, with hands and feet. These were big, broad characters the audience was invited to laugh at, not with. Arguably, the most memorable of the show's shooting gallery of goofballs was Jim Carrey's Fire Marshal Bill.

Fire Marshal Bill is a fire chief whose fire safety demonstrations inevitably involve making things explode. He's been burned so many times that he doesn't flinch at the prospect of catching fire again. Judd Apatow, who was close to Carrey back then, recalled seeing Carrey doing a version of Fire Marshal Bill onstage at the Comedy Store around 1988 or 1989.

"He started doing the burnt-guy face and complaining about how all of the electrical outlets weren't safe," Apatow recalled. "It was a great thing to witness." (Interestingly, Apatow and Carrey remained close collaborators while the latter worked on *ILC*. "Judd was my opening act on the road," says Carrey. "We'd write together. We might have written a couple of things for *In Living Color*. I'm not sure they got on, but I remember writing with him." David Alan Grier also recalled that Apatow "used to hang around *In Living Color* and try to pitch jokes.")

In an interview with writer Nelson George back in 1991, Carrey seemed to recollect the same night at the Comedy Store that Apatow did, saying, "Fire Marshal Bill is the product of a strange mood I was in at two in the morning at the Comedy Store. I was onstage and started showing different fire violations in the club. A writer saw me, and began building a character around this." However, during an interview with Bob Costas that same year, he also traced Fire Marshal Bill to a character in a proposed sketch called "The Make A Death Wish Foundation" that "didn't pass the censors, so we weaseled it in another direction." More recently, Carrey explained the original "Make A Death Wish Foundation" sketch: "It was a foundation for kids to get their posthumous wish, what they want to do after they die. I was the dead kid that wanted to go to Disneyland. So I'd be on rides with some celebrity or something, just flopping back and forth as a dead person, *Weekend at Bernie's*-style. I had that [Fire Marshal Bill] face for that character."

When the sketch got cut, he was commiserating with Bahr and Small—whom Carrey calls "one of the funniest human beings ever to walk the Earth"—and showed them the face he had for the sketch. "It looks like a burn victim," he says. The three of them began riffing until Fire Marshal Bill was born.

Carrey says that at its heart, the inspiration flowed from Peter Sellers's Inspector Clouseau. "The funniest thing was the Peter Sellers thing—the so-called expert that's always hurting himself. That concept is always funnier because you're making fun of someone's ego."

Still, there were issues. "The first time we did it," says Bahr, "when Jim came out of makeup, the Standards guy was like, 'No way.' It was disgusting. They made him really tone it down."

The Standards Department weren't the only ones with reservations. "I personally never cared for that sketch," says Sheffield. "We had a kid who worked on the lot who was a burn victim. He was horribly disfigured. When they first brought that sketch in, I said, 'Go pitch it to that kid. If he thinks it's funny, we'll go for it.' Nobody ever pitched the idea to the kid, but I was just trying to make a point by suggesting it."

The sketch was an immediate hit with viewers, however. It comes off as so cartoonish that it's hard to believe anyone would take it seriously enough to be upset. In fact, some did. The National Fire Protection Association wrote to Fox chairman Barry Diller asking that Fire Marshal Bill be removed from the show. A representative from the Saint Barnabas Burn Foundation complained that the show was "spotlighting dysfunctional behavior." William Schultz, president of the New Jersey Fire Prevention and Protection Association, asked for the character to be discontinued and an apology to burn victims from the network and the show. He warned that younger viewers would model Bill's behavior. "Children are going to be injured, they're going to die. It's going to come true, like fire waiting to happen." Local politicians in New Jersey pressured the show to reconsider the character.

Fox, for their part, mostly held firm. But as Sheffield recalls, "Every time one of those sketches would air, we'd get calls the next day from fire marshals around the country and they'd say, 'Kids are sticking knives in electrical outlets,' or whatever it was that Fire Marshal Bill had done the night before."

Most of the complaints found their way to Fox President Jamie Kellner. "Whenever you do comedy where you're really going for it, you're going to get people who get upset," he says. "I was in contact with one of the senators from New Jersey on a number of occasions because of Fire Marshal Bill. They were not pleasant calls."

The denunciations from outside groups seemed to have the opposite effect than intended. Fire Marshal Bill was one of the show's most popular characters, as well as one of its most utilized. The show did eleven separate Fire Marshal Bill sketches during the series' run.

"That was the character that put me over the top and gave me a film career and everything else," says Carrey.

Another character introduced in Season 2 that caused considerable hand-wringing was Damon's handicapped superhero, Handi-Man. On its face, Handi-Man just seemed patently offensive: He walks with a palsied limp and slurs his speech. When he declares "Up, up, and away" and flies out a window, he simply keels over and falls out of it. Damon knew it could work though.

"The fact I was born with a clubfoot gives me license to do that," he says. "I'd done it in my standup special on HBO, talking about how as a child I got into a lot of fights. I wasn't tough, I was just defending myself." In the special, he makes the point that you'll never find a handicapped bully. "From that came the idea of 'What if there was someone to protect those people, like a Handi-Man?'"

Bowman, who helped write the first Handi-Man sketch, says he'd had a similar idea at *SNL*. "But the *Saturday Night Live* version was a bit more tragic and didn't work," he says. "With Damon, because it was a really great performance, it did."

Still, the network smelled trouble. They covered their asses by screening the sketch for a disabled rights group.

"They loved it," says Sheffield. "When, in the sketch, he kicked that guy's ass for using the handicapped parking space, they were all over that. They said, 'It's about time we had a hero!' Even though a lot of people would look at it and say, 'My god! This is horrible to make fun of a handicapped person like that,' they thought it was great."

Damon felt vindicated: "When I know I'm operating from a good place, my conscience is clear. Handicapped people want somebody to make jokes about them but in a respectful way. What's more respectful than making them superheroes?"

Although many of the newest characters leaned toward the broad, the silly, and the easily franchise-able, the show didn't turn its back on politically charged material. Multiple Homey the Clown sketches in Season 2 brought the same reliable mix of angry black militancy and rank absurdity, and four different Brothers Brothers sketches grew more barbed as the season progressed.

There were hard-hitting new ideas too. "1-900-YT-GUILT" gave Damon a chance to break out his Farrakhan impression again, this time as an operator at a phone service that white people call to be browbeaten for their internalized racism. The sketch plays like a Paul Mooney standup bit come to life. Later in the season, "My Dark Conscience" worked similar themes, lampooning recent films like *A Dry White Season* and *A World Apart*, which attempted to tell the story of black suffering in Apartheid-era South Africa through white eyes. Playing like a commercial for an art film, the sketch features a narrator who makes the point explicit: "*My Dark Conscience*, a true story of the pain of watching somebody else suffer, and wanting to do something about it, but not really wanting to get involved, and then feeling a little guilty about it. Sort of."

These were still, arguably, what *ILC* did best—holding up a warped fun-house mirror to society's even more warped ideas about race. But many of these sketches became part of a long-running wrestling match with Fox's Standards Department. "They were always afraid of whatever black content the show had," says Bowman. "Using their own white liberal judgment, they found a ton of stuff offensive. Keenen would really have to push them into it."

Few probably realized that many of the most racially incendiary sketches were written, at least in part, by white writers.

"They never publicly acknowledged the writers a whole lot," says Sheffield. "They didn't really want it known that most of us were white. That wasn't good for the show's image. We could understand that. We were able to get away with a lot because we were working under Keenen's aegis. He put the black stamp of approval on it."

19

"We Got a Problem. I Want the Other Girl."

Rosie Perez was run ragged on *In Living Color*. In addition to choreographing the Fly Girls—with increasing help from her assistant, Arthur Rainer—she was also charged with choosing the music they'd dance to, and eventually she directed their segments too. She was also building her own acting career. She had a significant role in Jim Jarmusch's 1991 film *Night on Earth*, and leads in both 1992's *White Men Can't Jump* and 1993's *Untamed Heart*. On the weekends, she'd often be clubbing in New York.

One night, at a pop-up club called Carwash, she saw Leaders of the New School performing. The group featured a charismatic rapper named Busta Rhymes, who stalked the stage like a linebacker looking for someone to hit. His delivery was equal parts gruff, forceful, and goofy, and kept the audience on edge. Perez was blown away, and struck with an inspiration: These guys should be on the show. So should Public Enemy, KRS-One, and Queen Latifah. There weren't really any other shows—certainly none on in prime time—that showcased live hip-hop. *In Living Color* could be that show.

She took the idea to Keenen, who, she says, was lukewarm on it. Other producers were too. Musical guests cost money and they didn't have a lot of that to go around. Perez persisted. She pestered. Finally, Keenen caved.

"He goes, 'All right. Book them,'" she recalls. "He was like that. If your idea sucked, it didn't make the grade," but if he trusted you, he'd give you a chance to prove yourself. He told her she had one shot at this. (Keenen, for his part, insists that live music "was always part of the plan" for the show.)

Perez immediately approached Leaders of the New School, but the group was still ironing out the details of their record contract. They couldn't do anything until that was sorted out. She called other record companies. None wanted to let their established acts be the first to appear on what was then still a pretty new show. Eventually, she settled on a Los Angeles–based rapper named Def Jef. He closed out Episode 11 of Season 1 with a performance almost no one remembers.

Perez worried she'd blown her chance at this, and begged Keenen for another. When she promised she could get Queen Latifah, he was sold. Latifah's roof-rattling performance of "Mama Gave Birth to the Soul Children" at the end of the first episode of Season 2—while Public Enemy's Flavor Flav danced with the cast onstage—was proof Perez's idea was a good one. It didn't go unnoticed either. "After her performance," Perez said, "every hip-hop act wanted to be booked." That second season included performances from Monie Love, KRS-One, 3rd Bass, and the original apple of Perez's eye, Leaders of the New School. The season's musical highlight was Public Enemy's three-song medley ("Black Steel in the Hour of Chaos," "Buck Whylin'," "Fight the Power") that closed out an episode in April. With Ice Cube onstage alongside them, the performance felt like an *event*, and, in retrospect, a defining moment for the show. Hip-hop was still considered dangerous then, particularly artists like Public Enemy and Ice Cube, who were openly contemptuous of authority—be it corporate, governmental, or otherwise.

"They were the most controversial rap group at the time," Keenen said of Public Enemy. "Everybody was afraid of them but everybody loved them. For me to have the opportunity to break that door down was great."

Their appearance was the equivalent of Keenen throwing down his marker and choosing sides. It went a long way toward cementing the show's central place in hip-hop culture.

"*In Living Color* was one of those shows where we all grew together in the middle of that artistic renaissance," says Public Enemy's front man Chuck D. "The Wayans understood that black people could get some eyeballs in prime time. They felt like they could get away with [having us on]. It worked and was greatly appreciated."

———————

In Living Color was drawing more than twenty million viewers on its best nights, and by the middle of the second season, Keenen wanted to build on his success. He signed a contract with Fox in late 1990 to produce new films and television shows. One of his first ideas was *Kick It with the Fly Girls*, an *ILC* spinoff, hosted by Shawn Wayans, that would feature live music and dancing.

"I wanted to take the Fly Girls to the next level," he says. He envisioned them making pop albums, going on concert tours, maybe even launching their own fashion line. As Lisa Marie Todd puts it, "I jokingly say we were the Spice Girls before the Spice Girls."

All of this, Keenen realized, would require more hands—or feet—on deck. A decision was made to undertake a well-publicized, heavily marketed search for a new Fly Girl, someone who could not only dance but sing. It's easy to see how nowadays, in the age of *The Voice* and *So You Think You Can Dance*, this Fly Girl talent search would've become a reality show in and of itself. Eric Gold, who helped orchestrate it, admits it was a "stunt."

"The Fly Girls were hot," he says, "so we decided to use it to drive awareness and publicity."

At the New York audition, thousands of girls waited in a line that wrapped around the block. Keenen realized that auditioning them all would be a logistical nightmare so, according to Perez, he started going through the line and eliminating the ones who were, in his parlance, "busted." Not all of them took being dismissed based on their looks in stride. One took a few swings at Keenen before being escorted out by security.

On the second day of the New York auditions, Perez recalls seeing a "curvy, heavyset, big-ass beautiful girl" from the Bronx named Jennifer Lopez. "She wasn't the best dancer," as Perez writes in her memoir, "but definitely had an immense amount of star quality and a stunning face." Perez insists she told Keenen repeatedly, "That's the girl," and that Keenen didn't agree. She says he called her "chubby and corny." At the Los Angeles auditions, a brunette named Carla Garrido stood out.

The plan was to announce the show's choice at a televised event. Keenen insists that, contrary to what Perez claims, Lopez was always his first choice. At the event, though, he did something exceedingly out of character: He had the Fly Girls vote on their new member.

"I let what normally was a dictatorship become a democracy and the votes were not in Jennifer's favor," Keenen says. The Fly Girls chose Garrido. "We were on national TV when it happened, so I couldn't do anything except accept the votes."

Deidre Lang, one of the original Fly Girls, says Keenen seemed to be giving Lopez a lot of attention during the auditions, but she and a few other dancers already knew Garrido. Carrie Ann Inaba says, "Carla just seemed like she fit into the group really well."

Gold believes there was already a sense among the Fly Girls of Lopez's potential star power. Garrido seemed like less of a threat. "Jennifer was better by far," he says. "Keenen called me right afterwards and said, 'We got a problem. I want the other girl.' So, he ordered me to get Fox to put Jennifer under a holding deal, to hold her for a year until he could put her in. That's what we did."

The show also had a brief flirtation with bringing on male dancers. Several dance crews were invited to audition to be so-called Fly Guys. Tre Hardson was dancing as part of a four-man, L.A.-based crew called 2 Four 2 back then and already knew Perez. "Rosie was like our big sister," says Hardson. "She created the opportunity for us to compete. We had to make up a routine and go against different crews from L.A. We won."

The first thing 2 Four 2 was asked to do was dance alongside Jim Carrey's Vanilla Ice impression. The musical parody killed—in large part because Carrey was a dead ringer for Vanilla Ice—and the troupe was back a few episodes later, dancing with the Fly Girls during one segment and again at the show's close. But that was the sum total of it. The Fly Guys wouldn't be a lasting addition to the show.

20

"Some White Kid from Harvard Joking about Malcolm X-Lax—I Don't Think That Shit Is Funny"

Friday could be a very long day at *In Living Color*. Friday nights were show nights. Rehearsals would typically start around ten in the morning, and by two in the afternoon, audiences were often already lining up outside. Everyone would break for dinner at five, and if everything went according to plan, the cameras were rolling by eight. Everything rarely went according to plan. Unlike *Saturday Night Live*, which Lorne Michaels famously has said "doesn't go on because it's ready," but "because it's 11:30," *ILC*, since it wasn't broadcast live, had the flexibility to start the show whenever they felt like it. So they did.

"There was just a kind of 'screw-'em-they-can-wait' attitude that permeated the show," says Buddy Sheffield. Mark Curry, a comic who'd later star on the sitcom *Hangin' with Mr. Cooper*, was frequently charged with keeping the audience entertained while they waited. "Oh my god, I felt for the guy. He did every joke he knew four or five times." Occasionally, by showtime, the audience was worn out. Usually they rallied.

"When you'd go to tapings," says Bowman, "the audience were through the roof. People were dying. I've never seen an audience as hot."

Paul Miller, who, like Bowman, had worked on *SNL*, similarly marveled at the energy during those Friday-night shows. "The experience of shooting that show in front of an audience was something I'd never experienced before or since," he says. "They could've sold tickets and made a fortune." The tapings occasionally stretched into the wee hours of the following morning. "I remember going back to my car and the sun was coming up. It'd be five in the morning and the audience was still there. They were just this incredibly devoted fan base. They'd stay no matter how long we were there."

Although the show's ratings were solid, they weren't necessarily indicative of just how hot *ILC* was. It wasn't just how many were watching, it was *who* was watching. The audience was young, cosmopolitan, and energetic. *The Cosby Show* might've had many millions more viewers, but people weren't clamoring to hang out on the set when they were filming the latest installment of the Huxtables' mild-mannered adventures. The *ILC* set became a Friday-night destination.

"I remember going to the green room and everybody was there," says David Alan Grier. "Every famous person, all the coolest people wanted to hang out in that green room and in the hallways the first and second year." There was sometimes little rhyme or reason as to who might be there any given week. Some were famous—Bruce Willis, Whoopi Goldberg, Ricki Lake, Q-Tip, Rodney King—though many others were merely chasing fame.

"It was a party every week on that set," says Joe Davola, the VP who helped oversee the show for Fox. "Every agent in Hollywood, every hanger-on was there. There were cats from CAA, a ton of different groups of people." The scene got so ridiculous that it became fodder for a recurring sketch, "The BS Brothers," in which Grier and Tommy Davidson play two slimy showbiz leeches, faking it until they make it. "They took that exactly from what was going on while the show was being filmed every Friday night," says Davola.

During that second season, the cast members felt what it was like to be on a hit show. Dinner reservations were easier to come by. A short trip to the car wash could turn into an hour-long autograph-signing session.

"I remember going to visit Chris Rock at *SNL*," says Grier. "They treated me like a star. They were all over me. That was when I felt like, 'This show is really big.'"

There were career benefits too. Tommy Davidson was cast as the lead in *Strictly Business*, a romantic comedy that co-starred Halle Berry and reunited him on-screen with Kim Coles. Damon landed a starring role in *The Last Boy Scout*, a buddy flick in the *48 Hrs.* mold. "Having run Eddie Murphy's life and creative career," says Rawitt, "when Damon booked *The Last Boy Scout*, I thought, *Okay, Damon's going to be the next Eddie Murphy.*"

Grier scored a major supporting role opposite Murphy in the romantic comedy *Boomerang*, which was directed and produced by the *House Party* team, Reginald and Warrington Hudlin. Cast members also discovered that their newfound fame made them in-demand standups. Even those, like Grier, who weren't really standups. He was a classically trained actor, but once the show was a hit, standup offers started pouring in. "I was like, 'I don't perform in bars, gentlemen,'" he said, with mock haughtiness. "Damon goes, 'I made thirty-eight thousand dollars one weekend.' I'm like, 'Really? Dingleberries! Virginia Beach!'"

Michael Petok, one of the show's producers, says the rising profile had drawbacks. "When there's success, there's egos," he says. "Everyone's a diva."

Miller, with his background at *SNL*, as well as directing episodes of *Not Necessarily the News* and *Fridays*, was considered one of the show's steady hands. As Season 2 wore on, he saw familiar patterns emerge. "Success is a good thing, but it's also a trap," he says. "In the beginning when you're really hungry and trying to prove your point, there's a lot more discipline. As the show is getting to be more popular, there's a tendency to become less disciplined. People are late, people don't want to rehearse. Some of the cast are trying to take off days from rehearsal so they can do a standup gig. I had to deal with *So-and-so isn't going to be here today because they have an audition this morning for a movie.* Well, you have to rehearse. The set has to be built, cameras have to know what they're doing, lighting has to know what they're doing. So even though the show's a hit, you have nice careers that you didn't have two years ago, we still have a job to do. I sometimes found my role was being the taskmaster."

That could be trying. It was always Keenen's show and Keenen's vision, but Keenen wasn't the show's traffic cop. That responsibility fell generally on Miller, along with Rawitt, Petok, and another producer named Kevin Berg. Toward the end of Season 2, Miller felt that Keenen's focus was undergoing a subtle shift.

"First year, he was really hands-on," says Miller. "Second year, a little less so. I remember a couple instances where he wouldn't come in until the afternoon." The lines of communication between Keenen as the showrunner and Miller as the director were beginning to break down. Miller would sometimes be rehearsing sketches Keenen had already cut from the show, or preparing to shoot ones that needed to be heavily rewritten. He recalls one show day when the crew was getting ready to film but little or nothing was ready to be filmed. "Keenen said, 'Why don't you give the crew a break?' We went away for four hours while they rewrote everything. That was one of those nights we were there until four in the morning."

These weren't unusual challenges for a successful show. Egos grow, jealousies fester, friction develops—that's show business. For the most part, even as the spotlight shined brighter on some cast members than on others, the group's core camaraderie remained intact.

Coffield recalls that at some point a well-known standup comic made an appearance in a sketch that simply died in front of the live studio audience. The sketch, which never aired, made some reference to a chicken, and from that point on, "chicken" became the show's shorthand for jokes and sketches that failed, or just any general calamity. "Anytime something was remotely not funny, somebody would say, 'The chicken,' or plop down a chicken sandwich," says Coffield.

This inside joke eventually got a public airing. Grier had pitched an opening number for the show that involved him walking onstage in all black and singing a mock-serious "Tribute to Broadway." Keenen thought it was a terrible idea and told him so, but Grier insisted it would be funny, so Keenen relented. Sort of. He told him he could do it, and even when Grier had second thoughts, he reassured him.

"At the last minute, I tried to back out of it," says Grier. "He called me into his office and goes, 'This is going to be really special.'"

When Grier took the stage, the spotlight pulled close in on him and he began singing, a cappella. A few lines into it, a stage door opened behind him, and out walked a live chicken. Then another. And another. And another. The audience started laughing.

"He didn't see them," says Coffield of the chickens. "The audience was like, *What the hell?* They don't know this is a private joke." Eventually Shawn and Keenen collapsed onto the stage laughing at Grier, who finally noticed the live poultry around him.

"It was a setup," says Grier. "At the end, I walk offstage, and Carrie Ann Inaba goes, 'David, I really liked it,' which is like your fat aunt telling you you're handsome. It stunk." Amazingly, the sketch aired. "I don't know that America got the joke, but we got it."

Keenen seemed to revel in taking shots at his friends and rivals on the show. Over the course of his time in charge, the show jabbed, among others, Robert Townsend, Marsha Warfield, Byron Allen, Chris Rock, Oprah Winfrey, Sinbad, and the Hudlins. But the two contemporaries he mocked the most (and the most gleefully) were Spike Lee and Arsenio Hall.

Keenen and Lee knew each other and worked with many of the same actors, choreographers, casting directors, and crew members, but weren't necessarily friends. They were both picking apart black culture and poking at the question of what it means to be black in America, but doing so from different perspectives and probably for different reasons. For Lee, the drama, the story, and the sociopolitical message were the point. Laughs were welcome but incidental. For Keenen, the inverse was true. But it's easy to imagine each of them looking at the other's career and seeing a path not taken for themselves. It may not have risen to the level of actual envy—though Lee no doubt would've liked to have had Keenen's commercial success, and Keenen would've appreciated Lee's critical plaudits—but these were two New Yorkers planting and plowing in the same fields, just harvesting different crops.

"Spike's Joint," which surfaced three episodes into the second season, was conceived and written by Steve Tompkins, but endorsed by Keenen. Tommy Davidson does a note-perfect impression of Lee, who in the sketch is running a tchotchke shop in Brooklyn, selling cheesy merchandise he's lent his imprimatur to: the Mo' Better Butter Dispenser; Malcolm X-Lax; his Nike-imitation sneakers, Spikes; and the *School Daze* DVDs he can't even give away for free. The implication is that Lee is merely a huckster, packaging and branding revolution, turning it into a cheap commodity to sell to (mostly white) people. It pokes holes in Lee's

blacker-than-thou persona and dares suggest he's a sellout. Lee had recently criticized Eddie Murphy for not using his clout to get more black
performers and executives hired, so turnabout was, in this case, apparently fair play. As Tompkins puts it, "I definitely tried to do something a
little bit edgier when we took on Spike."

Spike didn't appreciate it one bit. When he ran into Keenen after the
sketch aired, he confronted him. "He came up to me at a party and was
chastising me for making fun of him," says Keenen. "I just let him know
everybody gets it. 'You're not special. When you do your thing, nobody dictates to you. When I do my thing, same here. I love you but you gonna get it.'"

In an interview with *Playboy* several months later, Lee explained the
root of his beef was that Keenen's writing staff was mostly white. "They
had thirteen writers and only three or four were black," said Lee. "The
rest were all these Jewish kids that went to Harvard. I just asked Keenen,
'What's up?' He explained to me all he's done for black people as far as
the show is concerned. I'm not going to dispute that. But if you have some
white kid from Harvard joking about Malcolm X-Lax—I don't think that
shit is funny. I don't think they'd allow a black person to make a joke
about [then Israeli prime minister] Golda Meir."

Tompkins took the dustup in stride. "He didn't think it was fair for
some white Jew from Harvard to write the sketch," he says. "Well, I'm not
Jewish." He laughs. "Obviously, I patently reject that notion. Anyone can
write about anything, black or white. You're telling me Shakespeare can't
write Othello?" He laughs again. "I'm not comparing myself to Shakespeare. It was Spike being Spike."

Davidson recalls getting a chilly reception from Lee when he ran into
him clothes shopping back in the nineties. "We were in a store in Brooklyn and he happened to be walking out," says Davidson. "I was so excited to meet him and said, 'Hey, I'm Tommy Davidson.' He's like, 'Yeah, I
know.'" Lee then reiterated the criticism he'd aired in *Playboy*. "He's like,
'Those white writers wouldn't let us talk about their leaders that way,'
and walked away." The two eventually patched up their differences. In
fact, Davidson—and Damon Wayans—ended up starring in Lee's 2000
film *Bamboozled*, which, incidentally, explored many of these same issues around race and identity.

But at the time the tension between Lee and the show was real.

Tompkins felt Keenen took the entire fracas to heart, and afterward was far less willing to "take potshots against other people like him who had made it." Keenen denies he ever went easy on anyone, and to be fair, Lee is targeted, albeit somewhat more indirectly, in another sketch in Season 3. But regardless of the accuracy of Tompkins's assessment, even he admits there was one major exception to this emerging rule: "Arsenio was the only guy Keenen seemed to relish going after."

Keenen and Arsenio had a complicated relationship. As Keenen himself says, "When both of us first came to L.A., we were best friends." But time and competition twisted that friendship some. Although both have steadfastly denied they were jockeying for pole position behind Eddie Murphy, to be his heir apparent, many who knew them back then say this was almost certainly the case, even if only subconsciously.

The two just seemed to be on a collision course. The fact that *The Arsenio Hall Show* tapped into the same cultural vein as *In Living Color* made Keenen and Arsenio natural rivals. With Kim Coles's dismissal, there was the suggestion Arsenio may have been trying to poach her from *ILC*. And Keenen's efforts to branch out with a potential Fly Girls television show was putting him into direct competition with Arsenio, who was in the process of producing a similar show with singer/actress Nia Peeples, called *The Party Machine*. All this added up to what one person close to the situation at the time referred to as a "virulent, competitive, tortured relationship" between Keenen and Arsenio. In an interview in late 1990, Keenen said there was no specific incident that caused the rift, but said, "Some friendships, you kind of outgrow." In another interview from around that time, Keenen called Arsenio "a parody of himself." He also felt Arsenio had taken jabs at him on his talk show.

Keenen's impression of Arsenio across four separate *ILC* sketches was withering and personal. He portrays Arsenio as a long-fingered, big-butted, empty-headed suck-up whose only interests are celebrity and his relationship with his "best friend" Eddie Murphy. A Season 2 sketch casts Keenen's Arsenio as a prosecuting attorney who even when questioning an accused felon on the witness stand still misses the point: "Now, your picture is up all over the post office. You're on the FBI's Top 10 list two years in a row. What the court would like to know is . . . has celebrity life changed you?"

All in all, it was an impression built on an almost intimate familiarity with its subject. Keenen understood Arsenio's soft spots and attacked them. He knew Arsenio was sensitive about his ample posterior. "That's something he hates," Keenen said around the time. "He tries to hide it with those long jackets." Unlike with other celebrities, who were usually parodied once and then left alone on the show, *ILC* was relentless with Arsenio. As Keenen put it back then, "Each time I do him, I try to do a different hit on him."

Arsenio was, according to multiple reports, not amused. In the *New York Times* in August 1990, Arsenio called Keenen's impression a "vendetta" against him. Two months later, *New York* magazine reported that he'd banned Keenen from his talk show. By December of that same year though, tensions had apparently cooled and Arsenio was claiming publicly that he wasn't offended at all.

Now, many years removed, it all seems largely like water under the bridge. Keenen says that through it all, he and Arsenio "remained friends. We definitely had our ups and downs. There would be potshots taken on his show, and it was like, 'Okay, you wanna play?' It's more of a friendly rivalry than animosity. It was just about who's gonna get the funniest laugh at the other person's expense." It's apparently a rivalry Keenen has not completely left behind. "I think I won."

In the final episode of the season, two of the show's most popular franchises ended on cliffhangers. Homey the Clown takes one million dollars from "The Man" to become the spokesperson for "Homey Wheats," a sugarcoated kids' cereal. He allows himself to be played for a fool in order to rake in the dough, and dine with his new Brooks Brothers–clad white partners at the restaurant that was previously a symbol of all he stood against, Chez Whitey. The sketch ends with Tommy Davidson, as one of Homey's fans, accusing Homey of selling out. "To Be Continued" flashes across the bottom of the screen.

The sketch is something of a crude metaphor for what was happening around *ILC*. The series was an unqualified success. Fox was riding high. They'd expanded their schedule to five nights a week and had turned a fifty-million-dollar profit in 1990. This, only a year after losing almost one hundred million dollars and nearly packing it in. Suddenly, at the show, there was pressure to repeat certain characters as much as possible. *The audience loves them! Let's give the fans what they want!* Conversations began about merchandising, about *building the brand*.

The sketch that followed Homey was "Men on Television." Damon's Blaine Edwards and Grier's Antoine Merriweather were among the show's most popular characters, but also among the most criticized, and not without some justification. Their flamboyant wardrobes and effeminate manner indulged persistent gay stereotypes, and some gay rights organizations complained. Keenen always maintained the sketches were never gay-bashing.

"We were having fun with gay culture because we put them in the power seat," he says. "Those characters were calling everyone out. They'd take a very straight situation and make everybody gay."

Despite the criticisms, the characters were a hit among actual gay men. "To this day," says Damon, "I get 'two snaps up' if I go in an area where there are gay people." The sketches were so popular that they were played on loops in gay bars around Los Angeles. "At this place called Revolver on Santa Monica Boulevard, they'd have 'Men On' night," says Damon. "Sunday nights, they'd all dress up as the 'Men On' guys."

As Grier saw it, there was a disconnect between older, more conservative members of the gay community, who often headed gay rights organizations, and younger gay people, who were happy to see a version of themselves, even a wildly exaggerated one, on television. "Those characters," says Grier, "the real key was they were comfortable with who they were. There was no hatred or anything like that about the writing or from our point of view. But the weird thing is, today, you couldn't do that."

Keenen agrees. In today's culture—where gay marriage is the law of the land, gays can serve openly in the military, and living life as a gay man or woman has been normalized to a degree almost unimaginable in the early nineties—the sketch likely wouldn't fly. And with more than twenty-five years of hindsight, Blaine and Antoine sometimes seem like relics from another era.

The final "Men On" sketch of the season begins routinely enough with Blaine and Antoine making jokes about several network shows including

The Fresh Prince of Bel-Air, *The Golden Girls*, and *Perfect Strangers*. At one point, Damon is laughing and quite obviously struggling not to break character, which was somewhat unusual for the show since any on-screen fumbles could simply be re-shot, but less so for the "Men On" sketches.

"We'd never tell each other what we were going to do," says Damon. "In rehearsal we'd rehearse it one way, but I knew David had stuff in his hip pocket and he knew I'd have stuff in my hip pocket. When it was time to shoot, we'd start trying to surprise each other and make each other laugh."

Grier makes a quick inside joke—"I just thought I heard a chicken!"—but Damon pulls it together. A few moments later Blaine is knocked out cold when a piece of falling equipment conks him on the head. When he comes to, he's lost his campy affectations. It's as if he's had the gay knocked right out of him. He wonders aloud why he's wearing these ridiculous clothes and angrily brushes Antoine's hand off his shoulder. Antoine is so distraught that he faints. The bottom of the screen tells viewers that this sketch is also "To Be Continued."

The characters' continued existence seemed to hang in the balance. No doubt, with the controversy they courted, retiring Blaine and Antoine would've been the path of least resistance. As the entire cast and crew filled the stage, fruity island drinks in hand, to wave goodbye to the audience and end the season, the show itself was at a high point, but also a moment of transition. Those cliffhangers seemed to be as much about the direction of *ILC*'s future as they were about the fate of its signature characters. Resolving Homey's and Blaine and Antoine's conflicts would be simple enough, but answering the deeper questions about the show's heart and soul was going to take time.

21

"If You Don't Bring Your A Game, Other People Are Happy to Do It"

Jamie Foxx was late. Five comics were slated to perform at the Laugh Factory as a final showcase for *In Living Color*, and he was supposed to be the first. The show wanted new cast members, and Foxx, who'd been performing at the Comedy Act Theater since moving out from Texas and already knew the Wayans siblings, looked promising.

"Jamie was a singer who did comedy just to get onstage so he could sing," says Keenen. "I watched him from the very beginning and always thought he was funny."

But Foxx was blowing the audition. It was time for him to go on, and nobody knew where he was. The showcase started without him. When he finally arrived, he found Tamara Rawitt. She was frantic.

"You're late! What are you doing? You're supposed to be here early! You were supposed to be first!"

"Oh, damn," Foxx replied. "Can I just go up last?"

"Yes, you have to! We've already started!"

Foxx didn't oversleep. He wasn't stuck in traffic. He knew what he was doing. He felt he'd flubbed the improvs at an earlier audition—"I just wasn't catching the right shit," he said—and wanted to ensure the standup portion went right. Which for him meant performing last.

Still, once he arrived and surveyed the crowd, he got nervous. He was an experienced standup but mostly played black clubs. This audience was mostly white people. He started thinking about tinkering with his act. He consulted Shawn and Marlon Wayans, who convinced him to "just do it like you do in the hood."

Onstage, Foxx swaggered and charmed. In one bit, he played Wanda, a bold, aggressive, hypersexual woman who seems to be the only one who doesn't realize she's ugly as sin. The bit had been born from some onstage ad-libbing.

"I said, 'All the good-looking ladies, clap your hands,'" Foxx recalled, "and then, 'Now, all the ugly ladies, let me hear you make some noise.' And it was quiet. All the ugly ladies was like, 'Hey, he ain't talking about me.' I said, 'Ain't that a bitch?'"

Keenen had invited the entire writing staff to the Laugh Factory for the auditions. Most were floored by Foxx. He did impressions, characters, standup—he could even sing. Fax Bahr recalls Keenen asking the writers afterward whether they thought Foxx was worth hiring. "We were all like, 'Oh my god, yeah. He's insane. He's so good.'"

The whole idea of adding new cast members was in many ways a function of the show's success. New players could pick up the slack as the existing cast took advantage of their new film and standup gigs, and ward off complacency.

"A lot of the people brought in were brought in to make the original cast work harder," says Les Firestein. "The idea was *There are people waiting in the wings. If you don't bring your A game, other people are happy to do it.*"

Rawitt: "You needed new characters at the table, new things for the writers to write for. You have to replenish the well, otherwise it runs dry."

This round of casting was even more competitive than the first time. Among the also-rans were Margaret Cho and Ellen Cleghorne, who'd already appeared in bit parts on *ILC* and was soon cast on *SNL*. One of the final five at the Laugh Factory was a Korean-American actor named Steve Park, recognizable from his memorable role as the grocery store owner in *Do the Right Thing*. He considered a spot on *ILC* a "dream job," but wasn't a standup and was concerned about auditioning.

"I remember coming in with a boom box," he says. "I did this thing making fun of Asian stereotypes, this whole Bruce Lee bit. I was doing bad lip-syncing so I had dialogue coming out of the boom box."

Bringing in Park would broaden the palette of ethnicities that the show could parody. The shooting death of teenager Latasha Harlins by a Korean grocery store owner in March 1991, less than two weeks after the Rodney King beating, highlighted the growing tensions between the African-American and Korean-American communities—something Lee had captured in *Do the Right Thing*. And wherever there was tension, there was infinite potential to cut that tension with humor. "The instinct was right to hire Steve," says Firestein.

The final addition to the cast was the least surprising but most controversial. Keenen had been grooming his brother Shawn for a spot in the cast since the show's beginnings. Keenen plugged Shawn into a few sketches in Season 2, mostly as a supporting player, and encouraged both Shawn and Marlon to develop their writing skills.

"They knew that when they were ready, I was going to guide them along," says Keenen. "Marlon and Shawn used to sit in a room with John Bowman and just write, in preparation for the day they got their shot."

Shawn felt like he'd paid his dues. He'd been doing standup since he was sixteen. He'd been the show's DJ, he'd worked as a production assistant, he'd been a writer trainee.

"I never wanted to rush into it," he says. "I'd learn how to write sketches and what the whole creative process was about." His best training, though, was mostly just hanging around his siblings. "I was around Damon, sitting in his dressing room while he wrote. Sometimes I'd be a sounding board."

Fairly or not, there were plenty at the show who felt that Shawn's ascension, preordained though it may have been, was a case of Keenen putting what was best for his family ahead of what was best for the show.

"Keenen's primary motive was to get his family into the limelight," says Tommy Davidson. "That doesn't make him a bad person and that doesn't make it a bad idea. Unless you're me."

Davidson had struggled from the beginning to score with breakout characters and recurring sketches. The competition for screen time often left him playing second banana roles. Now, not only was there more competition, but one of those he'd be competing with was another sibling of the guy making all the decisions. "You have a group of people that have been together for three years, [thinking] if they work their ass off, then eventually they're going to succeed on this show. Every year, you're going back trying to get your sketches on. Then they bring in somebody new and you go, 'Well, *fuck.'*" Davidson admired the love and commitment the Wayans siblings had for each other, but he'd been busting his ass and believed he "had a lot more talent than the majority of the family members." None of that seemed to matter. "That's called nepotism."

Keenen doesn't buy this criticism: "If you look at the show, everybody gets off. It doesn't become *The Wayans Show*. The truth was I was utilizing the ones who worked hardest, who came up with ideas."

In between managing the delicate egos of his cast and running the show, Keenen was also trying to build his own career. He'd never made a secret of his desire to make movies and, between Seasons 2 and 3, figured he had a chance to get back to it. He carved out time to go to London, to work on the film he'd written and which he was set to produce, direct, and star in, *Lloyd of London*. He was to play a D.C. cop in England working with a British detective on solving a series of murders and robberies. Aleta Chappelle, Fox's head of casting, helped cast the film, bringing in British comedian Lenny Henry to star opposite Keenen. The project had problems though. Universal wasn't willing to cough up the kind of budget to make *Lloyd of London* into an effects-heavy, high-gloss action flick in the mold of *Lethal Weapon* or, incidentally, *The Last Boy Scout*. And there were rumors Keenen's script needed considerable work. Faced with these issues and a tight schedule that exacerbated all of them, it fell apart.

"It shut down right before rehearsals were going to start," says Chappelle. "They just never could do it for the budget it was supposed to be. It shut down on a Friday and rehearsals were supposed to start Monday. I've never been on a project like that."

For Keenen, it was a lesson in obligations and priorities, and not necessarily a happy one. "I had to walk away from the movie because I had to go back to the show," he says. "Universal was very upset. We were in pre-production but too much time had gone by in the prep and decision-making. If the movie had gone over even a couple of days, I'd have been in conflict at the show, so I had to let it go. But it was a project I was really into and so was Universal. Those were the sacrifices you had to make."

As he returned to *ILC*, the show needed some freshening up. The first season had really only been half a season, thirteen episodes spread across a few months, but Season 2 had been twice as many episodes and twice as long. The cast, crew, and writers were fried.

"We had to re-staff every season because the grind was staggering," says Tamara Rawitt. "You were like in the witness relocation program when you came to work on the show. You'd stay there sixteen hours a day, four months at a time, and didn't have time to go to movies or watch TV. We had to drain people's brains to get all that stuff on the air every week."

Paul Miller had been directing the show since the pilot and was an experienced, steady hand. But by the end of the second season, he says, he and Keenen had "drifted apart." He felt Keenen wanted to "step back from the day-to-day operations of the show," in order to take advantage of other opportunities. Keenen had production deals and a movie career to nurture. "I think he was looking for me to step in and fill that void," Miller says. Instead, Miller left. Morris Abraham, a veteran director of talk shows, took over for a short spell before passing the mantle to Terri McCoy, who'd been Miller's associate director since the pilot.

The show lost both head writers after Season 2—John Bowman began working with comedian Martin Lawrence on creating the sitcom *Martin*, and Buddy Sheffield left to start his own show, a kids' variety series called *Roundhouse*—although Sheffield continued to contribute on a freelance basis. J.J. Paulsen left with Sheffield to work on *Roundhouse*. Paul Mooney had floated out of the show's orbit during Season 2—much later, he'd float back in—and Kim Bass's contract wasn't renewed. The writers brought in to replace them were a mixed bag. Michelle Jones was a young black woman who'd been answering phones at the *Hollywood Reporter* when she was hired. Harry Dunn had been writing, producing, and editing movie trailers. Fred Graver was a buttoned-up ex–*National Lampoon* editor who'd spent six years writing for David Letterman. Larry Wilmore was a former standup whose only previous writing experience was penning jokes for Rick Dees's television talk show, *Into the Night*. Wilmore was excited to even get a meeting with Keenen.

"It was a big break for me," he says. "We talked about our standup war stories and I spent my time just trying to make him laugh. We hit it off."

Rawitt also hired a charismatic Los Angeleno named Michael Anthony Snowden to be a writer's trainee. Snowden, a skinny twenty-one-year-old who wore glasses and looked a bit like Spike Lee, had never really written anything. He'd originally been discovered at a local hip-hop club and was asked to audition for the Fly Girls' TV spinoff as a dancer. He convinced the producers to let him submit sketch ideas instead.

"He wasn't a traditional writer at all," says Rawitt. "He was a hip-hop dancer, but the kid had wattage and street cred for days. He was wickedly funny. I brought him to Keenen and said, 'This is a guy who's going to make the room rock.'"

Snowden had a baby daughter at the time, and no one to watch her while he was at work, so he frequently brought her into the office. "She'd crawl around and all the girls in the office always watched her," he says. "She actually learned to walk at *In Living Color*. That's where she took her first step."

Snowden was learning too. Just before his first pitch meeting, some veteran writers told him that as a trainee, he was only supposed to listen, not actually pitch ideas, so Snowden came into the room, sat at the opposite end of the table from Keenen, and kept quiet. Each writer took his or her turn to pitch five ideas. Then Keenen turned to Snowden.

"What do you have?"

Snowden looked puzzled. "What do you mean?"

"Where are your pitches at?"

It was at this moment Snowden looked around the room and noticed the other writers stifling their laughs. Rather than admit he'd been the victim of a practical joke, Snowden stalled for time.

"Can you hold on? I'll go get them."

"Hurry up," Keenen said. "Don't make me regret hiring you."

Snowden ran back into his office, jumped over his baby daughter playing on the floor, grabbed the newspaper, scanned it, and quickly improvised five ideas. One was good enough to make it into the "packet" that week.

"I guess Keenen was impressed by the way I did that," he says.

It was the first time Snowden set himself apart from most of the show's writers in Keenen's eyes. It wouldn't be the last.

22

"All I Remember Is the Layer of Desperation That Hung in the Air"

Spike Lee grew up in Brooklyn and particularly early in his career, the borough was his muse. The Brooklyn that Lee sketched in *Do the Right Thing*, *Mo' Better Blues*, and *Jungle Fever*—which were released in the summers of 1989, 1990, and 1991, respectively—was one where racial strife both threatened and reinforced community bonds. Straying across the wrong intersection into a different neighborhood filled with different people and different cultural norms carried with it the implicit potential for violence. In August of 1989, almost exactly one month after the release of *Do the Right Thing*, Yusef Hawkins was shot to death in the predominantly Italian-American neighborhood of Bensonhurst. He and three friends had come to the neighborhood to answer a used car ad. There, they were set upon by a white mob.

Seventeen months later, the Reverend Al Sharpton was preparing to lead a protest march through Bensonhurst alongside Hawkins's parents, when an Italian-American man thrust a steak knife into his chest. Sharpton had been leading similar marches through Bensonhurst since Hawkins's death, calling for justice and, in the views of his critics, fomenting discord and further violence. As the trials of Hawkins's assailants progressed, Sharpton had warned that without guilty verdicts on murder charges, the jury "would be lighting a match to the end of a powder keg and telling us to burn the town down." "The clouds of violence," he said, "are over New York City."

Sharpton's agitating had helped topple mayor Ed Koch, who was defeated in a primary by the man who became the city's first black mayor, David Dinkins. Now it had gotten Sharpton himself stabbed. The wound was serious but not life-threatening, and after Sharpton was taken to a nearby hospital, Dinkins appealed for calm, promising that Sharpton echoed those sentiments. But one of Sharpton's associates, Alton Maddox, contradicted Dinkins immediately.

"The only person speaking for Reverend Sharpton is Alton Maddox and I'm not calling for calm," he said. Maddox called for more protests and promised to meet violence with violence.

Seven months later and five miles farther north, in Crown Heights, a car in a motorcade for Rabbi Menachem Mendel Schneerson, leader of a Chabad-Lubavitch sect of Hasidic Jews, was involved in an accident. The car collided with another car, then struck two black children on the sidewalk. One of the children, seven-year-old Gavin Cato, died shortly after. The incident, and the immediate aftermath, during which a Hasidic ambulance service removed the driver from the scene before Cato was extricated from the wreck by city ambulance crews, exacerbated existing tensions between the Jewish and black communities in Crown Heights and beyond. At Cato's funeral, Sharpton called the neighborhood's Jews "diamond dealers" and railed against the existence of an "apartheid ambulance service." A banner on display at the funeral read, "Hitler did not do the job." Three days of rioting and violence, mostly directed at the local Jewish community, led to one murder, nearly 200 injuries, 129 arrests, and close to $1 million in property damage.

Les Firestein grew up in New York, but was in Los Angeles getting ready for Season 3 when the Crown Heights riots kicked off in August. Firestein had been promoted to co-head writer, along with Pam Veasey and Greg Fields, for the new season. As a New York Jew, Firestein figured it was on him to wrench humor from the horrible events in Crown Heights. "Crown Heights Story," a send-up of "West Side Story," appears in the first episode of the third season, and features Jim Carrey as a Hasid named Menachem who falls in love with Kim Wayans. It unabashedly indulges Jewish stereotypes—"They bring knives, we bring lawyers," Carrey tells his gang, pre-rumble; "They bring guns, we bring more lawyers"—which, of course, was the point. The show's "unwritten rule," Firestein explains, was any writer had complete freedom to offend his own people. After the sketch aired, he got a letter from Stephen Sondheim, who wrote the lyrics for *West Side Story*. "One of my favorite mementos is a letter from Sondheim saying he really enjoyed the piece and thought it was better than his rendition," says Firestein.

In the season's next episode, another Firestein-penned sketch, "Jews on First," kicked at the racial tensions in New York and the rest of the country from another angle. Imagined as an excerpt from *The Al Sharpton and Lou Farrakhan Comedy Hour*, it's a spoof of Abbott and Costello's legendary "Who's on First?" routine, with Damon's Farrakhan and David Alan Grier's Sharpton filling the baseball team's ranks with names drawn from their stock-in-trade list of enemies and denunciations. "Jews on first, The Man at second, Mr. Charlie at shortstop, and It's a Conspiracy at third," as Farrakhan puts it to Sharpton in the sketch.

Sharpton, then a three-hundred-plus-pound man of the cloth who favored shiny track suits, gold medallions, and long, pressed hair in the style of his hero and former employer James Brown, was almost too ridiculous a figure to parody, and Grier wisely plays him mostly straight. The joke here is that for black leaders like Sharpton and Farrakhan, their catchphrase rebukes had become so numerous and interchangeable they'd been rendered meaningless and unintelligible.

"It was my favorite sketch I ever did on the show," says Firestein. "I have to give it up to those guys, especially Damon and Keenen. Keenen isn't in the sketch, but essentially Keenen is in every sketch. His kosher stamp of approval is all over the show. What was cool about those guys is that they'd mock the heroes of their community, which is a real threading of the needle. They realized conspiracy theory is a big part of the culture that they wanted to make fun of, and they wanted to make fun of it because having the ability to make fun of yourselves as a culture is a show of great strength. One of the things that was seminal about *In Living Color* was that black people enjoyed laughing at black people. That was the seismic change. You had an entire culture getting to the point where they said we're strong enough that we can laugh at the more ridiculous parts of our own culture."

The first two episodes of Season 3 also resolved the two cliffhangers that had ended the previous season. Homey the Clown's was the more satisfying of the two resolutions. Sitting at Chez Whitey, he proves his establishment bona fides by denouncing Farrakhan and telling his white hosts that "Rodney King was way out of line." He's then granted an audience with "The Man." But when "Whitey himself," as Homey calls him, asks Homey to kiss his ring, Homey smacks him on the head with his trademark sock, and tells him, "Homey's never played that." It had all been a setup: Homey just wanted to get close enough to The Man to bop him.

"That Homey sketch was really about how they buy your soul," says Keenen. If taken as a metaphor for *ILC*'s long-running battle with the establishment, it could be seen as a heartening promise to keep fighting the good fight, but on reflection, somehow it feels more like an endorsement of the show's status quo.

For "Men On," the denouement is less imaginative: Damon begins playing Blaine as the seemingly straight man he became at the end of Season 2, much to the horror of David Alan Grier's Antoine. But through repeated blows to the head, Antoine eventually succeeds in turning Blaine back into the effeminate gay man he used to be. It's certainly possible to read both sketches as a renewal of the show's commitment to controversial, uncomfortable comedy, except that the comedy here no longer feels controversial or uncomfortable. *ILC* deserves credit for helping to make that so, but ultimately, both sketches feel like a minimization of risk. If the show was in a transitional moment, the significant decision made here was following the less-than-inspirational mantra of "If it ain't broke, don't fix it."

Michael Anthony Snowden compared his introduction to *In Living Color* to the moment "Charlie Sheen first got out of the helicopter in *Platoon*. It was like being dropped off in Vietnam," he says.

On one level, things looked good for Snowden. Initially, he was just a writer trainee but Keenen clearly liked him. When Shawn Wayans was struggling to find his place in the cast, Snowden stepped up. "Me and Shawn started writing together because nobody would write for Shawn," says Snowden. "[The writers] could be mean sometimes, but with a reason. They felt Shawn was just there because of Keenen, due to nepotism. They had it in for Shawn but so unfairly. Shawn was really funny."

The first product of their collaboration was a parody of LL Cool J's hit "Mama Said Knock You Out." It was funny, if not exactly revelatory, but Keenen was pleased, and as the season progressed, it wasn't unusual to find Snowden tossing a football in the parking lot with Keenen and his brothers, or huddled with Keenen in his office, or even hanging out with him late-night at a club. He was quickly promoted from trainee to a full staff writer.

But Snowden soon discovered that ingratiating himself with Keenen didn't make him popular with the other writers. "I'd go out with Keenen and we had these extremely late nights, like four in the morning," he says. "Then I'd come back to the office and all the writers would still be there. They'd look at me, shaking their heads and I knew I fucked up."

The writers' room became more cutthroat in Season 3. There was intense pressure not just to produce good sketches but to defend those sketches, defend your jokes, defend your life.

"It was every writers' room I've ever been in but probably more so," says Fred Graver, who'd worked at *Late Night with David Letterman* and would later write for *Cheers* and *The Jon Stewart Show*. "It was very competitive. It could be very mean. One of the things that made the job really hard was we were in this office building and none of the windows opened. We were all there like twenty hours a day and the air was stifling. Maybe I was more sensitive to it than other people but it drove me nuts. I look back on those writers' meetings, and all I remember is the layer of desperation that hung in the air in this windowless office where people were spending eighteen to twenty hours a day trying to make each other laugh."

The grind of churning out material got more dramatic as Fox wanted more and more episodes each season. There could only be so many Fire Marshal Bill, Benita Butrell, and Homey the Clown sketches. The show needed fresh material all the time. The constant need for more pitches loomed over the writers like a dark cloud, morning, noon, and night. "The pressure of knowing you had to pitch every Monday would mean that even if you were home for the weekend, maybe you'd let yourself have Saturday as a little mental break," says Becky Hartman, "and then all day Sunday, you'd run to the newspaper stand and get every newspaper, every magazine, try to see movies. It felt like when you weren't at work, you never got that mental break you needed to recharge."

The long hours exacted a toll, and the subsequent physical exhaustion wasn't the only thing that often resulted in diminishing returns for the writers.

"It was not unusual for you to be there until well into the morning on weeknights, writing and rewriting, trying to get stuff on the air," says Larry Wilmore. "Once, Keenen was a little frustrated with some of our stuff, which wasn't unusual, and he was like, 'You guys need to pull more from your life. You need to get out.' I'm like, *Get out? This is our life! What are we going to pull from? Being here all the time is our life!*"

The very act of pitching had become a harrowing death waltz. Keenen would sit at the head of the table, eating his dinner, while, one by one, writers labored to make him laugh. "The pitch room atmosphere was hostile," says Firestein, "I'm going to say intentionally so."

Fax Bahr, who'd proven himself an important contributor during Season 2, says the show's routine grew more untenable in Season 3: "You'd hear at two that there was a pitch meeting at six. Then you'd wait until seven before Keenen would come in. We were all hungry and Keenen would have a full-blown dinner. He'd sit at the end of the table, eating, and we're just salivating. He was focused on his dinner and if he'd like something he'd go, 'Yeah, write that one.' If he didn't he'd be like, 'Next.'"

Time was a relative concept at the show. Nothing ever seemed to be running on schedule. "Meetings started late because Keenen did everything," says Graver. "He was in the edit rooms, in casting, in with the writers, in with the Fox executives, in everything. One day, he called a meeting for two in the afternoon and I knew this meeting wasn't going to start until four or five. So I bet a bunch of the writers I could go to the Beverly Hot Springs, get a massage, a hot spring, and a steam and be back in time while everybody else is sitting in these windowless offices, fuming. Sure enough, I got a massage, I soaked, I came back fantastically refreshed while everybody else is just walking into the meeting."

Because Keenen was juggling multiple tasks and projects, it could be hard to get his attention. By Season 3, he was around a lot less and, according to some I spoke to, not having much fun when he was there. It often seemed that he needed to be, or simply *wanted* to be, someplace else. Firestein recalls arriving at work five minutes late one day and being unable to find anyone. After walking around the office for a spell, he finally wandered into the gym that Keenen had had installed for himself. "Keenen was doing squats and the staff was pitching," says Firestein. "That's where the pitch meeting was taking place that day." Bahr says it was like "an acid trip. Keenen was benching some ungodly amount of weight while we sat around and pitched ideas to him."

At least a few times, writers pitched to Keenen via speakerphone. Even under the best of circumstances, Keenen seemed to make the pitching process as uncomfortable for the writers as possible.

"There was nothing more gratifying than making him laugh and nothing more terrifying than pitching a really crappy idea that he and the rest of the writers go to town on," says Hartman.

And Keenen was grudging with his laughs. Even his brother Marlon knew what it felt like to long to hear his big brother crack up. "Keenen always goes, 'Oh, that's funny,'" says Marlon. "It's rare he laughs."

For Keenen, not laughing in pitch meetings wasn't about being a curmudgeon. There was strategy behind it. "There's a psychology of laughter," he says. "Laughter in groups always works better. The writers would laugh at each other's sketches whether they were funny or not. I wouldn't laugh so I could hear what was really funny or not. I know the tricks. I wouldn't let them get away with their tricks. I'd just sit, I'd listen, and if it was funny, I'd say, 'That's funny.' Unless it was hysterical, then I'd laugh."

Writers had a short window to prove their worth and then had to prove it again and again. "Keenen didn't suffer fools," says Firestein. "If someone came on board and you could tell they didn't have it or weren't going to get it in time, I don't think Keenen had a great deal of sympathy. It was sink or swim. There wasn't a lot of hand-holding."

For someone like Michelle Jones, who'd come from a receptionist job at the *Hollywood Reporter*, there was no time to learn the ropes.

"Keenen didn't have a problem telling you if he thought something wasn't funny," says Jones. "To his credit, he wouldn't just say, 'This sucks.' He'd say, 'This is wrong because of this, this, and this.' He had it in his head what would make it right."

The stakes were clear. "If you didn't do your job, a lot of people got fired," says Wilmore. "So you felt like you could be fired anytime. I felt that every single day."

Keenen's own characterizations of the environment at the show and his attitude as its leader more or less conform to this portrait. The pressure he put on the writers was the same pressure he felt. "Once you set a standard, you can't go backwards," he says. Pitches had to be good. They had to be creative. Sometimes they weren't. "I knew when people had been fucking off on the weekend. You come in Monday with bullshit, it was like, *Okay, we will shut this down and get back together at four and you guys better have some sketches.* There were days like that."

It was a hard job because putting together a show like this *was* hard. There were no shortcuts. "I remember one night we were taping and the writers had gone home," says Keenen. "They thought, *Our job is done.* I had everybody called and brought back to work. As long as I'm here, you're here, because we'd continue to write while we were shooting. If something wasn't working, we had to fix it right there. Even if you didn't have a sketch in the show, you had to be there."

Pitching was tough, he says, not just because of him, but because of the writers themselves. "The writers were brutal to each other," he says. "They would break up laughing in the middle of your pitch because it was that bad. If you were bombing, there was no mercy. The writers' room was far more cutthroat than the performers. The guys especially were tough on the women. There was a lot of—I don't want to say harassment—but kind of like hazing."

It wasn't as if these elements hadn't been part of earlier seasons, but with the show now a hit, the pressure was cranked up. Unquestionably, as the show's leader, Keenen deserved a significant portion of the responsibility for the atmosphere, but he wasn't the only one. Under Sheffield and Bowman, the writers' room had been run with a gentler hand. Their replacements, Firestein, Fields, and Veasey, were tagged as equals, but it was Firestein—who relished the blood-sport aspects of comedy—who set the tone.

"Me and Les started doing a Wall of Shame," says Snowden. "Everything that was pitched that was really bad, we'd put it on the wall. Every time a sketch would bomb Les would pin it on the wall." When people got fired, their photos went on the wall too.

"It started as bad sketches but then it just became the Wall of Shame generally," says Firestein.

Some writers adapted to the comedy killing fields better than others. Michelle Jones and Harry Dunn shared an office and both struggled. "Most days, I went to work afraid," says Jones. "Afraid I'd lose my job, afraid I wasn't funny enough, just always scared. It's hard to be funny when you're scared." She knew her job was to please Keenen but wasn't sure how to do it, and no one was going to tell her. "It felt like high school," she says. "There are the *ins* and there are the *outs*." She was an *out*.

Dunn was even further *out*. He and his wife had just had a baby, and as with Jones, *ILC* was his first TV job. "I came in with a Pollyanna attitude because it was like, 'Oh my god, I got this great job. I just had a baby,'" says Dunn. "It was a good start for the year. I didn't know what I was walking into. I didn't know how to survive in a room like that." Television writing staffs, he says, are like *Lord of the Flies*. "They try to figure out where the weak link is and then target them."

He was the weak link. He wasn't contributing much each week. Most of his original ideas never made it to air. Desperation set in. He came to dread pitch meetings as regularly scheduled public humiliations. Firestein recalls seeing Dunn actually faint during one of his pitches, though Dunn insists it wasn't that bad. "After weeks and weeks of failed pitches, an idea started to get traction," he says. "For some reason, in the middle of it, I just froze. No fainting, I just froze."

Jones says her office with Dunn "was kind of dubbed the loser office." She accepted that she didn't fit at *ILC*, but Dunn fought hard to gain a foothold. The other writers, she says, "bagged on him behind his back. Harry was *out* like me but worked really hard to get *in*."

The low point for Dunn came after he brought in a photo of his newborn to share around the office. "Les took the picture, Xeroxed it, and drew dicks going in my baby's mouth with the caption, 'Baby's first teething,' then posted it all over the office," says Dunn. "At that point, I didn't know what to do. Do I fight the guy? Do I try to top this guy? I don't have that instinct where I can just attack. From that point forward, I realized I wasn't destined for this job."

Firestein saw the whole idea of Dunn passing around baby photos as a "survival move" that deserved a degree of scorn. "Plain and simple, Harry wasn't getting stuff into production. Showing his baby's picture to Keenen, I think the idea [was] that might help him not get fired. That wasn't the culture at that show. The only thing that was going to keep you there is if you were productive." Dunn was not and his baby photos, whatever their intention, didn't save him. He was let go halfway through the season. So was Jones.

The freewheeling, anything-goes vibe that Firestein—and to a lesser extent, Fields and Veasey—cultivated served a purpose, or at least was intended to. The hope was that the writers would feel liberated to pitch anything, no matter how outlandish or in poor taste.

"The humor in that room was so dark," says Wilmore. "A lot of that never got on the air but we had to go through that to get to the stuff that was on the air because a lot of that humor hadn't been on television before."

Of course, the freedom to say anything cut both ways. Arguments and debates among writers—over humor, culture, race, or where to order lunch from—were frequent and encouraged.

"There was a lot of tension," says Graver. "The tension was multiracial. It was some of the most intense arguments I saw between people. It was okay for somebody to call somebody else out on being whatever ethnic minority they were and behaving like a stereotype. Being a suburban white guy from Chicago, there were little things I became aware of very quickly." He felt like some things he did and said became perceived as racially insensitive or just generally not okay. "People looked at me like *Here comes Mr. CBS.* I remember the fourth or fifth time we were going to do 'Homeboy Shopping Network,' I went, 'Seriously? Are we really going back to this cliché of guys selling shit off the truck again? Isn't this a bad thing at some point?' Everybody looked at me like, *You're not allowed to blow the whistle on that. We'll blow the whistle on that when we're ready to."* For Graver, the open spirit of inquiry was more stifling than liberating. "I felt I was being very careful every minute of the day."

Ultimately though, as Graver sees it, the main conflicts among the writers didn't break along racial lines. "The divisions in the writers' room came more out of the way we approached our work," he says. "You had some Harvard boys, some New York Jews, a couple of white trash guys, some California surfer types, several black writers—one of whom was completely street, one of whom was probably a hustler operating a business out of his office—you had Pam Veasey, who was very professional and terrific. I always felt like the underlying conflicts were about *Are you lazy? Does your work suck? Does your sucky work take up room that my good work could be in?* The biggest arguments I ever had were when I was asked to rewrite somebody's stuff and just was like, 'This isn't good from the get-go. Why am I spending my time on this?'"

Larry Wilmore's brother Marc was hired as a writer midway through the season. He was an immediate contributor, well liked among the rest of the staff, but was only marginally happier at the show than the people he'd replaced. "It certainly wasn't fun," he says. "Keenen was hard on the writers. It was his show, so when your name's on the marquee, you're going to be tough on people."

ILC was Marc Wilmore's first television writing job, and a few months into his tenure, Fields took him aside to explain something important to him. "He said, 'Look, man, I want you to know I've worked on a lot of shows and don't think every show is like this,'" Marc says. "'This is the worst show I've ever been on.' It was just very, very dark. The working conditions were horrible. We didn't know Keenen was violating WGA rules. We'd leave after midnight, sometimes at four in the morning, and come back at ten in the morning. That's against Guild rules. There's like a ten-hour or twelve-hour turnaround that no one bothered to think about or enforce. It was so stressful."

23

"Jamie Fucking Scared Me"

Jamie Foxx was lying in bed on his side, a wig of frizzy black hair on his head, wearing a pink nightgown. Shawn Wayans was spooning him. They were filming a sketch called "Muttco's Coyote Ugly One-Night Stand Escape Kit." Foxx was playing the one-night stand that Shawn was willing to chew off his arm to escape. Neither actor has any lines in the sketch, and at first Foxx's identity isn't visible to viewers. The whole sketch essentially turns on one moment, the reveal when Foxx rolls over and the camera focuses on his face. His eyes are closed, his lips garishly contorted. His mere appearance draws huge laughs.

The whole sketch is over in under a minute, but it was probably Foxx's most memorable appearance during his first few months on the show. Everyone recognized Foxx as a prodigious talent, but like with Jim Carrey, it took a while to figure out what to do with him. Foxx appears pretty sparingly in the first half of Season 3, mostly in supporting roles. Even when the show needed someone to imitate Ray Charles—a job for which Foxx later won an Oscar—David Alan Grier, not Foxx, got the call. He had funny moments but wasn't minting any characters that required a repeat engagement. He felt like he was floundering, and despite his outward bravado, he was a little taken aback by the talent around him.

"They had already been doing the show for two years when I was hired, so when I saw Damon walk in and Jim walk in, it was like fucking Jurassic Park," he said. As he put it, "I was the eighth-funniest person in the room at any given time. I had to be quiet sometimes to learn my way."

That "Coyote Ugly" role pointed the way forward. It was, in a way, a wordless version of Wanda, the ugly woman he did in his audition. Keenen had suggested Foxx do something with that character but Foxx wasn't sure what. He invited Michael Anthony Snowden to his apartment to try to figure it out. There, the two began to hash out a sketch for Wanda on a blind date with Tommy Davidson.

"We wrote the sketch and it destroyed [at the table read]," says Snowden. "People were on their backs. Keenen was drinking water and shot water out of his nose."

According to Foxx, although Wanda was from his standup, it took a village to bring her to television. "Keenen reached in this box, gave me this blond wig and said, 'Try that on,'" Foxx recalled. "Then David Alan Grier goes, 'Hey, man, you've got to say, 'I'll rock your world.' Then this character was born. The first time we did it, when I came out in that dress, with those lips and the eyes, that character took off."

In Foxx's hands, Wanda is aggressive, obnoxious, and winningly oblivious to her aesthetic flaws, but also sad and lovably weird. When she tries to break the ice with Davidson on that blind date, her opening line is the kind of pure, sublime nonsense you might expect in a Monty Python sketch: "Do you like alligators?"

Ultimately, it's her interplay with Davidson that puts the sketch over the top. They're a study in contrasts: She's broad-shouldered, muscular, intimidating; he's delicate, refined, petite.

"That was Jamie's sketch," says Davidson. "He rocked that. But one of the things I learned at *In Living Color* was how to play the straight man."

Davidson and Foxx had a natural comedy dynamic, and the show exploited it. For another Wanda sketch later in the season, Davidson strips down to a towel and lies facedown on a massage table. Wanda is his masseuse. Larry Wilmore wrote the sketch, and for him, it was a lesson in comedy minimalism.

"Tommy was facedown the whole time so he couldn't see Wanda," he explains. "I thought the reveal of that would be really funny. It was a breakthrough for me as a comedy writer, constructing a sketch that was just about that premise. It didn't need all these one-liners and jokes. That setup alone got the laughs and one of the biggest laughs I've ever seen on the show, especially that reveal. Jamie's chasing Tommy around in his little underwear and the audience was just stomping."

"When I did that character, that's when it changed," Foxx said. "Because I was trying to find my bearings. I was there for a trial basis. Nobody knew who I was but they knew this character was slamming. That gave me my stripes."

For all that Foxx brought to the show, he also subtly changed the dynamic among the cast. Jamie was an aggressive, type-A personality, and joining a cast that already had two seasons under their belt, he came in with something to prove.

"Jamie fucking scared me," says Davidson. "Jamie was so talented, it was like, *Whoa.*"

The cast had always been competitive, but once Foxx arrived, that competition took on a sharper edge. "The banter was nonstop and kind of crazy," says Kelly Coffield. "The boys would make fun of each other in a big way. Jamie was trying a bit more to get his licks in. Once he came on the scene, there definitely could be some mean-spiritedness with it. There was nothing they wouldn't tease each other about." Davidson, she says, often got the worst of it. "Jamie picked on Tommy a lot because the other guys would laugh."

Keenen, for his part, didn't seem inclined to tone it down. "Jamie's the guy who loves to tease, loves to push," Keenen said. During filming, "Jamie would do things to Tommy that would make Tommy crazy. Tommy would always be looking to me to cut, and I'd never cut. I'd force him to stay in the scene. It would just be so much fun."

As cast members got more outside acting gigs, there was a sense, at least to Coffield, that the cast's internal hierarchy was starting to become based on who had the most going on in their career. Those who *needed ILC* were at the bottom of the totem pole. "There was this sense that the point was getting out there and doing as many other things as you possibly could," she says. "There was a lot of pointed joking, especially if somebody did something that wasn't a big hit."

Kevin Berg, the show's line producer, increasingly had to juggle the cast's outside commitments. It wasn't just film auditions, standup gigs, or promotional jags that Berg had to schedule around but also the cast members' growing sense that their time was valuable.

"Not only did they have places to be, they didn't like to hang around anymore when they weren't actually working," says Berg. "They expected a call time to coincide with them going to work, not coming in and waiting an hour or two."

Amid this less familial atmosphere, Davidson was struggling, and it didn't go unnoticed. According to Rose Catherine Pinkney, then a young studio executive working on the show, "Keenen was really hard on Tommy." Many in the cast saw Keenen as a father figure, she says, but "he ruled with an iron fist. He can be very specific about what he wants, whether that's what he wants to eat and how he wants it arranged on his plate, or how he wants the sketch to flow. He was tough on those guys but I believe people felt Keenen was hardest on Tommy, like when a parent is meaner to one kid." There were rumors Davidson was dabbling in drugs, which didn't sit right with Keenen, who was a relative model of clean living. "I don't know what came first," says Pinkney. "Whether Keenen being hard on him led Tommy to drugs or whether he was hard on Tommy because he knew."

Davidson says he was feeling the strain of work and family issues. The whole vibe at the show, he says, was "very, very tense. It had become a fight for who's going to get something on." He developed a drug habit and became less reliable. "I had a hard time showing up. I became very uninspired."

T'Keyah Crystal Keymáh also became somewhat detached, frustrated with her perennial second-tier status on the show. "I was probably the lowest person on the totem pole on that show," she said. "I was rarely given characters to do. It would be 'Okay, Jim, here's the piece where you play such-and-such a character, and Crystal, you're the woman that comes in. Week after week, I'd create characters that were 'The Girl,' 'The Woman.'" After a while, she said, "I spent a great deal of time in my dressing room crying."

That's not to say the cast was imploding. Far from it. This was more the everyday dysfunction that comes with lots of successful creative endeavors. But, as Coffield says, the vibe had changed.

"It's not like that crazy time when we were all starting," she says.

"It wasn't the old gang going to lunch together. Now it was like, *Okay, so-and-so isn't going to be there next week because they're doing this and that or being flown here and there*. People were giving interviews or having meetings with publicists. In that third season, things didn't split off because we were all pissed at each other. The real world came crashing in."

24

"I'm Better Than Any of These Girls and You Know It!"

I f Jennifer Lopez wanted to be a Fly Girl, she had to slim down and get a haircut. At least, according to Rosie Perez, whose memories of that time—via a 2015 interview and her own 2014 memoir—don't always line up with those of her colleagues at the time. Lopez was under a holding deal with Fox, but Perez says those were the two stipulations surrounding her joining the show.

"Keenen said if she loses some weight and cuts her hair, let's roll with it," Perez says. "That's the honest truth. Why would I lie about that? I said, 'Don't make her cut her hair. She's Puerto Rican. You can't do that.'" Others suggest the pressure on Lopez regarding her weight came at least equally if not entirely from Fox. Regardless, Lopez was feeling the strain from the minute she arrived at the Fly Girls' rehearsal space. It didn't help that two of the troupe's dancers, Carla Garrido, who'd initially been picked over Lopez for Season 2, and Michelle Whitney-Morrison, had been let go to make room for her.

"Those two are friends of mine and I was sad to see them go," says Carrie Ann Inaba. "I'm sure it was really hard for Jennifer to come in and be the new kid on the block. I think she always struggled with that. It created not a friendly welcoming."

Lopez also rubbed some of the dancers and crew the wrong way. Some bristled at her naked ambition. There was a feeling that Jennifer Lopez seemed most interested in what was best for Jennifer Lopez's own career as opposed to what was best for the group or the show.

"Within less than two weeks," Perez writes in her memoir, "every day almost, all the girls were coming into my office, complaining how she was manipulating wardrobe, makeup, and me, all to her advantage." (Lopez, through her publicist, declined to be interviewed for this book.)

To be fair, Lopez got along with some dancers better than others. She and Deidre Lang were tight. Lisa Marie Todd used to drive Lopez to rehearsals and go out to eat with her a fair bit. "I've read we were catty to her and all that," says Todd. "That wasn't the case for me." Cari French admits she was "never close" with Lopez and felt that by Season 3, "the tight-knit thing we had in the beginning was definitely not there."

Inaba, for her part, doesn't mince words regarding Lopez: "Jennifer and I never really got along. Jennifer is a very strong personality. That sometimes made it challenging for all of us, including her. She unabashedly goes after what she wants. It's not my style, but I was always impressed with how much she wanted certain things and how she went after them with no apologies."

Ultimately, it was Lopez's relationship with Perez that seemed to cause the most problems. Perez says she found Lopez to be ambitious, hardworking, and very professional, and insists the main source of their issues was that the rest of the Fly Girls "didn't click with her." "I got caught in the middle," Perez says. "I was immature and didn't handle it well."

That's probably underselling it a little. Perez worked Lopez hard and Lopez didn't always appreciate her criticism. Arguments weren't uncommon. The rest of the dancers certainly weren't oblivious to the friction.

"It would be more annoying than anything," says Todd. "Like, *Why are we wasting time on that instead of trying to be the best we can be?*"

According to Perez's memoir, at least some of her criticism of Lopez was really coming from Keenen. "He would always call me on the red phone reserved for producers during live and pretapings, telling me to take her out of a certain number if he thought she looked fat that week or too clunky." Perez would obey her boss's wishes, pass along the harsh words but conceal their source. During one rehearsal, Lopez stormed into Perez's office, apoplectic.

"You pick on me, me and only me, every fucking day!" she screamed. "Every fucking day! I work my ass off, deliver, and you keep pushing me aside, treating me like I'm shit! I know I'm good! I'm better than any of these girls and you know it!"

Eric Gold, who later managed Lopez for a spell, recalls that at another moment early in her tenure, she and Perez nearly came to blows.

"Rosie wasn't a benevolent dictator," says Gold. "Rosie ran it like a real dictator. She's bossing Jennifer around, and Jennifer's like, 'Fuck you! Let's go in the parking lot right now!' This turns into like a Bronx-Brooklyn thing. Rosie's like, 'Fuck you! I'll kill you!' And they're going in the parking lot to fight. Somehow Keenen intervened and it worked itself out."

Keenen says it never got quite that bad—"Jennifer was a very smart girl and made very smart choices and that's not a choice she would've ever made"—but, regardless, there was no denying the bad vibes between them.

It was clear to most that Lopez saw dancing as a path to other things, not an end in itself. Les Firestein says she made no secret of her desire to act on the show, but found her ambitions stymied in that direction. "She used to ask me about it all the time. My understanding was that Keenen wanted the Fly Girls to be the Fly Girls, end of story."

Perez insists that over the years, the beef between her and Lopez has been overblown. "I will say that in her time there, there were a few rifts, settled and squashed, and we moved on." It's clear that, at the very least, they reached an uneasy détente. Whatever static there was between them, it didn't negatively impact the Fly Girls' performances. In fact, many felt the sparks behind the scenes gave the group more creative fire. They were certainly more popular than ever.

Nonetheless, the troupe's bid for a syndicated spinoff TV series, *Kick It with the Fly Girls*, flamed out. After producing a sizzle reel and shopping it around at the annual National Association of Television Program Executives conference in early 1991, the plug was pulled despite getting commitments from affiliate stations across 56 percent of the country. However, energy was still poured into turning the Fly Girls into a singing group. Perez was enlisted to help manage the group's musical career, alongside Gold.

"I said yes because I felt I owed it to Keenen because he was wonderful to me," says Perez. "But I didn't like the job. I wasn't good at it. I was too young to take on that amount of responsibility. They needed a professional manager. It wasn't fair to the girls."

The whole music project had begun a year earlier, before Lopez even joined. Gold had contacted Jeff Ayeroff, a music executive who'd cofounded Virgin's U.S. label, and told him about this idea to turn the Fly Girls into pop stars. Ayeroff had some experience with such transformations. One of his first signings at Virgin was former L.A. Lakers cheerleader-turned-choreographer Paula Abdul. Ayeroff and Gemma Corfield, who worked in A&R at Virgin, came to a rehearsal to hear the Fly Girls sing.

"I have to be diplomatic about it," says Ayeroff, laughing. "They couldn't sing, weren't the right age, and weren't as attractive as I'd like. So, I said, 'You gotta go find some other people to do this.'"

Not long after, Ayeroff got another call from Gold. "I found the girl," Gold told him. He meant Lopez.

At that point, both Ayeroff and Corfield thought there was potential. But the recording project seemed to aggravate already existing tensions within the group. Keenen charged Perez with deciding who should be the lead singer. Deidre Lang had experience as a singer, but Perez thought she sounded "too Broadway." Carrie Ann Inaba had been a pop star in Japan in her teens, but Perez found her voice "too pageant-sounding." Lisa Marie Todd wasn't a trained singer, but was game to try. Cari French wasn't too enthused about the entire prospect: She suggested turning her microphone off. That left Lopez, whom Perez felt was "very pitchy but had a commercial tone." In the end, Perez passed the decision to Keenen, who decreed that Lopez, Lang, and Inaba should share lead singing duties. Seth Riggs, a vocal coach who's worked with Michael Jackson, Prince, Barbra Streisand, and Madonna, was enlisted to help iron out the considerable kinks.

"We were having individual sessions as well as group sessions," says Todd. "They weren't playing around. There was a game plan of how we're going to formulate this group and merchandise it all."

Perez helped recruit producers and songwriters, including Dallas Austin, who'd worked with Boyz II Men, Bell Biv DeVoe, and Janet Jackson.

"We flew to New York and had a meeting at Virgin," says Todd. They met with a young Sean "Puffy" Combs and A Tribe Called Quest's Q-Tip. "This was before Puffy was P. Diddy. I didn't know who he was. I was like, 'Puffy and Q-Tip? What kinds of names are these?'"

The group spent time practicing and even recorded some demos. As to the quality of those recordings, Perez didn't think much of them. "It was bad," she says. "That's what I remember about it. Some of the girls were into it, some weren't. I wasn't."

According to Gold though, it wasn't the music that sank the Virgin deal, but rather an incident so absurd, it's hard to believe any part of it could be true. In Gold's telling, the Girls had a meeting with Ayeroff at Virgin's Beverly Hills offices. At the time, Paula Abdul was one of the label's top artists: Her 1989 album *Forever Your Girl* had spawned four number one singles; the 1991 follow-up *Spellbound* had gone triple platinum, and she'd become a national spokesperson for Diet Coke. Most of the Fly Girls knew her personally, at least in passing, as did Perez. In fact, at the 1990 Emmys, after Perez lost to Abdul for Best Choreography, Abdul tracked down Perez to graciously tell her the award should've been hers. As Keenen recalled, Rosie's response was simple and to the point: "I know."

Despite Abdul's huge and somewhat unlikely success, recently she'd been beset by bad PR. In April 1991, one of her backup singers sued Virgin, saying it was actually her voice, not Abdul's, singing the lead on several of her hits. *In Living Color*, as the show was wont to do, piled on. A vicious musical parody of Abdul's hit "Promise of a New Day," retitled "Promise of a Thin Me," mocked her troubles, her struggles with her weight, and her romantic relationship with Arsenio Hall. (Sample lyric: "My voice is bad and my singing's a joke/I still make millions off of Diet Coke/How do I sing on key?/Others do it with me.") Perez says she begged off choreographing the sketch, which featured a few Fly Girls, handing the work to her assistant.

"It was kind of cruel," she says. "I respected Paula so much. Keenen was like, 'Get over it. It's comedy. It's not personal.' But I was like, 'If that was me, I'd die.'"

The irony, of course, was that the transition Abdul had made—from dancer to pop star—was exactly the one the Fly Girls were attempting.

As Gold recalls, during a break from their meeting with Ayeroff, some of the Girls went to the bathroom.

"The girls go into the bathroom and start talking shit about Paula Abdul," says Gold. As karma would have it, at that very moment, in one of the other bathroom stalls, was none other than Paula Abdul. "Out of the stall comes Paula, who walks into Jeff Ayeroff's office and says, 'They go or I go.' Virgin dropped them."

Keenen laughs when asked about the story, and is cagey about his memory of it. "It wasn't the Fly Girls, but there was someone who was part of this whole situation that was in the bathroom talking shit about Paula," he says. "And Paula *was* in the bathroom."

Though Gold swears by it and Keenen somewhat confirms it, neither Todd nor French has any memory of the incident. Nor does Ayeroff or Corfield. But like most myths, there might be at least a grain of truth in it.

"I'm sure if Paula heard about us signing another girl group she would've been pissed," says Corfield. "Certainly, when we signed Janet Jackson, we had to give Paula her own label."

To Ayeroff, the idea of Abdul freaking out about the Fly Girls being on the label is completely plausible. "That makes total sense. The fact she was in the bathroom while they were talking smack, that's like something from a bad Jon Cryer movie." He says that they would've likely had a discussion with Abdul before finalizing a deal with the Fly Girls, "because you don't want to kill the goose who's laying the golden egg."

Even with the Virgin deal dead, the Fly Girls' prospects as recording artists weren't totally smothered. According to Gold, Benny Medina—then best known as the inspiration for Will Smith's character in *The Fresh Prince of Bel-Air*—brought the group to Warner Bros. and their odyssey continued for a while.

The persistent interest in the Fly Girls had as much to do with *In Living Color*'s exalted status as an arbiter of black culture as it did anything else. Perez's batting average on Season 3's musical guests was even better than in past seasons: Performers included A Tribe Called Quest, Eric B & Rakim, Jodeci, and Black Sheep. Big Daddy Kane, whose performance of "Ooh, Aah, Nah-Nah-Nah" featured dozens jammed onstage with him, says that the show had earned real respect within rap circles.

"Keenen kept it hood," says Kane. "He had a DJ. He had chicks in biker shorts doing hip-hop dances. It was introducing a lot of elements of hip-hop to people that weren't aware of hip-hop."

The show had earned a reputation as, if not quite a star-maker, then certainly a necessary stop on the way to stardom for aspiring rappers. "It was huge for us," says Black Sheep MC Andres "Dres" Titus. "There weren't many accolades higher than that. Getting asked to perform on *In Living Color* or *Arsenio* was the pinnacle as far as a hip-hop event. It was a bridge and helped us a great deal as far as middle America and putting a face with the artist."

Perez says Black Sheep's performance of what was then barely a hit but later became one of the era's defining songs, "The Choice Is Yours," was among her favorites in the show's entire run. "It was the first time the entire cast got into the performance. They joined in the part, 'Engine engine number 9 . . .' It was just so fantastic."

Dres remembers the thrill of watching the cast dance along with him. "I remember seeing Jim Carrey dancing and it making me chuckle," he says. "It was kind of obvious he was a standout amongst their cast. Seeing him so animated to something we created, to me, was really funny."

After the performance Dres says Jamie Foxx invited him to his dressing room. "He had a keyboard set up with an amp," says Dres. "He wanted me to hear him sing." Dres was skeptical. "Then when he started playing and singing, I was blown away."

Foxx buttonholed many musical guests, singing or pressing demo tapes on them. At one point that third season, Teddy Riley, who was then part of the R&B group Guy, but had also produced and written for Keith Sweat, Bobby Brown, Heavy D, and Big Daddy Kane, was backstage during a taping. Foxx spotted him just as he was leaving.

"I grab my demo cassette tape, but I'm dressed as Wanda," Foxx said. "So I'm running down the hall. 'Yo, Ted!' This nigga turns around and sees titties and size twenty-one pumps. He's like, 'What the fuck?' I said, 'Yo, Ted, I want you to check my music out. I do music.' He goes, 'Impossible.'"

In one of the season's more electric moments, Heavy D & the Boyz perform a raucous rendition of "You Can't See What I See," with Flavor Flav chiming in on the chorus, and Tupac Shakur and Sean "Puffy" Combs—both then still young unknowns—nodding their heads, dancing, and occasionally shouting along in the background. Toward the end of the song, Tupac and Combs—who later became such bitter rivals that Combs was accused by some of having Shakur murdered—are arm in arm, bouncing up and down ecstatically.

"It was the Golden Era," says Dres. "Hip-hop at the time was still very new to commercial airwaves. It was the beginnings of this happening, the beginnings of an ad agency being able to look at our genre as something more than something played on radio in inner cities late at night. *In Living Color* was one of the bridges making it accepted, a platform to perform for South Dakota or Minnesota or Florida—places that wasn't going to get it otherwise."

By the third season, *In Living Color* had become almost like a salon where the people who were important in black America and the people who wanted to be important came to hang out, laugh, be seen, make deals, and swap ideas. Rappers on the come-up, like Tupac and Biggie Smalls, stopped by, as did once and future R&B stars, like TLC and Mary J. Blige. It was also a hangout of choice for young actors and comics, like Denzel Washington and Martin Lawrence. Leroy "Twist" Casey, a childhood friend of Shawn Wayans, who took over as the show's DJ when Shawn was promoted to the cast, recalls that the next generation of black comics, guys like Chris Tucker, Chris Spencer, and Alex Thomas, were often backstage soaking it all in.

It wasn't just entertainers. Michael Anthony Snowden recalls seeing Mae Jemison, the first black female astronaut, and Angela Davis, the iconic black power activist who'd once been on the FBI's Most Wanted List for her alleged role in a dramatic 1970 kidnapping and shootout in a California courthouse. (She was later acquitted.)

"Angela Davis came and what was funny is I had on a Malcolm X T-shirt," says Snowden. "She looked at the shirt and just [approvingly] shook her head."

One person who never really stopped by was Eddie Murphy, but in a way, he was there all the time. His influence was all over the show. In some ways he was its silent godfather.

"If Eddie Murphy didn't emerge on *SNL*, there would be no *In Living Color*," says Tamara Rawitt, who had first met Keenen while working for Murphy. "He gave Keenen the idea for *Sucka*. Eddie was supportive of Damon and Chris Rock because he believed in their innate talent. All things emanate from Eddie Murphy. Eddie is the Plymouth Rock for this generation of comedy."

———

While the show was basking in the loving glow of the black community's approval, it was simultaneously trying to broaden its audience. Steve Park was hired in part to make *ILC* less of an African-American-centered sketch show. The first two seasons had been sketch comedy from a black point of view, but there were generally only two possible targets of their satire: black people or white people. The reasons to open up the scope probably had more to do with giving the writers and cast fresh ideas than any sort of nod toward broader representation, but at any rate, Park put more ethnicities on the table. He played a kung fu master, a ninja, Connie Chung, and the comically narcissistic Tommy Wu, based on a real-life infomercial star. In one of his best moments on the show, he plays the head of a Korean family who opens a bodega next door to a restaurant run by the Hedleys, the hardworking family of Jamaican immigrants featured in previous "Hey Mon" sketches. Park's character is basically an extension of the shopkeeper he portrayed in *Do the Right Thing*, but this time he plays the industrious Korean immigrant archetype purely for laughs. He had some mixed feelings about conforming to pre-existing notions about Asians, but also knew what he'd signed up for.

"That was the nature of that show," he says. "We were doing stereotypes completely in your face so I felt like I had to dive in headfirst. I couldn't be lukewarm about it. I had to commit to these characters I was playing." Still, at times, he was ill at ease. "I remember feeling a lot of responsibility to the Asian-American community to have as much integrity as I could and not let myself get used to the point where I was doing something insulting. That was a really fine line I was always walking."

Besides walking that line, Park was dealing with the garden-variety difficulties of being a new face on the show. "It was extremely intimidating," he says. "It's like going to a party and everybody knows each other. Just getting comfortable, being completely star-struck by everyone, and then trying to perform in the middle of that was really challenging. I was dealing with massive insecurities and that atmosphere was extremely competitive."

He gravitated toward the show's other new guy, Foxx, and the two hung out a bit, but they were decidedly different personalities. Foxx, a former star high school quarterback, seemed to thrive in the hyper-aggressive environment, while Park constantly felt like "whatever I was doing I needed to amp it up 100, 200, 300 percent. That's not something that comes naturally to me. It was a little traumatic."

The show had also hoped to bring in a Latino cast member and by most accounts had their sights set on John Leguizamo. In early 1991, Leguizamo began performing a one-man show in New York called *Mambo Mouth*, in which he played an array of Latino characters. Tamara Rawitt and Keenen flew out to New York to see *Mambo Mouth* during its first week.

"Leguizamo was dazzling," she says. "Versatile, fearless, fierce—all his characters and his entire body of work is based on his ethnicity. He could've carried a third of the show on his back with all his characters."

All signs pointed toward him joining the cast. Eric Gold confirms that the show "tried very hard to get Leguizamo to come in." Firestein says that the courting was a long, drawn-out, will-he-or-won't-he process.

"We'd always hear the name Leguizamo around the hallways," Firestein says, "because Fox was always looking for *What's the next big thing?* I'm going to overstate it and say he was like a holy grail because as the show was going to grow over time, it wasn't just going to be African-American culture. We wanted to expand the show to Latinos, so he was like the golden goose." Writers were even assigned to write sketches for Leguizamo in hopes of enticing him.

Leguizamo himself had few reservations. "I was a huge, huge fan," he says. "I wanted to do it, they wanted me to do it." Yet, it never happened. He says, in retrospect, the people around him scuttled the deal. "Your representation talks in your ear and the whole thing gasses up your head," he says. "My handlers at the time said, 'You're blowing up, John! You've got to do your own thing! You've got to have your own show! You gotta do you!' I got talked out of doing it. I was young and gullible."

25

"We Were Horrible to the Censors"

O n September 28, 1991, Jesse Jackson appeared on *Saturday Night Live*'s "Weekend Update," reading from Dr. Seuss's classic children's book *Green Eggs and Ham*. Jackson's performance is note-perfect: He's stern-faced and serious throughout, at one moment removing his glasses for effect, and at another banging his hand on the desk for emphasis. It got big laughs. Most everyone saw the cameo as a well-conceived, well-executed, if ultimately lightweight, bit. Keenen saw something more sinister.

He'd already taped a remarkably similar cold open for *In Living Color*. In it, Keenen plays Jesse Jackson selling a line of Dr. Seuss–like children's books with titles like "Hop On Cop," "Horton Hears a Ho," and "Green Eggs and the Guv'ment Cheese." The sketches aren't identical, but the joke at their core is. Larry Wilmore, who wrote *ILC*'s Jesse Jackson sketch, recalls watching *SNL* that night in disbelief.

"I'm like, 'You've got to be fucking kidding me! How could this happen?'" he says. "I'd already written my sketch and we'd already shot it, but our show wasn't live." His Jesse Jackson sketch aired two weeks after *SNL*'s. "But I wrote it like a month before."

At the time, some writers said Keenen was convinced *SNL* head writer Jim Downey had bugged his phone and stolen the idea. Even more than twenty years later, Keenen still finds the whole incident highly suspect.

"Two people don't get that idea at the same time," he says. "*Saturday Night Live* didn't make fun of black celebrities. They didn't have people on the show they utilized in that capacity. It didn't seem consistent with *Saturday Night Live*. I'm not accusing them of stealing but it raised that suspicion." A *Spy* magazine story from a couple years later painted Keenen's paranoia about *SNL* as part of a larger pattern of wild theories that included the belief that certain vegetables enhance sexual prowess, watermelon helps prevent hair loss, and that, in addition to *SNL*, Keenen was also being watched by the CIA. Les Firestein says the magazine story was "mostly true," but also notes that while Keenen had plenty of seemingly odd ideas about food and health, he might've been onto something. "As a result of Keenen's *paranoia*, today he looks younger than when we did the show."

To most people who knew him, certainly those at the show, Keenen was a bit of an enigma. Though even his family members describe him as a tough boss and a taskmaster, Keenen didn't yell and wasn't prone to on-set tirades. He wasn't rude and didn't browbeat. He mostly held his cards close to his chest and seemed to play them carefully. Keenen was a guy comfortable with what others might deem uncomfortable silences. Several people described him as "mysterious" and "calculated." He was the kind of guy who seemed to be playing chess, while others were toiling at checkers. Some assumed this was all part of some Sun Tzu *Art of War*–inspired strategy ("Be extremely subtle, even to the point of formlessness. Be extremely mysterious, even to the point of soundlessness. Thereby you can be the director of the opponent's fate."), but according to Keenen, there was a lot less to it than that.

"What's funny is you don't know how other people perceive you as a person," he says. "I'm quiet, not because I'm mysterious, just because I'm shy. I just don't know what to say. I'm much more an observer than I am the life of the party. If I'm performing I feel comfortable, but not in a social setting." That said, he's learned to recognize and appreciate how his natural reserve can unnerve others. "People misread me but it has actually worked. Everybody thought I was this mysterious guy but really all it was is I'm not very gregarious."

Despite the increased emphasis on recurring characters and broader comedy during Season 3, the show didn't lose its appetite for the incendiary and the racially provocative. In a sketch from the season's first half, Kelly Coffield plays Sheila Peace, a cheery, clueless, unapologetically racist real estate agent. She tells Tommy Davidson the apartment she's showing would be ideal for him because there's a "Golden Bird Fried Chicken on the corner and a crack house over on Seventh." She tells an Asian couple that the first-floor apartment is ideal because they won't disturb their downstairs neighbors "with all that karate stuff." She tells an Arab boy he must be looking forward to growing up and owning a 7-Eleven, "just like your father."

Then there was "Timbuk: The Last Runaway Slave," a piece Damon adapted from his standup. Timbuk's family has been hiding in a cave since the Civil War. When his father dies, he's forced out into the world for the first time. Damon plays Timbuk as a cowering, ignorant heir to the racist Stepin Fetchit stereotype that dominated Hollywood in the pre–civil rights era. In the sketch, he runs into David Alan Grier, who's dressed in a suit. Grier's character quickly begins to lose his patience with Timbuk's trembling mien and tries to walk away.

"You must be one of them house niggers," Timbuk tells him.

Grier tries to set him straight. "You must be from the South. Brothers up here don't act like that."

When a white jogger bumps into Grier, Timbuk is overly apologetic—"Sorry, suh, we just mosey out your way"—but Grier confronts the jogger: "Man, what the hell is the matter with you?"

Timbuk is horrified. "Is you crazy, man? You don't be talking to no white man like that! They want to be right even when they wrong."

After the jogger leaves, Grier scolds Timbuk: "This is 1991, man. All that handkerchief head stuff don't play up here. This is America! We are free! We can do what we want!" At that point, the white jogger returns with two white police officers. Timbuk cowers as Grier confidently explains the situation. The cops don't want to hear it. They throw Grier to the ground and arrest him. The message is clear, contemporary, and harsh with intent: The more things change, the more they stay the same. As if to drive home the point, Timbuk says, "Freedom don't seem to last too long around here," before a "To Be Continued" flashes across the screen.

Damon used to do a whole monologue in his standup as Timbuk. "It was probably inspired by something I heard Richard Pryor do," he says, "this amazing monologue at the end of the *Bicentennial Nigger* album that always resonated with me." In that monologue, Pryor plays a shucking and jiving two-hundred-year-old slave who recounts the horrors of slavery, but with an upbeat spin, so as to not make white people uncomfortable as they celebrate the nation's bicentennial.

In spite of the promise at the sketch's end that it would be continued, the adventures of Timbuk ended there. According to a couple of the show's writers, Damon caught a lot of flack for Timbuk's buffoonery from people in the black community who apparently missed the sketch's satirical edge (or were offended, regardless). The overall response to Timbuk was lukewarm anyway.

"The narrative was different back then," says Firestein. "This isn't the time of Jon Stewart. There was a sense sometimes, at least among the writing staff, that if the show got too real or too political, it could be a turnoff."

———

Unlike at *SNL*, where cast members and writers frequently shared offices, there was, generally speaking, a clearer dividing line—and division of labor—at *ILC*. Writers hung around their offices and cast members congregated around the soundstage, the rehearsal space, and the dressing rooms downstairs. There were exceptions. Damon spent a lot of time with the writers, in part because he did a lot of writing himself. Jamie Foxx also hung around the writers' offices a lot, pitching ideas, trying out new characters for them. But the only cast member who actually had an office with the writers was Jim Carrey.

Carrey's sensibility was very much in line with most of the writing staff. "I loved the writers," he says. "So many of them were just phenomenal talents. Les Firestein was truly hilarious and one of the sickest human beings I've ever met. He curled my toes." Carrey worked frequently with Fax Bahr and Adam Small, and much of what they crafted was infused with a demented, anarchic spirit, though sometimes it was simply too de-mented and anarchic for the show. One such example that was a Carrey favorite was an anti-abortion ventriloquist and his puppet Feety.

"It was a little fetus finger puppet," he says. "I'd pull a hanger out and Feety would go crazy. I'd go, "Feety, Feety, I'm just going to hang my coat!" We'd have an argument about whether he's a living thing or not. I'd say, 'You don't have arms and legs, and you just got a little black dot for an eye. You don't look like a human at all.' He'd say, 'I will, if you give me a couple of months, you son of a bitch!'" It wasn't hard to imagine what the public reaction would've been to Feety. "Keenen was like, 'Brother, they will burn down the studio.'"

Policing such matters of taste generally fell to Fox's Standards and Practices Department. The department was run by Don Bay, who looked about what you'd expect the vice president of Standards and Practices at a television network to look like. He was tall and slim, with blond hair that was going gray and a conventionally handsome, patrician bearing. It would be tempting to characterize him as the physical embodiment of "The Man"—and it's true that his job was to be, essentially, the voice of the establishment—but Bay wasn't so easily caricatured. He was a law-yer by training, and prided himself as a fair, open-minded guy. As the person charged with telling the writers, cast, and producers when they'd gone too far, his relationship with them was, by definition, antagonistic, but he was well liked and respected.

"Don was actually a great dude," says Keenen. "The censor's job is to keep the network on the air so there's always going to be conflict, but we couldn't have done what we did if he hadn't been supportive."

In the show's early seasons the responsibility for dealing with Stan-dards and Practices—or "the censors," as many called them—fell mostly on Keenen and Tamara Rawitt. One of the main frustrations for Keenen was that the censors' decisions seemed subjective and somewhat arbi-trary. According to Bay, that's not exactly right.

"FBC [Fox Broadcasting Company] did have guidelines that were gen-eral in nature because specifics would've been impossible," he explains. "My philosophy was that very little was prohibited because there was usu-ally a way to present an objectionable line another way and still preserve the punch. I endeavored to allow Keenen to do his thing without interfering

any more than was necessary. They'd present their rationale for a particular line to which I expressed a concern, and I'd weigh it against our policy
before giving my decision. It was all very businesslike."

That notwithstanding, when initially faced with a tall white man telling him what he could and couldn't do, Keenen's reaction was to try to
undermine him. "We were horrible to the censors," he says. When negotiating the language for a particular sketch, Keenen tried to take advantage of the gaps in Bay's knowledge: "He knows nothing about street
language." So Keenen purposely inserted nonsensical phrases like "lemon
and lime" into sketches and instructed the cast to laugh hard at the lines.
"He'd get nervous and go, 'No, you can't say that.' So I'd go, 'Oh, we can't
say 'lemon and lime.' Can we say, 'Toss your salad'? He'd go, 'Yes, I guess
that's fine.' So we had an episode where we talked about tossing salad
and he had no idea. We'd do shit like that all the time and he'd get his ass
handed to him the next day."

Bay doesn't recall "ever being flummoxed or ignorant on a subject."
"Nothing," he says, "caught me by surprise."

Keenen eventually figured out a better way to work with the Standards Department. Instead of Bay shutting down ideas deemed unacceptable, Keenen asked him to "come to me with some alternatives. We
started to negotiate and found a sweet spot where we could work together."

Nonetheless, the battle between the show's creative team and Bay's
Standards Department remained an elaborate chess game. The writing
staff took pride in slipping dirty jokes past the censors. "No one," recalls
Steve Tompkins, "was better at this than Les Firestein. He had a way of
working the censors like I've never seen."

The Standards Department read all the scripts, and watched the
rehearsals and tapings, so there was no way to elude them completely.
But Firestein had all sorts of feints, dodges, and other techniques to keep
them off guard.

"There was a whole art to that," he says. It wasn't just about choosing
words carefully, it was about choosing when to use them. "Writers would
have something really funny and I'd go, 'You can't put that in the script
today. That's a Friday joke. You can't put it in on Wednesday, because the
censor will have too much time with it.' You want things to be too late in

the game, where [Standards] would have to kill a sketch" to make the cut they want.

Another Firestein ploy was to have the staff write "decoy sketches," material so beyond the pale that they knew it had no chance of airing. The idea was that the censors couldn't shoot down everything, so if they fed them these "sacrificial lambs," as Firestein calls them, that would throw them off the trail of the sketches they really wanted to keep.

"If that was a strategy, it's one I didn't recognize," Bay admits. "I treated each script as if they were intending the material and dealt with it on that basis. If they were doing that, I can imagine they must have been surprised on occasion," when a supposed "sacrificial lamb" actually made it to air.

In fact, Tompkins recalls one of the show's filthiest sketches began as an idea no one believed would ever be broadcast. "Les would do this thing where he'd resubmit a sketch that had been rejected, again and again, just to wear them down," says Tompkins. "I remember one, it was so outrageous and inappropriate: It was about a powdered drink mix like Tang, that when reconstituted with water tasted like female vaginal juices. It was for men who didn't have access to actual pussy juice—guys in prison, the Pope, astronauts in space. It was called Poon-Tang. He submits the sketch and of course, it's utterly unacceptable. So, every few months he'd rewrite it and we'd just come up with a different name: Pie-C, Minute Maiden." The persistence paid off: The "Minute Maiden" sketch ran in late October.

Creative input from the network was generally unwelcome at *In Living Color* and actively resisted, but occasionally the suits stumbled on a decent idea. During Season 3, they pushed to invite Sam Kinison to guest star. During sweeps weeks, it's not uncommon for network executives to do what's known as stunt casting and this certainly fell into that category, but it was something more too.

By late 1991, Kinison was a huge standup star who toured arenas and had killed in a supporting role in the film *Back to School*, but also a self-destructive force of nature, who'd amassed a crew of followers and hangers-on that included actors, porn stars, and many fellow comics. The fact that his guest appearance that season went off without a hitch seems noteworthy. He only performed one sketch, playing himself, so there wasn't a lot being asked of him. Kinison was also, at that point, newly sober, which likely helped. At the end of Season 1, Kelly Coffield had done a "Samantha Kinison" impersonation—imagining a female version of Kinison—so having her dust it off opposite the actual Kinison made sense. The results were genuinely funny.

Kinison had been tight with Carrey when both were young standups in Los Angeles, but according to Carrey, they'd had a falling-out prior to his guest spot on *ILC*.

"Sam and I had a bit of a rough end," says Carrey. "He wanted a gang and wanted me to join up and I was like, 'No, I'm going my own way.' Sam didn't like hearing that. It was a bit of a contentious moment we had together at the Improv one night where it got a little nuts and we kind of drifted apart. Him coming on the show was a catalyst for us to become friends again. It was nice to get to know each other again, re-up our love for each other." Sadly, five months later Kinison died in a head-on collision on a desert highway in Southern California.

Although the Kinison guest spot worked, it was perhaps a worrying harbinger of things to come. This was the first time a guest star had played such a significant role on the show, and the relative success of the experiment seemed to embolden executives at Fox to try it over and over as the show moved forward. It would rarely be as fruitful again.

26

"I Started Laughing So Hard That I Forgot to Do My Job"

In 1986, Richard Pryor was diagnosed with multiple sclerosis. For a while, his physical deterioration was gradual, but by the fall of 1991 it had accelerated. He was thin and frail, and had developed serious heart problems. CBS's special that November, *A Party for Richard Pryor*, was widely interpreted as a sort of Lifetime Achievement Award, or—less graciously—a slightly premature wake.

Eddie Murphy helped to orchestrate the event at the Beverly Hilton Hotel, and it served as something of an informal public reunion for most of the Black Pack's core members. Keenen, Arsenio, and Robert Townsend helped write the special and were all in attendance, sitting close to the man who'd been their primary inspiration for going into comedy in the first place. As Eddie put it that night, "If there were no Richard, I wouldn't be here."

Less than five years had passed since Keenen, Arsenio, and Robert had been struggling standups, best known for being Eddie's friends. Since then, they'd fought to establish themselves and, really, to establish a beachhead for black comedy and black creativity in Hollywood. By the time they were sitting together to fete Pryor, it looked like they'd succeeded. Along with Spike Lee, who, by then, was working on his next film,

Malcolm X, they'd played a fundamental part in altering the landscape for African-Americans in the entertainment industry.

A sea change had taken place over the course of the last decade: It wasn't just *In Living Color*, *The Arsenio Hall Show*, and whatever film Eddie lent his presence to. *The Fresh Prince of Bel-Air* and *A Different World* were Top 10 shows. *Roc*, a black family sitcom, had recently debuted after *In Living Color* and was regularly pulling in fifteen million viewers a night. Martin Lawrence was working with ex-*ILC* scribe John Bowman prepping his sitcom, *Martin*. *Def Comedy Jam*, which would take the Comedy Act Theater's underground vibe aboveground, was months away from its debut on HBO. John Singleton's *Boyz n the Hood*, which starred Ice Cube and a couple of then unknowns, Morris Chestnut and Cuba Gooding Jr. (who got his start, not coincidentally, in *Coming to America*), had dropped the previous summer like a cultural atom bomb. *Juice*, which was written and directed by Spike Lee's cinematographer Ernest Dickerson, was about to open number two at the box office despite a cast with no bigger star than Tupac Shakur. In July, *Mo' Money*, a film Damon had written based loosely on a job he had after dropping out of high school, working in the mailroom at a credit card company (he was arrested for stealing preapproved credit cards but got off with probation), opened huge, making more than seventeen million dollars in its first weekend. Perhaps there was no better sign of the new normal than the fact that a month before the Pryor celebration, *House Party 2* opened number one at the box office. Surely, when black filmmakers too can rake in dough making uninspired sequels to films that had only been mildly entertaining the first time around, something real has been achieved. So, the night celebrating Pryor had the feel of a victory lap, as well as being a tribute to the guy whom all roads led back to.

Pryor himself hadn't always been comfortable with the adulation of his younger acolytes. He'd reportedly been cold and brusque throughout the filming of *Harlem Nights*, which Eddie wrote largely for the purpose of working with him. As Eddie put it in 2011, "Richard felt threatened by me. It was this weird, *I like this motherfucker, but is he going to take my spot?* We got in the mix when they still did one nigger at a time in Hollywood."

Surely though, this night, and the array of African-American comics who'd carved their own pieces of the pie alongside each other was proof part of Pryor's legacy was that the system was changing. Pryor seemed to have softened too. As Arsenio recalled, "I remember standing with Damon in Richard's house and he talked about how much he appreciates Eddie and all of us who give him love. I don't know if this would be [him being] insecure, but Richard said, 'Sometimes when y'all say stuff about me, I'm thinking like, *You have to be teasing or joking.* Then it dawned on me, y'all motherfuckers for real.'"

Keenen hadn't met Pryor before that night at the Beverly Hilton. That, in itself, was a little odd, and something Keenen acknowledged in his speech from the stage. Pryor was the reason Keenen got into comedy, but he'd practically avoided him in person until then.

"I had had my opportunities to meet him when he'd come to the Comedy Store," Keenen explained in a later interview. "Eddie was very good friends with him and wanted to introduce me. My brother Damon had met him and wanted to introduce me. I didn't want to. I never wanted to meet him as a fan. I wanted to achieve something and then be able to say, 'This is because of you.'" At that point, he felt he finally had. "I was at the height of *In Living Color*. It had won the Emmy. He knew who I was. So, I was then able to humble myself and thank him. I went over and hugged him."

That hug was an important moment for Keenen. He'd gone from discovering Pryor after being chased home from school by a bully to standing with his arms around him as—if not quite his equal—certainly his peer. It was, along with his first appearance on *The Tonight Show*, a marker of his progress. "If I were going to bookend my career, it would be those two moments," he said. "*The Tonight Show* and being able to thank the guy who showed me what I was going to do with my life."

———

Every Tuesday morning, twenty-five to thirty top Fox executives would meet in a conference room for a free-form staff meeting. Many of the execs looked forward to the meetings. At a network and in an industry so tightly focused on day-to-day ups and downs, this was a chance to think long term, to discuss trends in film, in television, in entertainment broadly. Anybody and everybody was encouraged to speak. On a Tuesday in 1991, Fox president Jamie Kellner began musing about the Super Bowl. CBS had the rights to the next one, and in fact, the rights to the next few Super Bowls were already locked down by other networks.

"Jamie started talking about how nobody watches the halftime," says Dan McDermott, a Fox programming executive assigned to *ILC*. "I remember thinking, *Where is he going with this?* He said, 'We should do a live episode of *In Living Color*. We'll make a big deal out of it. We'll convince America to turn the channel at halftime.'"

The Super Bowl was then and remains the most viewed television event of the year. At that point, it was consistently watched by more than one hundred million people in the U.S. The conventional wisdom was it wasn't worth it for the other networks to sink money into programming opposite the game. There just weren't enough viewers left over to make it worthwhile. But if Fox could get just a fraction of those Super Bowl viewers to change the channel, Kellner argued, it'd be a coup. They'd been promoting themselves as the "Bad Boys of Television," irreverent upstarts with no respect for age-old industry norms. What better way to prove it?

"It was wholly consistent with everything we stood for," says Sandy Grushow, who by then had been promoted to EVP of Fox's Entertainment Division. "I used to refer to us as guerilla-like. We'd rush in there, throw a punch, then run out before the competition knew what hit them. That's exactly what this was designed to do."

The idea had its roots in a phone call from a guy named Jay Coleman to *ILC*'s executive in charge of production (and Keenen's manager), Eric Gold, a year earlier. Coleman was the president of Entertainment Marketing and Communications International, and a pioneer in bringing together pop stars with corporate brands. He'd paired Michael Jackson, Lionel Richie, and MC Hammer with Pepsi, Rod Stewart with Canada Dry, and gotten Jōvan Musk to help underwrite a Rolling Stones tour. Coleman told Gold that he'd recently been at the Super Bowl in New Orleans, watching the halftime show—which featured three local college marching bands performing odes to the host city—bored out of his mind. This was hardly an unusual feeling during Super Bowl halftimes. The year before, the main act was an Elvis impersonator named Elvis Presto.

The years before that, performers included aging entertainers (Chubby Checker, George Burns, Mickey Rooney), the cultish, morally hectoring singing ensemble Up with People, and more college marching bands. Through his boredom, Coleman, who died in 2011, saw an opportunity.

He told Gold he wanted MC Hammer to perform on Fox during halftime of the game. In between songs, he wanted fresh *In Living Color* sketches. He'd find a corporate partner to sponsor the entire program and foot the bill for production and promotion. Gold liked the idea, but only to a point.

"I said, 'Jay, I love you, but here's my thinking: 'We should do an *In Living Color* halftime show and have MC Hammer do the musical number,'" he says. Discussions wore on, and the idea was pushed a year, by which time MC Hammer had dropped out, and Coleman had signed Frito-Lay to sponsor the whole thing. Coleman met with Kellner, who brought the idea to the Tuesday meeting. It went over big. Keenen loved it too.

"I thought, *This is genius*," he says. "*The Super Bowl was the biggest thing in television. No one would dare take on the Super Bowl. We have to do that.*"

CBS's fusty plans for the 1992 game were ripe for the picking. They'd hired Disney to produce something called "Winter Magic," really little more than a thinly disguised promo for their Winter Olympics coverage the following month. It featured ice skaters Brian Boitano and Dorothy Hamill, along with a thirty-foot inflatable snowman. As Fox began promoting the hell out of *ILC*'s alternate halftime show on Fox, CBS seemed spooked and hastily broke with their theme, booking an additional performance by Gloria Estefan and Miami Sound Machine.

CBS weren't the only ones who were nervous. Frito-Lay was willing to fork over a reported two million dollars to the network and the show, but the brand was concerned about the show's content, particularly since it would be broadcast live.

"Everybody's interested in doing exciting things but they're also interested in protecting their brand," says Kellner. He agreed to broadcast the show on a delay. (Various people disagree on exactly how long the delay was, but it was somewhere between five and ten seconds.) Not only would Fox's Standards VP Don Bay be in the production booth with his hand poised over a button to bleep out any objectionable content, Kellner himself would be in the booth beside Bay, to watch over him.

Rose Catherine Pinkney, then a young executive at Twentieth Television who covered *ILC*, says there were many ways the live show could go awry, but Fox's chief worry was that the cast would take advantage of the situation to slip things past the Standards Department that would get everyone in trouble.

As preparations began, there was an all-hands-on-deck feeling. Fox's marketing and promotions teams were working overtime, flooding the airwaves with promos, getting media coverage for the event, and sending out invitations to the famous and the not-so-famous to ensure the live shots of the studio that night looked like a genuine party. John Bowman was convinced to pause his work on the *Martin* pilot and take a pass at a "Men on Football" sketch.

On Super Bowl Sunday, the studio filled with guests, including Kirstie Alley, Pauly Shore, Sam Kinison, and Blair Underwood, who mixed with cast members. There was an open bar. The party atmosphere didn't quite extend to the writers, who were rewriting and tweaking sketches right until showtime.

The Super Bowl show leaned heavily on franchise characters. Damon and Keenen revived "The Homeboy Shopping Network," which hadn't been seen since early in Season 2, and set it inside a football locker room. Fire Marshall Bill visited a sports bar. Background Guy—a Jim Carrey character that grew from his inability to fade into the background of any scene—appeared outside a Super Bowl locker room. Strictly speaking, the show wasn't all "live"—sketches like "Fire Marshal Bill" were essentially short, complicated, pyrotechnics-filled films that often took hours to shoot—but the most memorable moment was: Damon and David Alan Grier's "Men on Football."

It's may be unfairly harsh to say that the sketch itself was largely a parade of coy double-entendres and gay innuendos, but that was sort of the characters' stock-in-trade. Bowman had written the initial sketch, which was then rewritten by the show's staff, but the most enduring moments were ad-libbed by Damon and Grier. After a reference to Joe Namath wearing panty hose in a TV commercial, Grier's Antoine notes that Namath is married. Damon, as Blaine, responds: "Well, so is Richard

Gere and you should've seen that gerbil in the wedding dress." The line was a nod to a well-traveled urban myth that Gere had once stuck a live gerbil up his ass as part of some gay fetish play.

"That was one of the jokes I put in my pocket because I knew the censors wouldn't let it go," says Damon. He wanted to surprise Grier, make him laugh. He did. He also made Jamie Kellner laugh, which was why the joke made it onto the air.

"Don [Bay] and I worked up this scheme where anytime I felt something had gone over the line, I'd pound him on the back, so that within the ten seconds, he'd be focused on it and could hit a button and drop audio to solve the problem," says Kellner. "I started laughing so hard at the Richard Gere thing that I forgot to hit Don on the back. I forgot to do my job."

Damon wasn't done. Toward the sketch's end, Antoine mentions he's excited to see sprinter Carl Lewis at the upcoming Summer Olympics. "You know why Carl runs so fast?" Blaine responds. "You can run but you can't hide from your true self, Miss Lewis." The line also went out unmolested by the Standards Department.

"I had five seconds to make the call and quickly decided not to delete the reference," says Bay. "Lewis's being gay was openly discussed in Hollywood. Jamie asked if I'd cut it, to which I replied, 'No.'" Lewis's lawyer threatened legal action, but none materialized. Gere's agent called the show incensed and threatened to cause problems but mostly didn't.

For a few days afterward, the sketch was all anyone in Hollywood seemed to be talking about. The decision to air the lines about Lewis and Gere was controversial, even among those at Fox. Shortly afterward, the company's chairman, Barry Diller, said, "I'm not so sure they shouldn't have pushed the delay button." Keenen was at peace with the way it played out.

"There was a six-second button Fox had the option of hitting," says Keenen. "I didn't have control over that. That was the reason they had their guy there. If there was anything they didn't feel was appropriate they could've hit that button. I wasn't the guy to take heat for a decision I didn't make."

In the end, the show had hit a sort of sweet spot: just enough controversy to get people talking, not enough to incur legal action. Certainly, the show's monster ratings made it easier to soothe Fox's nerves. Nearly twenty-nine million viewers tuned in that night, and the Super Bowl's ratings for the second half crashed by ten points.

That's not to say there was no fallout at all from Damon's ad-libs. The Fox halftime show had been the first part of a larger overall marketing deal the show had made with Frito-Lay's parent company, Pepsi. There were plans for some of the *ILC* characters, including Homey the Clown, Blaine, and Antoine, to be featured in Pepsi "taste test" commercials.

"When the chairman of Pepsi watched the halftime show with his conservative friends, he was so appalled he canceled any further involvement," says Gold. "He killed the deal right there."

Other tangible consequences weren't so bad.

"Somebody sent us an actual gerbil to the show," says Michael Anthony Snowden. "[Fans] always sent us stuff—everything from death threats to insane, crazy shit—but somebody sent us an actual gerbil. Les bought one of those little plastic gerbil balls, and for the remainder of the season that gerbil rolled around the office."

Perhaps the most far-reaching effect of *ILC*'s Super Bowl halftime show was on Super Bowl halftime itself. Never again would the NFL hire an Elvis impersonator, figure skaters, or the members of Up with People. The following year, they hired Michael Jackson, then the biggest entertainer on the planet. His five-song halftime miniconcert was one of the most viewed television spectacles of all time, and pointed the way toward a future filled with big-budget concert blowouts, the world's most famous wardrobe malfunction, and Katy Perry riding a giant, golden lion.

"We swooped in like pirates and took over that halftime half hour," says Carrey. "We're the reason why you see all that amazing entertainment at Super Bowl halftime now."

27

"This Show Isn't Just a Money Spigot"

With the success of the Super Bowl experiment, the show hit a new high, but once the buzz wore off, the hangover set in. In retrospect, Super Bowl Sunday was the top of the mountain for *In Living Color*. Almost immediately it began its long, slow descent.

In February, Barry Diller resigned his chairmanship at Fox. Although many have debated whether he's been given—or took—too much credit for the birth of Fox as a fourth network, Diller had successfully steered the network out of its seemingly terminal late-eighties mire toward legitimacy. His decisions—along with those of Peter Chernin, Sandy Grushow, and Jamie Kellner—to push Fox toward "alternative" programming, toward the "Bad Boys of Television," had proven to be the right one. At the time of his departure, the network was programming five nights a week and was on line to post a profit of forty million dollars for the fiscal year.

Many were stunned by Diller's resignation, but the famously confrontational, hard-charging executive had been increasingly chafing against the strictures of his position. He'd been the chairman at Fox, but still had to answer to News Corp boss Rupert Murdoch, who never entirely bought into the idea that Fox needed to compete as scrappy underdogs. As one Fox executive puts it, "Rupert couldn't understand why we were settling for a small piece of the pie, when you can have the whole pie."

The day Diller announced his resignation, Murdoch called a meeting with his five top remaining executives, which included Kellner, Grushow, and Chernin. He told the group, "Now that Barry is gone, we can really get this network firing on all cylinders." When the remark got back to Diller, who at this point was still in the building, he chuckled to himself and noted that he always sensed Murdoch hadn't appreciated what they'd achieved. Murdoch took over Diller's position as Fox chairman himself, and almost immediately became more hands-on in the network's decision making.

Although Diller had often been a tough internal critic of *ILC*'s brash humor and a check on its most outlandish instincts, ultimately he was a supportive presence who'd been there since the show's beginnings. Now he was gone. Keenen began to feel the reverberations of the shakeup. His show was a huge hit, at the height of its influence, yet he was feeling squeezed. "As regime changes happen, it always seemed like [we] were having to start all over again," he says.

Murdoch had previously been a looming presence; now he was an active one. "When Diller left, Rupert was playing catch-up," says Gold. "He was nowhere to be seen until all of a sudden he was." Fox's attitude toward *ILC* began to shift. There was colder calculus going on.

"When you have a show that's a big hit making you a lot of money, it's going to get more attention," says Rose Catherine Pinkney. "So there were decisions made as we went along that were definitely much more business than creative."

Fox began filling holes in their schedule with *ILC* reruns. They pushed hard for more appearances from the show's franchise characters. There was pressure to produce more episodes, to package together clip shows to extend the season. The grind of dealing with the Standards Department grew more intense.

"We're like, 'Give us twenty-eight episodes,'" says programming exec Dan McDermott. "'Give us more "Men on Film."' 'Let us do compilation episodes.' All that sort of stuff designed to make the network more money. I understand that would be upsetting to a guy like Keenen, for whom this show isn't just a money spigot. This is his blood, his heart and soul."

As Pinkney explains, rather than looking at *In Living Color* and seeing a well-functioning hit show that should be largely left to its own devices, the network, and to some extent, the studio, saw a profitable enterprise with which they wanted to be more deeply involved. "The more the network and the studio tried to become another chef in the kitchen, the less interesting it was for Keenen."

And not just Keenen. Cast members began to grumble at what they felt was unwelcome meddling. "It was just more and more network involvement," says Kelly Coffield. "More people saying, 'You can do this but you can't do that.' 'You can say this but you can't say that. And while we're at it, could you please do six more of this hilarious character because we have it on a T-shirt?'"

Keenen's reaction to all this was predictable intransigence. "I never gave in because I didn't think they knew how to run the show," he says. "I'd listen but make as little compromise as I had to. There was a constant push and shove, give and take."

The production team worked on an extremely tight turnaround. The final cut of the show was typically finished and turned in to Fox less than a day or two before the Sunday night when it aired. At that point the network and the Standards Department reviewed it to ensure there wasn't anything objectionable. "We were frequently delivering the cut to Fox Saturday night or Sunday morning so they wouldn't have time to [request] changes," says the show's editor Kris Trexler. "Then we were always under the threat that they'd bleep us. There were times I'd have to go in Sunday morning or Sunday afternoon. There would be some relenting and compromising done so we could at least get the show on the air, last-minute."

Trexler recalls at least one time when someone at Fox personally made sloppy edits to an episode of the show. "They made the kind of cut that I would've taken my name off the show," he says. "It makes the editor look bad."

As the season dragged on, the cast and writers grew increasingly weary. In the last few months of the season, the network ran four shows' worth of repackaged, previously aired sketches, and even the new shows increasingly became a parade of franchise characters, many of whom were low on creative juice. There were multiple, not particularly funny Head Detective, B.S. Brothers, and Benita Butrell sketches. They even seemed to be running out of things to do with Fire Marshal Bill, who was put on a space shuttle in one sketch, and Homey the Clown, who was made a kindergarten substitute teacher. The show still had teeth—Keenen and Damon's "Brothers Brothers on the $100,000 Pyramid" was among the hardest-hitting sketches the show would ever do; Tommy Davidson finally got his chance to roll out his Sammy Davis Jr. impression in a spoof of the hit film *Ghost*; Jim Carrey and Kelly Coffield did a very clever parody of *Fatal Attraction* as a soft-focus coffee commercial—but the show's batting average was dipping. By the tail end of these long seasons, the writing staff simply didn't have much left in the tank.

"[Fox] would come to us in the spring, when we're winding down and everybody is on their last sprint to the finish line and say they want six more shows," explains Firestein. "It's like you've been pacing yourself for a 26.2-mile marathon and at mile 25, people say, 'Can you run six more miles?'" Often, more shows meant the cast and crew canceling vacations or other plans. People got edgy. "All the petty grievances that were going on during the season, when you're just going, *I'll just get to the end and then we'll be on hiatus*, when they'd extend the season, everyone would blow up at each other. They could hold it in for one more week but not four."

Which might be one way of explaining perhaps the most entertaining bust-up in the show's history, a showdown between Carrey and Keenen, over a sketch, that may or may not have nearly turned violent. The conflict stemmed from a sketch in which Carrey played Sergeant Stacey Koon, one of the cops accused of viciously beating motorist Rodney King. The sketch was filmed but shelved and Carrey was unhappy about it. He thought it was funny and timely, and that Keenen was shutting down his ideas, not giving him a fair shake. A few weeks later, Carrey's Koon impression was written into a different sketch, but this time, in a small part, playing a foil to someone else. Carrey was furious.

Cut to the table read for the sketch. Keenen is at the head of the table, Eric Gold is on his right, and Carrey on the other side of Gold. The cast, writers, and other staff fill out the long conference room table. When it's time for Carrey's first line, he stands up, points his butt in Keenen's direction, and reads his part from his ass.

"I've got his ass in my face, pointing at Keenen, and he's moving his ass muscles," says Gold, who at the time was managing both Carrey and Keenen. "Keenen's a very dignified man, and by the way, about six-foot-four. He gets up, he's ready to take Jim out. Jim gets up. He, too, is six-two or six-three and not afraid of anything. These guys are going to come to blows." The room went silent.

Steve Tompkins remembers the sound of Keenen's chair pushing back. "He was sitting there and everyone was kind of joking, but then all of a sudden, his chair went back and he stood up," he says.

Gold says he put himself between Keenen and Carrey to defuse the situation. Keenen poked his finger hard into Gold's chest several times and told him he better control his client. Then he stormed out of the room.

Firestein says the context is important. "Keenen and Jim had been grinding gears," he says. "He was quashing some of Jim's work that Jim thought was really good, and the more he complained, the more Keenen started using Jim as a utility player." As Tompkins puts it, "There were days when the court jester, Jim, displeased the king and his head was on the chopping block. Jim wasn't showing proper deference."

Some have suggested that Keenen harbored resentment that Carrey, the show's token white guy, was rapidly becoming its biggest star, though that's probably unfair. Regardless, the idea of confronting Keenen in such a public way was unheard of.

"No one ever stepped to Keenen," says Firestein. "Keenen ran a tight ship and was pretty well feared within the building. So nothing like this had ever happened, nothing even close. I remember Jim started doing it and there was no air in the room." After Keenen disappeared into his office, Firestein says he was enlisted to play peacemaker. "Eric said, 'If Jim doesn't apologize, he's going to be fired.'"

Carrey's memory of the confrontation follows the contours of the aforementioned narrative with key exceptions.

"It wasn't a Stacey Koon sketch," he says. "It had nothing to do with that. I came up with a character—I don't remember what the character was—but I'd written a sketch for it and Keenen canceled the sketch. Sometimes when you create a character, you get your nose out of joint if it doesn't make it on the show. Keenen had relegated the character to one line in another sketch and I was pissed." He also says he was actually sitting right beside Keenen. "When it came time to do my line, I took my time, got up from my seat, turned around, put my script on the seat, bent over, and said my line in Keenen's face, through my ass."

He doesn't remember nearly coming to blows with Keenen, but the tension certainly made it a possibility. "I remember turning around and all the writers and cast were completely silent with their eyes downcast. I was taking my life in my hands, but I'm that way when I get my dander up. Less so now, but I'd say ridiculous things to people that could kick my ass. By all rights, I should be dead, because Keenen's no one to trifle with." He recalls Keenen simply getting up and walking out. Later, he was asked to see him in his office. "He was sitting there with his eyes bugging out of his head on the other side of the desk. He said, 'Do you like this job?' I said, 'Yeah, man, I'm sorry. I was just angry, but I love this job.'"

Once Carrey apologized, Keenen says, "everything was cool."

Some who recalled this incident remember it happening at the beginning of the fourth season, not the end of the third, but whatever the exact moment of the skirmish, it was a sign of the heightened tensions, fraying nerves, and disintegrating relationships. However, the story's coda is comic and almost heartening. The incident provided fuel for Carrey's breakout big-screen role. "That was the creation of the ass-talking for *Ace Ventura*," he says. Yes, against considerable odds, talking out of his ass would become a classic Carrey signature after he incorporated it into the script for 1994's *Ace Ventura: Pet Detective*. "The thing about it is, that's where the best stuff comes from—extreme emotions, those moments where you're set free either by anger or joy." As silly as it is, he thinks there's something a little profound in the act of bending over and letting your ass speak for you. "Talking out of your ass to me was the perfect expression of rebellion. It's actually kind of a brilliant way of handling it. It's as disrespectful as you get."

⸻

As the season wound toward its close, another dismaying personnel issue loomed: Damon was planning on leaving the show.

Many speculated that the relationship between Keenen and Damon grew strained over the course of the show's first three seasons. Circumstantially, there were things to point to. It was Keenen's show but Damon was the first breakout star. Once new opportunities beckoned, Damon was less and less available. As one Fox executive puts it, "Keenen was trying to make a television show which was very valuable, and here was Damon negotiating to do fewer sketches by the day because he wanted to pursue a movie career."

What's more, a case can be made that Damon deserved a production credit and maybe even a share of the show's profits, but instead had been signed to a series of—as he remembers them—not particularly lucrative short-term contracts. It was easy to blame Fox for that, but at a certain point, couldn't the show's creator do something about it?

"At the end of the day, Damon was working for Keenen," says Firestein. "That's a hard thing to sort out when your brother is saying, 'This guy is making so much more money than I am,' or 'My brother has to approve my raise.' That's tense."

One person who worked on the show for a long time felt "Keenen suffered an enormous amount of sibling rivalry with Damon" and was jealous of Damon's natural talents. But Gold, who managed both brothers, saw it the other way around.

"Damon was always much more envious of Keenen," he says. "I've found that Keenen was a selfless, incredibly paternal, loving head of the family. Keenen only wanted the best for Damon at every single point. At every single point of conflict, it was Damon who always seemed a bit removed. Long after the show, you had Keenen, Marlon, Shawn, and Kim. Damon's the one who's not always involved. He was the black sheep. He was always a problem." Gold admits that he and Damon "have had [their] issues," and Damon fired him several times. "But I'm not saying this in a prejudicial way. I'm just saying as I remember it."

Some think it's all a lot of smoke and no fire. Most everyone agrees the brothers and the entire family were incredibly close, closer than your average family. Keenen denies any sort of jealousy or rivalry. "Damon and I are in different lanes," he says. "If you look at our careers, you can see that. I'm more behind the camera, he's more in front. Damon is a stronger performer than I am. I am a stronger creator than he is. When he broke out, I was happy. I knew he was a star, that's why I hired him. There's no competition. That was the goal—for all of them to become stars."

According to Damon, it was simply time for him to leave. He was in the process of finishing *Mo' Money* and had offers and ideas in the hopper for more films. "Keenen's manager was my manager," he says. "Keenen's lawyer was my lawyer. Both were telling me, 'It's time to go. You've got a movie career.'" All the way back to his initial contract negotiations for the pilot, Damon never felt valued by Fox. He says the company always treated him like Keenen's little brother. "I had no allegiance to the show because of how I was treated. There's no commitment to me, so why should I be committed to them? That was Fox's fault. They were thinking out of allegiance to my brother, I wouldn't go. They were playing the family card."

But Joe Davola recalls a phone call from Rupert Murdoch asking him to help convince Damon to stay: "Rupert called me up ready to shovel money into Damon's hands to have him stay."

Ultimately, it may not have been money Damon really wanted. "I thought my love for my brother trumped everything and show business would never come between us," he says. "If Keenen would've said, 'Hey Damon, I need you to stay,' I gladly would've stayed. But Keenen didn't say that, so I thought I had his blessing."

To judge by the heartfelt send-off Keenen gave him at the end of the season's final episode, he did. As the cast and crew gather onstage, Keenen announces, "It's a very bittersweet moment here on *In Living Color*. We want to say goodbye to one of our cast members, Damon Wayans, on his way to a superstar movie career. We had great times and of course we wish him the best. Come back and visit sometime. Love you." With that, Keenen kissed his younger brother on the cheek and embraced him warmly at center stage. The camera pulled back and then followed Damon as he walked through the backstage area, out the door of the studio, across the parking lot, and into the night.

28

"It Just Seemed Like Nothing Was Ever Going to Be Funny Again"

A crowd gathered outside the East County Courthouse, a bland, municipal building in Simi Valley, California, on April 29, 1992, awaiting the verdict in the trial of the four police officers who'd been videotaped beating Rodney King at the side of highway a year earlier. The court announced at 1:00 p.m. that the jury had reached its decision. At 3:15 p.m., the "not guilty" verdicts were read in the courtroom, and not long after, the four police officers made their way from the building, through the assembled throngs. It was a chaotic scene, with bystanders screaming "Racists!" and worse at the cops, and sheriff's deputies keeping the crowd from attacking Sergeant Stacey Koon. *Boyz n the Hood* director John Singleton heard the verdict on the radio in his car. He was on his way to the set of his next film, *Poetic Justice*, but instead drove straight to the courthouse and joined the angry protestors. Shortly after arriving, he was interviewed by a news crew.

"The judicial system feels no responsibility to black people—never has, never will," Singleton told them. "By having this verdict, what these people have done is they've lit the fuse to a bomb." In light of what happened next, Singleton sounded prophetic, but it didn't take a prophet to sense the mood in Los Angeles.

Black residents had felt under the LAPD's thumb for a long time and at the mercy of a justice system that was, at best, indifferent to their plight, or at worst, actively against them. There had been no accountability for officers when Eulia Love, a thirty-nine-year-old mother of two, had been shot eight times and killed after a dispute over a gas bill escalated into a physical confrontation. When a Korean-American grocery store owner gunned down fifteen-year-old Latasha Harlins, the killer was sentenced to probation, community service, and a five-hundred-dollar fine. Now the idea that video evidence of cops kicking and clubbing a black man wasn't enough to compel a jury to convict them was too much for some in the black community in Los Angeles to take.

The city exploded into three days of rage and mayhem. Looting was rampant, white and Latino motorists were dragged from their cars and beaten, sections of the city were set ablaze. Firefighters were attacked and shot at when they attempted to respond. Police were unprepared, and in many places forced to retreat. In Koreatown, which police had abandoned, Korean-American shopkeepers organized into armed security squads to defend their businesses. Much of the anarchy was captured by news crews and beamed to the rest of the country and the world. Viewers watched in shock as shopkeepers exchanged gunfire with looters, and a white truck driver, Reginald Denny, was pulled from the cab of his truck and beaten within an inch of his life by a black mob. It was chaos.

On the first night of the riots, Paramount urged Arsenio Hall to cancel his show. Tim Kelleher, who was a writer for *Arsenio* then and later for *In Living Color*, says Paramount closed their lot at noon and told everyone to go home. While he and his fellow writers were packing up, the show's production team delivered a memo.

"They said, 'We're doing a show tonight, everyone has to stay, no one is allowed to leave,'" Kelleher recalls. Arsenio ventured with a camera crew into the heart of the city and urged calm. The only guest on the show that night was L.A. mayor Tom Bradley. "It was just Arsenio and Tom Bradley with no audience. There was a dusk-to-dawn curfew. I remember driving home that night, all the windows were smashed, and at that point it just seemed like nothing was ever going to be funny again. You just couldn't make jokes and we didn't probably for a couple weeks."

National Guard units were deployed on the second day of the riots, but the havoc and bloodshed continued. That night, as chance would have it, was the series finale of *The Cosby Show*, and NBC abandoned its round-the-clock riots coverage to broadcast it. Ratings for the show had dropped over the course of the previous few years, and particularly in this context, Cosby's moralizing tone and the Huxtables' image as white America's favorite black family seemed a relic from another era.

When an uneasy peace was finally restored, the toll was shocking: Fifty-five people had been killed, more than two thousand injured. Entire neighborhoods looked like they'd been carpet bombed. Property damage was near one billion dollars.

At the time of the riots, *ILC* had completed filming on the third season. The cast and crew were on hiatus. When they returned at the end of the summer, the shadow of what some called the L.A. Uprising still hung around like a pall.

———

A little over a month after the riots, Arkansas governor Bill Clinton appeared on *The Arsenio Hall Show*. This wasn't just a typical politician sitting down with a talk show host shilling for votes. (Though, to be sure, it was that too.) Clinton had sewn up the Democratic nomination for president the night before. Of all the places one might expect to see him the following night, sitting in with Arsenio's band, playing saxophone in a pair of dark Ray-Bans, wasn't one of them.

During the episode, Clinton spoke to Arsenio about the L.A. Riots but not in the law-and-order terms politicians running for office might be expected to mouth. Instead, he seemed to grasp—on an emotional as well as historical level—that the riots were the culmination of years of bitterness and frustration. He spoke of residents who, "day in and day out, they trudge through their lives, they live in substandard housing on unsafe streets, they work their guts out, they fall further behind, nobody even knows they're there until there's a riot." The appearance helped cement a lasting connection between Clinton and African-Americans. But his appearance on the show was also another indication that Arsenio— and by extension, Keenen, Spike Lee, John Singleton, and others—weren't feeding a niche market. They were playing in the big leagues. In much the same way *ILC*'s Super Bowl special had been a statement about the show's reach, Clinton's *Arsenio* turn was confirmation that what once was fringe was now mainstream.

Ratings didn't always reflect that reality. *ILC*'s had been strong through the first three seasons, averaging around twenty million viewers. By the standards of today's bifurcated television market, those are huge numbers, but for the 1991–92 season that only made *ILC* the forty-eighth most popular show on television. (Although, it's worth noting it was third among black viewers.) Some of this comes down to the fact that Fox was still struggling to gain a foothold in some markets, where it was relegated to UHF feeds with spotty reception. But despite middling Nielsen numbers, *ILC* had the highest Q-rating of any show on TV. Q-ratings measure the audience's familiarity with and good feeling for a program. Essentially, the highest ratings go to the shows that the most people know and like, regardless of whether they watch every week. They're a good measure of a show's influence. *ILC* may have begun to show cracks in its creative foundation at the end of Season 3, but as the staff was reassembled for Season 4, it had never been more popular or influential.

The show's stature made its players valuable commodities. This included the Fly Girls. Although the Virgin deal had fallen apart, Warner Bros. picked up the thread, and Keenen still saw potential for the troupe as a multimedia juggernaut. As such, he was very interested in protecting—or maybe, better put, controlling—their image. But the dancers themselves weren't under contract to the show between seasons, so when four of them—all but Jennifer Lopez—saw a casting call for a Budweiser commercial soliciting "Fly Girl types" during the hiatus, they figured as actual Fly Girls, they'd be shoo-ins. They were right. All four were offered the commercial. Keenen called the Girls in for a meeting.

"Keenen was like, 'You can't do it,'" says Carrie Ann Inaba. "I was like, 'I'm sorry, you don't actually get to say that.' We weren't on retainer."

Cari French felt the same way: "We have to make money on the months we're off from this show. We can't sit around between seasons and not work."

The problem wasn't that they were working during the hiatus. It was that if all four of them did the commercial, even if they weren't billed as

"The Fly Girls," they might as well have been because everyone would recognize who they were. So essentially Budweiser was getting the Fly Girls on the cheap.

"They were getting paid scale," says Keenen. "At the same time, we were negotiating a Sprite commercial where they were going to get $350,000. But they didn't have the patience to wait for the Sprite commercial."

Keenen gave them an ultimatum: the commercial or the show. Inaba, French, and Lisa Marie Todd picked the commercial. "I just said, 'Look, I'm done,'" says Inaba. "The energy of the group had changed a little. It wasn't as exciting. It was time to move on."

Deidre Lang stayed with the Fly Girls, leaving just her and Lopez. Two new dancers, Josie Harris and Lisa Joann Thompson, were hired, but Keenen seemed frustrated and disillusioned with the way the plans for the Fly Girls—the TV spinoff, the recording project, the whole brand—had gotten derailed. "After we hired new girls, Jennifer and I went to Keenen and said, 'Are we still going to do the recording?'" says Lang. "He was like, 'It's changed now. I don't want to.' So it ended up falling apart."

Another consequence of the show's popularity was that its stars wanted to renegotiate their contracts with the studio. Jim Carrey felt he deserved more than seventy-five hundred dollars an episode.

"Jim says he wants twenty-five thousand dollars an episode, which isn't a lot, really," explains Eric Gold. However, because the original contracts were "favored nations," Carrey's demand triggered a domino effect. "David Alan Grier says, 'Well, if Jim's gonna get twenty-five, I want twenty-five.' And Tommy says, 'If you guys are getting it, I want it.' And Kim is like, 'Well, what about me?'"

Keenen backed his cast's salary demands, even as production on Season 4 was beginning and they were threatening to hold out until a deal was reached. The studio head at the time was Lucie Salhany, who'd taken over the year before, after having run Paramount's television division. Salhany, a college dropout, had started her career as a secretary at a Cleveland television station, then risen steadily through the ranks. She'd helped bring Oprah Winfrey's daytime talk show into syndication, and was instrumental in the creation of Arsenio's show. She was short, with dark hair and large eyes, and the fact she was a woman made her some-thing of a unicorn in the television industry's upper echelons.

According to Gold, during a meeting, Salhany proposed an idea for breaking the impasse with the *ILC* cast. "Lucie says, 'I got an idea: We're gonna fire Jim Carrey.' I'm in the room. I'm like, 'Are you out of your mind?'" Gold implored her, saying that talents like Carrey aren't easy to find.

Salhany says that Gold "was very tough to deal with. Eric was a pit bull. From my standpoint, it was a nightmare," though she admits, for a manager, "that's who you want."

Ultimately, cooler heads prevailed. No one was fired, new contracts were signed, the cast got their raises, and all was seemingly well. But the dealings with Salhany left a bad taste and certainly weren't a good foun-dation for an ongoing relationship between her and the show's principals.

———

When the cast reconvened, Steve Park wasn't among them. His contract hadn't been renewed, which was devastating to Park and something of a surprise among the other cast members. Although he'd struggled to cre-ate recurring characters, he was a good team player, who was funny in his spots and worked hard. At the time, Park was simply told he wasn't invited back. "The circumstances," he says, "were always shrouded in mystery." Years later, he reconnected with and eventually married Kelly Coffield, who passed along to him the story she'd been told about his de-parture.

"Keenen said my manager was playing hardball, demanding more money," says Park. "I think Keenen was really struggling with Fox, and was like, 'Screw it. Just let him go.'"

For Park, the disappointment was personal, but also, particularly in the wake of the L.A. Riots and the tense relations between the Korean-American and African-American communities, it felt bigger. Having worked with Spike Lee in *Do the Right Thing* and Keenen on *In Living Color*, Park had been a part of two black cultural landmarks. He'd been a huge fan of both Spike and Keenen, and before ever working with either, had felt bonded to their work. "I had this feeling like we're all on the same page," he says. "Like we all had the same point of view as minorities in

American culture. Then when I worked with them, I realized that's not the case. I'm seen as the outsider. That was disillusioning. It was difficult for me to realize they don't feel as connected to me as I do to them."

Park's exit wasn't the loss the show felt most acutely, however. With Damon's departure, there was a huge, gaping hole right at the show's center. "We could replace him, but he was irreplaceable," says Pam Veasey, who along with Les Firestein and Greg Fields was promoted from head writer to co-producer for Season 4. "When he left, the show wasn't the same."

After a wide casting call to find two new cast members, one, predictably, was found closer to home. Marlon Wayans had been around since the show's beginning but had been pursuing a college degree. "I wanted to learn to be Marlon before I came to be a Wayans," he says. "That's why I went off to college and learned to be my own man."

Life at a historically black college wasn't always what he'd envisioned. "I went to Howard because I thought I wanted to be around my people," he said. "Then I realized that them niggas hated me. My professors would be giving a class and go, 'What we're going to do in this class is talk about dignity—unlike that show *In Living Color* which is a minstrel show.' And he'd be looking dead at me." Marlon had attended LaGuardia High School of Performing Arts in New York—the school famously featured in *Fame*—and always knew acting and comedy were in his future. He'd begun auditioning for movies while still at Howard. He was offered a role in *Juice* but turned it down. He was cast to play Robin in Tim Burton's *Batman Returns*, but Burton cut Robin out of the film before they'd even begun shooting.

Marlon's first film or television role—not including a cameo in *I'm Gonna Git You Sucka*—was in *Mo' Money*. Damon made him audition for a role that had initially been earmarked for Kadeem Hardison. Hardison passed, Marlon got the part, and the film was a hit. With Damon leaving *ILC*, that Marlon would take his spot seemed like a foregone conclusion, but he was conflicted because it would mean dropping out of college. He remembered his mother cursing Keenen out in the laundry room of their Chelsea apartment when Keenen left Tuskegee. When Marlon approached her with essentially the same issue, her tune had changed. As he recalled, she was "sitting on a whole new washing machine now, with her fur and diamonds, going, 'Baby, don't be a jackass. Do like Keenen. Go take yourself out there and become an actor.'"

Marlon's arrival occasioned the expected grumbles about nepotism, but there was also a sense that while nobody could replace Damon, Marlon was about as close as anybody was going to get. "Maybe Keenen gave Shawn more than Shawn had deserved at the time," says Gold, who by this time was also managing Marlon and Shawn. "But when Marlon comes along, Marlon is a breakout talent like Damon."

Ali Wentworth came to the show through the more traditional route. She was a young actress who'd been part of the L.A. improv and sketch theater group the Groundlings. Her agent told her the show "was looking for a black guy to replace Damon Wayans." Naturally, she says wryly, as a blond, white woman, she figured she'd be perfect. She went through several rounds of casting before meeting with Keenen, who by this point in time had shaved his head clean and taken to wearing dark sunglasses, even indoors.

"I went to his office and he was eating a weird salad," says Wentworth. "He had sunglasses on, the kind that you can't see his eyes. I remember thinking, I have to kind of sex it up. I have to look kind of trashy. I couldn't wear my white corduroys and cashmere turtleneck sweater. So, I went in a miniskirt and this tight tube top thing. We had a conversation. It was pretty short. I left and thought, *Well, forget it. That's not going to work.* I found out later that day I got it." She had no idea what she was walking into.

29

"It Was a Really Cold, Destructive Place to Work"

By the beginning of the fourth season, something had changed. Coming out to greet the audience at the beginning of the first episode wearing a dark black suit, dark sunglasses, and sporting a shiny bald pate, Keenen looked more like a professional assassin than a comedian. It would be his only time on-screen all season. While he never made it official policy—and the show's writers still wrote sketches for him—Keenen stayed behind the scenes for the rest of his time on the show. Most interpreted this as part of an overall effort to gradually step away from the day-to-day hassles of running the show. By reducing his responsibilities and promoting Les Firestein, Pam Veasey, and Greg Fields into producer roles, Keenen could concentrate more energy on taking advantage of other offers coming in for him.

"Keenen got hot from the show as a personality, but also as a film-maker/executive producer," says Eric Gold. He was being offered "once-in-a-lifetime opportunities to star, direct, produce, host. His desire was to transition the executive producing heavy lifting to the internal team."

Firestein thought this made sense and not just because it meant a promotion for him. "He probably wanted a system in place to keep the mothership alive and expand his empire," he says. "I don't know why he wouldn't. He wanted to follow Lorne Michaels's trajectory, which is *I don't need to be here doing this every day*."

Keenen denies he was any less invested in the show than in earlier seasons. "There's no truth to that at all," he says. "As the show progressed, it required so much more from me simply because each season gets harder, it doesn't get easier. You can't be at a distance on a show like that in Season 4. It's all-consuming. I had to be everywhere but nothing was coming together. There was a point where there was so much, I had to stop being in front of the camera. I had no time to be in sketches."

That first episode was devoted almost entirely to the L.A. Riots. By the time the writers assembled to start working in early July, the riots were a couple of months past, but the effects were still tangible around the city as the cleanup was in progress. It was a tragedy, no doubt, but if comedy is tragedy plus time, the sense was that enough time had passed. But it was a needle to thread. Mike Schiff, who was hired at the beginning of the season along with a writing partner, Bill Martin, says, "The marching orders were that the first episode was going to be all Riot stuff. We were looking for ways to make the riots funny, but we'd all lived through them and they weren't funny at the time. I remember thinking, *If we can do this right, anything that makes the show more relevant and less goofy would be good for a premiere*."

Larry Wilmore recalls, "I wrote a lot of sketches around the Riots. I pitched so many inappropriate jokes, a lot that I wished to God had gotten on the air but didn't."

One sketch was a fake PSA portraying Rodney King (David Alan Grier) and Reginald Denny (Jim Carrey) as shell-shocked and brain-damaged. Their message: "Stay in your car." In "Fire Marshal Bill Rebuilds Los Angeles," the character's goofiness is paired this time with sharp commentary. Carrey, as Bill, enters a recently rebuilt grocery store with a shotgun. "So I hear you folks like to take shots at firemen," he says. He takes jabs at police brutality, looters, racists, the Simi Valley jury, and the justice system. Carrey, who's a main character in all but one of the episode's sketches, says he returned from the show's hiatus "pissed off royally" at the King verdicts and the violent fallout, "chomping at the bit" to exact a little comic justice. The show, he says, "was the only place to be as far as taking that subject on."

A new writer, Rick Najera, the show's first Latino writer, had been caught up in the riots personally. He was teaching a class and hadn't heard about the King verdict. When none of his students showed up, he walked back to his car and started to see smoke, and hear gunshots and sirens. He was approached by a group of young black and Latino men. "They jumped me," he says. "They were hitting me, saying, 'Let's get this white motherfucker!' I'm a light-skinned Latino. I go, 'Motherfucker, why you calling me white?'" He yelled at them in Spanish and they backed off. Najera drove home through the center of the mayhem, not far, he says, from where Denny was attacked.

Najera wrote a sketch called "Edward James Olmos Does Yardwork" that lampooned the Latino actor's prominent role as freelance peacemaker and janitor after the riots, when television news crews followed him as he led volunteers, broom in hand, on a mission to clean up the mess.

"Eddie was a friend and still is—he's my children's godfather," says Najera. "After the riots, Eddie said, 'Rick, let's go clean up.' I went to where he was having people clean up. We were in a part of South Central that hadn't been affected by the riots. There must have been thirty, forty, fifty preppy Americans sweeping up someone's front yard. A woman walks out and goes, 'Hey! There's no riots here. That's my yard. Leave it alone.'"

That became the basis for Najera's sketch. In it, Carrey, as Olmos, earnestly leads a crew as they make renovations to Olmos's own house. The suggestion that the actor was grandstanding ("There is so much to do," he says in the sketch, "so very many ways to be seen.") seemed fair, but the shots at Olmos's pocked complexion were a little out of bounds for Najera. "Keenen's big thing was 'You gotta go harder on Eddie,'" he says. "In the end, another writer wrote, 'We have to clean up the biggest part of this mess: my face.'" Olmos was unhappy with the cheap shot. "In Latino culture we can be very sensitive because of the way we're portrayed in the media. I was in a [writers'] room with people that didn't understand Latinos. I talked to Eddie and said, 'Listen, everyone gets parodied on *In Living Color*.'" It was an early lesson for Najera in the show's credo. "The feeling with every sketch was *You can go further*."

By the beginning of Season 4, the atmosphere behind the scenes was, at best, tense and, at worst, downright poisonous. Keenen was unhappy with Fox, cast members were at odds with each other, and the writing staff had gone through a makeover that was extreme even by its own ever-volatile standards. The head writers, Firestein, Veasey, and Fields, were now producers, which led to the departure of one of the staff's most productive teams, Fax Bahr and Adam Small.

"Keenen put Les, Pam, and Greg in charge and we said we don't want to be a part of that," says Small. "We felt we should've been promoted."

Michael Anthony Snowden had written a spec script for a potential *Blade Runner* sequel. Keenen helped get the script to Warner Bros., where the project ultimately stalled, but suddenly Snowden was an in-demand screenwriter—quite a transformation for a kid who'd been discovered dancing at a nightclub a year earlier—and left the show to pursue it. Steve Tompkins quit ("I couldn't wait to leave," he says. "It was absolute slave labor.") to work on a short-lived sketch show called *The Edge*. Fred Graver got a job writing for *Cheers*. In their place, the show hired eleven new writers, including several standups, some sitcom vets, and strangely enough, two former network executives. The new blood didn't change the vibe.

"It was high stress, very competitive," says Nancy Neufeld Callaway, who had been a VP in the film division at Fox before taking the writing gig. "We'd stay until two, three in the morning. I wouldn't say it was a warm, fuzzy room." A couple months into the season, Najera says, "people were falling apart physically." Such a big writing staff brought in more ideas, but also created other problems.

"We had 3 EPs [executive producers] and a gazillion writers," says Steve Oedekerk, a standup who'd been recruited to the show by Larry Wilmore. "The more people you have to manage, the harder it is to have a core symmetry." The writers cleaved into cliques. Oedekerk was friendly with Carrey from the Comedy Store, so he ended up sharing an office with him and writing almost exclusively for him. "It was very compartmentalized. I showed up there most excited about working with David Alan Grier. I didn't work with him on one sketch the entire season."

Marlon arrived at the show to find the same problems Shawn had.

"The writers didn't really write for me and Shawn," says Marlon. Some of this, he thinks, was a matter of him being new to the show. The writers didn't know his capabilities. Shawn thinks there was more to it than that.

"New people came on and they had their gripe with Keenen pushing them as writers," says Shawn. "Me and Marlon took the backlash. People were mean to us, which was good because it motivated me and Marlon to become the writers we are."

Bill Martin doesn't recall Shawn or Marlon being frozen out by the writing staff. "We were there for no other reason than to make Keenen happy and what made him happy was getting his brothers in the show," he says. "So we wrote tons of stuff for those guys."

Shawn and Marlon did quickly score with some original characters, two neighborhood wannabe thugs, Snuff and Roam, based on two guys they'd known growing up. According to Marlon, most of the sketches he starred in he wrote himself, including an over-the-top parody of *Def Comedy Jam*. One of Shawn's more memorable moments was portraying Chris Rock in a commercial parody for a credit card called Anonymous Express. According to Mike Schiff, the sketch was commissioned by Keenen. Schiff recalls sitting in his office one day and watching Rupert Murdoch walk past his door with Chris Rock, on their way to a meeting with Keenen. "I don't know what was said in that meeting but [afterward] Keenen called a pitch meeting and the word went out, 'Keenen wants to parody Chris Rock,'" says Schiff. "The words may have been, 'He wants to go after Chris Rock.'"

The sketch skewers Rock's near-invisibility at *Saturday Night Live*. When Shawn as Rock encounters a tour group being shown around the 30 Rock studios—one of whom is, ironically enough, played by future *SNL* cast member Molly Shannon—they try to guess who he is. One guesses he's Eddie Murphy. Another thinks he's Damon Wayans. "No, he got fired from his first season," Shawn answers, as Rock. "Now, he's on that other show, the one I should've been on in the first place."

Rock wasn't thrilled with the sketch. It cut close to the bone. "There was a whole cultural thing going on that I was kind of a part of but that I couldn't really express on *SNL*," he said in 2004. "I'm on *SNL*, and *In Living Color*'s on, rap's on MTV, *Def Comedy Jam* is happening, *Martin* is happening, all this black stuff is happening. I was like Charley Pride or some shit."

Shawn was tight with Rock at the time, and the sketch made things dicey between them. "I learned the New York comedy club ropes from Chris," says Shawn. "I had to call him and tell him we were doing him and how the joke wasn't really on him, the joke was on *SNL*. We're cool now, but at that time, it was a little tough."

Ali Wentworth found her place on the show pretty quickly, playing, in her words, "a lot of hookers, strippers, and Hillary Clinton." But in sharp contrast to her smooth on-screen integration, behind the scenes Wentworth found her introduction to the show harrowing. David Alan Grier and Jamie Foxx were warm toward her, but as a white female, she felt Kelly Coffield saw her as a threat. "I was welcomed by the men," she says. "I was shunned by the women."

Much of Wentworth's discomfort had very little to do with her. Upon her arrival, she walked into a tangled mess of alliances, rivalries, and hostilities she didn't understand. "I wasn't aware of the kind of in-depth fighting," she says. "There was not only a rift between Keenen and Fox, but there started to become a rift between the Wayans and Jim Carrey too. It got to a point where Jim and the Wayans weren't speaking to each other."

Carrey admits the vibe had changed considerably by this point: "Season 4 was a turning point. A lot of people started thinking about *Where am I going from here?* It becomes like a family. There's certain people in my family I'm not so close to because we've just had too much time together in a high-pressure situation. And Keenen wasn't an easy boss to work for. A lot of times he made us dig a hole, fill the hole, dig the hole, and fill the hole. There was a little infighting going on. There were a couple times I'd show up in a sketch with black sunglasses on and completely bum the sketch out. Then Kim would show up in one of my sketches wearing black sunglasses obviously not committed at all."

For Wentworth, who didn't know the other cast members and had never worked on television before, all the quiet hostility and passive-aggressive sniping made the working conditions dreadful. "I had a pit in my stomach every single day I went to work," she says. "There's nothing harder than having to be funny amidst all that. I didn't know what was going on. I very much tried to keep to myself. When we weren't rehearsing, I'd stay in my dressing room. It was a really cold, destructive place to work. I felt like at any moment somebody was going to lose their shit."

Oedekerk had known and liked Keenen and Damon from standup, but when he arrived at *ILC*, he barely recognized the guys he'd known. "At that point, Keenen was bald, always wore these dark glasses—so dark I was wondering if he could actually see well inside 'cause it wasn't a brightly lit place," he says. "When I showed up, it was sort of like, *My gosh, you've become Colonel Kurtz. What happened?*"

Tommy Davidson continued to struggle amid the tense atmosphere and fierce competition. A few episodes into the season, he departed to get treatment for substance abuse. *SNL* was infamous as a den of iniquity, where drug abuse was not just common, but was practically a job requirement, but *ILC*'s backstage culture was comparatively straitlaced, which made Davidson's mounting problems stand out even more. He's intentionally vague on the details—though he's spoken, at times, of his problems with cocaine—but says everyone on the show could see what was happening with him. "It was all the not-good things you do when you start getting strung out on something. I was late. I went from being an A-1 professional guy to a guy who wasn't showing up." Eventually, he just cracked. "I had a meltdown. I had to go get some help, get some new tools to live." Many of his issues were personal, but his experiences at the show also played a part. "That was the source of a lot of frustration and pain. It was a contributing factor."

Although Keenen was the source of some of this angst, Davidson says he was also part of the solution. "Keenen was a supportive dude," he says. "He treated me like family. He said, 'Do what you gotta do and take care of yourself. I love you.'"

Behind his chilly exterior, Keenen hid a surprising reservoir of empathy. One of the new writers, Robert Schimmel, who'd been hired along with his brother Jeff, was dealing with a horrifying situation at home: His young son was dying of cancer. The situation was excruciating. Robert—who died in a car crash in 2010—often walked out of his office, or a writer's meeting, to go cry in the building's stairwell. Every weekend, he flew home to Arizona to be with his family.

"Keenen came to my brother and said, 'I know what's happening with your son and it's horrible,'" says Jeff Schimmel. "'Go home and be with your kid. The show is going to be here. Come back when you want to come back.'" Robert was concerned if he left the show, he'd lose his salary and his family's health benefits. "Keenen said, 'You're not fired, you're not quitting, everything is here for you. Your job's not in jeopardy, your benefits aren't in jeopardy. When you're ready to come back, you're welcome to.' I've been in the entertainment industry for twenty-eight years. It's rare to see that.'"

———

Ratings dipped during the first part of the season, not precipitously, but enough that it didn't go unnoticed. The show had done good work—the L.A. Riots sketches; "The Black People's Awards," which pointedly honored African-Americans' work on television in such esteemed categories as "Best Black Sassy Next-Door Neighbor" and "Best Scared Brother on a Police Show"; "Juice Mania," an off-the-wall infomercial written by Schiff and Martin that featured Carrey hamming it up as an insane octogenarian peddling his juice maker's magical powers—but something was missing. When Damon left, he took all his characters with him. This meant no Homey the Clown, no "Men on Film," no Anton Jackson, no "Homeboy Shopping Network," no Brothers Brothers, no Handi-Man, no Oswald Bates. The solution to *ILC*'s troubles was obvious, particularly to Fox: Get Damon back.

Fox offered him a deal he couldn't refuse: seventy-five thousand dollars per sketch. According to Gold, the deal made Damon the highest-paid actor on television. The schedule was set so Damon didn't have to be there all the time. He could film multiple sketches in an afternoon. "He'd make two hundred twenty-five thousand dollars in a day," says Gold.

As Damon sees it, "This was me getting paid what I deserved, or making up for the times when I wasn't." When Damon returned, playing Anton Jackson, a mere five weeks into the season, the episode spurred a nice uptick in the ratings. But Damon didn't come back pretending to just be one of the guys.

"He had a bodyguard," says Oedekerk. "A really nice guy named Willy. That cracked me up."

Oedekerk may have been taken aback by how much Damon and Keenen had changed from the guys he knew from standup, but he kept his head down, worked hard, and quickly earned his keep as a writer. Early in the season, he and Carrey began making the most of the long hours in the office. Carrey's agent asked him to read a script for a film called *Ace Ventura: Pet Detective*. The script had been bouncing around for a while—both Rick Moranis and Chris Farley had reportedly passed on it—and it was easy to understand why. "It was a piece of shit," Carrey says.

Carrey gave the script to Oedekerk one weekend to confirm his assessment. "I read the script," says Oedekerk, "and came back on Monday and said, 'You'd be crazy to do this, man. It's absurdly unfunny.'"

As they talked about it though, they began to see a way that maybe they could make it work. "I made a deal with the company that I'd get paid to rewrite it," says Carrey, "but if it ended up being something I don't want to do, I wasn't obligated. I had a back door out of it that gave me a lot of freedom to do whatever I wanted in a really extreme way. So, me and Steve decided to rewrite from page one together."

Oedekerk was also working on a draft of a screenplay for the film *Nothing to Lose*, which would eventually star Martin Lawrence and Tim Robbins when it finally made it to the screen in 1997. "We'd finish *In Living Color* somewhere between eleven and midnight, then we'd work on *Ace Ventura* until like three in the morning," says Oedekerk. "Then I'd drive back to Laguna Hills. On the drive, I was finishing up *Nothing to Lose* on a tape recorder. I'd sleep for two hours, then drive back."

The long hours seemed to benefit the writing. Sometimes, they couldn't tell whether what they were conjuring was genuinely funny or if they were just overtired and punch-drunk. "We were howling with laughter," says Carrey. "I'd go, 'Okay, what do people love?' 'Fuckin', uh, shark attacks!' 'Okay, let's do a shark scene.' It was a total expression of disrespect for the medium of movies. We had the greatest time hanging out until four in the morning every night, writing this stupid movie."

Schiff's office with Martin was next door to Carrey and Oedekerk's. "Jim would come into our office late at night and ask which punch line we liked best, but he'd never give us the setup," says Schiff.

Carrey and Oedekerk spent seven months—essentially the entire fourth season—rewriting *Ace Ventura*. There was mounting pressure on Carrey to re-launch his film career with the right project. If his next film bombed, there might not be any more. As he and Oedekerk worked, he was growing increasingly confident that this script—the same one he and everyone else dismissed as a "piece of shit"—was the way to go. "Once I got into writing it," he says, "I realized I have to do this movie."

———

Tamara Rawitt had been something of an invisible hand at the show since its inception. She was more than just a traffic coordinator, making sure things happened on time; she was involved in just about every aspect of the show, from casting and staffing to dealing with the network and the studio. She also had a tight relationship with Keenen, whom she seemed to understand better than most outside his family, and who, in return, seemed to trust her implicitly. But like a lot of things about *ILC*, that was beginning to unravel in Season 4.

Rawitt was part of the writing process but wasn't, officially, a writer. As she puts it, "I did a lot of writing on the show. I fixed many things and made them much funnier behind the scenes." But she wasn't credited as a writer, and felt like, in general, her contributions were being overlooked. To remedy this, she asked Keenen for a writing credit. This, according to Firestein, didn't sit well with the writers.

"She'd never written anything for the show whatsoever and hadn't really offered to write," says Firestein. "Basically, the writers were asked, 'Are you okay with Tamara having a writing credit even though she doesn't write on the show?' which to many people seemed like saying, *We want to make this person chief of surgery at Cedars-Sinai even though they don't have a medical degree.* The writers were like, 'No, we're not okay with it.'"

Eric Gold says that Tamara's relationship with the writers grew worse over time. "She started to insist on writing credit," he explains, for her supervisory involvement in the writing process. He also felt she was too close to the network executives, particularly considering the amount of friction there was at the time between Keenen, the show, and the network. The situation grew untenable, and after close to four years working alongside Keenen, Rawitt left the show, she insists of her own accord. Other than losing Damon, it was arguably the most significant departure the production had suffered to that point.

Rawitt was angry that Keenen didn't have her back in the dispute over the writing credit. "That was one of the sore subjects between Keenen and me," she says. "I did an enormous amount on that show and I wasn't given credit for it."

30

"They Were Trying to Commandeer the Show"

On Election Night 1992, Fox broadcast its first Tuesday night of programming in the network's history. As befitted Fox's brand at the time, they weren't on the air to cover the election, but to amuse those who didn't care about it, with new episodes of *The Simpsons* and *Herman's Head* sandwiched around *Martin* and *In Living Color* reruns.

"We used to pride ourselves on being the ultimate counterprogrammers," says Sandy Grushow, then Fox's EVP of entertainment. "The best way to grow the network was to program aggressively when the other guys weren't."

The counterprogramming experiment was a minor success. *The Simpsons* finished second in its time slot, and even though both *Martin* and *In Living Color* finished fourth, they were competitive, drawing about sixteen million viewers who weren't interested in seeing Bill Clinton become the forty-second president of the United States. Not everyone was happy. Keenen was growing increasingly annoyed at Fox's eagerness to plug *ILC* reruns into their programming slate whenever they wanted. He believed that more runs of the show lowered its potential value in syndication.

Financially, syndication is the holy grail for a television show. Whatever money a producer or show creator might make in an initial deal pales in comparison with the potential income from syndication. Individual stations, or groups of stations, buy the rights from the studio to air reruns, and they pay per episode. There are more than three hundred independent television stations across the country, and the rights to air a single episode can reach hundreds of thousands of dollars per station; it can add up to a lot of money very quickly. Generally, a series needs to have one hundred original episodes before it has value on the syndication market, and *ILC* was on pace to pass one hundred episodes by the end of the fourth season. Keenen's belief that rerunning the show extensively before then would harm its syndication value is not exactly settled science. Jamie Kellner, Fox president at the time, says that in his experience, the shows "that had already been viewed by the highest number of people did the best in syndication." So far from undermining its value, additional reruns of *ILC* might actually increase its worth. Keenen didn't see it that way, and it's not clear anyone tried to sell him on that explanation anyway.

He had other headaches with Fox too. He'd recently batted away an attempt by the network to move the show from Sunday night to Saturday night based on a marketing report that indicated black viewers watched television on weekend nights in greater numbers. Keenen insisted to Fox that *ILC*'s audience wasn't simply black people, it was young people, and most would be out on Saturday night. Beyond arguments over scheduling, there seemed to always be network notes asking for more of this character or less of that one, friction with the Standards Department, or unwelcome input on possible guest stars.

"Sometimes the network would make requests of things they thought would work but they were things we'd already tried and confirmed didn't work," says Firestein. "Of course, Fox wouldn't take no for an answer." At one point, someone from the network "got caught fishing dead sketches from our recycle bin."

As the weeks passed, clashes between Keenen and Fox grew more pronounced.

"They were trying to commandeer the show," says Kelly Coffield. "They wanted stuff to be more marketable, more recognizable, to have even more buzz around particular characters and sketches."

Sandy Grushow doesn't dismiss these concerns but maintains that some of it was more a matter of perception. "There wasn't anybody in the Programming Department trying to rein the show in creatively. If there was any attempt to do so, it would've come from Broadcast Standards, Ad Sales, or Network Distribution. I had no sense Keenen was frustrated creatively. He and his manager, Eric Gold, had a direct and, as far as I could tell, positive relationship with Jamie Kellner. So, he may have been expressing that to Jamie, but I never got yanked into those dynamics."

For his part, Kellner says Gold "would call me and we'd try to find common ground," but that Grushow's boss, Fox Entertainment Group president Peter Chernin, "would've been the person responsible for maintaining that relationship" with Keenen and the show.

As the season dragged on, Keenen's patience for the seemingly constant battles wore thin. He was around less and less, and although he denies it, it was pretty apparent he was eying the exit door.

"He was clearly distracted sometimes, and disinterested," says Mike Schiff. "Honestly, I think he resented being there a little bit." Marc Wilmore says he can recall Keenen telling the entire writing staff, while they were all sitting around the conference table, that he didn't want to be at the show anymore.

At the time, Fox was in the process of rapidly growing its television footprint. The network was planning on expanding to seven nights of programming in January 1993, and was working on launching a cable channel, which would eventually become FX. The company was hungry for content that would bring guaranteed viewers with it, and naturally wanted to acquire said content as inexpensively as possible. *In Living Color* fit the bill near perfectly. Keenen and company had already produced more than seventy-five episodes across three-plus seasons, the show had a loyal fan base, and perhaps most enticingly, it was produced by Twentieth Television. That meant acquiring its rights would involve Fox negotiating a deal with its own TV studio arm, which is exactly what it began to do. When plans regarding the potential FX deal reached Keenen, he was furious.

This was the kind of situation the financial syndication rules, or finsyn, were put in place to prevent. The rules put limits and prohibitions on networks broadcasting shows they themselves owned. But the rules were being weakened by the late eighties when Twentieth took over producing *ILC* from HBO, and would be eliminated entirely by 1994. At the very least, though, the idea of a company selling the rights to one of its shows to another arm of the same company created a serious perception problem. As *ILC*'s producer and part-owner, how could Keenen know FX was paying a fair market price for the rights? As Kellner himself admits, "When the studio and network are under one ownership, it's easy to assume you're being cheated."

Flash forward to late November, when Fox canceled one of its Thursday-night shows, a forgettable twentysomething drama called *The Heights*. In its place, they decided to run what they were calling *In Living Color: The First Season*. Keenen says he was told at 7:30 p.m. on a Friday that this plan was going to be announced on Monday. The reruns would start running that Thursday. He was stunned. Not only did he see the negative impact on the show's syndication value, but the implication of rerunning sketches from Season 1 was that the show's best years had passed.

"That's when the big fallout started to happen," says Keenen. "I could see syndication going bye-bye, and that was your rainbow. I was working so hard, I'm killing myself and these guys are doing this?"

Keenen felt like he'd given up opportunities to star in and produce films because of the show, and now he'd been cut off at the knees. As Gold puts it, "You're leaving millions on the table, you're under pressure every day, and you're doing it because you believe you have a big upside. Then they took the upside away."

Putting aside whether the Thursday-night reruns would genuinely damage *ILC*'s syndication value, it seems fair to say Keenen and Fox— both the network and Twentieth Television—had been on a slow-moving collision course for a long time.

"There was the network, there was the studio, and there was Keenen," says Fox programming exec Dan McDermott. "This big asset was of enormous value to all three but in different ways. There was a lot of conflict over who had actual control of it and who was going to exploit it for their own financial gain to the detriment of other parties. The network's instinct—not only instinct but the network's stated desire— when you get a successful show is to exploit it as much as you can, as broadly and financially lucratively as you can. We wanted more episodes, we wanted to run repeat episodes and classic episodes. Keenen felt like his baby wasn't being treated well by other partners in the mix."

Amid all this, Fox's executive ranks were in transition. On November 2, Peter Chernin was named the chairman of the company's film division. Chernin, like Barry Diller, had been one of the executives who'd put the show on the air, and Keenen felt an allegiance with him. Now he'd no longer be around. Sandy Grushow was promoted into Chernin's place, but not until November 30. Kellner was getting ready to resign as Fox president at the end of the year. Lucie Salhany, who was running Twentieth Television, was quickly named Kellner's replacement.

It's not entirely clear whose decision it was to run *In Living Color: The First Season* on Thursday nights, but it didn't matter. The network's contract with the show gave them the right to do it and they did. What clearly fell through the cracks was having someone at Fox consider how Keenen would react to the plan but having a tight enough relationship with him to figure out a way to make him comfortable with it. Maybe that should've been Kellner, but he already had one foot out the door. Maybe it should've been Salhany, but she had no real personal relationship with Keenen. (As one exec puts it, "If you were to look at one hundred people and say, 'Who do you want having these conversations with Keenen?' Lucie would be your hundredth choice.") Maybe it should've been Grushow, but he says he was mostly unaware of the problem.

"It was on everybody's plate and yet it was on nobody's plate because of all the shifting going on," says Grushow. Ultimately, it's probably something that would've fallen to Diller or Chernin—or maybe even Joe Davola—but none of them was in the picture anymore. McDermott admits that the absence of Diller and Chernin, in particular, was a problem.

"Barry and Peter were not just MBAs solely concerned with bottom line," he says. "They loved the creative process and were very creative themselves. They had a real love of the show. Keenen and these guys were helping define American culture with this show, creating a wave of hip-hop culture that was going to be very dominant. Barry and Peter were respectful and frankly excited about the show and Keenen and all the folks working on the show. Subsequent people came into the network who didn't have the previous relationship with Keenen and their group, and looked at the show more as an asset they wanted to strip-mine."

Rose Catherine Pinkney recalls a meeting around this time with executives from the studio and the network. "It was in a gigantic conference room that I was in maybe four times in my five years at Fox—like the grown-up important conference room," she says. "All the top studio brass was coming and all of us who worked on the show, the day-to-day folks, were coming. Nobody was sure Keenen was going to show up. It was really funny because when he came, he sat at the end of the table with all the lower-level people, the people he saw on set every day. He clearly did it on purpose because there was a seat at the other end for him. But he didn't want to be there, didn't want to hear what they had to say. It was his way of being quietly defiant. It was like a Martin Luther King move."

As all this was going on, there was still a show to produce. But even that was getting completely engulfed by the bad vibes, particularly with regard to the Standards Department. When the network wanted a line of dialogue in that week's episode changed, Keenen and the producers went into foot-dragging mode, figuring if they held on to the tape of the episode long enough, Fox wouldn't have time to make the change. So, they wouldn't give up the tape.

As Firestein recalls, "Network lackeys were saying stuff like, 'It's our property. We actually own the show. We may just come and get it.' They were saber rattling like they were literally going to come and take physical possession of the episode."

Keenen had had enough. It wasn't about one line of dialogue. It wasn't even about not giving them the episode. It was about the totality of it, these various streams—repackaged episodes like *The First Season*, this bullshit FX deal, this feeling of being censored—merging at a critical moment. He couldn't let Fox screw him on the syndication stuff, push him around, *and* tell him what to allow on his show. He had to make a stand. He, Firestein, and producer Kevin Berg needed a plan for what to do if Fox made good on their threat to retrieve the tape of the episode.

"There was a story about how Keenen hid the master tape in the ceiling somewhere," says Rose Catherine Pinkney. "I think it's an urban legend."

Actually, as Keenen explains, laughing, this story is true. "I didn't physically hide the tape, but I told Kevin not to turn it over, to tell them he couldn't find it. Kevin was the one that hid it in the ceiling."

All the offices had drop ceilings with lightweight panels that could easily be removed and replaced. "It was a big one-inch tape, in those big blue cases," says Berg. "We thought if they came looking for it, we gotta hide it somewhere, so we literally stuck it up in the ceiling tiles."

If Keenen's goal was to piss off the Fox brass, mission accomplished. "It was a mess," says incoming Fox chairwoman Lucie Salhany. "Rupert [Murdoch] came into my office and said, 'That's a felony! You can't do that!'"

It was a Mexican standoff. Without the tape, Fox had no new episode to run. But Keenen had played the only card he still held. He was out of moves. He held out for a while, but with the intervention of lawyers, he was eventually convinced of the futility of his situation and delivered the episode. With that one concession, he acknowledged he'd lost control not just of the creative decisions on the show but of the entire direction of the show. He was exhausted. His relationship with Fox felt irretrievable. As he saw it, they thought they could run the show without him. Let them. He was done with it. No one at Fox, he says, tried to convince him to stay.

"They were under the impression it was a writer-driven show and that that's all they needed and the show would be just fine," he says. "So they were like, 'Yeah, cool, let him go.'"

McDermott says he thought Fox, whatever their problems, recognized Keenen's value. At the very least, he did. "I never felt it was preferable to do the show without Keenen," he says. "If I was ever asked and had the chance to weigh in—and I was and I did—my attitude was always that he's of material importance to the show. He *is* the show. There might have been decisions made above my pay grade that it's not worth the hassle or the money it's costing us or that it will cost us if we make a new deal. But I wasn't privy to that stuff."

On Friday, December 4, one day after the first airing of *In Living Color: The First Season*, Keenen called the cast and writers into the conference room. He walked to the head of the table, turned his seat backward, and sat down. Fighting back tears, he told them he was leaving the show.

"This isn't something I want to do, it's something I have to do," he said. He says he asked them to cooperate with whoever took his place. "This won't be the last time you see me," he told them. "We'll cross paths at a later time."

The very sight of the show's stoic leader struggling to stay composed as he walked away from the project that had been his life's work was shocking to many of those assembled, especially those who knew him best. "Keenen isn't a guy that cries a lot," says Marlon. "When he drops a tear, everybody drops one. It was sad. We all cried like babies."

Even those who were relatively new to the show found themselves caught up in the emotion of the moment. Writer T. Faye Griffin was hired that season as part of the network's diversity program and had just recently been bumped up to full staff member when Keenen announced his departure.

"It was like Daddy left," she says. "That's what made his going-away speech so impacting. His voice was quivering and one of the last things he said was, 'When I land, I'm coming back for all of y'all.' So, every time I see him, I say, 'Daddy, I'm still waiting for you to come get me.'"

Although Keenen says he told the staff to play nice with the next regime, some heard a different message entirely. "He certainly didn't say, 'Soldier on and make this the biggest hit you can,'" says Bill Martin. "Our sense was he would've enjoyed it if the place had caught on fire. He felt so disrespected by the network. His baby had been taken from him and there was a lot of ill will. There was nothing explicit but clearly the show was dead to him."

In fact, Schiff says, far from advocating a smooth line of succession, he remembers Keenen telling the writers they shouldn't feel obligated to stick around. "He took us all aside and in a very friendly way said, 'You guys know your contracts were to work on *my* show, so you're free to leave once I'm gone. Just tell your agent you can get out of this because this isn't what you signed up for.' It was nice of him to say, but we were all thinking, *No, we need these jobs. Thank you for your generous offer that I quit my first good job in television.*"

That night, Keenen made another farewell speech in front of the entire crew at dinner. Then, it being a Friday night, there was—believe it or not—a live show to do. The audience was already in their seats. "It was pretty somber that day," says Berg. "It was hard to go shoot a show after that."

For most of the episode, the cast kept a lid on the behind-the-scenes emotional bloodletting, at least until the final musical segment. The plan was for the entire cast and all the Fly Girls to gather around a piano while Jamie Foxx sang the Donny Hathaway song "This Christmas." There was no joke to the segment—this was planned as a rare moment of earnestness, a warm Christmastime send-off before the group went on a holiday hiatus. For Foxx, who'd been trying to hip the world to his musical talents since he arrived at *ILC*, it was a big chance to perform for twenty million viewers.

The segment opens with each of the Fly Girls, decked out in Santa hats, taking a few seconds to wish "Happy Holidays" to family and friends. When the camera pans to Wentworth, she looks shell-shocked, and just shrugs, "Merry Christmas." T'Keyah Crystal Keymáh smiles and says "Hi" to her grandmother. Carrey is the only one who attempts a joke, wishing a "Merry Christmas" to "all the spineless little weaklings I had to crush to get where I am today." As Jamie Foxx stands center stage amid this row of relative good cheer and begins singing, the rest of the cast—Shawn, Kim, Marlon, David Alan Grier, Kelly Coffield, and DJ Leroy "Twist" Casey—stand stone-faced behind them, in dark sunglasses and dark hats, looking to all the world like the Black Panthers have crashed the festive holiday proceedings.

"All of us that were displeased stood in protest," says Marlon. "We didn't smile. The cameras were trying to go around us. Everybody was like, 'Come on! Cheer up!' and we were like, 'No. This Christmas isn't happy for us.'"

After the show that night, there was a going-away party back in the offices. Keenen walked around with a bottle of Patrón. Most everyone on the writing staff sympathized with him, even those who might not have seen eye to eye with him as a boss. He seemed to be standing up for artistic integrity, for the little guy, refusing to be bullied by a big corporation. There were, however, a quiet few who felt like Keenen's brave stand was more of a smoke screen, an excuse for ditching a project he'd lost interest in a while ago. According to Marc Wilmore, Fox wasn't forcing Keenen out. In fact, the network wanted to expand *ILC* to an hour.

"Fox was begging him to stay," he says. "Rupert Murdoch routinely came to our offices. Keenen said he backed up the Brink's truck for us to go to an hour. Keenen didn't want to."

Gold agrees Keenen did want out or at least a chance to pursue other opportunities, and build a production company. But he doesn't recall any discussion about the show expanding to an hour, and says that while Murdoch was "always surprisingly nice and gentlemanly, Rupert never backs up the Brink's truck, especially for a show they didn't believe had residual value."

Many people blame Salhany for the deterioration of Keenen's relationship with Fox, and it's true she didn't have any personal connection to Keenen or personal investment in the show. As the studio head, many say she was heavy-handed with *ILC*. Unquestionably, she could've managed this asset better (or perhaps just managed it less). That said, the decision to run reruns on Thursday nights was almost certainly not hers, and even if she had a hand in selling the rights to FX, ultimately Murdoch himself was the one ruthlessly pushing to make deals to grow his company. In the end, there's plenty of blame to go around: Salhany, Kellner, Grushow, Chernin, Murdoch, Gold, and Keenen himself all could've handled the situation better. Far from being intractable, Keenen and Fox's problems were eminently solvable, something that, with hindsight, even Keenen sees now.

"I regret I didn't have better advice," Keenen says. "I was a young, passionate artist. I wasn't a businessman. I knew the business I was being presented wasn't favorable and it was going to ruin any opportunity of a back end. But had someone presented a way to make this situation favorable—which it could've been—it could've been a different negotiation. Everybody would've won. But I took a position, Fox took a position, and there was no mediator. Fox and I could've worked out that situation and *In Living Color* could've lived on. But with all the tension and the *'Fuck you!' 'Fuck him!'*—when you get into that and there's no mediator, there's only one outcome."

31

"It Was a Bunch of Scared People Left Trying to Save a Sinking Ship"

Fox quickly decided the show would continue without Keenen. There wasn't any serious discussion about simply closing up shop. It was a hit show, and as Sandy Grushow explains, "We were smart enough to know those were hard to come by."

Kevin Berg thinks there was a "big frustration factor" in Fox's decision making. "Fox stood up and said, 'Okay, we'll show him. We won't kill the show. We'll succeed without him.'"

At the studio, Rose Catherine Pinkney was concerned about the show's future, post-Keenen. "Nobody wants to lose your visionary producer," she says. "It's such a big deal that the person that came to you with an idea, convinced you there were one hundred episodes in it, explained how it could work season after season, when this person leaves, there's generally a void."

But Fox was committed to carrying on. "You have situations where actors or actresses leave shows all the time," says Jamie Kellner, who was himself resigning at the end of the year but was technically still Fox's president as all this went down. "Sometimes you replace them and it's successful. At times, you can't. You never want it to happen, but when it does, you just do the best you can."

Keenen admits, "I didn't want the show to continue without me," but the network immediately began making plans to do just that. Marlon says Fox offered him "a bunch of money" to stay on, but he refused. "At the time, I had a nine-hundred-dollar rent and seven hundred dollars in the bank, so I left with nothing. But at the end of the day, that's my brother."

Damon also had financial reasons to think twice about following his brother out the door. "I'd just made the deal to come back and they were paying me seventy-five thousand dollars a sketch," he says. He'd only shot a handful of those sketches when Keenen "decided we're leaving. So not only was I surprised, I was pretty upset because this was my comeuppance." Once Keenen quit, Fox upped the ante. "Fox said, 'We'll give you two hundred thousand dollars extra per show to take over as executive producer.'" It was the equivalent of offering Damon a gold-plated dagger to plunge into his older brother's back. Damon refused and walked out alongside Keenen and Marlon.

As Keenen notes, "That was a huge sacrifice. It was like, *You going where and you want me to do what?* But my family is a family. Come one, come all, leave one, leave all. So, I didn't have to say anything. Everybody said to themselves, 'If he's not here, I don't wanna be here even if you're gonna pay me this kind of money.' Damon, we laugh about it to this day. He was pissed. But he was my brother."

Kim and Shawn were under contract for the season and Fox wouldn't release them. "We all wanted to leave," says Kim. "We were heartbroken. We didn't see how you could remove the creator of a show, a show as specific as this, a show as sensitive in a lot of regards as this, and just expect to stick somebody else in there and everything is going to be hunky-dory."

Kim was right about the enormous challenge of doing the show without the guy who'd created it. That said, Keenen had been gradually ceding day-to-day responsibilities to the three co-producers, Les Firestein, Pam Veasey, and Greg Fields, so in some sense, there was a succession plan. But the reins didn't automatically pass to them.

"The network was struggling with, 'What do we do?'" says Veasey. "We didn't want them to bring somebody from the outside in. Myself, Les, and Greg said, 'We want to be the people to step up and carry on with the show.' It was difficult to convince the network. I remember going through a lot of tap dancing on that. We showed them the sketches the three of us were responsible for writing. We argued that we had been there. We were like, 'If you want it to be as close as possible to what exists, let us run the show. We are from Keenen's school of thought. He taught us.'"

Firestein thought the decision to continue without Keenen was "bizarre." "You're basically pulling the heart out of the show, and what you have left is a zombie," he says. "We were missing half our pieces, but Fox wanted us to do the same thing." Once Fox asked them to, though, his only choice was to carry on or to walk away from his own contract, "which at that point, I didn't feel like doing."

"I actually went to Keenen when he was leaving and asked how he felt about the three of us continuing without him," says Firestein. "He was like, 'You guys should do what's good for you. This is between me and Fox.' So, I felt like I had his blessing. I've seen Keenen since then and dealt with him and we're fine."

From Fox's standpoint, separating Keenen from the show wasn't as simple as changing the locks after he stormed out. Keenen had been an executive producer with an ownership stake in *ILC*. And while Fox may have been well within their contractual right to air *In Living Color: The First Season*, whether Twentieth Television could sell *ILC*'s rights to FX (Fox's new cable channel) for whatever price they deemed was fair was less clear-cut. Keenen and Gold claimed this was "self-dealing," and threatened a lawsuit over it. After meetings with lawyers and depositions, a settlement was hammered out. While the exact terms remain confidential, Fox bought Keenen out of his share of the show—most people I spoke to put the figure around or just above five million dollars, though one person had it as high as twenty million—and a formula was devised for repackaging future compilations of sketches and episodes. "I didn't want them to take my work and mix it up with shitty work produced after me and present it as my work," Keenen says. Ultimately, however, Fox was free to do with the show more or less what it pleased. And while many questioned the long-term syndication value of a rude, irreverent, of-the-moment sketch show, time has mostly answered that question. *ILC* was a staple of FX when the network launched in 1994, and for years was nearly inescapable on the channel. Reruns continued to air on its sister channel FXX until 2017. As of the fall of 2017, two upstart cable networks, Aspire and Fusion, were, somewhat ironically, using the show to plug holes in their own schedules: The former was airing reruns six days a week for between two and seven hours a day; the latter, three times a week for up to six hours a day.

Reactions to Keenen's departure varied among the cast. Kim and Shawn were essentially being held hostage to their contracts against their will. Others, like David Alan Grier and Kelly Coffield, felt a loyalty to Keenen and a disillusionment with the direction the show seemed to be headed. Carrey was grateful for the opportunity Keenen had given him, but in interviews around that time made it clear he was ready to turn the page.

"Keenen and I butted heads against each other," Carrey told the *Los Angeles Times* in March of 1993. "He was going off and doing other things and I felt the ship needed a captain. His heart just wasn't in the show anymore. You can't do a show like that halfway."

The show's longtime editor, Kris Trexler, says he was considering walking out with Keenen, and recalls Carrey as one of the leading voices keeping the show on track. "Jim said, 'Hey, we've got a show, let's rally, let's stick together and keep it going.' He was great."

Newer cast members, like Wentworth and Jamie Foxx, were distressed with the drama around Keenen's exit, but also just looking to get on with it. Feelings among the writing staff and the crew similarly ran the gamut. It was on Firestein, Veasey, and Fields to patch all this together into a cohesive show. It wasn't easy. "We didn't want audiences to think, *Ugh. They're gone so the show's a dud*," says Veasey. "We were hoping we could keep what existed, what was so special about *In Living Color*, alive."

As the revamped production team got their bearings, they relied some on sketches produced before Keenen's exit but which had been put on the shelf for later. "We always had a lot of sketches in the bank," says Firestein. "But remember, the sketches in the bank are the sketches we don't feel are great, otherwise they're not in the bank. Generally, it's stuff that's just okay."

Once the initial shock of Keenen's exit wore off, the show actually ran more smoothly without him. Keenen was, as Kevin Berg described it, a "bottleneck" that made the production inefficient. He was fickle, ornery, stubborn, and rarely punctual. Lots of time was wasted waiting for him to be available to make a decision. When he did make decisions, it often meant more work—a sketch that everyone else liked needed to be rewritten, a new set needed to be built, new props needed to be located because the ones used in rehearsal were distracting. Many writers felt like the job immediately got easier without Keenen. Fewer late nights, less unpredictability.

"It freed up the creative process somewhat because Keenen had very strong opinions about what we should and shouldn't do," says Bill Martin. "He had an encyclopedic memory of every pitch he ever rejected. So, there was a certain sense of, *Oh, all that stuff we didn't think he was going to like, let's pitch it now!* It definitely was a bit of a spring awakening creatively because we could try anything."

On the other hand, after more than seventy episodes, Keenen more or less knew what he was doing. His whims may have annoyed the writers and producers, but collectively his whims *were* the show's vision. If *ILC* was an inefficient machine under Keenen, it was inefficient by design.

"For all the aggravation of his bottlenecking," says Kevin Berg, "his bottlenecking was for a reason. I love the people who were there after he left, but some sketches that aired he never would've aired. We did some things that Keenen would've said, 'Don't shoot that. It's not funny.'"

Beyond his creative role, Keenen was also a figurehead that gave the writing staff cover to do more racially charged humor. Since the show's earliest days—when Keenen had told Fox in no uncertain terms that he didn't need consultants from the NAACP or the Urban League to validate his blackness—Keenen always served as a buffer, protecting the largely white writing staff from charges of racism or, at the very least, insensitivity. But now, without his imprimatur, some writers felt more exposed.

"However aloof he might have been, Keenen was the voice of the show," says Mike Schiff. One question hanging over the show now was "Could we still get away with things on a racial level without Keenen as our shield?"

A couple of weeks after Keenen's departure, *Los Angeles Times* critic Howard Rosenberg seemed to answer that question: "If TV's ethno-insults were confined to remnants of the past perhaps they would be more bearable. But they're not. The cleanup of stereotypes has not been complete—witness, for example, the ridicule that African-Americans are relentlessly subjected to on Fox's black-produced, increasingly unfunny satirical series *In Living Color*. The justification here appears to be that bashing one's own is acceptable—a sort of family affair—even though in this case the TV audience laughing at the black bashing is substantially non-black. Of course, *In Living Color* also targets other minorities such as people with disabilities and gays, and recently presented a particularly offensive, stereotype-feeding sketch about gays in the military showing mincing males in the barracks." (The Gay and Lesbian Alliance Against Defamation protested the latter sketch.)

Kim Wayans noticed a change in tone on the show almost immediately. "Keenen was able to get away with stuff as a black man in charge of a show like this, determining what's okay and what's not," she says. "That was no longer there. Now you have people giving you sketches to perform that you actually find offensive. Because now it's not you making fun of your own culture, it's somebody else who's not of your culture making fun of it and telling you that this is funny. It wasn't."

To be fair, the writing staff had five African-American writers on it, including one of the co-EPs, Pam Veasey, and the sketches produced during the second half of the season, if anything, were milder and took fewer chances with explicitly political or racial humor. But it was a problem of perception. When David Alan Grier plays Silky, a seventies-era pimp who's been cryogenically frozen for two decades, in "Forever Silky," his stereotypical portrayal—"Bitch, where's my money!"—is certainly no more offensive than any number of similarly stereotypical parts in earlier seasons (or similar roles in *Hollywood Shuffle* and *I'm Gonna Git You Sucka*, for that matter). "The Black People's Show" skewers the lack of opportunities for African-Americans in Hollywood by making fun of black actors playing raisins and intergalactic hookers; the tone is nearly identical to "The Black People's Awards," which was produced during Keenen's tenure. Similarly, Kelly Coffield's amiable racist Sheila Peace is no more bigoted than she was in Season 3. What had changed was the context.

"I was on the show almost from the beginning, so I don't think my material changed," says Firestein. "I don't think any of the other long-term writers' aesthetic or taste changed. I don't think it became making fun of black culture. We may not have had the guns to execute as well as we used to. Stuff isn't quite as funny because maybe the performers weren't as charismatic."

Perhaps the most pressing issue during the second half of Season 4 was that there were barely enough cast members to cast the sketches. Marc Wilmore, who'd begun appearing in scattered sketches at the end of Season 3, was suddenly on-screen a lot more. T'Keyah Crystal Keymáh and Ali Wentworth became more high-profile players. David Alan Grier and Jamie Foxx became stars. Still, they were shorthanded.

Even before Keenen's departure, the show began using more so-called "day players" to play smaller supporting roles simply because the main cast started to see such parts as beneath them. After he left, reliance on these day players increased even further; a few, like A.J. Jamal and David Edwards, were given short "tryout" contracts.

"I was there to do a job," says Edwards, a standup from Washington, D.C. "They just told me what to do. 'Hey, we need you in this sketch.' I wish they would've used me more. I remember being sad because I really wanted to make people laugh and they just weren't using me the right way."

Edwards had a seven-week contract, but never felt he was given a chance to prove himself. The gig carried a certain status though, and he sometimes invited one of his closest friends to come hang out backstage, a fellow standup named Dave Chappelle. "He used to come to the set," says Edwards. "He'd hang out and watch some of the tapings, hang with me in the dressing room, because we watched *In Living Color* in high school, and here I was on the show. It was a great moment for me, for bragging rights."

Eric Gold recalls that Chappelle "wanted to be on that show more than anybody, begged to be on," and says he probably would have been eventually if the show had stayed on the air longer. Edwards wasn't invited back after his seven-week run. Later in the year, he was cast on MTV's *The Real World*, and shortly after became infamous as the first person ever evicted from the cast's house.

Jenifer Lewis also had a short run on the show around this time, but she arrived with a little more cachet and was the star of several sketches. Lewis brought with her a handful of characters from a one-woman cabaret show she'd been developing. T. Faye Griffin says she and her writing partner, Al Sonja Rice (who's name is now Al Sonja Schmidt), were assigned to be Lewis's personal writing staff.

"All we did was cannibalize what she was already doing, the characters she walked in the door with," says Griffin. "We didn't really create anything new for her, we just customized for *In Living Color*'s style." Lewis's characters worked pretty well on the show, but there was a sense Lewis was auditioning *ILC*, as much as the other way around, perhaps fishing for a deal of her own from Fox. In the end, she didn't stick around.

Kim and Shawn were obligated to be on set but made no secret of their displeasure at being there. Some describe them as being "on strike," but they were more dragging their feet than actually refusing to work. The two occasionally played supporting parts in sketches, but had mostly stopped trying. In a sketch poking fun at the *Cosby Show* spinoff *A Different World*, Shawn is barely even going through the motions, muttering his lines with evident disinterest.

"I was angry," says Shawn. "The soul of the show was gone."

As Kim puts it, "The whole spirit had walked out the door. It was a bunch of scared people left trying to save a sinking ship. Nobody really knew what they were doing. The show felt adrift and desperate. It was no fun going to work anymore. I didn't want to be there."

It was an impossible situation. Kim and Shawn were perhaps justified in their resentment at being forced to perform for the company their brother just had a very public falling-out with, but on the other hand, the show needed warm bodies. Most people sympathized with their protest, but Kim and Shawn half-assing it was having an evident effect on everyone else's work too. "They're not that good as it is," says Marc Wilmore. "We're not dealing with Laurence Olivier and Kate Hepburn here."

The producers kept trying to use them. A script for a new Benita Butrell sketch made the packet one week, but when Kim read it, she found it offensive and racist. "I refused to do it," she says.

Berg had to deal with the situation. He walked down the hall and knocked on the door of Kim's dressing room. Kim was in there with Kelly Coffield. "She refused to come out of her dressing room to do the sketch," says Berg. "That was her way of saying, 'I'm done.'" Berg felt caught in the middle. He'd been with the show since the first season, had been promoted up the totem pole, and this was where it had gotten him. "I had to say, 'Look, if you're not going to do the sketch, you're in breach of contract and officially suspended from production. Feel free to go.' She was sitting there with Kelly and they were just crying. I was like, 'This is crazy. This is not something I want to do.'"

Kim wouldn't budge. "They were like, 'If you don't do it, we're going to hold you to breaching your contract. I was like, 'Do what you have to do.' I had to get lawyers and all that stuff. Eventually, we wound up settling out of court. I was released from my contract but not without some drama."

———————

The behind-the-scenes turmoil and even Keenen's eventual departure didn't necessarily dent the show's cachet among the hip-hop community, at least not immediately. Gang Starr, Onyx, Arrested Development, Digable Planets, Naughty by Nature, Mary J. Blige, Pete Rock & C. L. Smooth, and the Pharcyde all performed during Season 4. Digable Planets appeared on the show before their first album had even been released. It was a big deal for the group.

"It got the needle off zero," says Ishmael Butler, one of the group's MCs. "The show came from a hip-hop point of view. It was fast, it was streetwise, it dealt with current subjects that didn't necessarily have to cater to white audiences. It was a good look."

Arrested Development performed right around the time when all the drama with Keenen was going down, but the group's front man Speech says none of it spilled into their experience there. "The vibe was very positive," he says. With or without Keenen, *ILC* was important to the rap world. "It literally introduced hip-hop to a large segment of the American population. Hip-hop wasn't fully vetted yet. A lot of people weren't convinced it was going to last. They thought it was a fad. The show was a great platform to legitimize this art form, to get our music out to the entire world."

The season's most memorable performance—at least, in Rosie Perez's opinion—was one that never happened. In early March, Tupac Shakur was booked to perform. Tupac was a good friend of Perez's and, by extension, of the show. He'd just released his second album, *Strictly 4 My N.I.G.G.A.Z.*, which would eventually sell more than a million copies and spawn two iconic singles, "Keep Ya Head Up" and "Holler If Ya

Hear Me." Sitting in a limo outside of the production office before his scheduled performance, Tupac and several friends decided to spark up a joint. Nobody bothered to ask the limo driver if he was okay with that. He wasn't. An argument ensued, and when the driver walked toward the trunk of the car, Tupac assumed he was getting a gun. Fearing for their lives, Tupac and his friends pounced on the driver. A fight ensued. When the melee cleared, Tupac decamped to the show's green room, which is where the police found him when they arrived. "The driver called the police," says Perez.

The scene grew more intense. The Fly Girls were told to stay in their dressing rooms, because as Lisa Joann Thompson explains, "Tupac was causing a scene, yelling, fighting, and being obnoxious. Rosie was so pissed. She was yelling. Tupac was throwing his hands around. He was all hyped up."

Deidre Lang recalls Perez in hysterics: "Rosie was like, 'Tupac, no! Tupac, don't fight him!'"

David Alan Grier had been napping in his dressing room when he heard the commotion. "I get up and go out my door and there are a bunch of policemen running up and down the hallway," says Grier. He was annoyed. "I'm like, 'Why are these extras allowed back here in our dressing room?' I complained to the stage manager and he's like, 'No, dude. Those are real police.'"

Finally, after several minutes of mayhem, the cops subdued Tupac. "The police slam Tupac up against the wall, handcuff him, and cart him off to jail!" says Perez. "I was flabbergasted. It was crazy town." Tupac's performance was, needless to say, canceled. Heavy D & the Boyz performed in his place.

"That was a typical night of *In Living Color*," says Grier.

———

It took the public time to catch up with the show's problems. While the ratings dipped some in the weeks after Keenen, Damon, and Marlon left, they stayed reasonably strong until early April. Then the bottom fell out. Suddenly a show that had been reliably delivering seventeen to twenty million viewers was struggling to reach twelve or thirteen million. Fox's solution: more guest stars. The back half of the season included a glut of cameos. Some of them made a certain amount of sense (Mario Van Peebles, Sherman Hemsley), some a little less so (James Brown, Rodney Dangerfield), some none at all (Super Dave Osborne).

"Generally, when you see something incongruous to a show," says Firestein, "and you're like, 'What the fuck is that person doing there?'— go back to the network and somewhere there's a memo about sweeps, unquestionably." There were these sorts of "fishing expeditions," as Firestein calls them, to try to net someone the network could highlight in on-air promos. Almost always, the biggest names declined until "eventually as you're edging toward shooting, it's like, 'Super Dave is willing to do it.' Then Fox goes, 'We love Super Dave!'"

This was the kind of stuff Keenen had generally refused to submit to. On a personal level, Keenen had intimidated some of the Fox executives in a way that Firestein, Veasey, and Fields did not. As the show's creator and part-owner, he also had more leverage. Now, when Fox wanted Super Dave, Fox got Super Dave.

Guest stars often felt shoehorned into the show in a way that flattered neither the show nor the guest. Case in point: Dangerfield. His appearance seems completely contrived, and not very well contrived at that. The sketch opens with David Alan Grier and Jamie Foxx as cops who believe they've just pulled over Rodney King. But then Dangerfield emerges from the car—Grier actually says, "Wait a minute! It's Rodney Dangerfield!"— and essentially just does a minute and a half of his standup act, reeling off a half dozen or so one-liners on little or no pretext. It's not that the jokes weren't funny; they simply made no sense in the context of the show. It felt like the writers and the cast around him were barely trying.

"That was kind of a down time," says Larry Wilmore. "Morale was down. It just never quite felt the same when Keenen was gone."

The show was limping toward the season's finale. It was as if Kim and Shawn's protest—or at least their attitude—was contagious. In an interview a couple months after Keenen's departure, Grier didn't bother masking his disdain.

"I said a long time ago that if Keenen ever were hit by a car on the way to the studio, we wouldn't last six weeks," he told a newspaper reporter. "It was his show. It was his concept. His idea. He pointed us in a specific artistic direction. Right now, we're doing shows, but we don't have that artistic point of view any longer. It's like we're in the water, but we really don't have a rudder."

Grier's public badmouthing undermined the new production team and hung their dirty laundry out for the world to see. But it was an accurate reading of the cast's mood. Coffield too wanted out.

"I felt like I'd gotten to this place in terms of the different characters I was playing and the characters I wanted to play, but suddenly I didn't have an advocate there anymore," she says. "I realized that was what Keenen did. Suddenly, when he wasn't there, there was all this pressure from the network to serve up a particular kind of humor. Everything was becoming very two-dimensional. Things were being asked of me that I just didn't think were funny. I was gonna be doing old-lady fart jokes for the rest of my life. We didn't have a leader anymore. It felt messy and labored and a pain in the ass, really. I just thought it was getting really stupid. So, I went to the network and said, 'I don't want to come back next year.'"

At the taping of the season's final episode before the show went on hiatus, David Alan Grier stood at center stage and addressed the studio audience. It had been an extraordinarily long season, and not just measured in months or episodes. The show had endured incredible turmoil, losing not only its creator, but also several cast members and its vision. Its future was in real doubt. It could've been a solemn moment, but *ILC*—and Grier, in particular—didn't really do solemnity. Except, perhaps, with a heaping dollop of sarcasm.

"Ladies and Gentlemen," Grier said with hushed fake reverence, "during the hiatus our very own Jim Carrey is going to be shooting a film called *Ace Ventura: Pet Detective*." The project had been a punch line around the show all season. A lot of people knew that the script had been bouncing around for years. Most knew it sucked. His co-stars were going to be Dan Marino and Tone Lōc. It was a bomb in the making, and choice ammunition in the chest-puffing game of one-upsmanship that often went on among the cast. "Let's all wish him well," Grier continued, laying it on thick with the studio audience. "We're expecting big, big things." The audience roared with laughter at Carrey, who could do little but sit there, red-faced, and take it.

Before Carrey left for Miami to begin shooting, he had lunch with Sandy Grushow at the Ivy, a notorious industry hot spot. Grushow had recently taken over for Peter Chernin as the president of Fox's entertainment group, and the purpose of the lunch was to feel out Carrey's future on the show, and by extension, *ILC*'s future on Fox. Carrey was under contract for a fifth season, but as the show had learned during Season 4, holding people to contracts against their wishes didn't make for a happy, productive workforce.

"I remember sitting on the patio of the Ivy and asking him, 'What are you doing this summer?'" says Grushow. "He told me he was going to make this movie. He was telling me Dan Marino was going to be in it. I just nodded my head. I didn't think much of it." That said, Grushow felt Carrey was "the lynchpin" to *ILC* continuing. Of the most popular characters remaining after the Wayans family's departure, almost all were Carrey's. "The ratings obviously had slipped significantly, but there was enough air left in the thing for me to explore Jim's interest," says Grushow. "Without Jim there would've been no reason whatsoever to bring the show back. With Jim Carrey, it was a discussion." At the Ivy, Carrey told him he was enthusiastic about coming back for another season. He hoped *Ace Ventura* would launch his film career, and if it did, he might not be as readily available as during the first four seasons, but he liked the idea of having the show as a home base to come back to.

Not too long after this lunch, Grushow had a programming meeting with network chairwoman Lucie Salhany and News Corp boss Rupert Murdoch to discuss the fall season. Murdoch stood at a big magnetic board while Grushow and Salhany sat at a conference table. On the board was the proposed fall prime-time schedule. Each potential show was represented by a small magnetic tile with the show's name on it. The three of them could shuffle the tiles around the board like a puzzle to fit them on the schedule in a way that worked for the network. The tiles that didn't end up on the board were shows that would be canceled.

When the discussion turned to *In Living Color*, Grushow made a case for renewing it. Yes, the ratings were down, but they were still decent. And although the show had taken a serious blow with the departure of Keenen and his family, there was still a talented core cast—Grier,

Foxx, Tommy Davidson, and of course, Carrey. It could work. "I think Jim Carrey is star," Grushow said.

Murdoch looked down imperiously at him and then up at the board. He plucked *In Living Color*'s tile off the board, then turned back to Grushow. "Jim Carrey is no star," Murdoch told him. With that, he dropped the *ILC* tile into a small wastebasket at his feet.

32

"We Didn't Land on Chris Rock.
Chris Rock Landed on Us."

In Living Color was renewed anyway. It wasn't some impassioned speech or a great epiphany that convinced Rupert Murdoch to change his mind, just the intrusion of harsh reality: Fox didn't have another show to take its place. "Look, the show was riding on fumes," says Sandy Grushow. "It no longer had a raison d'être but we picked it up because we knew we could rely on a certain baseline of performance. We needed ratings."

The show that would be returning needed to be significantly rebuilt. Along with the exodus of the Wayans siblings during Season 4, Coffield left the show as she'd promised.

"We did a big search," says Pam Veasey. "It wasn't about replacing the Wayans. We knew that wouldn't happen. It was about trying to find the next round of cast members, the same way they do on *Saturday Night Live*." Once again, the possibility of hiring John Leguizamo surfaced but never materialized. Instead, the producers fanned out across the country that summer. They hit comedy clubs in New York, Chicago, Atlanta, and Los Angeles. Al Sonja Rice recalls going to the Comedy Store with Greg Fields one night to see a handful of comics that included Dave Chappelle. "That was the first time I'd ever seen him," says Rice. "He wasn't killing but he didn't care. I was going, 'This guy's really got something, but something ain't clicking.'"

At the end of the search, three new full-time cast members were hired: Jay Leggett, Carol Rosenthal, and Anne-Marie Johnson. Leggett, who died in 2013, was a heavyset improv actor who'd studied with the legendary Del Close in Chicago. Rosenthal had already been a cast member on the short-lived Fox sketch show *The Edge*, which counted several *In Living Color* alums, including Buddy Sheffield, Steve Tompkins, J.J. Paulsen, and Nancy Neufeld Callaway, among its writers. "When *The Edge* went off the air, I was offered *In Living Color*," says Rosenthal. "I didn't even have to audition for it, which was just unbelievable."

Johnson didn't audition either. She was a veteran actress who'd been working steadily for more than a decade by the time she took the *ILC* gig. She'd been a regular on the mideighties reboot of *What's Happening!!*, had worked with Keenen in *Hollywood Shuffle* and *I'm Gonna Git You Sucka*, and had just finished a five-year run as a lead in the CBS TV drama *In the Heat of the Night*. Tommy Davidson, who she'd starred alongside in *Strictly Business*, had helped bring her to *ILC*.

Davidson himself was returning to the cast after being gone for most of the tumultuous fourth season dealing with his drug problems. He'd had his issues with Keenen, and wasn't completely sorry to see him go. "I was relieved to have air to breathe," he says.

Marc Wilmore, who'd been appearing in sketches since late in Season 3, was officially added to the cast, and a black standup named Reggie McFadden was brought in, initially as a recurring supporting player.

Perhaps the most surprising addition was Chris Rock. Rock, of course, had a history with the show, or at least with its creator. He'd been a latecomer to Eddie Murphy's so-called Black Pack, and had a small but memorable part in *I'm Gonna Git You Sucka*, but was passed over by Keenen for a spot in the original *ILC* cast. He got hired at *SNL* instead, where his stagnation made him the butt of an *ILC* sketch.

Hiring Rock was reportedly the brainchild of Peter Roth, who'd taken over as the president of Twentieth Television in June of 1993. Few of the cast or producers seemed enthusiastic about the decision. "At the time, his stock wasn't high," says Firestein. "*Saturday Night Live* wasn't great at that particular time and they didn't write well enough for him. He was considered a funny guy, but I don't think they were equipped to make Chris productive on *Saturday Night Live*."

Rock though was anxious to join *ILC*. At *SNL*, he'd felt out of place and misunderstood. As he told Marc Maron in 2011, "I had these instances where they wanted me to do certain things at *SNL*—whatever slave sketch or Ubangi tribesman—and I was like, 'No, I'm not doing it.' Not that I thought they were racist but if you're the only black face that's going to be seen for an hour and a half, it *feels* racist." To Rock, *ILC* seemed like the center of the black comedy universe. "The decision was like, *The culture is changing and I'm not a part of it*," he said. "This shit is getting hip, this shit is getting blacker, this shit is getting *rap*-ier. [On] *SNL*, I was the first black guy in, like, eight years. I wanted to be in an environment where I didn't have to translate the comedy I wanted to do."

According to one Fox exec, Rock's reps "essentially begged us to put him on the show." But Rock wasn't a great sketch performer and his aesthetic wasn't necessarily a match for *ILC*. In years to come, he'd develop into a blistering, charismatic standup with a sharp observational eye, but that wasn't the show's bread and butter. Nonetheless, some Fox bigwigs were convinced he was the answer.

"I don't think Fox was so nuanced on how they viewed the show or maybe even how they viewed the African-American community," says Firestein. "They didn't care that Chris Rock hadn't succeeded at *SNL*. To them it was another funny black person they knew the name of or that they thought black people liked." Rock was brought on as a recurring guest star. "Our joke at the time," says Firestein, "was *We didn't land on Chris Rock. Chris Rock landed on us*."

The Fly Girls were also undergoing a transformation. Both Rosie Perez and Jennifer Lopez split after Season 4. Perez had a loyalty to Keenen, but she'd hardly been there much anyway lately. Both *White Men Can't Jump* and *Untamed Heart* had been released during Season 4, and she'd arguably become a bigger movie star than any of the cast members. "I was leaving my assistant in charge, more and more," she says. "That's not fair to him." In the end, her assistant, Arthur Rainer, took over as the choreographer.

Lopez left after she'd begun landing acting roles, including one on a new Fox dramedy called *South Central* which was created by *Married with Children* writer Ralph Farquhar, who'd also written the classic hip-hop film *Krush Groove*. The Fly Girls themselves became somewhat diminished in the post-Keenen era. Laurie-Ann Gibson replaced Lopez, and several other dancers who worked more as day players than permanent members of the troupe also flitted in and out.

"It was sad because we were Keenen's baby," says Deidre Lang, the only Fly Girl who lasted all five seasons. "When he ended up leaving, they put us on the back burner. We weren't as important to the show, not to the writers or whoever was doing it at the time. They'd say, 'Oh, girls, you don't have to come in today.' We were like, 'Wait a second. We're part of this show too.' It got a little sad."

Besides the new cast, there was a bevy of new writers brought on to replace the nine who'd departed at the end of the previous season. Among the new hires were Tim Kelleher, who'd spent three years writing for Arsenio, and Colin Quinn, a standup who'd worked as an announcer on the MTV game show *Remote Control* in the late eighties. Buddy Sheffield, who'd left after Season 2, was lured back to become the show's head writer. "Basically, they offered me a whole lot of money," he says. During his prior stint as head writer, "the most I ever made was $7500 a week, which, to the average person sounds like a hell of a lot of money—and it is—but as far as that position goes, it wasn't that much. They offered me much, much more to be head writer the fifth season."

The show also brought back director Paul Miller, and gave him more creative responsibility, part of an overall effort at regaining some of the magic of the show's earlier seasons. "I was coming in as a producer and director," says Miller. "I was looking forward to the challenge of trying to resurrect it and bring it back to what it had been in the beginning."

At the start of the 1993–94 season, the television landscape looked very different than it had when *In Living Color* debuted. Three of Fox's seven nights of programming were built primarily around so-called black shows. The network was airing the largest crop of programs produced by African-Americans in television history. It'd be nice to think this was the result of more progressive-minded executives or a commitment to diversity, and while that may have played a part—the fact is it was just good business. As the nascent cable industry grew, it grew more quickly in white households. Black families watched more network television than other families. The older networks were less responsive to these changing viewing habits, but not totally unresponsive. Midseason, ABC added *Sister, Sister* to a Friday-night lineup already anchored by two black sitcoms, *Family Matters* and *Hangin' with Mr. Cooper*. NBC was still pumping a lot of promo into *The Fresh Prince of Bel-Air* and scoring big numbers as a result.

ILC wasn't simply incidental to this development. Of Fox's "black" shows, *Martin* was co-created by former *ILC* head writer John Bowman, and co-executive produced by two other former *ILC*ers, Matt Wickline and Sandy Frank. *Living Single* had an original *ILC* player, Kim Coles, as one of its stars. A former *ILC*er, Michael Petok, was a producer on *The Sinbad Show*. Three ex-*ILC*ers—Franklyn Ajaye, Barry Douglas, and Rick Najera—wrote for Robert Townsend's variety show, *Townsend Television*, and *ILC*'s two main directors—Miller and Terri McCoy—helped direct it. McCoy also directed episodes of *South Central*, a midseason replacement that included former *ILC* scribe Michael Anthony Snowden among its writers and Jennifer Lopez in its cast. The only black show on Fox not directly sprinkled with *In Living Color*'s DNA was *Roc*, but even that had benefited from *ILC*'s success. For its first two seasons, *Roc* occupied the Sunday time slot immediately following *ILC*. Jamie Foxx was also a recurring guest star. Fox looked very much like the House that Keenen Built.

Over on ABC, Keenen's influence was hard to miss too: *Sister, Sister* was co-created by another former *ILC* writer, Kim Bass, and *Hangin' with Mr. Cooper* was built around the comic who used to warm up the crowd before *ILC* tapings, Mark Curry. Even *Family Matters* had a connection: One of the show's stars, Reginald VelJohnson, was Keenen's good friend from his days as a New York standup and had been part of the first performances Keenen and Damon ever filmed with the Kitchen Table.

When Fox set their prime-time schedule for the 1993–94 season, they shifted *In Living Color* to Thursday night at nine. Sunday night's slate was now filled with the show's spiritual offspring: *Martin*, *Living Single*, and *Townsend Television*. The move to Thursday was curious. The show now ran head to head with *Seinfeld*, which, after a slow start, had picked up considerable steam during the previous season and was consistently a

Top 5 show. What's more, slotting another black sketch/variety series into the Sunday lineup, a show run by Keenen's old friend and writing partner Robert Townsend—the same guy Garth Ancier tried to pitch on doing a "black *Laugh-In*" even before meeting with Keenen about it—certainly made it look like Fox was hedging their bets on *ILC* and scouting for a like-for-like replacement, if not actively trying to stick it to Keenen.

Townsend didn't sense any ulterior motives. He just wanted to do his show. "I'd pitched the show to other places, ABC, NBC," he says. "Fox was the only one that wanted to do it. I never look at it like, *There's only one black show*. I had already been in the sketch comedy world with *Partners in Crime*. It was an extension of what I do." He says he wasn't sure what Keenen thought of all this, because by that time, he and Keenen weren't talking on a regular basis. "Once you're in the Hollywood thing, everybody's doing their stuff. So, it wasn't like, 'Hey, let me check in.'" Besides, competition was always part of the game, particularly among comics, and particularly among Keenen, Robert, Arsenio, and the rest of the guys they'd come up with. "We're all big boys," says Townsend. "It's just business. We're in an industry where they try to pit us against each other, but we're all family. Keenen is one of my best friends."

Nonetheless, in December, Keenen filed a lawsuit against both Townsend and Fox, after a sketch, called "The Bold, The Black, The Beautiful," that the two worked on together for *Partners in Crime*, appeared in a September episode of *Townsend Television* without Keenen's permission. Fox had suggested using the older clip and Townsend told them he didn't have a problem with it, "as long as legally everything is fine." Fox reassured him it was okay to use the *Partners* sketch. "I guess it wasn't."

Keenen still had ongoing disputes with Fox regarding the use of his name and his work when packaging and rerunning *ILC* episodes. The lawsuit claims Fox and Townsend were aware of Keenen's "very strong desire not to have anything to do with Fox and of his desire not to be associated with any television series broadcast by FBC."

"I think there was a bigger game going on with Fox and Keenen that I wasn't privy to," says Townsend. The conflict was eventually resolved, but "whatever the settlement was, that was between Keenen and Fox. I never got involved."

33

"We Were Getting a Sense It Just Wasn't Working"

The conventional wisdom is that the fifth season of *In Living Color* was awful. That judgment fits a tidy narrative that once Keenen and his family were gone, the whole enterprise fell apart and became worthless. It's a narrative that's certainly been pushed by the Wayans siblings themselves and isn't without some truth. Much about the show changed when Keenen left, and many of those changes weren't for the better. But there was still a ton of talent at the show, and viewed in hindsight, Season 5 has more to recommend than even some of those who worked on it might remember.

In fact, the first episode of the season could stand comfortably alongside some of the better work from earlier seasons. The commercial parody for "Russell Simmons' Def Strawberry Jam" is a clever premise—as the voice-over explains, "One bite will turn your family into a fresh, fly, hip-hop crew"—that's very well executed. David Alan Grier, dressed in a conservative gray suit, eats a little jam on his toast and then suddenly explodes with a flurry of bleeped expletives. "Yo, it's about tiiiiime you served some good food, bitch!" he tells his wife, played by Anne-Marie Johnson. "Hey, hey, hey!" Johnson answers. "Your ugly ass ain't the only motherfucker who likes this shit! Those motherfucking kids be putting it on their waffles and shit!"

Grier also scored in a sketch as Sammy, a ventriloquist with a Korean hand puppet named Kim. Grier dances on the edge of offensiveness, adopting a choppy Korean accent for Kim, a bodega owner who repeatedly screams, "You buy something now!" at Sammy. The sketch simultaneously indulges and attacks stereotypes in a style the show practically invented a few years before.

"Seinfeld in the Hood" could be interpreted as a shot over the bow of their new Thursday-night competition, though as Tim Kelleher, who wrote it, explains, it was really "more in response to *Seinfeld* being a New York show, yet there were no black people" on it. Jim Carrey does an over-the-top Seinfeld impression, Jay Leggett magnifies all of George Costanza's most irritating traits, and Carol Rosenthal does a decent Kramer, particularly considering she had only an hour to prepare for it.

The sketch points up the gulf between two shows' comic sensibilities. *Seinfeld*'s observational humor was the product of privilege and comfort, something Les Firestein says "was so *not* the experience of most of our audience." As a New York Jew who had grown up on the border of Harlem, Firestein's sense of humor resided on that border, "with *Seinfeld* people on one side of the street and *In Living Color* people on the other."

The sketch, as Mike Schiff notes wryly, "failed to take *Seinfeld* down." In fact, that week *Seinfeld* clobbered *ILC* in the ratings, pulling in twice as many viewers and setting a pattern that would only get worse as the season progressed.

The rest of the season was rarely as good as that first episode, but there was plenty to recommend. T'Keyah Crystal Keymáh and Tommy Davidson's sketches as two precocious kids, Deronda and Pookie, whose games of pretend mimic the grown-ups in their lives, was a very funny commentary on the persistent childishness of the adult world. The *All in the Family* parody "All Up in the Family," which reimagines Archie Bunker and his clan as a black family, got better and better as the season wore on. David Alan Grier's "Insensitive Therapist"—who laughs at his patients' problems, reveals their innermost secrets in public, mocks their grief, and complains, "You people are so selfish!"—tapped into a gut-level disgust with the *feel my pain* culture that had taken hold in the nineties.

Ali Wentworth was great as Candy Cane, a hot mess of a children's show host, and Jamie Foxx's version of Wile E. Coyote as an unfairly targeted, increasingly assertive societal outcast was just the right mix of clever and stupid.

Then there was Jim Carrey, whose role on the show grew more dominant in the Wayans family's absence. Some of his older characters, like Fire Marshal Bill and Vera De Milo, felt a little tapped out, but others, like Background Guy and his Overly Confident Gay Man, were just finding their groove. One-offs, like the musical parody of the white Canadian dancehall star Snow's hit "Informer" (retitled "Imposter") and his maniacal school guidance counselor—kind of a cousin to Grier's Insensitive Therapist—were vintage Carrey. And one of the season's best new characters was his Umbilical Barry, a college-aged kid who has *literally* never cut the cord between himself and his overprotective, overly doting mother, played by Rosenthal. The character had actually been created the season before by Carrey's office-mate Steve Oedekerk, who thought it "could never be on the show in a million years." In fact, it was on twice and, according to Buddy Sheffield, there was at least one more in the works.

"We were trying to come up with the last one of those and Jim said, 'He's got to be sucked back into his mother.' They found some set that could look like a womb, and we were starting to shoot the thing. He's on the floor in the fetal position and he just stopped everything. He said, 'Oh my god! For this to work, I've got to be completely naked.' He stripped to nothing right there in front of all the crew and shot the closing of that sketch. He'd do absolutely anything."

Although the friction between Carrey and Keenen created great sparks, more than any other cast member, Carrey seemed to blossom in his absence. "He had a lot of ideas of his own and nothing was holding him back," says Bill Martin. "Jim's stuff got crazier and bigger. He felt less restricted."

With Oedekerk gone, Carrey shared an office with one of the new writers, Nick Bakay, and an iguana. "I'd say Jim was gone 70 percent of the time," says Bakay. Carrey had filmed most of *Ace Ventura* during the summer hiatus, but there was still a lot of work to be done—pickup shots, voice work, promotional duties—before the film's February release.

"I remember Jim leaving to do *Ace Ventura*," says Colin Quinn. "I read that script. I was like, 'Poor guy. What a mistake, man.' I felt like he was going off into obscurity."

Carrey was burning the candle at both ends juggling *Ace* with *ILC*. "Jim's office was right next to mine and he didn't have a sofa," says B. Mark Seabrooks, one of the new writers on the show. "I'd go in my office all the time and the cushions would be off my sofa because Jim would take them into his office and go to sleep."

When *Ace* was released in early February, the reviews were pretty terrible but it didn't matter. It topped the box office for three weeks. Everyone at *ILC* had to eat crow. They also had to contend with Carrey's increased absences. He quickly had three more films lined up, *The Mask*, *Dumb and Dumber*, and *Batman Forever*. Not all of that work could be done during a summer hiatus or in off-hours from the show. Carrey was under contract, which obligated him to be on set, but Eric Gold, who was still one of his managers, worked out a deal in which Fox gave Carrey some extended time off to shoot *The Mask*. In return, Carrey signed on for a sixth season of the show.

"Jim was very, very committed," says Pam Veasey. "We accommodated the schedule so he could do movies, but he was there enjoying doing Fire Marshal Bill even after *Ace Ventura*. I remember when he came in my office and told me he got *Dumb and Dumber*. He was like a kid. He was so excited."

———

When Firestein, Veasey, and Fields took over in the middle of the fourth season, they were doing emergency first aid. Their primary job was to keep the show alive. During Season 5, they were hoping to rebuild it more deliberately for the future. "The first thing we did was try to eliminate competition, so more people wrote together," says Veasey.

In some sense, simply not having Keenen's intimidating presence relieved a bit of tension, at least for the writers. A Ping-Pong table near the elevators became a good repository for competitive juices.

"There was a certain fear and panic the writers all had when Keenen walked in the room, and that was gone," says producer Kevin Berg. "If

Keenen said I want to meet all the writers at four, the writers would be assembled at four. If Keenen didn't show up until ten, those writers sat there waiting for him. It was a fear that he'd come in and rip them head to toe, tell them what he hated about every single sketch. Pam, Greg, and Les didn't invoke that fear."

Everything was done by committee now, so if you didn't like the decision one of the showrunners made, you still had a chance to convince the other two. Most of the staff liked the changes, at least on a day-to-day basis.

"A real darkness had been lifted," says Marc Wilmore. "It was like going from Rikers Island to a federal penitentiary with tennis courts, just one fence, and no guard in the tower. People appreciated your work and you left to go home early—'early' being ten o'clock, but it's better than midnight."

Quinn, who later worked as both a writer and cast member at *Saturday Night Live*, felt like the vibe around *ILC* was low-pressure and low-stakes.

"Everyone was so mellow," he says. "It was really hilarious. I was like, 'Hey, I wrote this sketch. I think it's really funny.' And they're like, 'Yeah, man, that's good.' They had their system down and there was no reason to get all hot and bothered about it. It was such a good environment. We'd just bust each other's balls. There were couches all over the office, and anytime you'd be lying on the couch, writing, Les would come and pick up the couch—just fling it. He was a strong guy. It was so funny watching a man flip a couch."

Not everyone appreciated Firestein's office antics the same way. If he'd perhaps dialed down the cutthroat vibe that rattled through the staff in earlier campaigns, he hadn't lost his taste for the outrageous. "Les was pretty infamous in terms of the wild shit he'd say and do," says Seabrooks.

One day, Firestein was playing Ping-Pong and spotted a new writer, Mary Williams-Villano, walking through the offices accompanied by a man she was talking to about being her agent. Villano, a somewhat skittish white woman in her midthirties, didn't really fit in at the show, and Firestein took great joy in tormenting her. As she was ushering the agent into the elevator, near the Ping-Pong table, Firestein paused the game.

"Mary, you forgot your diaphragm in my apartment," he told her, straight-faced. Then he returned to playing Ping-Pong. As the elevator door closed, she stood there, embarrassed and dumbfounded.

Villano recalls the incident slightly differently. "Les said, 'Why does it burn when I pee?'" she explains. She didn't remember the diaphragm comment but admits, "He may have also said that." Firestein picked on her, she says, "perhaps because he sensed I'm too sincere or too open. I've always been teased, my whole life." Sometimes she could shrug it off. Sometimes she'd end up in tears.

The office was not a place for the faint of heart. Firestein had framed photos of children with horrific deformities on his desk. For a while, his walls were heavily decorated with gay porn. "This is pre–hostile work-place environment lawsuits and stuff like that," he says.

In the middle of one workday, Seabrooks heard loud groans coming from Firestein's office. The door was open so he walked in. There were four people standing around, mouths agape, watching a video of a man with a handlebar mustache wearing a captain's hat, hanging from a sex sling, while another man had his foot literally in the man's ass. The video was playing all day.

"My joke about Les was if he wasn't a comedy writer, he'd be a serial killer," says Villano. "He definitely tried to give out that vibe." (Interestingly, Firestein, in an unrelated email exchange, offered that he "always said that the only differences between comedy writers and hatchet murderers were hatchets and courage.")

Firestein unreservedly took delight in making people squirm, but he points out that the gay porn in his office wasn't completely his idea. At the time, he says, Carrey was frequently pulling all-nighters and sleeping on the couch in Firestein's office. "In the middle of the night, he went out to Hollywood with Martin and Schiff and bought very hardcore gay porn," he says. "Then Jim wallpapered my office completely with that porn, from floor to ceiling. He went so far as to line the drawers of my desk. Say what you will about Jim, he commits to the bit. I left it up for weeks, if not months, because that was just part of the atmosphere there. *Anything goes* was kind of the idea. I remember Greg Fields came up to me one day and he's like, 'Les, I think you should take this shit down. It's starting to fuck with your head.' I took it down a couple days later. The next day, Rupert Murdoch just randomly came to my office."

Many of the show's new writers adapted to the environment more easily than Villano. Two brothers, Todd and Earl Richey Jones, had started as writer trainees in the network's diversity program during the previous season, and seemed to get the show's culture immediately. "It was a great environment," says Todd Jones. "Throughout tape days and run-throughs, people were constantly playing Ping-Pong. My brother and I didn't want to leave. We'd stay there until three in the morning."

Colin Quinn, Tim Kelleher, Nick Bakay, and T. Sean Shannon had all started as standups and hung around the office together a lot. Villano called them the Irish Mafia, and individually and collectively, they made their presence felt. "That's a pretty intimidating group of guys, particularly in the low-sperm-count world of comedy writing," admits Bakay. "We definitely had no problem bagging on each other and everyone else in our path. Then again, we all arrived at writing via the [standup] comedy gauntlet as opposed to the Ivy Leagues."

Shannon, Kelleher, and Bakay were all pretty instant contributors, but Quinn says he struggled. "I wouldn't call myself the greatest attribute that ever existed on the show. I wrote a parody of [Canadian dancehall star] Snow for Jim Carrey, 'Imposter,' but they just used a couple lines of it." That was a pretty common occurrence for him. He'd write a sketch, and only a line or two would get used. At first, he was annoyed, but after a while, he adjusted his expectations. "When you're writing, you pick your victories." Shannon says Quinn is being modest: "That guy's such a great joke writer. He contributed."

The so-called Irish Mafia definitely fit the no-holds-barred aesthetic Firestein sought to cultivate, and seemed to flaunt their disregard for convention.

"Me and Colin wrote 'nigger' in a sketch once," says Shannon. "It was just one joke. It got pulled out of the sketch before anyone read it." Shannon was told unequivocally that, "We don't do that here." He wasn't really chastened. "I never worried about offending people. That's where all the joy of comedy is, that danger zone."

Todd Jones says that as a black writer working in network television, he's accustomed to these kinds of things. "If you're on a black show, there are going to be white writers and those white writers are going to pitch things that sometimes cross lines," he says. It might be creating characters that conform to old stereotypes or it might be worse. "If you're offended by stuff a white writer may pitch that goes too far, I don't know how you're going to write in Hollywood."

Without Keenen as the ultimate arbiter of racial politics, this tension remained constant. Faye Griffin felt like the show was in danger of losing its core blackness. At pitch meetings, she'd sometimes cringe at ideas that promoted the same negative images of African-Americans that Keenen and Townsend had faced when they first arrived in Hollywood. "There was a little buffoonery being pitched around, but there were enough of us in the room—me and Sonja, the Jones boys—to squash anything that wasn't cool."

Of course, these were the same criticisms Keenen himself faced early in the show's run. "The Homeboy Shopping Network," Anton Jackson, Timbuk—these were all built on disparaging stereotypes even as they sought to subvert them. But as Paul Miller had noted way back during the first season when he sat in the control booth watching the first "Homeboy Shopping Network" sketch, those characters were only okay because they were coming from Keenen. A black man was fully entitled to make fun of his own culture in a way a white man wasn't. Comedy purists have often struggled with this concept. Why shouldn't T. Sean Shannon or Les Firestein be allowed to make the exact same jokes as Todd Jones or Faye Griffin? Under Keenen's aegis, they could, because from a perception standpoint, when he was running the show, all the jokes were his, no matter who wrote them. Now those lines weren't so clear.

Perhaps nothing illustrated this point better than a character Jamie Foxx had been trying to get on the show since Season 4. He pitched it to several writers, including Jeff Schimmel and Mike Schiff. The idea made Schimmel so uncomfortable that even more than twenty years later he didn't want to describe it. Schiff says the character was called Mono Monkus, and the most important thing to know about him was that he was a monkey.

"Jamie had ideas and could act it out," he explains. Foxx showed Schiff and Martin an ape-like walk he'd developed for the character and a way of grunting. They quickly stopped him.

"We can't touch that," Schiff told Foxx. "We can't write you as a monkey."

"No, it's not a race thing," Foxx insisted. "I just want to play out-of-the-box characters."

But for Martin and Schiff the idea was a non-starter. "We were just too scared of it," Schiff says.

Would Mono Monkus have gotten a chance during Keenen's tenure? Hard to say. Moreover, was the fact white writers wouldn't accede to a black cast member's request to play a monkey without a black figurehead's approval a sign of progress or regress? The show's tangled racial dynamics were growing more dizzying by the day.

Early in the season, Sheffield wrote a spoof of the John Singleton film *Poetic Justice*. The film stars Tupac Shakur and Janet Jackson, and features poems written by Maya Angelou. Sheffield says he wrote "stupid-ass poetry that seemed to be satirizing what was in the movie." But there was backlash at *ILC*. "It was like, 'We can't make fun of Maya Angelou and Tupac.' It was all sacrosanct because this is some big black icon we have to treat reverently. Before, we didn't treat anything with reverence."

———

There was plenty that was, in fact, pretty awful about Season 5. Jamie Foxx's Wanda character was egregiously overused. After appearing six times in the previous season, Wanda was already feeling played out, but because she was one of the show's remaining signature bits, the producers doubled down with nine more—including an interminable six-part series about the search for her baby's father. With some cast members only available part-time, multiple sketches for the show's favorite characters like Wanda or Fire Marshal Bill were often written and filmed in bunches. While that might be an efficient use of time, the process of having to churn out so many iterations of the same thing could be creatively deadening.

Chris Rock didn't exactly blossom at *ILC* either. Almost all his appearances were playing Cheap Pete, his character from *I'm Gonna Git You Sucka*. "Chris Rock seemed very nice, but at the time he didn't impress me as very talented," says Griffin. She and her writing partner, Al Sonja Rice, "wrote some Cheap Pete sketches and it was the same joke over and over. 'Good Lord! I don't wanna pay for drinks. I can just take the bar rag and wring it out.' I thought, *This guy's career has got to be toast.*" Somehow, six separate sketches were squeezed from this thin premise. The rumor was Peter Roth, the Twentieth Television president, loved the character.

As with the previous season, Fox insisted on lots of guest stars. The parade of cameos almost felt like a meta-comedy routine itself. Although a few, like Tupac and Marsha Warfield, fit in fine, most felt as if they were plucked at random from a list of reasonably well-known black people: Gary Coleman, Barry Bonds, Johnny Gill, Fred "Rerun" Berry, Biz Markie, Luther Vandross. The main thing all these people had in common was that they'd said yes when asked. In fact, sketches were frequently written with a blank spot for whatever fill-in-the-blank guest star could be confirmed at the last minute.

After a certain point in the season, it felt like some cast members and writers stopped trying. "The Dirty Dozens," initially a pretty clever adaptation of the classic playground tradition into a game show, gradually devolved upon repeated exposure into a lazy collection of tired "Your mama . . ." jokes. Most of the jokes had been floating around for decades, and in a few cases the same exact jokes were repeated over the course of the six different iterations of the sketch that appeared during the season. Carol Rosenthal thinks the cast was too big. There were "too many people to please, so everything was getting diluted. At a certain point toward the end of the season, I felt like jokes were being recycled."

For better or worse, the vibe at the show had gotten considerably looser.

"The cast were always trying to make each other laugh and break character," says Firestein. "With Keenen out of the building, they were more free to fuck with each other. No one was watching over their shoulder. It's like the parents were gone."

A divide developed between the new cast members and the veterans. Many of the latter had one foot out the door. Johnson says the place felt "sad," and for her, quite lonely. It was also a boys' club, she says, despite there being more female cast members than there had ever been. She had a particular issue with Foxx.

"I didn't get along with Jamie," she says. "I think he was used to speaking to women in a particular way. He really tried to push the enve-

lope, push the female button, and I had none of it. We did have words, because I demand a certain level of respect. I think he was trying to test me.
I don't play that game. I wasn't afraid of him. Now I'm sure he's changed,
but he was young."

Firestein describes the process of making the show during that fifth
season, "without the Wayanses and with the spotty availability of Jim
Carrey," as "arduous." Criticism became louder as the season progressed.
Rosenthal recalls walking back from lunch one day with Veasey and spot-
ting a vulture flying high up in the sky above the studio lot. "I remember
saying to Pam, 'Oh, look, the show is dying,' We were getting a sense it
just wasn't working."

As Firestein notes, "There was such a groundswell of *It's not as good.
They're not innovating.* The truth is you still had half the cast members,
you still had the head writers who'd been there from the beginning.
There's no reason we couldn't continue to put out as good a show. But
there was also a sense that it wasn't the same because the Wayans' fin-
gerprints were all over that show."

To compound matters, that fall, Fox very publicly wooed Chevy
Chase to the network to do a late-night talk show. When the show was
pronounced dead on arrival, and canceled within six weeks, the network
replaced it with—what else?—*ILC* reruns. Once again, the show was
having to compete with an earlier version of itself. Frustration mounted.
As Greg Fields put it at the time, "Not that we don't miss the Wayans and
others who left, but *Saturday Night Live* people come and go. I know if
people would give the new cast a chance, they'd see things they'd like."

———

Sketch comedy is a notoriously difficult art. Most shows would be thrilled
if 35 to 40 percent of their sketches were consistently hitting. Was *In
Living Color*'s gem-to-dud ratio in Season 5 as good as the best moments
of the first few seasons? Probably not. But, in spots, it was just as funny.
It could certainly hold its own alongside *SNL*, which, at the time, was
going through one of its periodic rebuilding seasons. The bigger problem
was that it was becoming more and more indistinguishable from *SNL*.
Umbilical Barry, Candy Cane, David Alan Grier's Insensitive Therapist

all made for good sketches, but nothing about them made them *In Living Color* sketches. Particularly as that fifth season wore on, *ILC* was just becoming a pretty good sketch show.

It wasn't just that the show had lost the Wayans family. It was that the writers, producers, and players who were becoming more dominant—Firestein, Fields, Sheffield, Schiff and Martin, Bakay, T. Sean Shannon, Jay Leggett, Ali Wentworth, and most of all, Carrey—didn't have the same specific (read: black) perspective. Now, it's a little unfair to single out a bunch of white people as the reason for the show's loss of identity, particularly when at least four of them—Firestein, Fields, Sheffield, and Carrey—were a big part of the show at its best. Just as important was that cast members like Grier, Davidson, Keymáh, and Johnson—all of whom were on-screen a lot during Season 5—may have been great comic actors, but weren't necessarily generating their own material. They could take a sketch and make it better, but they weren't generally in the writers' offices putting their own ideas on a blank page. Lost it seemed was a willingness to risk offensiveness, to take shots at everyone, to give voice to a point of view that hadn't been heard before. By Season 5, those boundaries had been pushed, everyone had already been offended. As Bill Martin puts it, "The show seemed to matter less." It was a victim of its own success.

It's hard to know how much to attribute the ratings decline during Season 5 to bad press around the Wayans siblings' departure, to an actual decline in the show's quality, or to simply being in an unwinnable time slot on Thursday night. Going head to head with *Seinfeld* was certainly a tough ask. It's tempting to look at Fox's decision to schedule *ILC* when it did as a vote of no confidence, essentially turning the show into cannon fodder. Fox President Sandy Grushow insists that wasn't the intention.

"I don't think we were consciously throwing *ILC* to the wolves on Thursday, which every network had been known to do on a frequent basis," he says. It was more about believing the show had a core audience that would stick with it and help deliver some sort of decent rating. "We were probably being very realistic about its performance but confident it was the best we were going to do on a highly competitive but high-revenue night."

The calculation Fox made wasn't necessarily incorrect, but it seemed to put a low cap on the show's potential. By December, *ILC* was averaging around eleven or twelve million viewers per episode. When *Seinfeld* is pulling in around thirty million, there simply aren't many more eyeballs to fight over. Some saw *Seinfeld* as the whitest show on television, one that few black viewers cared about, and that may have been true, but its inverse was not. *ILC* had a huge black fan base, but in its prime, it also had a huge white fan base. There were a lot more people like Firestein, whose sense of humor straddled both worlds, than anyone had previously realized. Beyond that, the show had introduced all this black humor and culture to white people who just liked comedy. By scheduling *ILC* opposite *Seinfeld,* the network forced all those people to decide what to watch, and most of them chose *Seinfeld*.

"Any player hate we had toward *Seinfeld*," says Firestein, "might be rooted not in direct competition but in the fact that *Seinfeld* was poorly rated for a few seasons but the execs stayed with it because the show was reflective of the execs' lives. On the other hand, whenever *ILC* or any 'urban' shows like it hit a speed bump, execs would throw their hands up like parents not understanding rap music."

Grier admits that by Season 5, mentally and emotionally, he'd checked out. "Familiarity breeds contempt," he says. "You pray for success. 'Dear God, I've been acting for ten years, give me one hit. I'll never complain again.' You get the hit. 'Dear God, please get me off this shit.' That's the actor's plight."

Grier's attitude was indicative of a growing sentiment. "People were done with it," says Wentworth. "Everybody had other stuff going on. Jamie, Tommy, David, and Jim were all antsy to do the next step of their career." The feeling seemed to filter down to the crew too. "When Keenen was there, there would be all these perks and gifts coming in, free stuff or a catered dinner. Then, towards the end, people were basically stealing toilet paper."

As the season drew toward its conclusion, a gallows humor started to take hold. In the penultimate episode, during "Deronda and Pookie Play Party," Davidson, playing the pre-adolescent Pookie, suggests to his young playmate, "Let's play 'Positive Black Role Models on Television'!" Keymáh's Deronda enthusiastically agrees and sticks her head inside their cardboard television. "Hello, everybody!" she says, looking out of the box. Pookie quickly drapes a blanket over the television. "Sorry, you're canceled."

In the final episode, as a sketch called "Prison Cable Network: Lights Out with Angel" winds down, Carrey, playing a sidekick on a jailhouse late-night television show, offers, "Good news from the warden! We've just had our show renewed for another ten years." The joke wasn't subtle. *In Living Color* was hardly a prison, but for some of the show's old guard it was starting to feel like it. The last segment of the season is a musical performance from a long-forgotten rap trio with a name that, in hindsight, feels like an ironic joke: To Be Continued. As the group takes the stage, they try to hype the audience up: "Ain't no party like an *In Living Color* party 'cause an *In Living Color* party don't stop!" But this party was about to stop for good: About a minute into their performance, the credits begin to roll, and then a minute after that, without so much as a goodbye from any of the cast members, the screen fades to black.

34

"It Was Time to Fold Up the Tent"

Despite low morale and slumping ratings, most people around the show assumed *In Living Color* would be renewed for a sixth season. After all, Jim Carrey, who'd become a bona fide movie star, was under contract for another season, as were pretty much the entire rest of the cast. Carrey alone would've been enough to draw in a respectable audience. That this ostensibly black sketch show hinged largely on the return of what had once been the token white guy seemed either ironic or dispiriting, but still, the idea of canceling the show right as Carrey was becoming such a massive draw was practically inconceivable. "It would've been tantamount," says Les Firestein, "to canceling *Saturday Night Live* after Eddie Murphy did *Beverly Hills Cop*."

There was even a plan in place to address one of the show's glaring weaknesses. With Keenen's departure, the show had lost both a singular voice and a symbolic figurehead. In some sense, it had lost its blackness. The solution, according to Firestein, was going to be to turn that visible leadership role over to Chris Rock, who'd been woefully underused in Season 5. Rock would run the show alongside Firestein. (Veasey had already decided to leave the show to transition to working on television dramas, and Fields had taken a gig as a producer on *Full House*.) "Fox was like, 'It has to be you and a black person,'" says Firestein. "I'd never presume I could do that show on my own."

That plan never made it past the upfronts in late May. The upfronts are an annual event at which network television executives show advertisers their planned slate of programming for the upcoming season. As they approached that year, word came down that instead of twenty-two new *ILC* episodes, Fox was only going to order thirteen. A day before the big event in New York, even the thirteen-episode order was starting to look shaky.

Firestein says he'd just been waiting to find out what the budget was going to be for Season 6. "Then at the upfronts, they said at the last minute, 'Oh, we're not doing *In Living Color.*'"

Sandy Grushow hardly remembers the thought process at Fox that led to canceling the show. "The decision would've been *The ratings are down. The show is not remotely what it once was,*" he explains. "I don't think any of us regretted picking up the show [for the fifth season] because frankly we probably needed it. But the original intent of the show no longer existed with Keenen and Damon gone. It was time to fold up the tent."

Grushow is right about all that. But still there was pretty iron-clad logic around renewing it too. All the talent was coming back. The ratings were down but still better than about half the other shows Fox had on in prime time, including *The X-Files*, which hadn't yet taken off. Dan McDermott, the VP of current programming, says it would've been down to either Grushow or Fox chairwoman Lucie Salhany to make the final call on bringing the show back, though Salhany says it wasn't that straightforward.

"This wouldn't have been one person's decision," she says. "This would've been Sandy's and the whole network's, because you never made a decision alone. Rupert [Murdoch] was always in there. So, if *In Living Color* went, it was all the way from Rupert down. That's who made the decisions."

ILC didn't go down alone. The casualties at Fox that season included *Townsend Television, Roc, South Central*, and *The Sinbad Show*, leaving many to question if there was a broader strategy afoot. "There was this sense that Fox was cleaning out the black shows a little," says Ali Wentworth. "'Ethnic cleansing' was the term they would've used back then."

As Firestein puts it, "Fox was trying to change their complexion. They were trying to change their brand."

In December, the network had pulled off a huge coup, outbidding CBS for the rights to air NFL games starting in the 1994–95 season. Most of the top executives who'd helped position Fox as an "alternative network"—Barry Diller, Peter Chernin, Jamie Kellner—were long gone, and one of the last remaining believers in that strategy, Grushow, would leave Fox in September. The network was thinking big now. Murdoch didn't want a slice of the pie. He wanted the whole thing.

This "ethnic cleansing" didn't go unnoticed. "We were used as laborers to build up Fox, and once that was done, we were let go," says Anne-Marie Johnson. "It was like, 'Okay, hired help, the indentured servitude is over. We are releasing you and thank you for building the mansion.' Everybody knew that in the black community." The Reverend Jesse Jackson threatened boycotts—not just of Fox, but of the four major networks—over what he saw as "institutionalized racism." *South Central* producer Ralph Farquhar and the show's star, Tina Lifford, enlisted the support of the Congressional Black Caucus. New York congressman Ed Towns hammered Fox for what he perceived to be "plantation programming." Fox, he said in a press release, built its network on black programs, but "apparently, as the network moves to become more mainstream, its attitude to positive black programs is we don't need nor want them anymore." For *In Living Color*, it was quite a turnaround from its early days as the black establishment's pariah to being its cause célèbre.

Grushow, Salhany, and McDermott all say the cancellations weren't race-related. "*Roc* ran for three seasons and just, ratings-wise, we didn't have the juice in the tank to keep going," says McDermott. "*Sinbad* never really gelled creatively. Robert Townsend either. We definitely weren't getting out of urban half hours." The network still had both *Martin* and *Living Single*, and one of the new shows the following season was *M.A.N.T.I.S.*, about a black superhero.

Salhany, who resigned in July of that year, says "there was no outward racism" regarding the cancellations, nor any decision made that "we don't want any more black programming," but she acknowledges that "Rupert wanted to broaden the advertiser base," and that a lot of big brands had deeply ingrained institutional biases. "When I went to sell

Arsenio Hall to Chrysler, the guy in charge said a black comedian will never work late-night because no man wants their wife watching a black comedian in bed."

Interestingly, Arsenio's show aired its own final episode just a week after the *ILC* finale. In the face of more competition on late-night television, Arsenio's ratings had been declining, and not too long after a much-criticized, show-long interview with Louis Farrakhan, the decision was made to pull the plug. As Arsenio said at the time, "Everything must change, and it's time."

If there was one person definitely not sorry to see *In Living Color* go, it was Keenen Ivory Wayans. He was prepping his next film, *A Low Down Dirty Shame*, but couldn't help feeling vindicated watching *ILC* careen off the tracks and into a ditch. "I was glad they had to shut it down because it wasn't reflective of what I had created," he says. "If it had been successful without me, I'd be in an institution."

Many of the cast members had more nuanced views of the show's demise. Even some who felt like their time at the show was up were disappointed.

"It should've gone on," says Carrey. "It's ridiculous that it didn't. I didn't want to go on with it, but the franchise should've been a continuous thing. It was a huge opportunity lost there."

A few months after *ILC* was canceled, Firestein got a call from an executive in charge of specials at Fox. "This person said to me, 'We want to do a couple of *In Living Color* specials,'" he explains. "The idea was Jim had become so mega-huge, they're like, 'We still have a contract with him. Let's make him do these specials.' I said, 'I'm pretty sure your contract is null and void. Once you don't pick up the show, it's done.'" This seemed to be news to the executive but it drove home a point for Firestein. "There were people at Fox who still believed there was some mutation of *In Living Color* they could do. That, of course, turned out not to be true at all."

There is a school of thought that *ILC* could've been retooled into something that could've run for many years, or even decades. Certainly, *SNL* has had many down years and even lived through the departure of its creator Lorne Michaels, though he eventually returned to the show. Fox could've ridden out some lean years. They might've been able to lure Keenen back into the fold. Or maybe Chris Rock would've stepped up in

Season 6 and given the show the strong voice it had lost. Some point to the relative success of *The Chris Rock Show*, starting in 1997, as a sign that Rock may have been up to the task. But *The Chris Rock Show* was a much different show than *ILC*—more talk, more politics, a lot less sketch—and was on HBO, where it didn't need the same sort of viewership numbers as on a network. There were rumblings that Fox was hoping to transition *ILC* from prime time to late night, which could've insulated it a little from the constant pressure for ratings. That could've worked.

Is Fox's failure to stick with *ILC* as NBC stuck with *SNL* an indication of the same inherent prejudice Firestein bemoaned regarding *Seinfeld*? Were white shows given chances black shows weren't? Possibly, although there's a compelling case to be made that while deep-seated biases play into these decisions, they don't explain everything. Sometimes decisions are made more as shrugs than proclamations.

Rob Edwards, who was a writer on the *ILC* pilot, later worked on *The Fresh Prince of Bel-Air* during that show's first season. The show's ratings that first season were middling at best, and according to Edwards, few NBC executives really got the show. Most of the cast figured it wouldn't survive more than a few episodes.

"I just remembered, having lived through *In Living Color*, saying, 'Just have heart. The audience will find the show,'" says Edwards. But the attitude around NBC was that they should've stuck with the Cosby model of black family sitcoms. *The Fresh Prince*, built around rapper Will Smith, was too out there for mainstream America. *Too black*. Edwards says the show very well might've been canceled if not for one fan: NBC president Brandon Tartikoff's young daughter. "Brandon's daughter was a huge fan and couldn't wait for Dad to bring home tapes. She'd come to the tapings, dance on the set, and do all kinds of stuff during breaks. We all said, 'That little girl is the most important person on the stage.' That's what it took. She said, 'Daddy, don't cancel my favorite show.' That's how these shows survived."

35

"Does Anybody Say NBC Has All This White Programming?"

J ust a couple weeks after *In Living Color*'s cancellation, the entire country sat transfixed on a Friday in June watching the television event of the decade: A cavalcade of LAPD cruisers in extraordinarily low-speed pursuit of a white Ford Bronco carrying ex-football-star-turned-accused-murderer O.J. Simpson. As the chase crawled up the 405 Freeway near Los Angeles, news helicopters followed overhead, and crowds gathered along the route to gawk, cheer, and wave signs reading "Go Juice Go" and "We love the Juice."

The chase, the murder trial that followed—the entire O.J. saga—seemed both a surreal historical anomaly and a pointed encapsulation of the country's feelings about race, celebrity, the justice system, and the media. For a lot of former *In Living Color* writers and cast members, the events hit them the way the start of a new baseball season might hit a recently retired ballplayer: They longed to be back on the field. Within minutes of the Bronco chase, Les Firestein was getting calls from old colleagues essentially pitching sketches for a show that no longer existed. *Imagine if we redid the famous Hertz commercial with O.J. sprinting through the airport, but this time the LAPD would be on his tail? What if we crossed the chase with the new Keanu Reeves film* Speed, *and Keanu had to drive less than 50 mph or the Bronco would explode? What if Rodney King was driving instead of O.J.'s buddy, Al Cowlings?*

The following April, months deep into the public circus that was the televised trial, Damon Wayans hosted *Saturday Night Live*. The gig was undoubtedly a big deal for Damon. This was a triumphant return to the show that had fired him nearly a decade before. Damon revived two *ILC* characters for the appearance: the homeless drunk Anton Jackson and Blaine Edwards, his half of the "Men on Film" duo. Anton shows up at the O.J. trial, wearing clothes O.J. discarded into the trash can Anton was living in.

There's not much to the Anton sketch, at least not much in the way of social commentary, which was typical of *SNL*'s treatment of the O.J. saga. Far from ignoring the events, *SNL* went all in, with new O.J. sketches every week or two, and "Weekend Update" anchor Norm MacDonald going so hard on O.J., it eventually contributed to his dismissal from the show. But *SNL*'s sketches treated the saga much the way it would've treated any celebrity scandal—rarely, if ever, touching on the stark racial divide the trial exposed. Perhaps it wasn't surprising: *SNL* had no black writers at the time, and their two black cast members, Tim Meadows and Ellen Cleghorne, were definitely more Garrett Morris than Eddie Murphy. If Damon's very appearance on the show playing Anton and Blaine was an acknowledgment of *ILC*'s impact on pop culture, the show itself was a reminder that real fundamental change is often so gradual as to be imperceptible in the moment.

Damon's post-*ILC* career did not blossom as nearly everyone had predicted. He starred in a parade of forgettable films (*Major Payne*, *Celtic Pride*, *The Great White Hype*, *Bulletproof*), before finally finding a modest hit, back on television with a surprisingly Cosby-ish ABC family sitcom called *My Wife and Kids* that lasted five seasons and has done well in syndication.

In 2000, Damon starred in *Bamboozled*, Spike Lee's fascinating if flawed film that imagined the rise of a modern blackface minstrel show. The film asks hard questions about how blacks are portrayed in the media, and African-Americans' own role in this portrayal. *Bamboozled* is perhaps a better idea than it is a movie, but for Damon, who'd lived out these questions for most of his career, it seemed a particularly apt satire. Unfortunately, New Line buried the film, and to those not paying much attention, it just looked like another flop for Damon. His next film, *Marci X*, in which he plays a cartoonish gangsta rapper, made it feel like he either didn't get the point of *Bamboozled* or didn't care. As Spike Lee himself put it a few years later, "One thing I don't understand is that Mr. Damon Wayans can do this film and then go do *Marci X*, the type of film of which *Bamboozled* is an indictment."

Keenen seemingly had designs on becoming an action hero after *ILC*, but audiences didn't take to him as one. His first film, *A Low Down Dirty Shame*, an action-comedy that was a little short on both action and comedy, didn't make much of a splash. Two more films, *The Glimmer Man*, opposite Steven Seagal, and *Most Wanted*, with Jon Voight, became unintentional punch lines. His attempt at a talk show, *The Keenen Ivory Wayans Show*, in 1997 was ill-conceived, if for no other reason than the fact that, as his brothers quickly pointed out to him, Keenen did not particularly like talking to people. Aimed at capturing the audience that had been abandoned when Arsenio's show went off the air, it ended up competing for that audience with two other shows, the Quincy Jones–produced *Vibe*, hosted first by Chris Spencer and then by Sinbad, and Paramount's *Magic Hour*, with Magic Johnson. In the end, all three shows went down in flames quickly.

As Arsenio put it, "The guys who came after me were simply capitalizing on economics they saw or projected. They canceled each other out by all hitting at the same time. Sinbad, I love him dearly, but the most incredible joke ever written was when Damon Wayans said Sinbad thought that a talk show meant that he talked all the motherfucking time. Keenen had a good barometer as to when to talk and when to shut up, but Keenen wasn't going to succeed while there were so many people going after the same urban audience."

Keenen's biggest win during those years was as a producer of *Don't Be a Menace to South Central While Drinking Your Juice in the Hood*, a film Shawn and Marlon co-wrote with ex–*In Living Color* writer Phil Beauman. Of all the projects the Wayans family worked on during the few years immediately after *ILC*, it was the one most similar to the show. It lampooned the hardened street dramas then in vogue among black filmmakers.

"When we wrote *Don't Be a Menace*, Keenen made us do nineteen drafts before we handed it in to the studio, and then we had to do six more," says Marlon. "He was tough." The Wayans brothers didn't see eye to eye with the film's director, Paris Barclay, and at one point, Keenen shut down production. When Shawn and Marlon looked at a rough cut of what they had, they were devastated. "The director messed up the movie and we had to rewrite a whole new movie and shoot it in ten days," says Marlon. The results were far from perfect, but the movie became a minor hit, making nearly forty million dollars on a budget of less than four million. The comedy was broad, and it sometimes felt more like a collection of sketches stitched into a movie than a coherent film, but the same could've been said about *Hollywood Shuffle* and *I'm Gonna Git You Sucka*.

Marlon and Shawn also developed a sitcom, *The Wayans Bros.* After the series debuted in 1995, it was accused of the same things *ILC* had been accused of five years earlier, the same things, in fact, that *Amos 'n Andy* had been accused of five decades earlier.

"There's a fine line between when people are laughing with you and people are laughing at you," Billie J. Green, president of the NAACP's Hollywood chapter, told the *Los Angeles Times*. "Right now, people are laughing at us." Green criticized several shows, but singled out *The Wayans Bros.* as the worst offender. "It is not a fair representation of black America. What we're seeing is like *Amos 'n Andy* and Stepin Fetchit. In fact, *Amos 'n Andy* was a better show than what we're seeing now."

The criticism was, as Marlon explained, "because we were physical. I believe black comics can be physical without being coons. We overuse the word."

It was a version of the same argument that had been going on for more than a generation. Did the nation's checkered history require that black and white comics be judged by different standards? As Shawn put it, "You never see white people going, 'Jim Carrey's a coon.' Never."

The show was the inaugural offering from the WB, a joint venture between Warner Bros. and the Tribune Broadcasting Company. The choice of the show as the network's first offering wasn't surprising, particularly considering that the WB's president and its chief programmer were both former Fox executives who'd help develop *In Living Color*, Jamie Kellner and Garth Ancier.

The WB launched around the same time as Paramount's entry into the world of network television, UPN. Again, it was a former Fox exec at the helm, Lucie Salhany. As Fox steered away from black programming and toward the mainstream, both the WB and UPN slid into the void that had been created. The WB seemed eager to hand out sitcoms to black comics: Besides *The Wayans Bros.*, early WB entries included *Cleghorne!* (Ellen Cleghorne), *The Parent 'Hood* (Robert Townsend), *The Jamie Foxx Show*, and *The Steve Harvey Show*. UPN appeared just as committed to serving African-American audiences, with shows like *Moesha*, starring the young singer-actress Brandy Norwood, the LL Cool J sitcom *In the House*, and *Malcolm & Eddie*, built around ex–*Cosby Show* star Malcolm-Jamal Warner and up-and-coming comic Eddie Griffin.

"We recognized there was a demand," says Kellner. "The black community wasn't being serviced by the big networks, and when you're starting out and you're a counterprogrammer, you're looking at what's not sewed up. We probably had the highest percentage of African-American-starred and -produced programs in history for a while on the WB, because we found a bunch of good producers."

A lot of them were ex–*ILC* hands. Sandy Frank and Larry Wilmore worked on *The Jamie Foxx Show*, B. Mark Seabrooks did *The Steve Harvey Show*, and Greg Fields, Franklyn Ajaye, Barry Douglas, Faye Griffin, Al Sonja Rice, and Michelle Jones all worked on *The Parent 'Hood*. At the UPN, Salhany admits to a similar counterprogramming mission as Kellner had, but bristles at classifying shows like *In the House* and *Homeboys from Outer Space* by the color of most of their cast members.

"It's unfair for people to say they're black shows," she says. "They were funky comedies. Everybody said UPN had all this black programming. Does anybody say NBC has all this white programming?"

The Wayans Bros. lasted until 1999, when it was abruptly canceled. Marlon and Shawn then teamed back up with Keenen and a handful of the writers from his recently canceled talk show to work on an idea for a film they'd begun thinking about years earlier, *Scary Movie*.

On paper, *Scary Movie* is a strange idea: It's a parody of films like *Scream* and *I Know What You Did Last Summer*, both of which are almost horror movie parodies themselves, full of nods and winks to knowing audiences. Much like *Don't Be a Menace*, *I'm Gonna Git You Sucka*, and

Hollywood Shuffle, Scary Movie—which Keenen directed and produced, and which Marlon and Shawn both had a hand in writing—feels like a collection of set-pieces loosely stacked around a paper-thin narrative. Keenen grew up a fan of Richard Pryor and blaxploitation films, watched up close as his friend Eddie Murphy broke ground with *Trading Places* and *48 Hrs.*, and was a part of the cultural renaissance that birthed Spike Lee and John Singleton's films, but *Scary Movie* was more in the tradition of another, no less prominent side of Keenen's personality, the one that loved the unadulterated silliness of Carol Burnett, Mel Brooks, Monty Python, and the Zucker-Abrahams-Zucker films (*Kentucky Fried Movie, Airplane!, The Naked Gun*).

The formula worked. Made on a modest budget of less than twenty million dollars, *Scary Movie* went on to earn nearly three hundred million dollars worldwide and spawned a lucrative franchise. Career-wise it was a home run, and it's informed nearly every project Keenen, Marlon, and Shawn have originated since then: *White Chicks, Littleman, Dance Flick, A Haunted House, 50 Shades of Black.* (The last two Marlon wrote and produced without Shawn or Keenen.) The Wayans brothers have become essentially a parody factory.

Scary Movie represents a fork in the career path for Keenen. His original goal, to perhaps become the same type of actor that Eddie Murphy was during the *48 Hrs./Beverly Hills Cop* years, hadn't panned out, but now he'd found something that did. Eric Gold says it was around this time he realized his plan for Keenen's career wasn't Keenen's plan. Gold wanted to position Keenen as a big mainstream comedy director not unlike Jay Roach (*Austin Powers, Meet the Parents*) or Tom Shadyac (*Ace Ventura, Nutty Professor, Bruce Almighty*).

"Keenen should've become one of the most important comedy directors in the world," he says. "He could identify great talent, had great points of view, understands editing so well, and could support a comedic personality. But instead of wanting to expand out of the family, Keenen, Marlon, and Shawn wanted to consolidate the family thing. They're very comfortable together, they love working together, they had their friends who were part of their circle. Their feeling was *I don't want to play that game. I want to build a brand with my brothers.*" Gold split with Keenen, Marlon, and Shawn after *Scary Movie 2* in 2001, and split for good with

Damon a few years after that. But Gold still thinks highly of them, particularly Keenen.

"Keenen hasn't been given his due," says Gold. "He showed such leadership early in his career. *In Living Color* launched a generation of showrunners and movie stars and it really goes back to Keenen. It was his eye. He's one of the most undervalued assets in Hollywood. The town is sleeping on him a little."

36

"No Matter How Funny a Black Comic Is, It Doesn't Mean Shit Unless He Makes the Right White Man Laugh"

The winter after *In Living Color* was canceled, Fox added John Leguizamo's *House of Buggin'* to its Sunday-night lineup. The show was frequently billed as a Latino *In Living Color*, and superficially they had much in common. Five *ILC* writers—Fax Bahr, Adam Small, Mike Schiff, Bill Martin, and T. Sean Shannon—contributed to *House of Buggin'*, Paul Miller was the main director, and all of those except for Shannon got producer credits too. But Leguizamo resisted following the *ILC* template.

"We tried to tell John how to produce a sketch the *In Living Color* way and he wasn't into it," says Small. "He wanted to do it like the theater, which meant no camera blocking. We'd rewrite a sketch on the day, and that night, he'd rewrite it back to the way it was." Small and Bahr were fired after two episodes.

Ultimately, none of that likely impacted the show's short life span. Schiff and Martin both feel America wasn't ready for a Latino sketch show. "In 1994, Latin culture hadn't seeped into mainstream culture the way African-American culture had," says Schiff. "*In Living Color* had huge swaths of things to parody that people were familiar with. At *House of Buggin'*, you'd look for things that enough people knew for it to be a network success. Frequently, we'd write sketches and the network would say, 'What is this?'" The show was canceled inside of a month.

Shortly after, Bahr and Small were tapped by Quincy Jones to adapt *MAD* magazine into a late-night sketch show on Fox. "Pretty much everything we did as showrunners was based on *In Living Color*, to some extent," says Bahr. "*MADtv*," says Small, "is marinated in *In Living Color*." Nearly half of the first season's cast members were African-American. Paul Miller directed sketches, Heavy D did the theme song, and a handful of *ILC*ers, including Mary Williams-Villano and Rick Najera, worked as writers there. Faye Griffin says the show even rehashed sketch ideas from the *ILC* writers' room.

Bahr and Small stuck around for three seasons, but the show endured for fourteen, a remarkable accomplishment, though *MADtv* never really broke out to become a water-cooler hit. Its long life feels like evidence that *ILC* could've survived indefinitely had it moved to late night. It's easy to imagine the final season of *ILC* as the beginning of the show transforming into something more like what *MADtv* became—less black, less newsworthy, still funny. But arguably, such a fate may have diminished *In Living Color*'s legacy more than enhanced it.

In Living Color, or at the very least its aesthetic, resonated in obvious and less obvious ways in the years that followed. Ice Cube has talked about the show as an inspiration while he was writing *Friday*. That movie's success opened the door for a wave of black comedies like *Barbershop*, *Big Momma's House*, and *How High*, which continued to prove the mainstream appeal of what had previously been thought of by the industry as strictly niche. *Friday* also launched Chris Tucker, who became a huge movie star very much in the Eddie Murphy mold, before retreating from the spotlight for a long spell and only reemerging periodically to play smaller, quieter roles.

"*In Living Color* was a pioneer," says Leguizamo. "It was a groundbreaking transition in television to proving that black comedy is so relevant and appealing to everybody in America. That show was groundbreaking for anybody of color."

As the network and cable dial expanded, the number of channels willing to take a flyer on sketch shows seemed to expand with it. But the prize of a zeitgeist-seizing hit like *In Living Color* or *Saturday Night Live* remained elusive. Dana Carvey, Andy Dick, and Jenny McCarthy—yes, that Jenny McCarthy—each fronted failed sketch projects in the second half of the nineties. *Upright Citizens Brigade* helped launch some careers (Amy Poehler, Matt Walsh, Rob Corddry) but never connected with the larger public during its three seasons on Comedy Central in the late nineties (though their improv classes and theaters would eventually become a huge force in comedy a decade later). A pair of black sketch shows—MTV's *Lyricist Lounge Show* and *Cedric the Entertainer Presents*—were occasionally funny but struggled to find loyal viewers. So when Dave Chappelle went in to pitch his idea for a sketch show to Comedy Central in 2002, the prospects for success seemed no more likely than they had for any of these projects.

Chappelle was hardly an unknown quantity. He'd been doing standup since the early nineties. He'd had small parts in a half dozen studio films, had co-written and starred in his own film, *Half-Baked*, and been through the wringer with network television. By the midnineties, he'd starred in so many pilots that were never picked up that Les Firestein once joked to him that someone should syndicate all his failed pilots. "There were about a hundred of them," says Firestein. "I had a sense people didn't quite know what to do with him."

In 1996, Chappelle starred in *Buddies*, an ABC sitcom in which he and fellow comic Jim Breuer were to play best friends. After ABC saw the pilot, they canned Breuer. Chappelle considered quitting in protest, but stuck it out for a season and came to regret it. Chappelle's character was frequently put in the position of defending the white establishment's good intentions against black people's prejudices.

"Chappelle had a strong point of view, very edgy, no fear with racial comedy, and I don't know that that's what that show was doing," says Todd Jones, an ex-*ILC*er who wrote on *Buddies*. "Chappelle would've been more suited to the *In Living Color* style of comedy."

After *Buddies* failed, Fox hoped to build a sitcom specifically for

Chappelle. He'd play a standup comic, and have more control over the project's creative direction. Fox ordered six episodes, but when the network—which at this point was a few years into repositioning itself as more mainstream and had recently shed its two remaining successful black sitcoms, *Martin* and *Living Single*—tried to recast the show's female lead, replacing a black actor with a white one, and add another white character, Chappelle quit. In an interview with *Variety* at the time, he explained what happened.

"They fly me out for a creative meeting," he said. "I'm in a room full of white people and they proceed to tell me why we need more white people on the show, so it can have a more universal appeal. This network built itself on black viewers, and what they're saying is white people are narcissistic. They don't want to watch black people; they want to watch themselves. It tells every black artist no matter what you do, you need whites to succeed." To Chappelle, this thinking perpetuated the kind of institutional racism that had pervaded the industry since its earliest days.

UPN offered to pick up the series. Chappelle declined. "I'm just so disgusted with TV," Chappelle said. "I don't care if I ever work in TV again."

All this is an important prologue to understanding *Chappelle's Show*. Chappelle created the show with Neal Brennan, a friend and comedy writer he'd worked alongside on *Half-Baked*. Because it was Comedy Central, ratings expectations were lower and Chappelle was promised a degree of creative autonomy he hadn't gotten in his previous at-bats with television. The result was a revelation.

In a sketch during the first episode that set the tone for the entire series, Chappelle plays a blind Klan leader named Clayton Bigsby who doesn't realize he's black. Untangling the threads of high and low humor here is instructive: There's the sight gag of a black man raising his fist, yelling "White Power!" to a collection of dumbfounded white supremacists. There's Bigsby's white friend who hides the truth from him. "If I tell him he's black, he'll probably kill himself, just so there would be one less Negro around," he says. There's the question of whether Bigsby's racist diatribes are less racist because he's black, even if he doesn't realize he's black. And there's the moment Bigsby unmasks himself in front of a roomful of his followers, who look on in shock, trying to work out if embracing Bigsby's message about hating black people now amounts to embracing a black person. It's sophisticated and silly, simple and complex, funny and serious all at once.

Chappelle's Show is undoubtedly the offspring of *In Living Color*, but the connection isn't necessarily direct. Chappelle's humor is harder, angrier, and more unforgiving than *ILC*'s. While it's easy to see how sketches like "The Wrath of Farrakhan" and "Timbuk: The Last Runaway Slave" could've fit in on *Chappelle's Show*, or how Chappelle's crackhead Tyrone Biggums and his broad Rick James impression could've sat comfortably on *ILC*, the tone of the two shows is very different.

"Dave is subversive," says Rusty Cundieff, who directed many *Chappelle's Show* sketches, including the Clayton Bigsby one. "*In Living Color*'s angle was more *Let's have fun with this.*"

Both Chappelle and his co-creator Brennan had been *ILC* fans—by chance, Brennan actually first discovered future *Chappelle's Show* cast member Donnell Rawlings while filming some *ILC* casting sessions around 1992—but it wasn't something they talked a lot about during the making of their show. Some of the difference in perspective between the two shows tracks to the personalities that created them. As much as *In Living Color* might've been the realization of Keenen's vision, *Chappelle's Show* was even more so an embodiment of Chappelle's worldview. He and Brennan wrote most of the series themselves, and Chappelle stars in nearly every sketch. But some of the difference between the two shows also comes down to the thirteen years of time in between their respective debuts. The landscape had changed dramatically. Black culture was more integrated into the mainstream.

It's also worth keeping in mind that *Chappelle's Show* was on Comedy Central, not network television, which freed Chappelle from the burden of having to—in industry parlance—"broaden the appeal." *Chappelle's Show* was a huge hit for Comedy Central, but a huge hit meant three million viewers. In comparison, *In Living Color* was averaging more than ten million when it was canceled. If three million viewers makes you a hit, you can take more risks. Still, Cundieff says, "There were plenty of sketches we did that the network didn't want us to do because either they didn't think they were funny or they just didn't get it."

Chappelle's Show was a phenomenon. It was a hit on Comedy Central. The DVD became the biggest-selling television show on DVD in history. As the third season was being prepped, Comedy Central signed Chappelle to a two-year contract worth about fifty million dollars. There seemed to be nothing but blue sky ahead. Yet before the third season premiered, Chappelle simply left, disappearing to South Africa for several weeks, and eventually walking away from his lucrative new deal.

Much has been written and conjectured about Chappelle's reasons for quitting. Many of the most salacious rumors—*He's on crack! He's in the loony bin!*—were baseless. Some other stories edged closer to the truth: He was fed up with Comedy Central meddling with the creative process. The huge payday suddenly put him in the uncomfortable position of no longer being an underdog. He feared audiences couldn't relate to him anymore, or maybe he couldn't relate to himself. And perhaps most interesting—though not necessarily most accurate—was the story about a sketch he'd been working on right before he left for Africa. In it, he played a magical pixie in blackface who tried to convince African-Americans to act out in the most stereotypically black ways. A white crew member reportedly laughed at the sketch, but something about that laugh struck Chappelle as wrong. It made him ask the same question of himself that had been asked of black comics since Stepin Fetchit: *Are they laughing with me or at me? Am I lampooning stereotypes or reinforcing them?*

"When he laughed, it made me uncomfortable," Chappelle said. "As a matter of fact, that was the last thing I shot before I told myself, 'I gotta take fucking time-out after this.' Because my head almost exploded."

Brennan says he doesn't have a problem with "anything Comedy Central has done in terms of me and Dave." He didn't think there was a conspiracy to silence the show or excessive interference by the executives. In fact, between *South Park*, *The Daily Show*, and *Chappelle's Show*, Comedy Central makes money by being subversive.

But for a guy who had been dicked around by the industry for a decade, who'd been made to feel like a sellout on *Buddies*, who'd sworn off television after his subsequent experience at Fox, something didn't feel right. Not only had the huge contract from Comedy Central not made Chappelle content with the first unqualified success of his career, it had done the opposite.

Chappelle's abrupt exit from his own show echoes the acrimonious departures of Keenen from *ILC* and Richard Pryor from *The Richard Pryor Show*. The individual circumstances differ, but the similarities between the demises of the three most important black sketch shows in history can't be mere happenstance. It's not just black show creators clashing with white executives—though it's that too. It's black comics struggling to bring their authentic voices to the mainstream, forced to question their own intentions in both success and failure. As Paul Mooney—not coincidentally, the only guy who worked on all three shows—put it to Pryor once, "The minute you hear white people applauding you, you get all pissed at yourself because you think you ain't being black enough."

If there's a definite pattern around the demise of the Pryor show, *ILC*, and *Chappelle's Show*, there's an even larger framework this pattern fits into. Consider the career arcs of many of the top black comics of the past fifty years. Flip Wilson had one of the most popular shows on television in the early seventies then abruptly quit and retired from show business. Pryor was the most important comic in the world then flamed out in mess of drugs, poor career choices, and actual flames. In the eighties, Eddie Murphy had one of the greatest commercial runs of any actor ever, but since the midnineties has quit doing standup and retreated from the public spotlight, generally only emerging to make really forgettable movies (with a few exceptions). Keenen walked away from *ILC* and since his talk show petered out has rarely been on-screen. Arsenio peaked in the nineties and spent most of the 2000s out of show business. At the height of Martin Lawrence's television success in the nineties, he was hospitalized and jailed multiple times, once after running in the street, waving a gun, and yelling things like "Fight the establishment!" at passing cars. Chris Tucker became a twenty-million-dollars-a-picture movie star in the second half of the nineties, but since 2001 has made only three films, a presumably contractually obligated *Rush Hour 3* in 2007 and then smaller parts in 2012's *Silver Linings Playbook* and 2016's *Billy Lynn's Long Halftime Walk*. Chappelle famously bailed on a fifty-million-dollar deal from Comedy Central and was dismissed as crazy.

These situations aren't identical, not by a long shot, and certainly not every successful black comic's career fits this pattern. Chris Rock has remained a cultural icon for decades, Kevin Hart appears to be managing superstardom well, and newer talents like Donald Glover, Keegan-Michael Key, Jordan Peele, and Hannibal Buress have adjusted to their expanding celebrity smoothly. But some of the parallels in the careers of those who have struggled or walked away are hard to ignore. Often, these comics fit for a moment in the box the entertainment industry creates for them then struggle to get out of it. At the very least, it seems that for black comics, there is a unique set of pressures that makes careers harder to maintain. Hollywood is still largely run by and *for* white people. As Chris Rock put it in 1993, "The sad truth is that no matter how funny a black comic is, it doesn't mean shit unless he makes the right white man laugh." Without question, the landscape *has* changed since Flip Wilson and Richard Pryor's days, but the question is *By how much?* Black audiences are given more consideration than they were pre-1990, but for companies like Sony or Warner Bros. or Fox, these days, it's less about straight-out racism than it's about math: They want to make products for the largest possible audience with the most disposable income, and at the moment, that's still white people. Black comics must balance these business pressures with the pressure not to disappoint black audiences. Then comes the pressure of their own creative instincts, which may be leading them in a direction that could let down all these audiences.

W. E. B. Du Bois observed something similar more than a century ago. In his 1903 book, *The Souls of Black Folk*, Du Bois wrote about the "double consciousness" with which African-Americans grapple. They could never avoid seeing themselves "through the eyes of others, of measuring one's soul by the tape of a world that looks on in amused contempt and pity." Paul Mooney described this double consciousness as having "one self for the master and one self that's 'just between us.'" That created a tug-of-war for guys like Pryor, Chappelle, and Keenen, who struggled to balance those two selves.

Not long after *Chappelle's Show* fell apart, Chris Rock got a call with an offer to do a show just like it. "They offered me a ton of money, just an insane amount," Rock explained in 2008. He took the offer seriously enough to go back and watch *Chappelle's Show* on DVD. "I put in Season 2 and was like, 'There's no way I'll ever do a sketch show again.' It was so funny." Sketch shows are best done by comics on the way up, people without much to lose. Pryor had way too much to lose. Keenen and Chappelle didn't—at least when they started. Once they did, they were gone. "The next guy to do a sketch show can't be me," Rock continued. "It's got to be some young kid that doesn't know any better."

37

"How Does *In Living Color* Fare in a World of *Key and Peele?*"

In Hollywood, a good idea never really dies. Once any television show or film achieves even a modicum of success, you can bet there are already teams of people scheming to figure out how to take that idea and repeat it, reboot it, copy it, set up a sequel, or spin it off into ten more projects. *In Living Color* is no exception.

Both during the show's run and after its cancellation, there was talk about spinning off some of the more popular characters—Fire Marshal Bill, Wanda, Homey the Clown, Blaine and Antoine from "Men on Film"—into movies. "We tried," says Keenen. "There was going to be a Homey the Clown film."

This was years after the show had ended, and the Homey film was well into preproduction. At the same time, Keenen, Shawn, and Marlon were trying to get another film, *White Chicks*, off the ground. "We pitched *White Chicks* and there was a bidding war that ended with Sony making the best offer," Kennen says. This created problems with Fox, which was developing the Homey film. "The guy who was at Fox at the time got pissed and pulled the plug on *Homey the Clown*. We were two days before shooting *Homey*."

As Damon recalls, "We got close. I wish we would've done it. I wish we still could do it."

Talk of and steps toward adapting other characters oscillated, with some getting farther along than others. Rumors of a Fire Marshal Bill movie stayed just rumors. Carrey says it wasn't physically doable. "Fire Marshal Bill, you can only do it for a minute and a half until my face would literally go into convulsions," he explains. Nonetheless, the lost opportunities aren't without their bright sides: *In Living Color*'s characters have thus far avoided the ignominious silver screen fate that befell such *Saturday Night Live* mainstays as Stuart Smalley, Pat, and Mary Katherine Gallagher.

Efforts at rebooting the television show itself, though, came perilously close to happening. By 2011, the legal issues between Keenen and Fox regarding syndication and charges of self-dealing had long been settled, and there was enough water under the bridge that both the network and the show's creator believed there was a way to make their relationship work again. That Keenen and Fox would want to revive *ILC* wasn't shocking. The original show had only grown in stature in the nearly two decades since it disappeared. Carrey, Foxx, and Jennifer Lopez were A-List movie stars; Rosie Perez, David Alan Grier, and Tommy Davidson were stars as well; and even once-lowly writers like Larry Wilmore and Colin Quinn had become household names. And it wasn't as if America had sorted out all those pesky issues regarding race that once bedeviled it. The first black president was a symbolic marker for racial progress, but also seemingly an incitement for those who nostalgically recalled a simpler (read: whiter) time. It was the age of Obama but also of Hurricane Katrina, Oscar Grant, birtherism, Mel Gibson, Fox News, the War on Terror. It was a time when a massively popular black rapper—one who'd famously proclaimed to a national television audience that a white president didn't care about black people—could interrupt the Grammys to protest a white pop star receiving an award he believed should've gone to a black pop star, and the black president would call him a jackass for it. *MADtv* had closed up shop in 2009, and *SNL* still struggled to integrate black comics into the show. (At the time, Kenan Thompson was the only African-American full cast member, and the show had exactly zero black writers on a staff of more than twenty.) Surely, the thinking was, there could be a place for *ILC* in this landscape.

The initial plan was to make two specials. Assuming all went well,

Keenen expected that Fox would pick up a full season of the show. The original cast members would do some sketches early on, but with the idea of introducing audiences to a new cast, who'd take the ball and run with it.

It didn't pan out as Keenen or Fox had expected. The show struggled to find the kinds of cast members Keenen was looking for. As he explained during a 2013 radio interview, "The talent pool is different. There's a lot of funny guys out there now but they don't do characters, sing, act. They do one thing. You look at a guy like Jamie Foxx: Jamie is super talented, doing drama, singing, comedy, standup. Those are the kinds of people you need to put a show like that together."

One of the biggest complications proved to be securing the participation of the original cast. Most had agreed—in theory—to do *something* for the new show. Turning that into reality was tricky, and cast a pall of uncertainty over the production.

"There were rumors among the cast: 'Is Jim Carrey really coming? Is it going to be David Alan Grier?'" recalls Josh Duvendeck, who was hired as one of the new cast members. "No one confirmed it because no one wanted to set that standard if they weren't going to be able to follow through."

The main issue with getting the original cast committed was money. According to multiple accounts, the offers Fox made to them were insultingly low.

"They were going to give me $2500 to do two specials," says Damon. "They wanted me to do a Homey sketch and a 'Men On' sketch, plus they wanted to own any new characters I created. I knew that when they started promoting it, it's going to be as if I'm in it throughout the show. I couldn't allow myself to be used like that. I can't work for $2500. I'm not going to let you disrespect me like that."

Carrey was willing to do a guest appearance but says Keenen found "studios aren't as generous as they used to be. That stuff was a lot of work if you're not going to get a payoff." None of the original cast members, besides Keenen, ended up filming anything.

Keenen himself had changed some since the original show, but according to Les Firestein, whom he'd brought in as a writer and producer for the reboot, that wasn't necessarily a good thing. "Keenen was much nicer," says Firestein. "He'd explain to people why he didn't want to do something. He didn't play as fearsome a role on the reboot, and as a result he was less feared, but that may have also made people less productive."

Maronzio Vance, a comic who was hired as a writer on the reboot, feels the kinder, gentler Keenen was pulling punches in a way his younger self never would have. "He didn't want to make fun of anybody anymore," says Vance. "He was like, 'That's mean.' He didn't want to go dark. I'm like, *This show is based on being dark and fucked up and making fun of people*. But he was older now. He had perspective."

As the staff worked on assembling a pilot episode, they were acutely aware of a looming presence, just overhead. Two former *MADtv* cast members, Keegan-Michael Key and Jordan Peele, were on the floor above them developing their own sketch show. "Key and Peele were on the third floor, we were on the second," says Vance. "It was weird. Key and Peele were the new kids on the block doing sketch about race and social issues. They could've bugged our room. We could've bugged theirs."

Firestein says they didn't talk much about Key and Peele around the production offices, but their presence seemed to underline a pervading issue. "The shows are different but the question is *How does* In Living Color *fare in a world of* Key and Peele?"

The production fell seriously behind schedule—Fox's senior VP of television production Joel Hornstock called the process "interminable"—and was way over budget, but eventually eight to ten sketches were produced. The cast members and writers' opinions on whether any of it was actually funny are mostly just conjecture. None of them ever saw the final pilot, and the writers didn't even see the sketches filmed. The set was closed to them.

One cast member, Milton "Lil Rel" Howery, says one thing he did see was the intro Keenen did for the entire show, which he says basically reenacted his acrimonious departure from *ILC* two decades earlier. "Fox couldn't have been happy with that," he says. "It was Fox telling Keenen he was never going to work on the network again. I was sitting there like, *Oh, man. That's how we're going to kick this off?*"

It's not clear whether Keenen intended it as a barbed joke—much like Richard Pryor's monologues about NBC during his run on *The Richard Pryor Show*—or whether it was just a sign that Keenen had given up on the reboot at that point. After the tape week, there wasn't even a wrap party.

By the end of April of 2012, the pilot was finished and the production office closed. For all the disagreements Keenen and Fox had over the years, they saw eye to eye on this one: The pilot was going nowhere. It had been time-consuming and expensive to produce—"I think it wound up being just under four million dollars," says Firestein—yet it felt lacking.

"It stunk," says Hornstock. "Who knows which incarnation I saw because it never had a final *final*, but it was terrible. It was embarrassing and it cost all those millions of dollars."

Publicly, Keenen said he thought the pilot was good, though he may have just been being polite. Ultimately, he didn't see how the series could sustain itself. "It's one of those things where the bar is set so high and if you can't reach that, you gotta let it go," he says. "If I'd been doing another sketch show with a new, young cast, it would've been fine. But once you called it *In Living Color*, and you've got all these former cast members who are icons that you're gonna be compared to, you can't fuck with that."

38

"It's That Moment When It All Ignited"

avid Alan Grier and Jim Carrey were sitting around the set of *In Living Color* one day early in the show's run, talking to kill the downtime typical on any television production. The show had recently debuted and was a hit—or at least a hit for Fox, which was still struggling to be taken seriously as a fourth network. Grier had grown up steeped in the Civil Rights Movement, having earned a master's from the Yale School of Drama and played Jackie Robinson on Broadway. Yet it was Carrey, a Canadian high school dropout, who seemed to intuitively grasp the importance of what they were engaged in.

"This is history," he told Grier.

Grier didn't see it. Maybe the decade he'd spent as a struggling black actor had hardened him, made him cynical. "You're fucking crazy," he said. "This isn't history. This is just another sketch show. After we're canceled, six months later, people will have forgotten about *In Living Color*."

People haven't forgotten *In Living Color*—at least not entirely—but assessing its legacy is tricky. Many of the cast have gone on to huge Hollywood careers. The show's writers and producers ran or at least had a hand in practically every significant comedy on television in the last twenty-plus years, including *The Simpsons, South Park, Seinfeld, The*

Bernie Mac Show, *The Fresh Prince of Bel-Air*, *The Daily Show*, *The Office*, *Cheers*, *Chappelle's Show*, *Friends*, and *Saturday Night Live*.

"*In Living Color* was a show that opened the doors to America, to look behind the screen of what [people] think is going on in the black mind, as opposed to what's really going on," says Kim Wayans. "People were surprised by how one culture perceives another and vice-versa. It wasn't just about black culture and how we see things, but also about how [white people] see things in relation to us. It opened up dialogue, and whenever you open up dialogue about things that were once taboo, it's a step forward."

In a very tangible way, Keenen and *In Living Color* helped to force open doors that had previously been barely cracked within Hollywood. "Keenen and I were like the first soldiers stupid and courageous enough to believe we can do it," says Robert Townsend. "Now people take it for granted that a person of color can write, direct, produce a movie or TV show. Back then, it was never heard of. Being a black writer-director-producer was like being a black quarterback in football. There weren't many of us."

Les Firestein, who went on to a long career in television as writer and producer, working with Drew Carey, Wanda Sykes, Norm MacDonald, and Jon Stewart, believes that *ILC* helped prove there was a potentially huge market for black entertainment. "There are a lot of people like Chappelle, like Key and Peele, that have to look back to this show as a form of Jackie Robinson," he says. "It was kind of the comedy equivalent of rap music, where you had something that jumped cultures and went widespread in America."

There's an obvious through line from *ILC* to *MADtv*, *The Chris Rock Show*, *Chappelle's Show*, and *Key and Peele*, but that only tells a fraction of the story. The entertainment landscape for the two and a half decades after the show debuted looks vastly different than the two and a half decades before it. Television and film are completely unrecognizable from what they were in the eighties. The playing field may still not be level for minorities, but people like Shonda Rhimes, Kenya Barris, Lee Daniels, Ava DuVernay, Issa Rae, Jordan Peele, and Donald Glover have found a way to tell a diverse array of distinctly African-American stories. The fact that black rappers and singers like Drake, Kanye West, Jay-Z, and

Beyoncé are among the biggest stars on the planet is probably less meaningful than the fact that white ones like Justin Timberlake, Taylor Swift, Justin Bieber, Eminem, and Adam Levine are often just as marinated in hip-hop culture. Even country music adopts a hip-hop pose these days. What was once so fringe that *In Living Color* was one of the few places a kid from rural Iowa could discover Public Enemy, has now taken over. Hip-hop *is* mainstream American culture. The astounding success of *Hamilton*, a hip-hop Broadway musical about the country's decidedly un-hip-hop founding fathers, seems like a final Rubicon crossed.

In the course of one generation, hip-hop culture has changed America. The final weight of its impact won't be tallied for a long time. But whatever hip-hop did to America, *In Living Color* was a part of it. Not just in spreading the music from urban America to the suburbs, the exurbs, and beyond, but in introducing one culture to another, in giving us permission to point at each other and laugh.

During his years on the show, Buddy Sheffield occasionally returned to the Gulf Coast of Mississippi where he'd grown up. When friends and relatives discovered he—a white boy from the Old South—wrote for *In Living Color*, they'd inevitably rave about it. "Some of these people weren't the most open-minded," says Sheffield. "I thought, *Well, if nothing else, for thirty minutes a week, I've got these people sitting down and loving a bunch of black people.*" That's not nothing.

"It's hard to look at it in a vacuum and say what *In Living Color* did for black performers," says Marsha Warfield. "It's a continuum." The period in the late eighties and early nineties that spawned *In Living Color*, *Do the Right Thing*, *Boyz n the Hood*, *Coming to America*, Arsenio's talk show, Public Enemy, and Tupac was an inflection point, a moment in time when the weight of two hundred years of history could no longer prevent the giant aircraft carrier that is American culture from turning. "That whole time was part of an evolution that got us to where we are now," says Warfield. "Nobody could've predicted a quote-unquote small show like *In Living Color* on an off network would explode. It anchored a whole new world not just for black entertainment but for entertainment period. It deserves its own place for being part of that revolution and evolution."

In Living Color wasn't just swept up in this sea change, it was an instigator for it.

"It was all happening at once," says Tommy Davidson. "It was a renais-sance period for urban entertainment. It's that moment when it all ignited, all came together. Out of that came *Fresh Prince of Bel-Air*, *House Party*, Run-DMC's 'Walk This Way,' *Yo! MTV Raps*. It was an explosion, and here we are now in the commercial age of that renaissance. Back then, it was new. Now, you can't sell a Sprite or an iPad without it."

Hip-hop—not just the music, but the culture—has been, in Keenen's eyes, "the bridge between black and white" in America. *In Living Color* helped construct that bridge. "I'd argue with anyone that Obama is the culmination of hip-hop," Keenen said in 2015. "That culture, that gener-ation is what brought our nation together." Politically, we may have en-tered a post-Obama era, but culturally there's no going back. The country may be split into warring factions that seem to have nothing in common, but that's not true. What's left of monoculture in our increasingly bifur-cated media world is a hip-hop-infused coalition that *In Living Color* helped assemble.

———

A few years after *In Living Color* ended, Buddy Sheffield was working on a pilot and was in the postproduction suite, when in walked an engineer who was in charge of juicing up the laughs. This is standard industry practice that goes back decades, substituting a pre-recorded laugh track for a subpar studio audience reaction. The engineer pulled out a cassette labeled, "This Ol' Box."

"Excuse me," Sheffield asked him. "What is that?"

"Oh, this is the audience's reaction I recorded a few years ago at *In Living Color*," the engineer said. It was from an Anton Jackson sketch in the show's first season.

"I wrote that sketch," Sheffield told him proudly.

"These are some of the greatest laughs I've ever been able to record," the engineer responded. "I use this all the time."

Sheffield paused, then smiled. "So you're basically taking our laughs from *In Living Color* and using them to sweeten unfunny shit all over Hollywood?"

If you want a demonstrable legacy, there you have it. Everything else is ephemeral. *In Living Color* was funny, and at its best so funny that it set a bar not often reached again in the years to follow. To see that only in terms of race may be reductive. Those big, loud, hard laughs came not just from being smart or clever or witty or black but from being outrageous, from putting things on television that viewers hadn't seen before. Not all of it has aged well, but when you watched the show back then, and saw Homey the Clown, Timbuk, "Men on Film," "Jews on First," and Fire Marshal Bill in real time, the audaciousness was real. This was a show willing to upset people in search of those big, loud, hard laughs. They said the un-sayable. That's a legacy that always needs periodic renewing, whether by *In Living Color*, *Saturday Night Live*, *The Simpsons*, *Chappelle's Show*, *South Park*, *Key and Peele*, or whomever.

It's a legacy Keenen himself can get behind.

"We were just young, dumb, and having fun," he said, reflecting on the show's legacy. "The agenda was just to be the funniest show on TV." At the time he said it, it sounded like a cop-out, a way not to have to consider the bigger questions about *In Living Color* and how it has reverberated down the ages. And maybe it was. But there was some truth in there too. Keenen understood history but was never trying to make it. He was a guy who consistently resisted the poignant in favor of the funny—which is a big part of how *In Living Color* ended up being both.

Acknowledgments

This book would not have been possible without the efforts and support of many people whose names don't grace the cover of it. First off, I am indebted to everyone I interviewed over the course of several years of research, many of whom submitted to multiple, sometimes quite lengthy interrogations and seemingly endless follow-up questions. It is their recollections and perspectives that shaped the narrative, and their generous spirits are hopefully reflected in it. In particular, I would like to thank Tamara Rawitt and Les Firestein, who both enthusiastically made themselves available for my constant queries and sent me original materials that I otherwise would never have been able to procure. This book is undoubtedly better for their involvement.

I'd also like to thank my publisher, Dawn Davis, whose belief in this idea made this book a reality and whose thoughtful insights improved it immeasurably along the way. Lindsay Newton offered notes and edits on early drafts that were both incisive and encouraging, and Albert Tang did wonders to turn my jumbled ideas about the book's design into something coherent and creative. My agent, Laura Nolan, has always been a great sounding board and provided invaluable guidance throughout the process. Thank you to Cynthia Colonna for her dutiful transcribing work, and to David Walters for unwittingly helping to birth this entire project by greenlighting a magazine story back in 2015. And, of course, thanks to all the family and friends who have been supportive—with your feedback, with your ideas, with your patience with my bellyaching—during the past couple years as I've worked on this book, a list that includes but is not limited to: Mark Yarm; Tom Siebert; Samira Jafari; Brad Feldman; Tracey Noelle Luz; Lynn Peisner; my parents, Arthur and Susan Peisner; and my kids, Graham and Molly Peisner.

Bibliography and Other Sources

Books

Acham, Christine. *Revolution Televised: Prime Time and the Struggle for Black Power*. Minneapolis: University of Minnesota Press, 2004.

Apatow, Judd. *Sick in the Head: Conversations About Life and Comedy*. New York: Random House, 2015.

Bianculli, David. *Dangerously Funny: The Uncensored Story of The Smothers Brothers Comedy Hour*. New York: Touchstone, 2009.

Block, Alex Ben. *Outfoxed: Marvin Davis, Barry Diller, Rupert Murdoch, Joan Rivers, and the Inside Story of America's Fourth Television Network*. New York: St. Martin's Press, 1990.

Chang, Jeff. *Can't Stop Won't Stop: A History of the Hip-Hop Generation*. New York: Picador, 2005.

DeBellis, John. *Standup Guys: A Generation of Laughs*. 920 Spot Books/Booklocker, 2012. PDF ebook.

George, Nelson. *In Living Color: The Authorized Companion to the Fox TV Series*. New York: Warner Books, 1991.

Gregory, Dick, and Robert Lipsyte. *Nigger*. New York: Pocket Books, 1990.

Grier, David Alan, with Alan Eisenstock. *Barack Like Me: The Chocolate-Covered Truth*. New York: Touchstone, 2009.

Hecht, Michael L., Ronald L. Jackson, and Sidney A. Ribeau. *African-American Communication: Exploring Identity and Culture*. New York: Routledge, 2003.

Henry, David, and Joe Henry. *Furious Cool: Richard Pryor and the World That Made Him*. Chapel Hill, NC: Algonquin Books, 2013.

Heron, Gil-Scott. *The Last Holiday: A Memoir*. New York: Grove Press, 2012.

Hill, Doug, and Jeff Weingrad. *Saturday Night: A Backstage History of Saturday Night Live*. New York: Beech Tree Books, 1986.

Kimmel, Daniel M. *The Fourth Network: How Fox Broke the Rules and Reinvented Television.* Chicago: Ivan R. Dee, 2004.

Knoedelseder, William. *I'm Dying Up Here: Heartbreak and High Times in Stand-Up Comedy's Golden Era.* New York: PublicAffairs, 2010.

Lane, Frederick S. *The Decency Wars: The Campaign to Cleanse American Culture.* Amherst, NY: Prometheus Books, 2006.

Lee, Spike, with Kaleem Aftab. *That's My Story and I'm Sticking to It.* New York: W. W. Norton, 2005.

Littleton, Darryl J. *Black Comedians on Black Comedy.* New York: Applause Books, 2008.

McCourt, Frank. *Teacher Man.* New York: Scribner, 2005.

Miller, James Andrew, and Tom Shales. *Live from New York: The Complete Uncensored History of* Saturday Night Live *as Told by Its Stars, Writers, and Guests.* New York: Little, Brown and Company, 2002.

Mitchell, Elvis, and Timothy Greenfield-Sanders. *The Black List.* New York: Atria Books, 2008.

Mooney, Paul. *Black Is the New White.* New York: Simon Spotlight Entertainment, 2009.

Perez, Rosie. *Handbook for an Unpredictable Life: How I Survived Sister Renata and My Crazy Mother, and Still Came Out Smiling (with Great Hair).* New York: Crown Archetype, 2014.

Pryor, Richard, with Todd Gold. *Pryor Convictions: And Other Life Sentences.* New York: Pantheon Books, 1995.

Saul, Scott. *Becoming Richard Pryor.* New York: Harper, 2014.

Stanley, Bob. *Yeah Yeah Yeah: The Story of Pop Music from Bill Haley to Beyoncé.* New York: W. W. Norton, 2014.

Watkins, Mel. *On the Real Side: A History of African American Comedy.* Chicago: Chicago Review Press, 1999.

Wayans, Damon. *Bootleg.* New York: Harper Paperbacks, 2000.

Zinoman, Jason. *Searching for Dave Chappelle.* Amazon Digital Services, 2013. Kindle edition.

Zoglin, Richard. *Comedy at the Edge: How Stand-up in the 1970s Changed America.* New York: Bloomsbury, 2008.

Zook, Kristal Brent. *Color By Fox: The Fox Network and the Revolution in Black Television.* New York: Oxford University Press, 1999.

Newspapers/Magazines/Web Content

Abbott, Jim. *Orlando Sentinel.* "After 'In Living Color,' Coles Gets on with Her Life," June 7, 1991.

Afro-American Syndicate. "Oprah Show Ends 2004 Proclaiming—'America's Funniest Family: The Wayanses,'" 2004.

Associated Press. "Q&A with Damon Wayans," June 20, 2005.

———. "TV Parody Inflames Group," April 3, 1991.

Bernstein, Jonathan. *Spin.* "Chris Rock," February 1993.

Booe, Martin. *USA Weekend.* "He's So Fresh," October 27, 1990.

Borders, William. *New York Times.* "Playground Plan Divides Chelsea," May 27, 1964.

Braxton, Greg. *Los Angeles Times.* "Hip-Hop TV's Leading Edge," November 4, 1990.

———. *Los Angeles Times.* "Where More Isn't Much Better," October 4, 1992.

———. *Los Angeles Times.* "Flip Side: Happy Not Being Funny," March 11, 1993.

———. *Los Angeles Times.* "Fox's 'In Living Color': Life After Wayans World," March 26, 1993.

———. *Los Angeles Times.* "Groups Call for Changes in Portrayals of Blacks on TV," February 8, 1997.

Bray, Hiawatha. *Detroit Free Press.* "Hyundai Drops 'In Living Color' Ads," December 25, 1992.

Buchalter, Gail. *Los Angeles Times.* "Eddie Murphy and the Black Pack," February 28, 1988.

Carter, Alan. *Entertainment Weekly.* "'In Living Color' . . . in Trouble," February, 14, 1992.

———. *Entertainment Weekly.* "Leaving 'In Living Color,'" January 15, 1993.

Carter, Bill. *New York Times.* "Frito-Lay and Fox Attempt to Outflank the Super Bowl," January 13, 1992.

Cerone, Daniel. *Los Angeles Times.* "Brought to You 'In Living Color,'" April 15, 1990.

Chambers, Veronica. *Vibe.* "Hip-Hop Hollywood: Poetry In Motion," Fall 1992.

Chaney, Jen. *Vulture.* "The Enduring Satire of *Hollywood Shuffle*'s 'Black Acting School,'" February 7, 2017.

Collier, Aldore. *Ebony.* "Fighting the Power in Hollywood," August 1990.

———. *Jet.* "Keenen Ivory Wayans and Family Star 'In Living Color,'" September 10, 1990.

———. *Ebony.* "Robert Townsend: A New Kind of Hollywood Dreamer," June 1991.

Craig, Jane. *Spy.* "Damon Wayans' Older Brother," September 1993.

Dawidziak, Mark. *Akron Beacon Journal.* "'Living Color' Enlivened by Irreverence, Fresh Perspective," July 22, 1990.

DeWitt, Karen. *New York Times.* "Minority College Attendance Rose in the Late 80s, Report Says," January 20, 1992.

Diaz, Angel, and Jason Duaine Hah. *Complex.* "And You Know This, Mannnnn: An Oral History of Friday," 2015.

Donoloe, Darlene. *People.* "In *Hollywood Shuffle* Comic Actor Robert Townsend Wields His Wit Against Movie Industry Racism," May 18, 1987.

Ebert, Roger. *Chicago Sun-Times.* "Review: *I'm Gonna Git You Sucka*," December 14, 1988.

———. *Chicago Sun-Times.* "Jim Carrey Laughs in the Face of Success," July 24, 1994.

Edgers, Geoff. *Washington Post.* "The Real King of Comedy," October 13, 2015.

Farhi, Paul. *Washington Post.* "A Television Trend: Audiences in Black and White," November 29, 1994.

Fein, Esther B. *New York Times.* "Robert Townsend Has Fun at Hollywood's Expense," April 19, 1987.

Firestein, Les. *Los Angeles Times.* "Two Gaps in the TV Tapestry: Dropping 'In Living Color' Leaves a Void. Where Else Could Viewers Find Satire Without Regard to Race as Long as the Skits Were Funny?" August 29, 1994.

Froelich, Janis D. *Des Moines Register.* "'In Living Color' Lives," December 19, 1993.

Fryer Jr., Roland G., Paul S. Heaton, Steven D. Leavitt, and Kevin M. Murphy. *Economic Inquiry* 51, no. 3. "Measuring Crack Cocaine and Its Impact," April 2006.

Gabriel, Larry. *Detroit Free Press.* "Names and Faces," February 10, 1992.

Geesling, Don. *Brooklyn Rail.* "An American Griot: Gil-Scott Heron," November 7, 2007.

Givhan, Robin D. *Detroit Free Press.* "No Joking Matter: Ethnic Humor Can Strike a Sour Note," September 6, 1990.

Goldstein, Patrick. *Los Angeles Times.* "Marketing the Color Black: Strategies for Crossover Films Fail to Stifle Charges of Racism," April 18, 1989.

Gunther, Marc. *New York Times.* "Black Producers Add a Fresh Nuance," August 26, 1990.

Hall, Arsenio. *Daily Beast.* "Arsenio Hall on Filming from L.A. Riots' Ground Zero," April 26, 2012.

Hall, Carlo. *Washington Post.* "The Color of Funny," July 1, 1990.

Hall, Steve. *Indianapolis Star.* "Wayans Finds Success Poking Fun at Stereotypes," July 15, 1990.

Herbers, John. *New York Times.* "Black Poverty Spreads in 50 Biggest U.S. Cities," January 26, 1987.

Herbert, Steve. *Los Angeles Times.* "Election-Night Alternatives," November 3, 1992.

Hesse, Josiah M. *Westword.* "Keenen Ivory Wayans on Dave Chappelle, *In Living Color* and Jehovah's Witnesses," September 20, 2013.

Hiatt, Brian. *Rolling Stone.* "Eddie Murphy Speaks," November 9, 2011.

Hill, Michael. *Baltimore Sun.* " 'In Living Color' Buzzes Like 'SNL' of Early Days,' " May 25, 1990.

Hirschberg, Lynn. *New York Times Magazine.* "How Black Comedy Got the Last Laugh," September 3, 2000.

Hirshey, Gerri. *Vanity Fair.* "The Black Pack: Eddie Murphy and His Sidekick, Arsenio Hall, Are Poised to Make It Big in Their Latest Film, *Coming to America*," July 1, 1988.

Hontz, Jenny. *Variety.* "TV's Race Card: Chappelle, Producer Call Foul Over Fox Sitcom," July 8, 1998.

Hood, Micaela. *SouthFlorida.com.* "The New Damon Wayans," November 7, 2013.

Jackson, Mandi Isaacs. *American Studies* 47, no. 1. "Harlem's Rent Strike and Rat War: Representation, Housing Access and Tenant Resistance in New York, 1958–1964," Spring 2006.

Johnson, Allan. *Chicago Tribune.* "Wayans' World: Damon Follows Eddie's Path to Stardom," July 24, 1992.

Johnson, Richard. *Palm Beach Post.* " 'In Living Color' Star Livid Over Firing," October 6, 1990.

Keough, Peter. *Chicago Reader*. "Hollywood Shuffle: How Robert Townsend Got a Good Part," April 2, 1987.

Kiesewetter, John. *Cincinnati Enquirer*. "Newport Roots Fuel Comedy Writer's Work," July 26, 1991.

Lanagan, Patrick A. *United States Department of Justice, Bureau of Justice Statistics*. "Race of Prisoners Admitted to State and Federal Institutions, 1926–86," May 1991.

Lee, Spike. *Spin*. "An Exclusive Interview with Eddie Murphy," October 1990.

Lyons, Douglas C. *Ebony*. "Blacks and the New TV Season," October 1990.

Marco, Bennet. *Spy*. "The Little Network That Could've," September 1991.

Mascitti, Al. *News Journal*. "Carrey Plans to Pull Out Comic Stops at Grand," March 12, 1993.

McFadden, Robert D. *New York Times*. "Slain in Prison, but Once Celebrated as a Fugitive," February 22, 2008.

McNally, Joel. *Milwaukee Journal*. " 'In Living Color' Casts About for New Tack," February 19, 1993.

McNichol, Tom. *USA Weekend*. "Comedy Is My Defense: Damon Wayans Plays on His Own Pain in This Month's New Comedy, *'Mo Money*,'" June 10, 1992.

McWilliams, Michael. *Detroit Free Press*. "The Color of Funny," June 23, 1990.

Miller, Patricia. *Asbury Park Press*. "Dover Official Inflamed by TV Fire Chief," April 4, 1991.

Millman, Joyce. *San Francisco Examiner*. " 'In Living Color' Closes Racial Gap in Hip TV Satire,' " April 27, 1990.

———. *San Francisco Examiner*. "Black Actors Now Star in More Diverse Roles," July 29, 1990.

Mills, David. *Washington Post*. "Obituary: Robin Harris," March 26, 1990.

———. *Washington Post*. "Saturday Night's Live One," September 29, 1990 (transcript via undercoverblackman.blogspot.com).

———. *Washington Times*. "Q&A: Chris Rock," 1989 (transcript via undercoverblackman.blogspot.com).

Mink, Eric. *St. Louis Post-Dispatch*. "Outrageous Humor on 'In Living Color,' " May 11, 1990.

Mitchell, Elvis. *Interview*. "Eddie Murphy," September 1, 1987.

———. *Playboy*. "Spike Lee: The Playboy Interview," July 1991.

Murphy, Austin. *Sports Illustrated*. "It's . . . Halftime!: How a Drum Major Known as Tommy the Toe Begat the Best (Bono, Jacko, Jagger) and Worst (Up with People!) Segment of Every Super Bowl Sunday," January 31, 2014.

Perkins, Ken Parish. *Dallas Morning News*. "Stuck in a Holding Pattern After 'In Living Color,' Kim Coles Is Now Flying High," September 19, 1993.

Pickle, Betsy. *St. Louis Post-Dispatch*. "In Living Color Is All in the Family," May 24, 1990.

Poe, Janita. *Chicago Tribune*. "Not In Living Color," July 8, 1992.

Rabin, Nathan. *AVclub.com*. "Chris Rock," November 17, 2004.

Randolph, Laura B. *Ebony*. "Arsenio Hall Talks About His Feuds with Roseanne and Madonna and the Rumors About Him and Eddie," December 1990.

Rangarajan, Sinduja. *LA Weekly*. "The Godfather of L.A.'s Black Comedy Scene, Michael Williams, Is Plotting His Comeback." September 23, 2014.

Richmond, Peter. *GQ*. "Eddie Murphy's Gilded Road to Ruin," July 1992.

Richmond, Ray. *Detroit Free Press*. "Foxy Moves Put 4th Network in the Same League as the Big Three," September 2, 1990.

Rosenberg, Howard. *Los Angeles Times*. "Living Color: Brash, Cruel but Funny," April 14, 1990.

———. *Los Angeles Times*. "Bigotry on TV: The Stain Still Lingers," December 16, 1992.

———. *Los Angeles Times*. "Is Stern Worse Than Fox's 'Color'?" December 21, 1992.

Russell, Deborah. *Billboard*. "Rapper 2Pac Faces Assault Charge in L.A. Altercation," March 27, 1993.

Sandomir, Richard. *New York Times*. "Fox Network Outbids CBS for Rights to Pro Football," December 18, 1993.

Scholtes, Peter S. *City Pages*. "Back to the Terrordome," April 21, 2008.

Schreiber, Lee R. *Los Angeles Times*. "Hey Chris, Where'd the Edge Go?: 'Saturday Night Live' Rookie Chris Rock Brought a Streetwise Sense of Humor That Has Been Somewhat Smoothed Out—For Now," March 10, 1991.

Siegel, Lee. *Slate*. "Spike Lee: The Director Talks About Movies, Race and Will Smith," December 1, 2005.

Smith, Dinitia. *New York*. "Color Them Funny," October 8, 1990.

Smith, Russell. *Dallas Morning News.* "Carrey Holding Aces with Hit," February 20, 1994.

Southgate, Martha. *New York Daily News.* "Comedy with a Snap," June 17, 1990.

Spigner, Clarence. *Crisis.* "Black Impressions: Television and Film Imagery," January 1994.

Telander, Rick. *Sports Illustrated.* "Senseless: In America's Cities, Kids Are Killing Kids Over Sneakers and Other Sports Apparel Favored by Drug Dealers. Who's to Blame?" May 14, 1990.

Waldron, Clarence. *Jet.* "TV Discovers That Black Shows Bring in Big Bucks," May 20, 1991.

Watkins, Mel. *New York Times.* "Flip Wilson, Outrageous Comic and TV Host, Dies at 64," November 27, 1998.

Wayne, Renee Lucas. *Philadelphia Daily News.* "Laughing in the Right Spot: 'Sucka' Creator Keenen Ivory Wayans Wants You to Know Blaxploitation from Parody," January 18, 1989.

Weinstein, Steve. *Los Angeles Times.* "Fox Tackles Super Bowl with Sly Plan," January 25, 1992.

Welkos, Robert, and Clare Spiegel. *Los Angeles Times.* "Three Bullets Haunted Officer to a Deserved Stress Pension," February 3, 1985.

Wild, David. *New York Times.* "The Family That Clowns Together," July 16, 2000.

Wilkinson, Tracy. *Los Angeles Times.* "Street Drama: Actor Edward James Olmos Plays Leading Role in Cleanup Effort," May 5, 1992.

Wiseman, Lisa. *Baltimore Sun.* "At First Glance, Rock and Davidson Might Seem Like Very Funny Bookends. Look Again. Comedy's 2 Extremes," August 19, 1994.

Wolf, Jeanne. *New York Times.* "'Blankman': Hero for the Hood," August 18, 1994.

Zehme, Bill. *Rolling Stone.* "Eddie Murphy: Call Him Money," August 24, 1989.

CNN. "Damon Wayans: Chat Books Transcript," May 20, 1999.

Entertainment Weekly. "The Subject Is Rosie—Fearless on Film and in Life, the Straight-Outta-Brooklyn Actresss Expands Her Turf," October 29, 1993.

New York Times. "Fulton Houses Dedicated At 9th Ave. Near 19th St.," October 16, 1962.

———. "City Accepting Applications for Two Housing Projects," October 27, 1963.

———. "Old Neighborhood, New Look," February 20, 1969.

———. "'In Living Color,' Urkel Beat '90210,' Cosby in Q Rating," June 8, 1992.

Paramount Pictures. "A Conversation with Chris Rock," 2015.

People. "Don't Mess with Eddie Murphy's Pal Keenen Ivory Wayans—He's Making His Own Movie, Sucka," December 12, 1988.

United States Census Bureau. "Persons Below Poverty Level in the U.S., 1975–2010" (via Infoplease.com).

———. "Income and Poverty in the United States, 2015," Report Number P60-256, September 2016.

———. "We the Americans: Blacks," September 1993.

Uproxx. "25 Years Later: How 'In Living Color' Broke Sketch Comedy's Race Barrier," April 15, 2015.

Variety. "Wayans, Townsend in Skit Suit," November 29, 1993.

TV/Films

Soul. George Schlatter Productions, dir. Mark Warren, 1968.

Later with Bob Costas. NBC Productions, exec. prod. Dick Ebersol, 1991 (interview with Jim Carrey).

The Arsenio Hall Show. Arsenio Hall Communications, exec. prod. Arsenio Hall, May 23, 1994.

The Keenen Ivory Wayans Show. Ancient & Modern Productions, exec. prod. Keenen Ivory Wayans, 1997 (interview with Shawn and Marlon).

Jimmy Kimmel Live! Jackhole Industries/12:05 Productions, prod. Chris Fraticelli, June 30, 2004.

Inside the Actor's Studio. The Actor's Studio, prod. Alice Christian, November 28, 2004.

The Oprah Winfrey Show. Harpo Productions, exec. prod. Oprah Winfrey, February 3, 2006.

Inside the Actor's Studio. The Actor's Studio, prod. Jeff Wurtz, March 13, 2007.

Why We Laugh: Black Comedians on Black Comedy. Codeblack Entertainment, dir. Robert Townsend, 2009.

CNN Presents . . . Race and Rage: The Beating of Rodney King. CNN, exec. prod. Stan Wilson, March 4, 2011.

Late Night with Jimmy Fallon. Broadway Video, exec. prod. Lorne Michaels, November 4, 2011.

Oprah's Next Chapter. Harpo Productions, exec. prod. Oprah Winfrey, March 3, 2013.

Inside Comedy. Carousel Productions, dir. David Steinberg, March 11, 2013.

The Improv: 50 Years Behind the Brick Wall. Spotted Dog Entertainment, prod. Tracy Green, Katie Petrachonis, Rocco Urbisci, December 6, 2013.

The Arsenio Hall Show. Arsenio Hall Communications, exec. prod. Arsenio Hall, April 22, 2014.

Windy City Live. ABC7 Chicago, July 25, 2014 (interview with Keenen, Damon, Marlon, and Shawn Wayans).

Good Day New York. Fox 5NY, December 19, 2014 (interview with Damon Wayans).

Finding Your Roots with Henry Louis Gates Jr. Ark Media, dir. Muriel Soenens, January 19, 2016.

Video/Radio/Podcast Interviews

Chris Rock, February 6, 1997, by Terry Gross for *Fresh Air.*

Kim Wayans, June 12, 2011, by Jeff Phelps for *Another Look.*

Keenen Ivory Wayans, July 9, 2011, onstage at the American Black Film Festival.

David Alan Grier, October 21, 2011, by Neal Brennan and Moshe Kasher for *The Champs.*

Chris Rock, November 3, 2011, by Marc Maron for *WTF.*

Kim Wayans, January 4, 2012, by Christine Aylward for *Reel Life, Real Stories.*

Chris Rock, August 8, 2012, by Terry Gross for *Fresh Air.*

Marlon Wayans and Shawn Wayans, November 20, 2012, by Neal Brennan and Moshe Kasher for *The Champs.*

Keenen Ivory Wayans, July 8, 2013, by Amy Harrington for the Archive of American Television.

Keenen Ivory Wayans, July 26, 2013, by Charlamagne Tha God, Angela Yee, and DJ Envy for *The Breakfast Club.*

Keenen Ivory Wayans, August 7, 2013, by Juan Epstein for *Rosenberg Radio.*

Chris Albrecht, October 7, 2013, by Stephen J. Abramson for Television Academy Foundation Archive.

Shawn Wayans, January 31, 2014, by Juan Epstein for *Hot 97*.

Arsenio Hall, February 4, 2014, by Neal Brennan and Moshe Kasher for *The Champs*.

Damon Wayans, Marlon Wayans, and Shawn Wayans, July 19, 2014, by Sway Calloway for *Sway in the Morning*.

Damon Wayans, November 10, 2014, by Leo Laporte for *Triangulation*.

Marlon Wayans and Shawn Wayans, January 17, 2015, by Sway Calloway for *Sway in the Morning*.

Jamie Foxx, April 21, 2015, by Sway Calloway for *Sway in the Morning*.

Jamie Foxx, May 12, 2015, by Snoop Dogg for GGN News Network.

Shawn Wayans, May 22, 2015, by Peter Rosenberg and Laura Stylez for *Hot 97*.

Tommy Davidson, May 25, 2015, by Marc Maron for *WTF*.

Damon Wayans, September 4, 2015, by Charlamagne Tha God, Angela Yee, and DJ Envy for *The Breakfast Club*.

Jamie Foxx, December 6, 2015, by Tim Ferriss for *The Tim Ferriss Show*.

Marlon Wayans, March 24, 2016, by Tom Vann and Daniel Dennis for *A Mediocre Time with Tom and Dan*.

Chris Rock, April 15, 2016, by J.J. Abrams for Tribeca Film Festival.

Marlon Wayans, April 21, 2016, by Adam Carolla for *The Adam Carolla Show*.

David Spade, May 26, 2016, by Dan Patrick for *The Dan Patrick Show*.

Eddie Murphy, August 20, 2016, by Scott Feinberg for *The* Hollywood Reporter's *Awards Chatter*.

David Alan Grier, July 26, 2017, by Marc Maron for *WTF*.

Author Interviews

Miguel Acevedo

Franklyn Ajaye

Garth Ancier

Jeff Ayeroff

Fax Bahr

Nick Bakay

Jennifer Bartels

Kim Bass

Don Bay

Kevin Berg

Sandra Bernhard

John Bowman

Neal Brennan

Kevin Bright

Ishmael Butler

Nancy Neufeld Callaway

Jim Carrey

Leroy "Twist" Casey

Sydney Castillo

Aleta Chappelle

Kim Coles

Jeanette Collins

Eve Szurley Coquillard

Gemma Corfield

Rusty Cundieff

Tommy Davidson

Joe Davola

John DeBellis

Harry Dunn

Josh Duvendeck

Carla Earle

Becky Hartman Edwards

David Edwards

Rob Edwards

Les Firestein

Martha Frankel

Mimi Friedman

Shauna Garr

Melvin George

Eric Gold

Maurice Goodman

Fred Graver

Dick Gregory

David Alan Grier

T. Faye Griffin

Madonna Grimes

Sandy Grushow

Argus Hamilton

Tre Hardson

Antonio "Big Daddy Kane" Hardy

Kali Hawk

Charles Hirschhorn

Joel Hornstock

Milton "Lil Rel" Howery

Carrie Ann Inaba

Ray James

A.J. Johnson

Anne-Marie Johnson

Michelle Jones

Todd R. Jones

Tim Kelleher

Jamie Kellner

Howard Kuperberg

Deidre Lang

Cari French Lather

John Leguizamo

Neil Levy

Bill Martin

Tajai Massey

Dan McDermott

T.J. McGee

Paul Miller

Michelle Whitney Morrison

Michael Moye

Charlie Murphy

Rick Najera

Steve Oedekerk

Judy Orbach

Kelly Coffield Park

Steve Park

Rosie Perez

Michael Petok

Rose Catherine Pinkney

Shari Poindexter

Alvin Poussaint

Colin Quinn

Tamara Rawitt

Carlton "Chuck D" Ridenhour

Toney Riley

Tom Rizzo

Carol Rosenthal

Lucie Salhany

Susan Sandberg

Mike Schiff

Jeff Schimmel

George Schlatter

Al Sonja Schmidt

Angela Scott

B. Mark Seabrooks

T. Sean Shannon

Buddy Sheffield

G. John Slagle

Adam Small

Dennis Snee

Michael Anthony Snowden

Aries Spears

Penelope Spheeris

Todd "Speech" Thomas

Lisa Joann Thompson

Richie Tienken

Liz Welch Tirrell

Andre "Dres" Titus

Lisa Marie Todd

Steve Tompkins

Robert Townsend

Kris Trexler

Rocco Urbisci

Maronzio Vance

Pam Veasey

Reginald VelJohnson

Mary Williams Villano

Marsha Warfield

Damon Wayans

Keenen Ivory Wayans

Kim Wayans

Marlon Wayans

Shawn Wayans

Alexandra Wentworth

Ken Wilcox

Michael Williams

Larry Wilmore

Marc Wilmore

Carmi Zlotnik

Index